India's Children

India's Children

Essays on Social Policy

edited by

A.K. Shiva Kumar

Preet Rustagi

Ramya Subrahmanian

OXFORD
UNIVERSITY PRESS

OXFORD
UNIVERSITY PRESS

Oxford University Press is a department of the University of Oxford. It furthers the University's objective of excellence in research, scholarship, and education by publishing worldwide. Oxford is a registered trademark of Oxford University Press in the UK and in certain other countries

Published in India by
Oxford University Press
YMCA Library Building, 1 Jai Singh Road, New Delhi 110 001, India

First Edition published in 2015

ISBN-13: 978-0-19-945528-7
ISBN-10: 0-19-945528-7

Typeset in Bembo Std 10.5/13
by SPEX Infotech, Puducherry 605 005

Note: In this volume, 1 lakh is equal to 0.1 million and
1 crore is equal to 10 million.

Contents

Part II: Macro Context and Policy Spaces

Part III: Gender, Family, and Marriage

Part IV: Social Exclusion and Human Development

Tables and Figures

TABLES

FIGURES

Foreword

Children constitute a sizeable proportion of India's population, that is, around 40 per cent, and will continue to do so over the next few decades. This demographic feature in an ageing world has been the focus of much discussion in India, given that enabling today's children to realize their full potential, while important in itself, can also accelerate India's development.

The prospects of sustaining India's economic growth rest considerably on how well the present and future generations of India's children are able to break the intergenerational cycle of deprivation and accelerate human development. This would call for addressing more effectively several conditions affecting their lives including malnutrition, poor educational and health outcomes, persistence of open defecation, lack of social mobility, and vulnerability to chronic and temporal poverty. Inequalities across social groups arising out of caste, class, ethnicity, geography, religion, and gender add to the social complexity. Tackling such inequalities requires rethinking of public policies from the perspective of social transformation and social justice. It also requires incorporating strategies for normative change that include large scale communication for raising awareness, mobilization of young and excluded populations, and creating a climate of accountability and transparency in the functioning institutions, both public and private.

The focus on 'social policies' in this volume draws attention to many dimensions of the policy environment that shape the future of children. These include the macro environment in which outcomes for children are shaped, rising food prices, and issues of resource availability or 'fiscal space'. Both income and non-income dimensions of children's deprivations need to be addressed in dealing with the challenges of measuring poverty and deprivation from children's perspective. India's policy commitment to 'inclusive growth' in the Twelfth Five-Year Plan needs to be unpacked in terms of the different facets of exclusion that constrain equitable human development outcomes. Gender issues in the sphere of family and marriage need to be examined as these are primary institutions shaping gender identity as well as the well-being of women and children. Finally, a focus on what is driving the 'new' India, including demographic change and impacts on youth employment need to be explored.

The essays in this volume offer an array of such perspectives and views for India's social policies in the years ahead. I would like to thank the authors for their inspiring and relevant contributions. The partnership between UNICEF and the Institute for Human Development on 'Child Well-being and Social Policy' is also gratefully acknowledged. I am sure that the volume will contribute towards enriching public discourse and strengthening public action to promote rights and results for children.

Louis-Georges Arsenault
Representative, UNICEF India
December 2014

Abbreviations

ADC	Autonomous District Council
ANM	Auxiliary Nurse Midwife
APL	Above Poverty Line
ART	Assisted Reproductive Technologies
ASHA	Accredited Social Health Activist
AWC	Anganwadi Centre
AWW	Anganwadi Worker
BCG	Bacillus Calmette–Guérin
BE	Budget Estimates
BMI	Body Mass Index
BPL	Below Poverty Line
BSY	Balika Samridhi Yojana
CABE	Central Advisory Board of Education
CBGA	Centre for Budget and Governance Accountability
CCT	Conditional Cash Transfer
CDI	Child Development Index
CDPO	Child Development Project Officer
CHC	Community Health Centre
CHIP	Childhood Poverty Research and Policy Centre
CLPRA	Child Labour Prohibition and Regulation Act
CMPO	Child Marriage Prohibition Officer

CPR	Common Property Resources
CRC	Convention on the Rights of the Child
CrPC	Code of Criminal Procedure
CSA	Child Sexual Abuse
CSR	Child Sex Ratio
DHP	District Health Plan
DISE	District Information System for Education
DLHS	District Level Household and Facility Survey
DPT	Diphtheria, Pertussis, Tetanus
DWCD	Department of Women and Child Development
EBB	Educationally Backward Blocks
ECCD	Early Childhood Care and Development
ECCE	Early Childhood Care and Education
ECD	Early Childhood Development
EFA	Education for All
ESNA	Extended System of National Accounts
FAS	Foundation for Agrarian Studies
FLPR	Female Labour Participation Rates
GDI	Gender-related Development Index
GDP	Gross Domestic Product
GEM	Gender Empowerment Index
GNP	Gross National Product
GoI	Government of India
HDI	Human Development Index
HRD	Human Resource Development
IAP	Integrated Action Plan
ICDS	Integrated Child Development Scheme
IFAD	International Fund for Agricultural Development
IFPRI	International Food Policy Research Institute
IIDS	Indian Institute of Dalit Studies
IMR	Infant Mortality Rate

IPCD	International Conference of Population and Development
ITDA	Integrated Tribal Development Agency
ITDP	Integrated Tribal Development Project
ITPA	Immoral Traffic (Prevention) Act
JJA	Juvenile Justice Act
JJB	Juvenile Justice Board
JSY	Janani Suraksha Yojana
KGBV	Kasturba Gandhi Balika Vidyalaya
MADA	Modified Area Development Approach
M&E	Monitoring and Evaluation
MDC	Mentally Deficient Children
MDG	Millennium Development Goal
MDMS	Mid-Day Meal Scheme
MGNREGA	Mahatma Gandhi National Rural Employment Guarantee Act
MHRD	Ministry of Human Resource Development
MIS	Management Information System
MLE	Multilingual Education Intervention
MLL	Minimum Levels of Learning
MLP	Micro-level Planning
MMR	Maternal Mortality Rate
MoHFW	Ministry of Health and Family Welfare
MoTA	Ministry of Tribal Affairs
MoYAS	Ministry of Youth Affairs and Sports
MTP	Medical Termination of Pregnancy
MWCD	Ministry of Women and Child Development
NAC	National Advisory Council
NCERT	National Council of Education Research and Training
NCEUS	National Commission for Enterprises in the Unorganized Sector

NCMP	National Common Minimum Programme
NCPCR	National Commission for Protection of Child Rights
NCRB	National Crime Records Bureau
NFHS	National Family Health Survey
NGO	Non-governmental Organization
NHSRC	National Health Systems Resource Centre
NPC	National Policy for Children
NRHM	National Rural Health Mission
NSS	National Sample Survey
NSSF	National Small Savings Fund
NTFP	Non-timber Forest Product
OBC	Other Backward Class
OECD	Organisation for Economic Co-operation and Development
OPEPA	Odisha Primary Education Program Authority
PARI	Project on Agrarian Relations in India
PC-PNDT	Pre-conception and Pre-natal Diagnostic Techniques Act
PDS	Public Distribution System
PESA	Panchayats (Extension to Scheduled Areas) Act
PHC	Primary Health Centre
PIL	Public Interest Litigation
PIP	Project Implementation Plan
PL	Poverty Line
POCSO	Protection of Children from Sexual Offences Bill
PPP	Public–Private Partnership
PQLI	Physical Quality of Life Index
PRI	Panchayati Raj Institution
PTG	Primitive Tribal Group
RBI	Reserve Bank of India
RCH	Reproductive and Child Health Programme

RE	Revised Estimates
RKS	Rogi Kalyan Samiti
RTE	Right to Education
SAARC	South Asian Association for Regional Cooperation
SC	Scheduled Caste
SNA	System of National Accounts
SRB	Sex Ratio at Birth
SRH	Sexual and Reproductive Health
ST	Scheduled Tribe
STT	Securities Transaction Tax
TFR	Total Fertility Rate
TSP	Tribal Sub-plan
UEI	Unfair Exclusion and Inclusion
U5MR	Under-5 Mortality Rate
UNCRC	United Nations Convention on the Rights of the Child
UPA	United Progressive Alliance
UTI	Unit Trust of India
VHSC	Village Health and Sanitation Committee
WPR	Work Participation Rate

Child Rights, Equity, and Social Policy

An Introduction

Ramya Subrahmanian,
A.K. Shiva Kumar, and
Preet Rustagi

This volume is a collection of essays[1] on social policy in India from the perspective of child rights. Children continue to constitute a sizeable proportion of India's population. As against 1.5 million babies born annually in the early 1950s, by 2012, around 25 million babies[2] were born each year. In 1951, there were 140 million children below the age of 14 years—constituting over 38 per cent of the total population. By 2011, their numbers had more than doubled to nearly 290 million children.[3] Since India's independence, massive investments in roads, railways, telecommunications, and in social and physical infrastructure, together with more than a fivefold increase in per capita incomes, have yielded many gains for children. Access to primary schooling has

[1] While we discuss the various chapters of this volume, the discussion in this chapter is thematic and does not follow the actual sequencing of chapters.

[2] Data from UNICEF website, http://www.unicef.org/infobycountry/india_statistics.html, last accessed on 5 October 2014.

[3] Census of India.

improved dramatically and is near universal. In 1951, about 538,000 teachers taught 19.2 million children enrolled in 210,000 primary schools. By 2011, about 135 million children were being taught by nearly 1.5 million teachers in close to 749,000 primary schools (Ministry of Economic Affairs 2014). Child survival has also improved significantly. In 2012, India's infant mortality rate (IMR) was 42 (Office of Registrar General of India 2013), down from 134 deaths per 1,000 live births in 1951. Partly responsible for this has been the large health infrastructure created by India, with the number of primary health care centres (PHCs) increasing from 725 in 1951 to nearly 24,000 by March 2011.[4]

Despite progress along many fronts, it is well known that Indian children continue to face many deprivations. Statistical indicators reveal that differences in well-being among children in India are narrowing, yet almost 43 per cent of children below 5 years were undernourished in 2005–6, and, even today, over a million babies die before their first birthday. Similarly, there are stark inequalities in the well-being of children across states, between rural and urban areas, and within communities. Discrimination on grounds of class, caste, and gender further adds to the vulnerabilities of children. The slow progress in ending deprivation is even more striking (and equally disturbing) because, in recent years, despite the far better economic performance, India has fallen behind many of its neighbours in South Asia. This was not the case in 1990 when India ranked under only Sri Lanka in the region on most human development indicators.

Through the entry point of new opportunities available to children in India and old challenges still faced by them, the volume raises several key questions that are central to policy debates in India: What does poverty mean when viewed from the perspective of access to basic services for children and realization of children's basic capabilities? How should it be measured? How do we address the challenges of investment in public service expansion and delivery required to ensure equitable outcomes for children irrespective of their economic means, social group, or geographical location? How do we ensure that dif-

[4] Government of India data taken from http://data.gov.in/catalog/building-position-sub-centres-primary-health-centres-and-community-health-centres#web_catalog_tabs_block_10, last accessed on 4 October 2014.

ferent institutions—families, the state and its different arms, and the community—work in concert to further children's rights? How can processes of social discrimination and exclusion, which have both shaped and affected India's development trajectory, be challenged and transformed? How do we best invest in today's children across the age spectrum in a way that strengthens their functioning as adult citizens tomorrow?

Underpinning this collection of essays is the centrality and importance of designing social policies with regard to children's rights. Children form a distinct group because of their status as dependants until they are 18 years old. However, it is equally important to acknowledge that a child faces different needs during the stages of infancy and adolescence and, in that sense too, children are not a homogenous category. The concerns of infants, adolescents, and youth have been given attention in this volume highlighting some key issues for policy attention.

Too often, investment in children's rights has been framed in terms of the returns to investment in children, where children are viewed purely as human capital, and investments today are measured in terms of returns to economy and society tomorrow. While it is clear that well-nourished, educated, skilled, and healthy children will become productive national assets after they transition into adulthood, this futuristic vision often fails to focus on the details of what is required today, in terms of services, programmes, and resources, to realize their rights as children. In short, a focus on children's rights during childhood and an understanding of the implications of life-course poverty—deprivations during early ages of childhood that have negative consequences for later stages of childhood—will sharpen policy and intervention efforts in the 'here and now', and compel attention to quality design and implementation in a way that can produce meaningful and immediate outcomes.

Many strides have been made to align national policies with India's commitments to uphold the 1990 United Nations Convention on the Rights of the Child (UNCRC), which it ratified in 1992. The recent publication of the National Policy for Children (NPC), 2013, replaces the one written in 1974. The NPC recognizes children as persons below the age of 18 years; the validity of childhood as a distinct stage of life with its own value; and the multidimensionality of the vulnerabilities faced by children in different circumstances.

A strong and unequivocal commitment to non-discrimination as well as special affirmative measures to bridge inequities marks this document, alongside a multisectoral set of commitments that should bring different sectoral ministries into a coherent policy framework of child rights. The long list of commitments listed in the policy are as much a testament to the will of the state to recognize child rights as the overarching principle for its policies and programmes for children as they are a recognition of the long road ahead to realize this principle.

From a rights perspective, the persistence of human poverty reflects a failure by the state to guarantee access to basic entitlements (to health, education, nutrition, and so on) that are guaranteed by the Constitution. Rights have the backing of moral consensus and legal obligations. However, do rights have any meaning if they cannot be legally enforced? Does the fact that some human rights are denied today make these rights redundant? Amartya Sen (2007) argues that these are the wrong questions to pose. He points to the distinction between human rights and legal rights and argues that human rights exist whether or not these rights are reflected in actual legislation. For instance, the enactment of the Child Labour (Prohibition and Regulation) Act, 1986, does not mean that there was no violation of child labour rights before that year. Similarly, an unrealized right is different from a non-existing right. Recognizing a right imposes an obligation on society to do something for the realization of the particular right even if it is likely to remain unrealized for several years. This is very different from not recognizing the right itself whereby society would be absolved of having to act against violations that have no formal recognition in the legal framework. Guaranteeing the right of every child to good quality elementary education under the Right of Children to Free and Compulsory Education Act, 2009 (which came into effect on 1 April 2010), may take decades, but passing the Act has triggered public actions to meet the commitment, which would not have been forthcoming otherwise. The language and frameworks of rights-based development thus provides a powerful rallying point for public action.

The urgency of getting it right for children today cannot be overemphasized. Three chapters in this volume (Rustagi et al. [Chapter 2], Swaminathan and Athreya [Chapter 3], and Kundu and Mohanan [Chapter 4]) establish the range and scale of children's deprivations across what can be described as basic material needs—education, health, nutrition, sanitation, shelter, and water, as well as domains of work and labour, where children and their families need to be enabled to complete education and obtain appropriate skills to improve their access to decent work and wages. All these chapters concur that both the absolute levels and the relative spread of deprivations across most socio-economic groups suggest the need for a radical overhaul of social policies and programmes. They primarily reaffirm the importance of integrated approaches—beyond 'convergence' of the given sectoral programmes to a more substantive reconfiguration of policies that recognize the multidimensionality of poverty and deprivation, as well as the interplays between psychosocial and material dimensions of well-being, economy and society, and family and state.

These chapters also reaffirm the importance of universality as a principle of policy and resource investment for children and their families, pointing to the deprivations that exist, albeit to a lesser degree, in even basic material needs in the wealthier quintiles. The analysis by Swaminathan and Athreya of five of the several villages they have studied in-depth reveals that apart from the top 10 per cent in these diversely situated villages, the rest of the population has deprivations in common, and the intensity and effect are clearly most felt amongst socially excluded groups and the poorest of the lot. Indeed, income inequality has its own pernicious effects on children's rights and development. However, poor public services can affect all children. A judicious combination of policies aimed at both strengthening the economic status of families and providing quality services to their children is required. Recognizing the diversity of the country, in terms of both geography and social group and circumstance, and nuancing these universal policies to allow for different approaches as required would also be important.

CHILD-SENSITIVE SOCIAL POLICIES

Social policy is not simple to define. In general, social policy is seen as an integrative approach to public policy, based on recognition of the interrelationship between economic policies, governance structures, social formations, cultural trajectories, and human development outcomes. Multidisciplinarity is a central aspect of social policy.

Social policy is often an area of analysis and study as well as referring to a set of policies and forms of social action that can have a transformative effect on diverse populations. In the singular, we use social policy to refer to both the study and the collective group of public policies that deal with social well-being. In the plural, we refer to social policies in terms of the diverse public policies that have an impact on child rights.

Social policies are broadly considered to be focused on the well-being of citizens, and the study of social policy can be consequently viewed as analysis of how different societies and institutions interpret social needs and challenges and identify ways to address those needs. Kabeer (2004) delves deeper into this terrain, when she argues that

> the 'social' dimensions of public policy relate to those aspects which bear on how societies reproduce themselves at different levels: at the micro-level of individuals and their capabilities; at the meso level of institutions and social relations; and at the macro level of the societal structures of production and reproduction. Institutions are critical within this understanding of 'social policy' because they mediate the processes by which societies translate the resources at their disposal into the individual and societal outcomes which are of interest to policy-makers.

Social policies that are child-sensitive or child-centric are necessary in order to address the specific requirements and structure of childhood in terms of physical and psychosocial needs, the structures of dependency, as well as transitions within the phase of childhood at various points of maturity and change. They are required to respond to the fundamental point that children's experiences of poverty and vulnerability are multidimensional and differ from those of adults. Children undergo complex physical, psychological, and intellectual development as they grow and are also often more vulnerable to malnutrition, disease, abuse, and exploitation than adults. Their dependency on adults to support and protect them means that loss of family care is a significant risk, which deepens in the context of conflict, humanitarian crises, and HIV and AIDS.

The analyses of social policies need to go beyond the state as a primary actor and focus also on the ways in which community and family structures are filters through which children's rights are determined and achieved. Children's primary location as dependants within families can obscure the extent to which intra-household discrimination can result in child poverty and hunger, lack of access to services, and abuse and exploitation. Gender-based discrimination exacerbates children's vulnerability, as women are primarily carers of children, and any reduction in their agency and ability to act can translate into greater vulnerability of their children, especially daughters. Membership of a social group can determine the freedom that children have to play, learn, and eat with other social groups and can irreversibly shape their self-perception and self-esteem when at the receiving end of discrimination and ostracism. Social identity can be a source of both great strength and great stigma and is a significant determinant of well-being outcomes.

Balancing the rights and responsibilities of different institutions that bear duty to promote child rights, given children's dependency on adult capabilities and will, is a fundamental challenge for social policy. How should governments balance the needs of children with those of parents? How can child rights be framed in a way that respects individual rights and yet recognizes the complexity of social relationships within the family context? Bajpai's chapter (Chapter 5) reflects on India's Herculean attempt to frame child rights from over 250 pieces of legislation that directly or indirectly deal with children, many of which define childhood in different ways, delineated by different age limits. Amidst all these legislative efforts, she argues, the fundamental question of 'who is a child' remains ambiguous. Legal and institutional reforms are required both to recognize dimensions of increased agency and independence in late childhood and early adulthood, as well as to address the practical challenges of determining age in the absence of comprehensive systems of birth and marriage registration. The rationalization of different age limits in laws that protect children should not be arbitrary, she argues, or based only on socio-cultural perception. 'If the best interest of the child is the consideration, one could perhaps err on the side of having a higher age limit for protective care and a lower age limit in respect of civil and cultural matters.' Her chapter provides a comprehensive account of India's legislative framework for child rights and the challenges of regulating family, society, and state actions for the protection of children.

Sound social policies depend, in turn, on sound and multidisciplinary analysis that can recognize the interplay of different structures on opportunities and challenges for children. Recognizing the interplays between different dimensions of economic and social life also involves change processes, to which the policymakers need to be alert. Children's realities change constantly as a result of economic, demographic, and political transitions. Changes in the economic domain can compel families to adjust their economic and livelihood strategies, resulting in changing patterns of migration, family headship, amongst others. These changes can have significant impact on children's ability to stay in school, or on their decisions about work, marriage, or other social arrangements. Staying alert to the implications of major demographic, economic, and other trends on social arrangements and on sustained investments in children are central to the social policy arena. S. Mahendra Dev's chapter (Chapter 6) traces the diverse pathways in which macroeconomic crises can impact women's well-being and child nutrition, illustrating both the complexity of pathways, and the linkages between the macro-, meso-, and micro-level institutions, identified in Naila Kabeer's definition of 'the social' in public policy, quoted earlier. Being aware of these pathways can lead to informed and sensitive social policies that protect households and individuals from insecurities that arise from wider economic processes.

Finally, social policies require strategic planning and a sound investment plan that can generate sustainable programmes and services. Jha and Das (Chapter 7) argue strongly for far greater investments in the social sectors and services that reach children. While in recent years, with the expansion of the economy, India has invested far more in the social sectors than before, the overall levels of investment look insignificant when compared with investment levels of developed countries, whose development outcomes we seek to emulate. Further, the investments are fed through a system replete with bottlenecks that prevents funds from actually being used for the desired purposes and on time. While administrative reforms are required to ensure that these bottlenecks are removed, there is a wider issue of resource availability that concerns the authors. The vulnerability of budgetary allocations to changes in macroeconomic conditions means that at a time of financial difficulty—as after the global financial crisis and recession that have led most major economies, including India, to face economic slowdown—the fiscal squeeze has resulted in low to moderate increases in social sector allocations. This leads the authors to call for much more progressive policies on taxation[5] to ensure that crucial human development investments, needed even more when there is a macro-economic squeeze, are not subject to the vagaries of global economic downturns. This point is endorsed by S. Mahendra Dev in his chapter, where he points out the importance of ensuring fiscal stimulus and higher investments at times of crisis to ensure that vulnerable households do not face catastrophic consequences.

EMBEDDING A CHILD-RIGHTS APPROACH

As argued earlier, a shift to a child rights–centred approach to social policy is necessary to ensure immediate transformations in the opportunities made available to children to not just survive, but also to thrive and flourish during the period of childhood. For these transformations to occur, there is an urgent need for reform both in the way social policies are conceived and the ways in which programmes are designed for implementation through India's specific institutional architecture. Saith and Wazir (Chapter 1) characterize the Indian understanding of child deprivation in relation to poverty measurement as 'largely locked in a cognitive time warp constrained by anachronistic epistemologies, methodologies and ideologies', especially in the way the understanding of children's multidimensional deprivations is reduced to a few measures of material deprivation and the conflation of children's poverty with household poverty. From this reductionist conception, a range of policies and programmes flow, which determine poverty targeting in a way that does little to address the deprivations that children face and has limited impact on child well-being outcomes. Indeed, as Rustagi et al. demonstrate through a detailed unit-level analysis of the available national data (the National Family Health Survey [NFHS] and the National Sample Survey [NSS]), many aspects of child deprivation, while concentrated among the poorer wealth quintiles and socially excluded groups such as the Scheduled Castes (SCs) and Scheduled Tribes (STs), are not absent even amongst the top 20 per cent (highest wealth quintile).

This finding is confirmed by Swaminathan and Athreya through their micro-level empirical analysis of diverse villages. A narrow

[5] A recent article in *The Economist* (2013) reported that about 2.5 per cent or 32 million Indians pay income tax.

income- or consumption-based definition of poverty, when extended to children, highlights household poverty as a dominant axis from which to view deprivation—an unsatisfactory basis from which to then develop policies. While wealth inequality is a considerable factor which needs attention in the form of redistributive policies, unless they are coupled with strong non-discrimination measures and universally accessible quality public services, the chances of such policies reducing child deprivation in India across all axes—gender, economic class, and social group—will be slim.

A significant contribution made by a multidimensional and child-centred approach, which measures all of these axes as above, is the demonstration of the insufficiency of using income poverty as the sole basis on which to establish a poverty line. Saith and Wazir argue this point conceptually; Rustagi et al. and Swaminathan and Athreya disaggregate different data sets and conclude the same. While, in recent years, India has seen a remarkable spate of social policies being put in place with legislative and policy backing (such as the Right to Education Act, 2009, the National Food Security Act, 2013, the effort to recalibrate, and also to recalculate, the poverty line, amongst others), many aspects of the public debate reinforce some of the challenges outlined so far in this chapter. These include questions of universality and inclusion and exclusion criteria, questions of targeting criteria, the definitional arbitrariness of both the poverty line and the definitions of poverty, and the challenges of a changing environment—for instance, where mobile phones are more easily accessible than toilet facilities. At heart, these questions reflect a debate on the meaning and measurement of 'poverty'. Shifting towards more actionable measures to capture deprivation may overcome some of the limitations of determining 'sufficiency' of measures, such as income and consumption, based on calculations of only 'need'. Saith and Wazir suggest using hard and objective measures, such as data on child stunting, to uncover the pathways to deprivation and, through this, support families that need attention.

Not all news is grim though; Kundu and Mohanan, in their analysis of urban India, show some positive developments. The data they analyse shows near elimination of gender gaps in elementary education as well as a marked decline in the overall child employment, especially children under 10 years of age, including children in rural areas. They attribute these developments to the improved availability of elementary schools especially in rural areas, a result of significant public investment through the Sarva Shiksha Abhiyan (the current 'Education for All' programme) and its predecessor, the District Primary Education Programme. However, the challenge of education in the transitional phases remains sharp. High dropout rates in the age group of 11–14 years indicate insufficient access to quality secondary schools, and low education enrolment rates of children in the age group of 15–18 years suggest continued vulnerability in terms of access to employment and work, which therefore compels trade-offs between schooling and employment.

The sharp gender differentiation in transition to work in the age group of 15–18 years also provides an important reminder of the gender inequalities that compel girls to leave school and prepare for marriage by engaging in non-economic activities within the household, while boys gravitate towards employment-related activities. The consequences for girls in terms of early marriage leading to unpaid care work, in the context of limited work opportunities, remain a significant factor in perpetuating the vicious cycle of gender inequality and female disadvantage in India. This is a theme picked up in two other contributions to this volume, Nanda and Khanna (Chapter 9) and Misra and Subrahmanian (Chapter 11), on unpaid care work and factors underlying early marriage, respectively.

More broadly, denial of children's rights to quality education means that children who leave school before getting sufficient education are entering the workforce with inadequate levels of skills, which thereby reduce their chances of moving towards better employment opportunities and of breaking the intergenerational cycle of poverty. Kundu and Mohanan argue, therefore, for social policies that both encourage continued education (whilst also offering skill-formation programmes for those children who are unable to stay away from the labour market because of family economic conditions) and provide other supportive economic measures aimed at vulnerable households, such as those engaged in casual labour. The complexity of issues is laid bare through close reading of data, and through this exposition the possibility of seeing the value of integrated and comprehensive approaches. Such an approach can help to harness India's very unusual demographic advantage of a young population.

As Saith and Wazir point out, 'ways of seeing influence ways of doing'. The link between concepts, measurement of outcomes, and the resultant paradigm of policy intent, programme design, and monitoring and evaluation is a central theme of social policy analysis. In their chapter, Saith and Wazir call for a 'double paradigm shift' with

> significant implications for modes of conceptualization and recognition, for the focus and substantive content of analysis, for the choice of methods and tools, for the framing and design of policies and interventions, and, more generally, for the scope of debates and discourse pertaining to the development rights of children.

GENDER, FAMILY, AND MARRIAGE

This volume comes at a momentous time of awareness and social churning on issues of gender-based violence in India. Unprecedented citizen mobilization and protest against rape, in the context of urbanization, greater participation of women in public life (particularly through education and reservations in decentralized governance structures), and a proactive media, among others, has contributed to greater public discourse as well as some rapid action on revising laws against rape in the past few months. Building on a growing body of work on 'safe cities'[6] for girls and women and the consistent work done by women's groups and feminist movements in the country over decades, gender-just social policies appear to be on the ascent in India.

Transforming social norms that underlie gender equality needs to be a chief objective of gender-just social policies. Gender-based violence stems from patriarchal social structures that devalue women and perpetuate inequalities between women and men across all domains. Nanda and Khanna point to several traditions that give rise to the prevalence of early marriage or child marriage in India, accounting for one-third of the world's total marriages of girls under the age of 18. The practice of dowry, the belief that a family's primary and final

[6] See for example, the work under the Safe Cities Free of Violence against Women and Girls Initiative, http://www.unwomen.org/2011/06/un-launches-initiative-to-make-cities-safer-for-women-and-children/, last accessed on 21 May 2013.

responsibility to a girl is to get her married, the investment of family honour in preserving a girl's chastity prior to marriage, are all interrelated cultural and traditional practices that contribute to the perpetuation of social norms that devalue girls and tie their fortunes and fate to the institutions of marriage and procreation (preferably of sons). Within this set of aspirations for their daughters, there are changes that place value on some extent of education for girls to encourage their independence and provide them with valuable skills that they can contribute to their marital homes. However, as Kundu and Mohanan's data shows, even in urban India, norms determining choices and opportunities for girls are slow to change after they attain puberty, and there is a marked orientation towards domesticity, marriage, and family reproduction.

Nothing illustrates the challenges India faces in achieving gender equality, in the face of powerful and enduring social norms, as much as the declining sex ratio. John's chapter (Chapter 8) provides data that show how India's child sex ratio (CSR) (measuring females per 1,000 males in the age group 0–6 years) has declined from 945 to 918 between 1991 and 2011 (GoI 2011) and in several states it has declined to levels in the 800s per 1,000 males. State-level disaggregation further shows that as per 2011 Census data, a few states, primarily in southern India (such as Tamil Nadu, Karnataka, and Kerala), have maintained their levels over the previous decade and in some other states (such as Gujarat and Delhi), there is a plateauing of the CSRs. States that had in 2001 some of the worst figures for CSR (such as Punjab, Haryana, Chandigarh, and Himachal Pradesh) have shown improvements in 2011, owing to some concerted public policy and civil society efforts. However, their performance is undermined by the continuing decline in other states of the country, which, John notes, represents a 'widening of the circle well beyond the so-called prosperity belt of north-west India to the poorer states'. Indeed, declining sex ratios, once seen as occurring mostly in prosperous states and amongst middle-class families, seem to be spreading to areas where the practice of sex-selective abortion was unknown. While district disaggregated data would be more relevant to pinpoint the trends in CSRs, these broad trends suggest that the spread of sex-selection technologies could be associated with the desire for planning smaller families and are linked to existing normative frames to worsen outcomes for girls and women and further entrench gender bias or 'daughter aversion'.

Girls born in such an environment of daughter aversion can only bear the burden of gendered expectations that have been set for them so well in advance of their birth. The notion of coping with the social disappointment of being born a female shapes the experiences of many young girls in India today—a psychological burden that is little explored and understood. Familial norms that train daughters to prepare for domesticity may allow for schooling, but not for exploring arenas, avenues, characters, and behaviours that are not deemed gender appropriate. These norms also build on a culture of taboos, where discussions about sexuality and the freedom to choose the partner are deemed unnecessary, given the dominance of arranged marriages and the supremacy of the marital institution in framing sexual experience and health. Jejeebhoy and Santhya (Chapter 10) shed light on the way in which social norms play out within the family domain, particularly through parent–child communication. Drawing on primary surveys conducted with parents in six states of India, especially in-depth interviews with parents and young people, their chapter provides both quantitative and qualitative insights into parent–child communication. While mothers predominantly act as a source of information for their daughters, it is striking that the extent of information provided, whether accurate or not, is limited only to puberty and menstruation. However, even more striking is the neglect of boys, both by fathers and mothers.

Jejeebhoy and Santhya draw attention to areas of public policy, which seldom, if ever, get discussed. Social taboos on discussing sexual matters permeate even the policy arena, as India's complex relationship with sex education demonstrates. Yet, the foundations of sexual and reproductive health are laid during childhood. Absence of dialogue within the home can only have negative impacts on young girls and boys, especially when other public institutions reinforce this silence. Parents interviewed in this study overwhelmingly felt that children would learn about sex once they were married. Discussions before marriage on sex were considered to be inappropriate. Preparation, for girls in particular, focused more on appropriate behaviour in and out of the marital bed. Lack of information, as Jejeebhoy and Santhya note, can make these experiences more difficult than they need to be: '...it is not surprising that many women described their daughters' first experience of menstruation as traumatic, characterized by tears, fears that their parents would be angry, and concerns that the blood signified their ill health'. Parents' lack of knowledge and confidence to discuss these issues is itself a significant contributory factor to the lack of parent–child communication.

Another finding that emerges is how ill-prepared young men are for the transition to adulthood. Because parents are reluctant to undertake a task they themselves feel ill-prepared for or are unwilling to perform, parental assumptions that children learn through media, their friends, and through their spouse at the time of marriage are often mistaken. Issues of masculinity and the lack of attention to boys and fathers in social policies are also a matter of concern. Nanda and Khanna point to the lack of investment in programmes that work with adolescent boys, as part of efforts to delay the early marriage of girls, when 'young boys can be a catalyst of change in norms of early marriage...some also realize the advantages of marrying girls who deferred marriage for personal development since they would have the maturity to handle the responsibilities of marriage better'.

The lack of attention to boys and men as gendered actors in social policies is reflected in the chapter by Misra and Subrahmanian. The chapter presents an argument in favour of establishing universal day-care services in order to alleviate women's responsibilities for childcare, and enable them to explore other domestic, productive, and leisure pursuits in their time-constrained lives. The lack of male contribution to childcare responsibilities is borne out not just in empirical accounts of the way the gender division of labour plays out in the majority of Indian homes, but also evident in data which disaggregates time use by men and women. Children's care needs are also significant, especially for children under the age of three years. These needs vary as they grow older, and meeting these needs forms the foundation for the healthy development of children. Indeed, the irreversible consequences of deprivations that children face in the early years means that quality care for young children is a non-negotiable requirement and one to which social policies must be focused. While much is known about the inputs that children require in order to flourish, there has been little attempt to address the time and labour required to provide those inputs—nutritional, health, cognitive stimulation, amongst others—and the trade-offs that this unpaid work within the home carry for the primary caregiver. Balancing both the right of women to free time and right of children to care requires purposive social policies that provide care alternatives to women and families that have multiple demands on the use of their time to maximize other aspects of survival and well-being. Misra and Subrahmanian lay out the different aspects of this policy domain and make a plea for expanding services with quality to support families and parents of young children, especially mothers.

The consequences of low investments in services for women and for the promotion of gender equality are several. Nanda and Khanna draw attention to the well-known repercussions of early marriage both for women and for their children. Early marriage of girls and their physical immaturity at the time of giving birth can have consequences on the health of their children as well as themselves, not to mention the effect of being withdrawn from school for marriage before completion of secondary schooling. The impact of multiple burdens on women's time on the health and well-being of both women and children are detailed in the chapter by Misra and Subrahmanian. Jejeebhoy and Santhya emphasize the globally accepted view of the importance of parents in helping their children learn about physical changes associated with puberty and about sex, pregnancy, and sexually transmitted diseases and HIV. All these point to the importance of accelerating progress in multiple areas simultaneously to address the interrelated aspects of normative discrimination against girls.

Several policy interventions that have been designed to address early marriage, sex-selective abortion, childcare services, sexual and reproductive health awareness, and general discrimination against females are reviewed by the contributors. John reviews the challenges of implementation of the law to prevent sex selection leading to sex-selective abortion through regulating the use of diagnostic techniques in preconception and prenatal phases. The requirement of cooperation from medical doctors, who stand to gain financially from the use of these technologies even for legitimate medical reasons, and the near impossibility of regulating what often goes on behind closed doors has made implementation of this law nearly impossible. To what extent is the law itself flawed? John acknowledges a widely prevalent view that without this law, and the few efforts to implement it stringently, the CSR in India may have been even worse. The use of this law as an entry point for communication strategies, vigilant bureaucratic action, as well as the use of the media to track and expose those in violation of the law, all demonstrate how the law may be used even if not enforced. However, her sharper critiques are reserved for the way the national population policy's encouragement of a two-child norm has been misused in many states to penalize families when they have more than two children. Measures such as curtailing freedom to stand for panchayat elections, or accessing government resources (such as the recent 'Conditional Maternity Benefit Scheme', the Indira Gandhi Matritva Sahyog Yojana, which provides maternity benefits to women bearing only their first or second child) are all, as she rightly argues, 'violations of human rights'. Such punitive measures have a demonstrable effect on family planning and furthering son preference, which is a prevalent cultural norm. Thus the link between policies aimed at gender equality and their impact on social norms and outcomes for girls itself needs to be investigated.

Sekher's analysis of the government's incentive schemes, aimed at encouraging families to have and keep their daughters, provides revealing evidence of the ways in which policies, in both design and implementation, can subvert the very causes for which they are created (Chapter 12). Conditional cash incentive schemes (different from the conditional cash transfers that are globally renowned, where families get regular monthly cash transfers in return for meeting a set of social conditions, such as immunization, schooling, antenatal check-ups, amongst others) are a uniquely Indian policy instrument, where cash is given perhaps annually to eligible girls (using poverty criteria or geographical criteria, depending on the scheme) or on attainment of adulthood, or both, to provide financial inducement and some support to their families to keep them in school and keep them unmarried until they reach the legal age of marriage. As Sekher notes, there has been very little evaluation of these incentive schemes in terms of the extent to which they do change parental strategies for their daughters' well-being. His is a rare desk-based review of these schemes, providing insight into some of the challenges of implementation, but also, fundamentally, the dangers of the design of the programmes. Conditionalities are often communicated in ways that suggest to parents that the use of these funds is for their daughters' marriages or contributions to the dowry kitty. Bureaucratic reinforcement of the very social norms that have required the intervention in the first place is ironic to say the least and it also demonstrates how little consensus exists between policy-shapers and the officials who are tasked to implement the programmes they design. Without giving proper attention to ensuring coherence in concept and execution, such government programmes will continue to drain resources with little impact on the social transformation that they claim to foster.

Programmes that do exist—such as for girls' education in the form of the Kasturba Gandhi Balika Vidyalayas—show much promise, though their spread is far from universal. Yet, they indicate that the government is serious in its attempts to use education and empowerment to take forward these initiatives. As Nanda and Khanna note, scaling up to cover larger populations still eludes some of the better designed and effective government programmes. Non-governmental organizations (NGOs) have contributed much into designing and carrying out empowerment and life skills programmes for young girls, but they are not evaluated rigorously enough to offer lessons for scale up. A similar situation rests with the Integrated Child Development Scheme (ICDS), which has the scale and resources to offer childcare services both for those under three years and under six years. Recent efforts to reform ICDS, so that the focus on children under three years becomes sharper than it has been so far, emphasize the role of combining both parent-support initiatives and home-based care for young children and also of providing day-care services for those who require institutional support for childcare in the course of their everyday responsibilities. As Misra and Subrahmanian note:

> Dual crises in women's work and the widespread underdevelopment of young children call for a gendered response that meets the intersecting needs of women and children. The provision of universal childcare in these circumstances needs to be seen as an essential right and entitlement for poor families. The delivery of community-based childcare services through crèches is a key intervention towards attaining long-term national goals of poverty reduction, social inclusion, and gender equity.

More efforts to support women through interlinked services based on fundamental and well-understood commitment to gender equality are required to create the foundations for girl child's rights and a better quality of life for boys as well.

DELVING BELOW THE SURFACE: TOWARDS INCLUSIVE SOCIAL POLICIES

Mediating the interplay between policy intent and well-being outcomes is not just about having a set of implementing institutions. There is also a significant interplay between social structures, social relations, and development aspirations and goals. Structures of gender relations and broader identities based on caste, ethnicity, and tribe have been significant factors determining both inequalities of resource distribution and initiatives of public policy to redress these historical injustices. Yet, as Jodhka points out in his chapter on the different discursive engagements of academics on caste, identity politics, and state policies in India, the assumption that modernization and urbanization would result in the demise of caste as a cultural ideology has been disproved (Chapter 13). However, as he argues, new opportunities and ways of understanding caste, as not a traditional cultural ideology but a 'system of power and domination...that has distributive and material dimensions, leading to diverse developmental outcomes for different categories of population', have led to the opening of new spaces of engagement in the policy arena. These spaces need to be understood and supported to promote meaningful inclusion in the process of development.

Jodhka's chapter is important for the application of different disciplinary lenses to a category of analysis that has received little attention in the development sector, beyond disaggregation of data to show disparities and inequalities. The shifting nature of caste, as well as disciplinary and other differences in how caste has been understood, forms an important context when debating the best ways and approaches to reduce inequalities and disparities. Conventional policy approaches have had some success, especially in expanding the Dalit middle class and political spaces for representation and participation. However, empirically and in human development terms, disparities remain significant. The weak link between the moderate pace of economic mobility and greater political mobilization, on the one hand, and the slower pace of change in human development outcomes, on the other, requires closer analysis. While there have been significant shifts including the weakening of some aspects of the caste system, the challenges emerging from caste as a social institution remain, in particular, through structures of domination. Jodhka points to the institutionalization of inequality, as reflected in the unequal distribution of resources leading to the kinds of disparities elaborated in this volume and also as reflected in a system of culturally and socially entrenched discrimination and denials.

These forms of institutionalized practices require substantive rethinking of policies with the aim to reduce inequality, particularly in the social sectors. They suggest that redistribution of resources alone cannot undo culturally and socially rooted norms and behaviours—they require transformative strategies across all domains.

Gill's chapter (Chapter 14) attempts to develop a framework for assessing the 'inclusiveness' of development programmes, drawing on the example of the National Rural Health Mission (NRHM), which is India's flagship universal health programme. Using the aspirations of the Eleventh Five-Year Plan (2008–12) as her analytical base, which first articulated the policy vision of 'inclusive growth', especially focused on reducing disparities in the social sectors, Gill develops a framework for assessing the extent to which social sector programmes take the challenge of inclusiveness forward, looking in detail at policy intent and resourcing, delivery systems and implementation structures, and the perspective of beneficiaries of the services. Her assessment draws challenging conclusions about the conflation of poverty with caste in targeting welfare programmes and expenditures, even when the effect of caste- and tribe-based exclusion on poverty is recognized, as well as the dominant preoccupation of national programmes with quantification of physical inputs rather than assessment of the quality of outreach and service delivery and its impacts on participants. Above all, she notes the lack of research and analysis on discrimination and disparities in access to government schemes, which have the reduction of inequalities in social development outcomes as an overarching aim. Without such research on discrimination and exclusion within public services, Gill argues, little will be known about 'its nature and extent, and the institutional processes which explain, at least in part, how and why development outcomes for certain groups continue to be consistently dire'.

A major contribution towards expanding this understanding is made by Thorat and Sabharwal (Chapter 15), who draw on the rich body of work undertaken at the Indian Institute of Dalit Studies to fill the gaps in knowledge to which Gill has drawn our attention. They note that

> the main difficulty is lack of a relevant theoretical concept of caste-/ethnicity-/religion-based social exclusion, indicators (or identifiers) of social exclusion, methods for measurement of social exclusion, and methods to capture the consequences of social exclusion on the poverty, livelihood, and human development of excluded groups.

Their chapter attempts to fill this gap by both providing a conceptual framework and suggesting possible indicators of exclusion that could be applied to policy analysis and the assessment of programme delivery. They distinguish between different forms of exclusion, some of which may be invisible or covert, and others, which may be more directly measurable and overt. They bring in the qualitative dimension of experience even in the process of 'inclusion', where there could be partial or unequal terms in inclusion, as well as the dimension of consequences of exclusion—the knock-on effects that lead to the spiral of denial in several spheres simultaneously. By building a conceptual scaffolding that captures the complexity of processes of exclusion and their consequences, Thorat and Sabharwal open up a world of indicators that can, and indeed need to, be used to assess how discriminatory India's public institutions are and to uncover the interlinkages between the private lives and public experiences of those from the excluded communities.

Three chapters in this volume deal with understanding the complex ways in which society and state policies and their interventions respond to the specific challenges faced by India's Adivasi or indigenous population concentrated in central India and a few other states. Xaxa (Chapter 16) locates the historically poor development indicators of children from ST communities in the wider political economy of development that has been pursued in ways that have dislocated these communities from their means of living and ways of life. In locating Adivasi engagement with the modern Indian state in the political economy, Xaxa is able to provide a historical context to the ways in which several practices followed by Adivasi communities have been disrupted and often with negative consequences for their development and well-being. The dominant lens on Adivasis has been the one that sees them as geographically and culturally isolated, and the dominant mode of intervention has been to end this isolation through building roads and railways to extend credit, land, and labour markets. This, Xaxa argues, has been largely for the purposes of exploitation, since equal efforts to extend social infrastructure in the form of irrigation, schooling, and health have been sorely lacking. Thus, despite a shift from welfare to development in government strategies for Adivasi communities, especially since the Fifth Five-Year Plan (1974–9), tribal poverty rates and their human development indicators continue to be the lowest in the country and are improving at a slow pace relative to others.

The 'modernization' hypothesis—that tribal communities are geographically and socially isolated and need to be integrated into the modern world—has underpinned much of state policy and can be seen at best as 'adverse inclusion', as emphazised by Thorat and Sabharwal in their chapter. Processes of integration have destroyed traditional practices, which were often protective of community health and nutrition. Other forms of integration have resulted in displacement and land alienation and denial of access to forests, which are the traditional habitats of Adivasi populations. Xaxa argues that unless deprivations faced by Adivasi children are seen in this wider perspective, solutions to this deprivation are unlikely to be effective.

Tukdeo, in her chapter, takes this theme further with a close examination of the representation and experiences of Adivasi children in the schooling process (Chapter 17). As she notes:

> For Adivasi children, opening their textbooks often means encountering isolation, images of themselves that are frozen in time, and histories that are invisible or at best, appear as tokens... With feathers in their hair, faces painted, the Adivasi communities are presented as 'being part of the jungle'—primitive in every sense of the term.

As per Tukdeo, the reduction of Adivasi communities to simple stereotypes invalidates their cultural heterogeneity and reinforces the 'broader histories of isolation, erasure, and invisibilization'. Locating schooling processes within broader processes of power relations at work, Tukdeo provides a historical context to the current day representations of

Adivasis and examines the consequences for Adivasi children's ability to flourish and participate in India's education system. The contradictions between the principles laid out in various policies to respect the autonomy of tribal regions, on the one hand, and the actions of the Indian State and other actors, on the other, highlight the tensions inherent in the approaches towards addressing Adivasi development.

Recent developments in education policy offer some hope. The Right to Education Act of 2009 has several components, such as an emphasis on localization that should, in theory, allow for more sensitive and responsive measures, especially in the tribal areas. However, an emphasis on standardization can run counter to the need for localized and experiential forms of schooling. These tensions are exacerbated by the lack of Adivasi voice in the policy processes that are designed to reach them and transform their experiences of education and governance.

Themes of Adivasi displacement, alienation, and the challenges of state policy continue in Mehta's close look at the policies and interventions in one state—Odisha (Chapter 18). Despite 45 per cent of the state being classified as a 'Scheduled Area' under the Constitution, which confers special privileges for areas with scheduled tribe majority, poor outcomes persist for children in the state. Mehta argues that tribal pauperization is a consequence of a range of policies and the widespread alienation of communities from traditional commons. Compensatory policies are little known or understood on the ground. In the social sectors, while much work has been done to spread basic services, such as the Integrated Child Development Services, staffing challenges mean high levels of absenteeism and non-functioning services. Where services exist, displacement due to conflict and forced migration due to extreme poverty undermine efforts made by the state and providers to plug gaps and make services available. Mehta notes that even though the incidence of disease among tribal children varies only slightly from, or may be lower than, those of their non-tribal counterparts, they are much less likely to receive treatment in a health facility than the latter. Poor infrastructure in the form of roads, and opportunity costs of taking children to health centres—all such factors contribute to high mortality.

Drawing on interviews with stakeholders, Mehta's chapter demonstrates that the weaknesses of the state's engagement with Adivasi communities and their development challenges are well understood. Setting aside the political economy issues that exacerbate deprivations, the lack of nuanced, community-based, consultative processes stands out as a continuing problem of state intervention. The lack of consultation, combined with generalized strategies that are not based on evidence and are not monitored regularly for lessons, contributes to lacklustre implementation of programmes. Space for innovation is not absent; but, Mehta argues, more engagement with NGOs that demonstrate effective ways to work with communities would help the state do better in the design and implementation of programmes, provided there is a willingness to recognize the time it requires to foster meaningful developmental processes. At heart, there is also the need for state officials to respect Adivasi communities and treat them as equals, '[h]owever, most importantly, they said it needed a mindset, an alternate path of treating tribals as part of us, not as some people living on the fringes'. True inclusiveness based on respect and recognition is then the foundation of the transformation of social policies aimed at Adivasi communities.

TOWARDS CHILD-CENTRED SOCIAL POLICIES

The issues and questions addressed in this multidisciplinary set of essays draw on a wide array of data sources. Primary and secondary data—quantitative and qualitative, numerical and textual—are marshalled by the contributors, who have not just raised questions, but also used evidence to provide informed opinions on the direction of India's social policies in the coming decade. While this volume does not offer detailed insights into particular social sectors, the aim is to step back and look more broadly at the policy environment and the social institutions within which prospects for child rights are being shaped. We very much hope that the offered perspectives contribute to the public discourse on fulfilling India's promises to its children.

We also hope that two key issues that chapters in this volume draw attention to—the need to *expand* programmes and services for children and the need to *improve* existing programmes in terms of both design and implementation—receive the national attention that they deserve. And, finally, as Guy Standing (2012, p. 22) observes, the basis for evaluating the effectiveness of current investments needs to shift to a 'rights-not-charity' principle:

> *A policy or institutional change is socially just if it enhances the rights of the recipient of benefits or services and limits the discretionary power of the providers.* This principle is also crucial for assessing the appeal of alternative social policies. A right is possessed as a mark of a person's humanity or citizenship and cannot be made dependent on some behavioural conditionality... Their social and economic entitlements should be rights, not matters for the discretionary decisions of bureaucrats, philanthropists or aid donors, however well meaning those may be. (Italics as part of the original)

REFERENCES

Government of India (GoI). 2011. 'Provisional Population Totals: India: Census 2011', Office of the Registrar General and Census Commissioner, Ministry of Home Affairs, New Delhi.

Kabeer, Naila. 2004. 'Re-visioning "The Social": Towards Citizen-centred Social Policy or the Poor in Poor Countries', IDS Working Paper 191. Brighton: Institute of Development Studies.

Ministry of Economic Affairs. 2014. 'Economic Survey 2013–14'. http://indiabudget.nic.in/es2013-14/estat1.pdf, last accessed on 4 October 2014.

Office of Registrar General of India. 2013. 'SRS Bulletin September 2013'. http://censuskarnataka.gov.in/SRS%20Bulletins/SRS_Bulletin-September_2013.pdf, last accessed on 5 October 2014.

Sen, Amartya. 2007. 'Children and Human Rights', *Indian Journal of Human Development*, 1(2): 1–11.

Standing, Guy. 2012. 'Cash Transfers: A Review of the Issues in India', Social Policy Working Paper Series-1, UNICEF India. New Delhi: UNICEF India and Sewa Bharat.

The Economist. 2013. 'A Walk on the Wild Side', 23 February 2013. http://www.economist.com/news/asia/21572224-government-borrowing-generates-inflation-widens-external-deficit-and-crowds-out-much-needed, last accessed on 1 March 2013.

Part I

Measuring Poverty and Deprivations from Children's Perspective

1 Recognizing Child Well-being

*The Need for a Double Paradigm Shift**

Ashwani Saith and Rekha Wazir

THE NEED FOR A DOUBLE PARADIGM SHIFT

Ways of seeing influence ways of doing; there is thus much to be gained potentially by a thorough stocktaking and interrogation of the habitual methods and techniques employed in the field of child poverty measurement in India. The basic argument of this chapter is that a double paradigm shift is urgently necessary: from the mainstream approach that focuses overwhelmingly on the material poverty and deprivation experienced by some children, which is deemed by definition to be those in households in poverty, to one that widens the field of vision to include both material and non-material dimensions of well-being of all children. Such a simultaneous shift carries significant implications for modes of conceptualization and recognition—for the focus and substantive content of analysis, for the choice of methods and tools, for the framing and design of policies and interventions, and, more generally, for the scope of debates and discourse pertaining to the development rights of children.

* The arguments of this chapter are more fully developed in Saith and Wazir 2010a and 2010b.

In developing economies generally, and certainly in India, child poverty and well-being issues have suffered serious collateral damage on account of being constricted within the straitjacket of the conventional approaches that dominate the space, imagination, and research. The ubiquitous monetary poverty line approach essentially treats child poverty as being coterminous with household poverty, and the incidence of child poverty is estimated by simply counting the number of children in households found to be below the posited poverty line; all issues of the specificity of child poverty, as distinct from that experienced by adults, get excluded at a stroke. The other dominant approach, that is, human development and its prime recognition device, the Human Development Index (HDI), promises much more than it actually delivers, with child well-being still being defined generally in terms of deficits in the domains of a few standard basic needs. Neither approach adequately acknowledges the full array of dimensions that constitute child well-being in holistic terms. Such straitjacket approaches need to be replaced by wider templates that include other relevant, often non-material, domains of well-being in which many children, whether from poor or non-poor families, suffer endemic and often debilitating deficits.

A few examples could help to carry and clarify the argument. Consider child disability, which afflicts children from all strata of society, not just the poor, and is not generally considered as an issue in its own right in the conventional child poverty agenda. Similarly, child abuse and violence are phenomena that also cut across the poverty boundary. If the two sets of issues are compared, it is reasonable to expect that child disability might impose a far greater cost on the parents and also on the child for families in poverty, because achieving well-being for a disabled child is often, though not always, dependent on economic resources. Disability, when combined with poverty, not only exacerbates problems but also curtails the ability of the individual to move out of poverty. But this does not render disability of children in non-poor households into a non-issue, and certainly not for the children concerned. In the case of abuse and violence, the poverty status of the household might have little relevance, since the issue is not structurally related in cause or cure to family resources, but to behaviour. However, both issues have several negative consequences on the well-being and healthy development of children.

Even for many standard constituents of 'poverty', such as education and nutrition, the focus cannot be exclusively on children in households in poverty. What about the girl child in a non-poor household who is not sent to school on account of conservative parental attitudes? With regard to nutrition, it might indeed be reasonably predicted that calorie and other nutrient deficiencies would be found primarily amongst poor children. But, what if the dimension of nutritional well-being is redefined as malnutrition? This would necessitate an assessment of not just the inadequacy, but also the inappropriateness of children's diets. It would permit, indeed require, the inclusion of children, usually from non-poor families, who suffer from obesity, with its known long-term negative consequences on health and well-being, including costs imposed on society in general.

The chapter is structured as follows: The second section provides an overview of the relatively well-developed state of the study of child well-being in rich countries and highlights several aspects of relevance for the Indian context. The third section provides a brief comparative review of mainstream approaches to assess their relative strengths in serving as vehicles for addressing issues of child poverty and/or child well-being. The location shifts from the global level to India in the fourth section, where some early shoots in the development of the child well-being field are briefly evaluated. How innovative are these? Do they discard the methodological shackles of the mainstream approaches? The fifth section provides a discussion on some crucial elements and dimensions that have to be addressed in developing an alternative wider approach to the recognition and measurement of child well-being in the Indian context. Finally, the last section provides brief concluding reflections.

GLOBAL PERSPECTIVES: FROM POVERTY TO WELL-BEING

Globally, significant progress has been made in moving away from a narrow poverty-related perspective to a wider multidimensional approach that encompasses both material and non-material aspects of children's well-being. A considerable distance has been traversed since B.S. Rowntree's pioneering and methodologically meticulous research on poverty in 1899 in the city of York. His focus was on absolute poverty defined using a primary poverty line that covered the bare 'minimum necessary for maintenance of merely physical health' (Rowntree 1902, p. 37). While specific aspects of child poverty were frequently commented on, the basic underlying premise and conclusion was that its incidence mirrored the poverty of the parents.

Development and material prosperity shift the experience and perceptions of poverty, and new social norms overtake the hard minimalist criterion of maintaining bare bodily physical efficiency. Once the hard basic needs norm is abdicated, poverty also becomes a relative issue. This has come to be reflected in the prevalent approach to the recognition and measurement of poverty in European countries. A standard way of doing this, as in current European practice (EC 2008) is to set the poverty line not in absolute terms but to peg it relative to the median income of the population. However, this would tend to ignore the wide range of factors that impinge on children's well-being in domains that are specific to the child per se. The material components of even a relative poverty line far from exhaust the list of factors and forces that influence the well-being or ill-being of children through life experiences, both within the ambit of the household and in domains and environments beyond it.

At present, a wide range of agencies, using a spectrum of approaches, are involved internationally in measuring and monitoring the status of children and constructing indices of child well-being through interactively developing a common core of dimensions that go well beyond the inherited 'poverty' and traditional 'human development' variables. A major impetus for this widening of perspective has come from the Convention on the Rights of the Child (CRC), which gives equal weight to children's rights to survival, development, protection, and participation. Parties from various states are required to monitor and report progress in implementing the CRC, which, by definition, requires them to gather information on a wide range of indicators that go beyond poverty.

Despite obvious lacunae and problems, the direction of change is unambiguous. On the basis of a review of 199 'status of children' reports from around the world, Ben-Arieh (2006) concludes that a majority of these reports refer to multiple domains of children's well-being, are about the whole child population, and, perhaps not surprisingly, were published in North America, with other Western countries coming in second place. In these countries, significantly more reports are compiled by advocacy groups and academic institutions rather than by international organizations. The direction in which the child indicators movement is evolving is summarized by Ben-Arieh (2006, 2008) as follows:

- From mapping survival to mapping well-being;
- From negative to positive indicators;
- From a focus on well-becoming (the status of the child in future) to well-being (the current status);
- From traditional to new domains;
- From using children as subjects of study to involving them as active participants;
- Towards a composite index of child well-being; and
- Towards a more policy-oriented effort.

Collectively, what has been generated through this very broad and dynamic movement is, first, that well-being has become the key point of focus in assessing the status of children. The notion of well-being is itself being tested and finding its boundaries, which are unavoidably porous and fuzzy in nature. Second, the active issue being debated now is how to conceptualize, measure, and monitor children's well-being in different contexts, how to make the exercise more participatory for the child, and how to incorporate children's subjective perceptions. There is a move to define the approach at more disaggregated levels that could be country-specific, or reflect the specialized mandates of different agencies, or focus in-depth on particular dimensions of well-being. The development and testing of such initiatives enhances the capacity of the general approach to take into account variations and specificities of cultural or country contexts.

Given the advanced level of the study of child well-being in rich countries and the very preliminary state of affairs in contemporary Indian research discourse and policy, it is necessary to take advantage of accumulated global knowledge rather than to set about reinventing the wheel. Such an interaction involves complex challenges, especially since the societal and development contexts are far removed from each other.

INDIAN POVERTY MEASUREMENT: HOW CHILD SENSITIVE IS IT?

In sharp contrast to the pace of progress at the global level, the Indian approach to the recognition of child deprivation seems to be largely locked in a cognitive time warp constrained by anachronistic epistemologies, methodologies, and ideologies. First, the diverse deprivations of children are reduced to dimensions of material poverty; and second, child poverty is usually conflated with household poverty. In general, this charge applies broadly to most mainstream approaches that are in use. It could reasonably be expected that the material deprivation and poverty experienced by any household unit would also characterize the children in it. As such, children in households in poverty could be deemed to be children in poverty. However, it is important to pay close attention to how household poverty is defined in the first place. Brief reflections follow on examples of three major approaches: the poverty line approach, selected social indicators of deprivation; and those using anthropometric yardsticks.

Poverty Thresholds

In India, clearly the worst-performing approaches and methodology are the mainstream ones that use poverty thresholds, whether in its traditional form of expenditure-based monetary poverty line, or in its reincarnation in the form of a multidimensional poverty-scoring template, that is, as in the so-called Below Poverty Line (BPL) household census (Saith 2005, 2007). Neither of these methods was devised for the specific purpose of measuring development deficits as experienced by children and, therefore, their immediate unsuitability should not come as a surprise; but then, neither should these instruments be employed to identify and estimate the incidence of child deprivation. While marginal improvements within the methodology remain possible, the fundamental flaw, from the point of view of capturing child-specific deprivation, is inherent in nature.

Saith (2005) argues that the conventional monetary poverty-line approach pits method versus meaning and the poverty line against the poor. The issue is not simply the usually abysmally low level at which the poverty line is set, but, more fundamentally, that the level of household per capita consumer expenditure cannot be conflated with poverty or well-being. A destitute household that sells productive assets to spend on urgent major health emergencies could get re-classified as being above poverty; so also, if poor parents withdraw children from school and send them to work, the household might well also jump over the monetary poverty line. These criticisms are but the tip of an iceberg. Earlier, Kabeer (1994) drew attention to the gender blindness and gender bias inherent in the household-level poverty-line approach. But this approach has not been similarly audited from the perspective of children. While neither the women nor the children of any household might be able to entirely escape the household's aggregate classification, it is relevant still to ask which kinds of deprivations are experienced in which kinds of manner and to what extent by them. The definition of material poverty and deprivation might itself be blind to important dimensions specific to the constraints and needs of women or children, reflecting a male-dominated professional imagination.

Various critiques of the recent BPL multidimensional scoring approach to the identification of rural households in poverty convincingly confirm its inability to capture poverty at the household level; further, the scheme of criteria and scoring provides very little usable information on the status of the children in the household (Saith 2007; Saith and Wazir 2010a, 2010b). Indeed, the methodology generates potentially pernicious side effects: for instance, by creating a perverse incentive for families to withdraw children from school, since doing so would bring them closer to their being recognized as BPL households and thus to eligibility for selected state benefits. The poverty reduction regime then functions instead as a poverty trap.

Mainstream Social Indicators

The early pioneering, but regrettably under-acknowledged, lead was provided in this area in 1979 by Morris D. Morris's Physical Quality of Life Index (PQLI), which pre-dates the HDI by more than a decade (Morris and McAlpin 1982).[1] Significantly, this initiative focused

[1] The methodological foundations of the use of social indicators for the measurement and planning of quality of life were explored earlier by Jan Drewnowski (1974).

directly on the Indian child. The index was developed for India, using state-level data, and displays several features that suggest superiority over the HDI juggernaut.

The recognition and measurement of human development in India has so far been dominated by well-known general approaches, only some of which take children as their particular focus. For example, the HDI and the related gender-specific version, the Gender-related Development Index (GDI), refer to entire populations, and an interrogation on their child-specific content finds them wanting. Another international indicator comes from UNICEF, namely, the Under-5 Mortality Rate (U5MR), which it has labelled the principal indicator of child well-being. Parallel to this, Save the Children has launched its own brand: the Child Development Index (CDI). Unfortunately, none of them scores particularly well from the specific perspective of children. For instance, the HDI is quite insensitive to hunger, even in the medium term. Worsening outcomes in terms of wasting and stunting are quite compatible with an upward drift in the HDI, arising from an improvement in enrolment rates, in improved longevity on account of public health initiatives, and growth of GNP per capita. As such, it is relatively useless in monitoring the nutritional or health status of children or of other members of the population, except in the most distant manner. This argument holds in general and also applies to the Indian reality. Applications of the social indicators methodology to child well-being, at least in the mainstream development field, remain well short of realizing the creative potential of this approach. While U5MR and CDI certainly do better, they still do not perform well enough.

Anthropometric Measures

Using anthropometric measurements represents a truly direct approach to the measurement of outcomes by focusing on the status of the human body; it cuts straight to the point. Various indicators can be used, the most common ones being wasting, stunting, body mass index (BMI), and measurements pertaining to anaemia and dietary and nutritional indicators, amongst others. In India, such data are generated by the five yearly National Family Health Surveys (NFHS) based on large-scale countrywide samples. The most recent survey of 2006 generated great interest since it allowed its findings to be compared with those of the last 1999 NFHS-2 survey. The interest was all the more intense since it covered a window of time when the Indian economy had posted a dramatic acceleration in the growth rate of GNP. So what do the different approaches roughly reveal? And in doing so, do they converge to any kind of credible consensus? Unfortunately not, considering the following four pieces of summary empirical evidence.

First, between 1999 and 2006, the per capita growth rate of GNP was an impressive 4–5 per cent per annum. Second, in 1995, India's HDI score was 0.551; it rose to 0.578 in 2000 and to 0.619 in 2005. Third, according to the Planning Commission's estimates, the incidence of headcount poverty using the national poverty line was 51.3 per cent in 1973–4, 36.0 per cent in 1993–4, and 27.5 per cent in 2004–5. Evidence from all three approaches agrees on steady progress, and that should please everyone. Unfortunately, the fourth item of evidence throws a spanner in the works. Comparing the findings of the NFHS 1999 with that of the 2006–7 Round, it is revealed that: in 1999, 51.8 per cent of Indian women between the ages of 15 and 49 years were anaemic; in 2006, this figure rose to 56.2 per cent. Among children between the ages of 3 and 6 years, 74.2 per cent were anaemic in 1999; in 2006, this figure was 79.1 per cent. Among children under the age of 3 years in 1999, 20 per cent were wasted; in 2006, this figure had risen to 23 per cent. These shocking findings have understandably induced dismay beyond the reach of methodological qualifications and quibbling.

The data sets from the NFHS are, of course, the ones that are most directly, and reliably, focused on children and use direct and anthropometric indicators. These findings undermine the credibility of the conclusions implied by the other three approaches: GNP growth, HDI changes, and headcount monetary poverty rates. If all four observations are empirically sound, the deduction must be that the rapid growth of GNP per capita, the steady improvement in human development, and the continued progress in the reduction of monetary poverty did not manage to make a dent in the crucial area of poverty as experienced by children and women.

This comparison confirms that it would be injudicious to accept trends in per capita income, HDIs, or headcount poverty rates as proxies for trends in child deprivation or well-being. There is no substitute for developing methodologies that directly address the status of the child, as well as that of the child's family, especially within an appropriately gendered framework. Here again, the wider template of NFHS, which could also be extended in the direction of non-material and non-conventional indicators of well-being, potentially offers a far more productive route than the inherently gender-blinkered methodologies of other mainstream approaches, especially those based on household-level poverty lines or score sheets. In this sense, these departures respond to Cecile Jackson's exhortation to 'rescue gender from the poverty trap' (Jackson 1996).

SOME FRESH INITIATIVES IN INDIA

At present, there would appear to be a propitious academic, activist, and policy conjuncture for the widening of the discourse on child deprivation in India—from one that has so far viewed child poverty within the straitjacket of household poverty reckoned in terms of the poverty line, towards the adoption of a wider template of well-being that incorporates various non-material, psychosocial, personal security, mental well-being, disability, and relational dimensions as well. Widening the agenda also leads to the incorporation of additional players and drivers, new stakeholders, and responsibility bearers. This conjuncture is created partly by the emerging reporting requirements and exhortations of the international development regime, including especially child-focused agencies (prominently UNICEF, but also others, such as Save the Children), international treaties (such as the relevant ILO Conventions, the CRC), and rights-oriented initiatives (such as Education for All and the Millennium Development Goals [MDGs]). But it is also fuelled by dissatisfaction over the inability of the existing methodologies to provide a meaningful, intellectual, or operational frame for contending with issues of child well-being in a holistic manner.

In India, there are a variety of initiatives that have recently emerged from and further propel such an agenda. These include the 'Bristol Approach', currently used by UNICEF for its ongoing study of child poverty in Asian countries, including India; the methodology developed by the UK-based Childhood Poverty Research and Policy Centre (CHIP) in collaboration with partners in China, India, Kyrgyzstan, and Mongolia; the approach used by the Young Lives Project—a partnership between Save the Children (UK), several British universities, and partners in Ethiopia, India, Peru, and Vietnam; and by HAQ, a non-governmental, child rights organization based in Delhi. While each initiative provides a welcome departure, it transpires that in several critical respects, they all eventually tend to get trapped in the dead ends of the mainstream reductionist interpretations of well-being.

While there is some rejection of the monetary poverty-line approach and while multiple deprivations are explicitly recognized, the entry point of most studies continues to be poverty, either income poverty or poverty in its multidimensional forms. In this, they share the basic perspective and objectives of the poverty-line approach, that is, satisfaction of basic needs, though this time with an improved methodology, which rejects the money-metric techniques of the poverty-line approach. They use social indicators instead, which directly verify whether the specific basic needs are adequately met. Useful as this move is, there is still a gap between where current approaches stop and where we need to go in terms of assessing the well-being of children.

While NGOs such as HAQ are attempting to go beyond this, they are constrained by the lack of data on a whole range of important but hidden issues such as abuse, disability, and violence. These non-poverty dimensions continue to be under-reported, but they are as persistent and debilitating as poverty and have a profound impact on children's well-being and development. These hidden domains are no doubt difficult to measure, but data collection is not an insurmountable problem per se. Several rich countries already collect data on children's non-material well-being, as well as innovative approaches to data collection on a range of children's issues, making effective use of new information and communication technologies that can be found in India as well.

TOWARDS MAPPING CHILD WELL-BEING IN INDIA

Child poverty studies in India have made some strides, as evidenced earlier in this chapter, but significant gaps persist. The following discussion offers a qualified justification and an initial sketch of the conceptual frame of a more holistic approach and engages with some of its important substantive elements and methodological requirements. The purpose here is not to provide a complete operational blueprint for a ready-made strategy to be implemented in India; as that goes beyond the scope of an individual chapter. The intention, rather, is to highlight the major reorientations and extensions that such shift in paradigms would entail at the levels of recognition, definition, and conceptualization; of the adoption of wider methods including subjective and perceptive methodologies; of the need to explicitly probe the specific circumstances and needs of vulnerable social constituencies; and of issues involved in the generation of relevant data to guide and monitor the process as a whole. While this discussion is pitched largely at an a priori level, it is inspired mainly by Indian realities and addressed primarily to the large and diverse community of researchers, practitioners, and activists in this field in India.

Need for a Holistic Vision

This chapter has argued for a widening of the conceptual and policy perspective from narrow interpretations of child poverty, reckoned in terms of material deprivation, to a broader framework that encapsulates child well-being more holistically. There are two powerful implications of such a shift at both the conceptual and policy levels. First, moving from material poverty to well-being includes many other forms of child deprivations and deficits, such as violence, abuse, participation, subjective perceptions, social exclusion, disability, malnutrition (rather than only under-nutrition), to mention but a few. Second, in view of the fact that these additional facets of well-being could characterize children independently of whether they belong to poor or rich households, the subject group is no longer children from households in poverty, but *all* children, regardless of the economic status of the households to which they belong.

The traditional approach is focused on A (Table 1.1). In order to identify and count the children in space A, the first step was to identify

Table 1.1 Holistic Framework for Mapping Child Well-being

	Experience deficits in the domains of:	
	Material basic needs	Holistic well-being
Children in poor households	A	B
Children in non-poor households	C	D

households in poverty in terms of basic needs and then to count the number of children in such households. The higher the percentage of such households, the higher was the incidence of child poverty, allowing for differences in the average number of children in poor, as against non-poor households. Most commonly, the methodology used was the monetary poverty line approach with all its problems, including blindness to intra-household distribution issues and its inability to check directly whether basic needs were met in reality even when the expenditure levels were in excess of the prescribed poverty line. The problems with the narrowness of focus and with the nature of the methodology have both come to be widely acknowledged.

The responses to this, at both conceptual and policy levels, have been varied. In rich countries, there has been a steady shift from a sole focus on A to including B, C, and D, that is, to a holistic inclusion of well-being dimensions for all children. This has implied the use of different concepts, methods, and data, different target groups, different stakeholders, change agents, and responsibility bearers. This was demonstrated systematically in this chapter.

However, for poor countries, including India, this dissatisfaction has had a different response from development researchers and practitioners. Here, as was argued earlier, the main shift has been in the methodology of recognition and measurement of child deficits. Disappointingly, though, while the nomenclature is often changed from child 'poverty' to child 'well-being', this shift usually turns out to be nominal, with the definition of 'well-being' still limited essentially to the conventional elements of basic needs, namely, nutrition, water, housing, education, health, and electricity. The monetary poverty-line approach is given up and replaced by the social indicators approach involving the direct verification and measurement of the degree to which these particular needs of children have been met—some at the household level (for example, electricity and clean water) and others at the level of the individual child (for example, education). Therefore, the result is *not* a shift in the substantive focus as much as a change of approach and methodology.

One could question the legitimacy of using the term 'well-being' when the content of this well-being remains limited to the elemental, basic needs basket. Such approaches have also sometimes portrayed themselves as examples of the application of the 'capability' paradigm. Within this paradigm, basic needs poverty has indeed been labelled as 'capability deprivation'. In our view, this is too narrow a view of well-being or of capabilities to be useful. Indeed, several of the new initiatives in the Indian context, as discussed earlier, could be so described and criticized: there is an explicit or implicit claim to having shifted from space A to space B, whereas a careful scrutiny of substance confirms that they are still lodged firmly in the former.

That said, it should be noted that giving up the monetary poverty-line approach opens up the possibility of some widening of perspective even within these approaches from A to C. This happens since the direct approach would surely find many children with educational or other deficits in households that are well above the monetary poverty line. The extent to which this happens depends on the specific norms applied to different basic needs. To the extent that the focus is on *extreme* poverty—defined as acute shortfalls in nutritional status, housing, education, and other such needs—it is unlikely, indeed, that the coverage would, in reality, expand significantly from A to C. If anything, the focus within space A might narrow even further to concentrate on children experiencing 'extreme' deficits for particular basic needs. Of course, if appropriate levels were set for the various basic needs norms, ones that duly reflected human rights considerations, there could be substantial shortfalls in meeting specific basic needs of children even in monetarily non-poor households: girls not sent to school because of gender bias; or boys sent out to work instead of to school; or neglect of the health needs of girls; or other more general deficits suffered by the household despite having cash to spend. This again confirms the active relevance of space C. Thus, there are legitimate grounds for concern that the 'new' agenda of child 'well-being' is still overly restricted to specific aspects of conventional poverty reduction.

In this matter, instead of rediscovering the wheel, it would be far more appropriate to reflect duly on the ground painstakingly covered by the well-being and social indicator movements in the rich countries. There, the agenda has, over time, reinvented itself involving a relocation from space A (in the manner that is perhaps currently construed in poor countries) into one which covers A, B, C, and D. That cumulative and dynamic body of knowledge needs to be used as a resource in making such a transition in the Indian context as well, albeit bearing in mind the implications of contextual specificity and the limits this places on the simple transference of understandings that are contingent on levels of prosperity and cultural mores.

In moving to such a wider frame, which still accommodates the issue of poverty at its core, there is no calling for a unique predefined rigid composite indicator of child well-being, à la the HDI, or the recently promulgated CDI developed by Save the Children. Indeed, neither aggregation nor uniqueness is particularly desirable. Disaggregated indices provide more information and insight: this is inevitably lost in the aggregation process of combining different indices on different sub-dimensions. As also, a unique measure cannot possibly capture the diversity that characterizes a large and complex society with its structured differences and inequalities; one size or description cannot fit or apply to all. As such, there is a need to explore the open space for contending and overlapping perspectives on what enters into and impinges on child well-being. Selective aggregations can no doubt be made, but then without acquiring a hegemonic status that suppresses the diversity of situations, perspectives, and meanings inherent in such a broad synthetic notion.

Self-perceived Poverty and Participatory Methods

Acknowledging additional non-traditional basic needs often takes the researcher and practitioner into non-commodity space—into the domain of behaviour, institutions, modes of exercising power, exclusion, and bias and self-perception by the subjects experiencing the deficits. There are serious epistemological issues involved here that need to be recognized. Doing so implies that the modes of enquiry and knowledge acquisition also have to change and adapt. This highlights the relevance of methodologies that use participatory techniques that use subjective and qualitative approaches. These may not lend themselves to quantification and measurement, but that does not devalue their profound relevance for a meaningfully framed project of achieving holistic child well-being.

Participatory methodologies are not useful for the *overall* estimation of the incidence of poverty, be it for the entire population or for any component of it, such as children. Nor can these be employed for making meaningful *comparisons* of deprivation across populations, such as residents of different villages, since the methodology is based on a direct mutual knowledge of the members of the reference group. However, the methodology can yield valuable qualitative information about the forms, nature, and experience of deprivation and can also be employed for investigating the responses of individuals, families, or groups to their circumstances, constraints, and aspirations. In a community setting, these methods, if used well, can be very effective in identifying those in poverty. There is a special premium on its use arising from the fact that adults cannot be assumed to be able to readily comprehend, appreciate, and analyse the worlds of children and the problems and desires as the children perceive them. However, this methodology raises special challenges in relation to children, especially for lower age cohorts. While this approach has considerable potential benefits when used creatively and with due sensitivity in appropriate contexts, a prime danger is that this method can be easily manipulated and misused. Such a distortion of method can occur all the more easily in case of children than in interactions with adults.

Thus far, the use of participatory methods involving children has been relatively limited in Indian research, and a highly substantial potential benefit remains to be derived from extending their use in exploring the perception and experience of well-being, happiness, exclusion; of the desires and aspirations of children; of the quality and deficits in the relationships of children as perceived by themselves. In this regard, rich countries are much more advanced and there is a substantial possibility of learning by studying this experience with an eye for Indian situations.

This highlights a special feature of the field of child poverty and child well-being, which is, that the discourse and debates, policies, interventions, and decisions are enacted almost entirely by adults on behalf of children. This has several implications. Despite sincere efforts at enhancing child participation in making decisions that affect their well-being, there are limits and problems in such attempts. The age at which participation becomes meaningful is obviously a serious, variable, and difficult to specify constraint. But even for older children, a meaningful participatory process is contingent on several preconditions of relative autonomy, of cognition, of awareness, of access to information and the analytical capacity to process it for identifying alternative implications of different courses of action. Such difficulties should not legitimize denial. Thus, in contrast to other subaltern categories—for example, gender and socially excluded groups, where affected adults can act as their own change agents—in children, there is a dependence on the enabling or disabling actions of involved adults, whether it is parents, teachers, or others. The process involved is thus rendered more complex and engages several additional categories of care-providers and stakeholders.

Further, it is important to avoid the danger of seeing 'children' with the same homogenizing vision that views 'the poor' as an undifferentiated mass. Almost no analytical argument or policy intervention carries validity and applicability across all children. There are many internal distinctions that need to be maintained, and keeping gender and age cohorts separately in mind is essential.

Social Exclusion

Social exclusion has rightly been given an increasingly prominent space in the study of deprivation. There are two broad and relatively distinct conceptual approaches to social exclusion; the difference between these is of special significance, since it also implies very different policy interventions. The first, as developed in the context of the paradox of social marginalization as a parallel process to the development of the French welfare state, focuses on factors and processes that account for this, especially with respect to particularly vulnerable social groups. This version shifts the focus from poverty and material deprivation as an outcome to the societal structures, relations, and processes that generate these outcomes. The second approach, while accepting the value of the above, goes beyond this—it does so by conceptualizing social exclusion as fundamentally reflecting discriminatory practices based on essentially immutable aspects of the identity of the individual such as race, caste, gender, and disability. A second layer of discriminatory bias could be rooted in other identity-related features which are mutable but which cannot be rendered socially invisible: language, age, ethnicity, and religion. This version of the social exclusion approach clearly adds value conceptually to the understanding of poverty and deprivation, since it highlights discrimination as a reason for both being and remaining in poverty; and also to the possibility of such discrimination persisting, despite the fact that the individual, household, or community being so victimized was economically well clear of the poverty line.

Such an identity-related discrimination approach has massive salience in contemporary India. While there has been considerable empirical and analytical research on the status of the Dalits, tribal populations, and other socially discriminated communities in Indian society, much of it has taken place within the framework of India's extensive affirmative action programmes, with the focus on such ascribed group identities such as Scheduled Castes (SCs), Scheduled Tribes (STs), and Other Backward Classes (OBCs).

Despite the sustained high-profile focus on this, it is remarkable how little specific research has been conducted on the experience of this despicable form of discrimination in the context of Indian children being born into this social reality. While recalling incidents in his life that shaped his thinking and outlook, Ambedkar (1990) includes several experiences of his childhood, one of which was that at school, he could not even help himself to a drink of water. It is known that significant social discrimination is still experienced by children, and this needs urgent study through the use of methodologies that focus on subjective perceptions of exclusion, humiliation, separation, and bias or the discovery of anger, injustice, dignity, and identity. An agenda of child well-being would prioritize these dimensions; one limiting itself to material deprivations would tend to exclude them by definition.

Gender Dimensions

A brief gender audit of the different approaches is also in order: the status of women, especially young mothers, has massive implications for child well-being through an array of causal linkages that have been clearly identified and studied in-depth; and such an audit could also shed some independent light on the sensitivity of the approach specifically to aspects affecting the girl child. The conventional monetary poverty line has been widely critiqued for its virtual gender blindness. The social indicators, including the Gender-related Development Index (GDI) and the Gender Empowerment Index (GEM) have been severely criticized for their reductionism. While GDI and GEM can be used to argue that there have been improvements in the situation of women, the direct evidence from the Family Health Survey rounds are sobering and point to persisting, even worsening, gender outcomes in India.

A more creative departure within the Indian context, and one that carries potential significance for the field of child well-being, is provided by gender studies of psychosocial and other non-conventional indicators of the well-being of women. Sonpar and Kapur (2003) have provided an insightful and nuanced treatment of gender disparities in the context of the process of structural reforms in India, focusing on mental well-being and life-quality issues. On an analogous track, Eapen and Kodoth (2003) take up wider and non-conventional dimensions of stresses in the lives of women against the backdrop of the gender achievements of the so-called Kerala model. These interventions highlight the importance of not limiting the rubric of concern and study to the conventional domains of basic needs, significant as these undeniably remain. Others have taken up the worthwhile challenge to investigate gender differences within households using non-monetary indicators (Cantillon and Nolan 2001). This and related innovative methodological interventions point to both the need and the possibility of extending the canvas to the analysis of children's well-being using these and similar approaches.

A Fresh Challenge: Newly Emerging Needs of Children

Beyond the traditional and more hidden domains of children's well-being, there is yet another dimension that needs to be given due attention, that is, the newly emerging needs of children (van Oudenhoven and Wazir 2006; Wazir 2008). At present, there are no mechanisms for forecasting, measuring, and responding to such needs, yet several of these are potentially ominous for children's well-being. The term 'newly emerging needs' is used to describe a loosely connected group of new challenges, problems, and opportunities confronting children that are important and relevant to their overall well-being and development. These 'new' needs are frequently juxtaposed alongside a pre-existing set of 'old' problems, frequently intensifying these by creating additional dimensions and interfaces on which all children can feel distress. In India, many children still live in poverty, child malnutrition remains an intractable problem, a large number do not go to school, and countless others labour from an early age. But the changes that are sweeping the country, as indeed the rest of the world, are bringing in fresh challenges that cannot be ignored. Researchers, policymakers, and practitioners have to be flexible, forward looking, and increasingly prepared for new and unfamiliar situations that are not yet clearly formed, but have the potential to become major threats for children in the foreseeable future.

The most obvious illustration of a newly emerging need is provided by the pandemic increase in the number of children born and living with HIV/AIDS. The sheer number of children affected by it and the multidimensional ways in which it challenges their well-being has forced this issue to the top of the agenda and made it a key priority for development aid. Governments, international agencies, and NGOs have been compelled to develop responses at the level of policy and practice. This is one of the new events affecting children, which receives some of the attention it deserves. But there are other issues as well that are jostling for attention—the rise in childhood diseases related to environmental pollution, lifestyle changes, diet, and stress; the challenges thrown up by new technologies such as mobile phones and unlimited internet access—and they all have the potential to become major threats for children. For example, diabesity, a combination of Type 2 diabetes and obesity, may become the new childhood epidemic, in not just the US, but also in countries like India and China that are more associated with starvation and inadequate diets (BBC News 2004).

Demographic changes, environmental pollution, medical interventions, increased interactions with other peoples and cultures, and globalization of the economy, information systems, and lifestyles are some of the interrelated processes that lie at the root of these newly emerging needs and pose new challenges as much as they create new opportunities. These processes, individually or combined, create a myriad of different conditions and situations, each of which may pose a unique challenge to children, create specific needs, and demand special attention. They affect all children—rich and poor, boys and girls—though the impact on the different groups of children will be quite different.

Counting and Measuring

The lack of relevant and reliable empirical evidence constitutes a major lacuna that is constraining all child rights endeavours and seriously compromising efforts at conceptualization, policy design, monitoring, and impact assessment. This gap is all the more damaging in view of the burgeoning role of the state in development design and finance.

At an international level, disproportionate effort seems to go into the construction of internationally comparable templates for a set of handy variables for which data are easily available. One genuine concern expressed regarding the millennium development goals (MDGs) is precisely that many important development deficits, which do not find space on the highlighted MDG pedestal, could be implicitly devalued by agencies, politicians, and bureaucracies (Saith 2006). This danger becomes acute when addressing the issue of child well-being. Quantifiable, measurable, deliverable targets have become symbols of significance. Yet, there is a lengthy list of vital dimensions of child well-being that do not meet these criteria of managerial acceptability, such as child abuse, violence against children, child disability, and subjective aspects of child well-being. Indeed, the more the definitional boundaries are widened—from the present focus on material poverty towards a fuller acceptance of multidimensional child well-being—the greater becomes the importance of not equating measurability with relevance and significance. Clearly, fresh epistemological and methodological challenges will have to be met with innovative and creative responses.

Lack of data on specific aspects of child well-being could also reflect a lack of concern, as for instance on child disability. The problem of invisibility is compounded by the stigma ascribed to such disability, which then tends to reinforce denial and silence at multiple levels. In turn, the lack of data lays the basis for a lack of policy. These areas of silence need to be addressed with urgency, possibly through qualitative synthetic mapping and monitoring of important non-measurable or not-measured dimensions. At the other end of the spectrum, there seems to be an overemphasis on high-profile statistics and measurement with respect to some more conventional dimensions of child well-being. Thus, for example, educational statistics, used as a yardstick of child well-being, provide some sobering insights. The primary focus has been on school enrolments, but there is little systematic information on crucial dimensions of the learning process such as quality, relevance, achievement, completion, or enjoyment. The recent e-Shishu project in Odisha suggests that it could be feasible to think of national templates of meaningful statistics that could be refreshed regularly.[2]

Despite the extensive institutional capacity of the Indian statistical system, the outcome with respect to the status of the child remains very patchy and unsatisfactory. What is also disappointing is the absence of any systematic drive to develop a more comprehensive databank that allows cross-sectional and inter-temporal comparative analysis. For setting a meaningful research and policy agenda for child well-being in holistic terms, it is imperative to undertake a comprehensive stocktaking of the national statistical system to critically inventory and evaluate the scope and quality of data available from all relevant sources at multiple levels. This would highlight gaps and needs for gathering or generating data at various levels for use by different players, with the responsibility of delivering on the components of child well-being. Clearly, fresh epistemological and methodological challenges will have to be met with innovative and creative responses in this process.

★ ★ ★

To return to the original motivational concerns of the chapter, while it can be re-emphasized that household poverty is indeed one crucial determinant of child deprivation, it was also argued that prevalent methodologies of the estimation of household poverty, including those practised in India, are seriously deficient. This has a knock-on effect in terms of subsequent inaccuracies in the estimation of child poverty—even within the terms of this approach. It was argued that the issue of child well-being is inherently far broader than the constrictive frame of reference imposed by the conventional household poverty

[2] The objective of the project, active since 2005, was to generate a database that would track every child in Odisha in the age group of 0–14 years, covering name, age, educational status, and other relevant details, using door-to-door household surveys—about 8 million in number. These forms, originally in Oriya and then translated into English, were then uploaded onto a web-linked database. The entire process was completed, apparently, in less than four months.

measurement approach. This calls for an acknowledgement of the full array of material and non-material dimensions that influence child well-being. Most of these dimensions influence *all* children, regardless of the poverty status of the households to which they belong. Recognizing these, in both discourse and the design of interventions, is central to any meaningful approach to addressing child rights on a holistic and universal basis. The well-being of all children cannot be limited by definition to the material deprivation of those children living in households in basic needs poverty.

Many creative and innovative initiatives—even though scattered, small scale, and unarticulated—have emerged. Efforts at widening the research and policy agenda from material poverty towards holistic well-being will need to learn strategically and selectively from the considerable body of knowledge, experience, and expertise that is available from the parallel communities of researchers, activists, and practitioners in the rich countries. Special attention is also necessary to widen the frame of reference from one that inventories deficits in the negative form of *ill-being* to perspectives that also actively engage with the positive space of factors that stimulate various forms of *well-being*. It is time to catch up—a goal that should not prove unrealistic, given India's impressive academic and professional infrastructure.

REFERENCES

Ambedkar, B.R. 1990. *Waiting for a Visa: Reminiscences*. Bombay: Siddharth Publications, People's Education Society.

BBC News. 2004. 'Chinese Concern at Obesity Surge', 10 December.

Ben-Arieh, Asher. 2006. 'State of the Child Reports and Indices of Children's Well Being: An International Perspective', Presentation for the MedChild International Conference on Tools for Measuring the Well-being of Children, Rome, 20 March. www.medchild.org/upload/News/Files/39_2006322_112923_asher%20ben%20arieh%20edchild.ppt.

———. 2008. 'The Child Indicators Movement: Past, Present, and Future', *Child Indicators Research*, 1: 3–16.

Cantillon, Sara and Brian Nolan. 2001. 'Poverty within Households: Measuring Gender Differences Using Nonmonetary Indicators', *Feminist Economics*, 7(1): 5–23.

Drewnowski, Jan. 1974. *On Measuring and Planning the Quality of Life*. The Hague: Institute of Social Studies and Mouton.

Eapen, Mridul and Praveena Kodoth. 2003. 'Family Structure, Women's Education and Work: Re-examining the High Status of Women in Kerala', in Ratna M. Sudarshan and Swapna Mukhopadhyay (eds), *Tracking Gender Equity under Economic Reforms: Continuity and Change in South Asia*, pp. 227–67. New Delhi: Kali for Women.

European Commission. 2008. *Child Poverty and Well-being in the EU: Current Status and Way Forward*, Social Protection Committee, Directorate-General for Employment, Social Affairs and Equal Opportunities, January.

Jackson, Cecile. 1996. 'Rescuing Gender from the Poverty Trap', *World Development*, 24(3): 489–504.

Kabeer, Naila. 1994. *Reversed Realities: Gender Hierarchies in Development Thought*. London: Verso Press.

Morris, Morris David and Michelle B. McAlpin. 1982. *Measuring the Condition of India's Poor: The Physical Quality of Life Index*. New Delhi: Promilla & Co. Publishers.

van Oudenhoven, Nico and Rekha Wazir. 2006. *Newly Emerging Needs of Children: An Exploration*. Antwerp: Garant Uitgevers.

Rowntree, B.S. 1902. *Poverty: A Study of Town Life*, 4th edition. London: Macmillan & Co.

Saith, Ashwani. 2005. 'Poverty Lines versus the Poor: Method versus Meaning', *Economic and Political Weekly*, 22 October, 40(43): 4601–10.

———. 2006. 'From Universal Values to Millennium Development Goals: Lost in Translation', *Development and Change*, 37(6): 1167–99.

———. 2007. 'Distortion and Downsizing of Poverty in India: The Perverse Power of Official Definitions', *Indian Journal of Human Development*, 1(2):247–81.

Saith, Ashwani and Rekha Wazir. 2010a. 'From Poverty to Well-being: Alternative Approaches to the Recognition of Child Deprivation in India', IHD-UNICEF Working Paper Series on Children of India: Rights and Opportunities. New Delhi: UNICEF.

———. 2010b. 'Towards Conceptualizing Child Wellbeing in India: The Need for a Paradigm Shift', *Child Indicators Research*, 3(3): 385–408.

Sonpar, Shobna and Ravi Kapur. 2003. 'Non-Conventional Indicators of Gender Disparities under Structural Adjustment', in Ratna M. Sudarshan and Swapna Mukhopadhyay (eds), *Tracking Gender Equity under Economic Reforms: Continuity and Change in South Asia*, pp. 24–63. New Delhi: Kali for Women.

Wazir, Rekha. 2008. 'Newly Emerging Needs of Children: Towards Widening the Policy Agenda in South Asia', *Indian Journal of Human Development*, 2(1): 183–201.

2 Child Well-being and Deprivations in India

Preet Rustagi, Sunil Kumar Mishra, and Balwant Singh Mehta

The well-being of children is a critical component of the human development of any country. India has the world's largest child population. Ensuring that children have access to adequate nutrition, good health, and education, and also that the households they live in have access to basic earnings, adequate food consumption, shelter, sanitation, and clean water, constitutes a core minimum set of material and non-material needs. The inequalities and deprivations faced by children highlight their vulnerabilities, and addressing these deprivations is of concern both nationally and globally.

The need to draw attention to children as a distinct group stems from their invisibilization in most policy discourses at the macro level. Also, the conflation of children's development indicators with that of the households they belong to as well as the strong association drawn between material poverty and deprivations faced by children warrant closer study. A shift from viewing children as mere dependants to viewing them as individuals with rights specific to them is attempted in this chapter through an analysis of the magnitude of children's vulnerabilities and deprivations.[1]

[1] For instances of inadequacies in the households approach of measuring poverty, see Rustagi et al. 2012 and Saith and Wazir 2010.

Material poverty of households weakens their access to basic amenities and facilities, such as shelter, sanitation, and water needs, and this adversely affects children in the households as well. Children experience not only deprivations that affect the households to which they belong, but also the non-material deprivations; non-material deprivations are invisible because children are perceived as dependants in the households and not as individuals in their own right.

The growing acceptance of the urgency to look at children as a separate, distinct group stems from the recognition that their physical, social, economic, psychological, and emotional needs have to be met in a time-bound way, given the narrow windows of opportunity to ensure this. Once lost in childhood, these opportunities can seldom be regained later, and the consequent deficits in the well-being of children are increasingly being recognized as having severe adverse consequences on their future as adults (Rees et al. 2012).

This chapter takes stock of children's well-being and deprivations, using latest available information from different secondary data sources. The variations across locations, states, gender, and social groups for a range of selected indicators—education, nutrition, immunization, shelter, water and sanitation—highlight both the inequalities prevalent and the extent of deprivations faced by children in India. The secondary data from National Family Health Surveys (NFHS) provide statistics on these variables, but they neither show us how children (those under the age of 18 years) are affected by deprivations, nor reveal the incidence of multiple deprivations faced by children. The approach of using unit-level data from NFHS to calculate the deprivations for a range of select indicators—both household and individual—reveals the incidence of each deprivation and thus helps to measure multiple deprivations.

This chapter is divided into five sections. A profile of children in India across age cohorts, states, and social groups is provided in the first section. The second section presents the material poverty profile of children across states, location, and household occupational categories. The incidence of deprivations faced by children, as individuals or as members of the household they belong to, is discussed in the third section. The extent of multiple deprivations affecting children (based on and limited to a set of six core deprivations—education, food, immunization, shelter, sanitation, and water) and characteristics of these children and households will be presented in the fourth section.

Finally, the concluding remarks highlight the key findings and the urgent need to focus on children affected by multiple deprivations in India. The need for appropriate social policies and to strategize how this can be achieved is emphasized in the chapter.

PROFILE OF CHILDREN IN INDIA

This section presents data on the share of children in the population of India and the major states; their share of population in the various social groups; and their age structure. Children are all persons under the age of 18 years, and they constitute two-fifths of India's population (37 per cent). In spite of the declining birth and fertility rates, India has a large proportion of young persons, and the advantage of this demographic dividend needs to be harnessed. Losing this window of opportunity will push large sections of India's population into deprivation for many years to come.

Numbers and Age Structure

In 2001, as per the Census, there were 423 million children in India. In spite of the gradual decline in fertility rates over the years, the total number of children show a higher figure in the 2011 Census. However, the 2011 Census reported a decline of five million children in the age group of 0–6 years from 2001 to 2011; there were 159 million children in this age group in 2011 compared with 164 million in 2001.

In the age group of 0–6 years, there has been a decline of nearly nine million children in rural areas, while in urban locations, there has been an increase of four million children.[2] Whether this is an outcome of natural decline and urbanization or a reflection of the poor livelihood opportunities in rural locations and the agrarian push-led migration are relevant questions to address, but they fall outside the purview of this chapter.

Nearly one-fourth of all children are in the age group of 0–4 years, while those in the age groups of 5–9 years and 10–14 years constitute

[2] While detailed information on child population (those under 18 years), including age structure-wise data, is awaited at the time of publication, this decline in the child population of the age group of 0–6 years in rural areas is spread across 29 states and 7 union territories (UTs).

30 per cent each. The proportion of child population is the comparator against which the proportion of deprived children is seen in order to assess the extent of deprivations faced by children and to identify the intensity across locations. The density of child population may be seen as also directly reflecting the larger incidence of deprivations faced by children in states like Uttar Pradesh, Bihar, Maharashtra, West Bengal, as opposed to a similar proportion of deprivation in Odisha, Jharkhand, or Gujarat.

Location of Children

Children may be in households, institutions, on the streets, or living on their own. Statistical information from secondary sources shows that the majority of children can be found living in family households. Three-fourths (75 per cent) of all households in India have children living in them.

There is some variation across rural and urban India. While rural areas have 77 per cent of households with children, urban areas report 68 per cent only. Three-fourths of all children in India live in villages and slightly under half are girls. The sex ratio among children of the age group of 0–6 years reports a decline in most states, and for the country as a whole it fell by 13 points—from 927 females per 1,000 males in 2001 to 914 in 2011.

Children by States

The states that have a high proportion of child population are Bihar, Uttar Pradesh, Rajasthan, Jharkhand, Madhya Pradesh, Uttarakhand, Chhattisgarh, Haryana, and Assam. As expected, a larger number of children live in geographically bigger states that have a higher population density and fertility rates than other states.

Analysis of the share of children in individual state populations (Figure 2.1) suggests, for instance, that while children comprise only one-third of the population of southern states like Kerala and Tamil Nadu, in states like Uttar Pradesh in the north and Bihar in the east, a substantial part of the population (50 per cent) is below 18 years of age.

Figures 2.2a and 2.2b give the proportion of households with children in different states of India, both in rural areas and in urban areas.

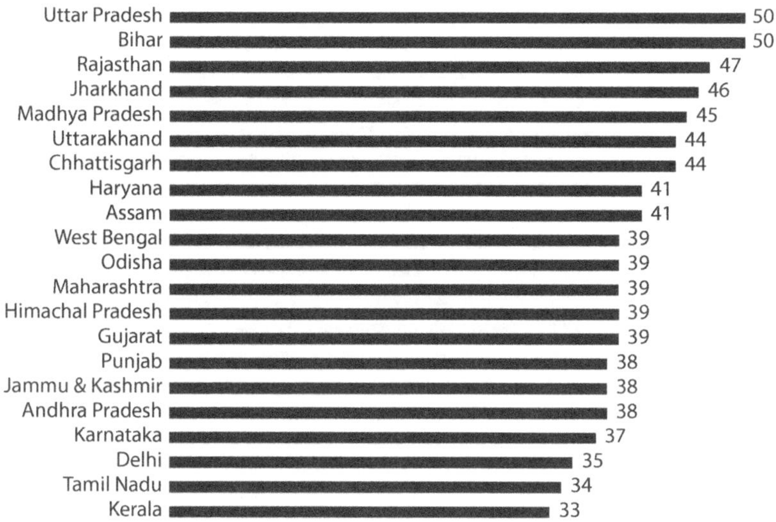

FIGURE 2.1 Percentage of Child Population of Select States
Source: Derived from NSS 2004–5.

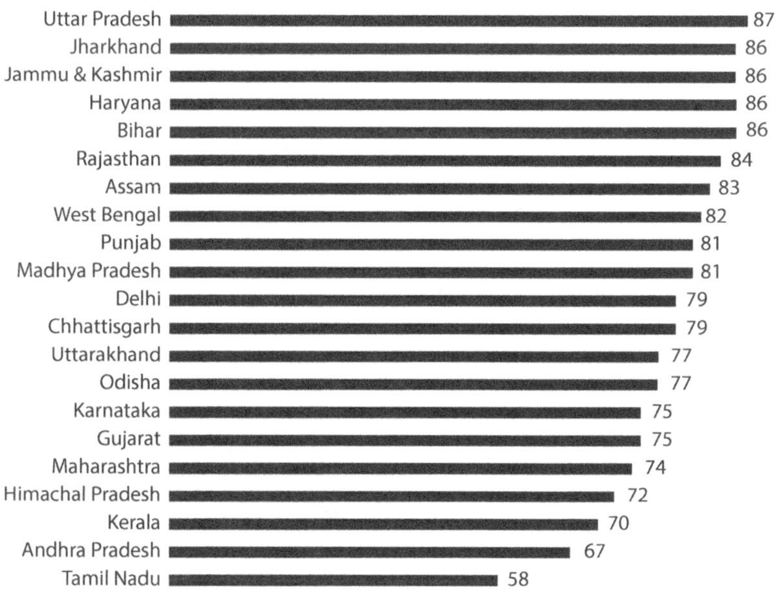

FIGURE 2.2a Percentage of Rural Households with Children, by State
Source: Derived from NSS 2004–5.

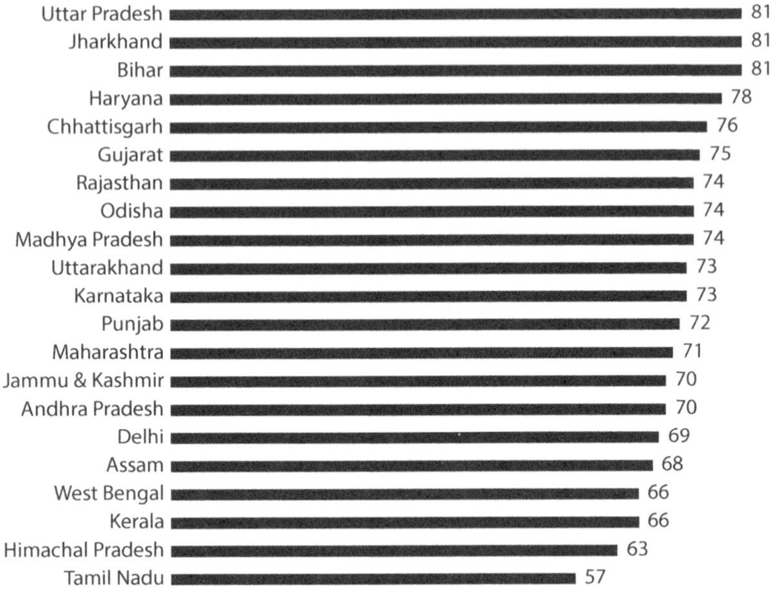

FIGURE 2.2b Percentage of Urban Households with Children, by State
Source: Derived from NSS 2004–5.

What is striking here is that Tamil Nadu has the least proportion of households with children. This holds true even for rural Tamil Nadu, where 58 per cent of households have members below the age of 18 years, a proportion lower than in any other state.

Children by Social Groups

Analysis by social groups shows that Scheduled Tribes (STs), Scheduled Castes (SCs), Other Backward Classes (OBCs), and other categories contribute, respectively, 11 per cent, 22 per cent, 42 per cent, and 25 per cent of children's population in rural areas (see Table 2.1). To the extent that STs and SCs are known to be historically poorer than other social groups, deprivations of children belonging to these groups are also expected to be the most entrenched.

MATERIAL POVERTY AND CHILDREN

Official poverty lines in India, defined in terms of consumption expenditure as a proxy for income, are very low by international

TABLE 2.1 State-wise Percentage of Child Population

Social groups	Total	Rural	Urban
ST	9	11	3
SC	20	22	15
OBC	41	42	37
Others	30	25	45
Total	100	100	100

Source: Derived from NSS 2004–5.
Note: ST: Scheduled Tribe; SC: Scheduled Caste; OBC: Other Backward Class.

standards. This means that a significant proportion of households that may by other measures be defined as poor may not be deemed as 'official poor', because they do not fall below this threshold. In rural India, for instance, about half of the population in 2004–5 lived on Rs 15 per person, per day, only Rs 3 more than the official rural poverty line (Rs 12 per person, per day, in 2004–5) (World Bank 2011). Children within such vulnerable households may be missed if one were to go strictly by the official poverty line.

For the purposes of this chapter, therefore, we consider households to be poor if their monthly per capita expenditure is below 1.25 times the official poverty line set using 1993 prices (Table 2.2). This is based on an approach followed by Sengupta et al. (2008).

Using this more fluid definition of poverty, this study finds that slightly over half (52 per cent) of all children in rural India live in households surviving on less than 1.25 times the poverty line (for the proportion of children across all six categories, see Table A2.1). This is more than the share of total rural population living in such households (45 per cent). Similarly, in urban areas, about half of the entire child population (48 per cent) lives in poor households.

In contrast, although middle- and high-income households account for only 20 per cent of the population in rural areas, their cumulative share in total child population is lower at 15 per cent (Figure 2.3). This divergence is even more striking in urban areas, where middle- and high-income households constitute 34 per cent of the total population, but house only 26 per cent of children. This suggests that poor households, in general, tend to have more children—a stylized fact that is well known, but is also worrying since it effectively means that about half of India's children live in poor households.

TABLE 2.2 Criteria for Classification of Households into Different Poverty Thresholds

Poor (less than or equal to 1.25 PL)	Extremely poor	Less than 0.75 PL
	Poor	Greater than 0.75 PL, but less than 1 PL
	Marginal	Greater than 1 PL, but less than 1.25 PL
Vulnerable		Greater than 1.25 PL, but less than 2 PL
Middle-income group		Greater than 2 PL but less than 4 PL
High-income group		Greater than 4 PL

Source: Using Sengupta et al. (2008) to reclassify poor for the purpose of this study.
Note: PL: Poverty line.

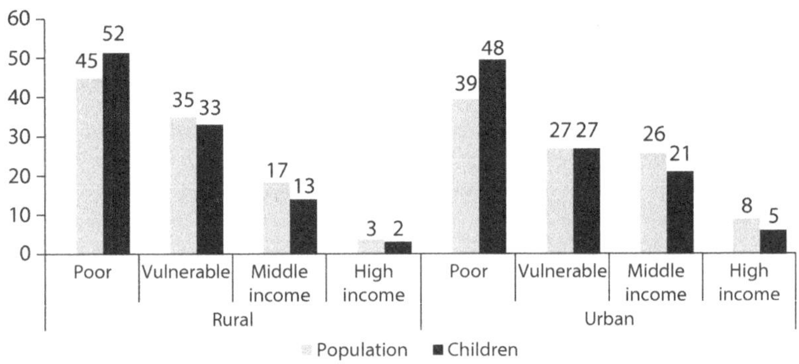

FIGURE 2.3 Percentage of Child and Total Population by Income Class
Source: Derived from NSS 2004–5.

However, there are variations across states. Three in every four children in Odisha, for instance, live in poor households (Figure 2.4). In contrast, in Kerala, children living in poor households account for only 20 per cent of the total child population in the state.

Variations exist by social group as well. For example, a substantial proportion of SC children—63 per cent—lives in poor households. In comparison, only 36 per cent of children from other social groups live in poor households. The gap is even wider for ST children, among whom nearly 67 per cent live in poor households (Figure 2.5).

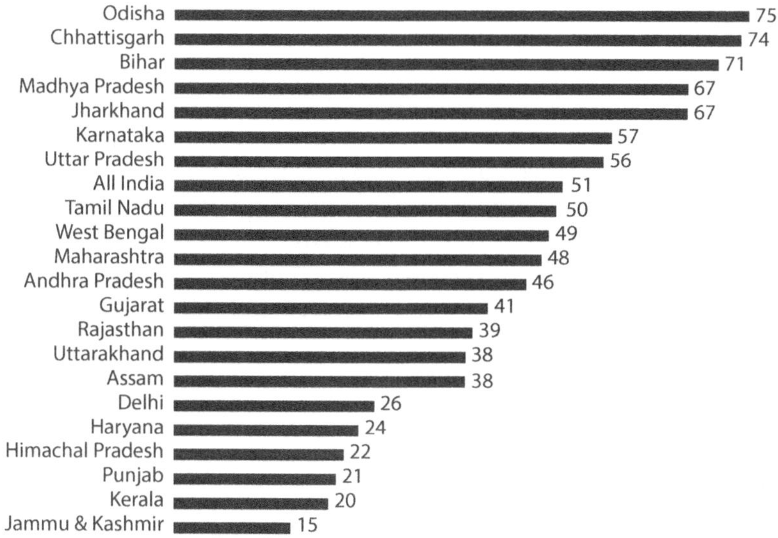

FIGURE 2.4 Percentage of Children Living in Poor Households, by State
Source: Derived from NSS 2004–5.

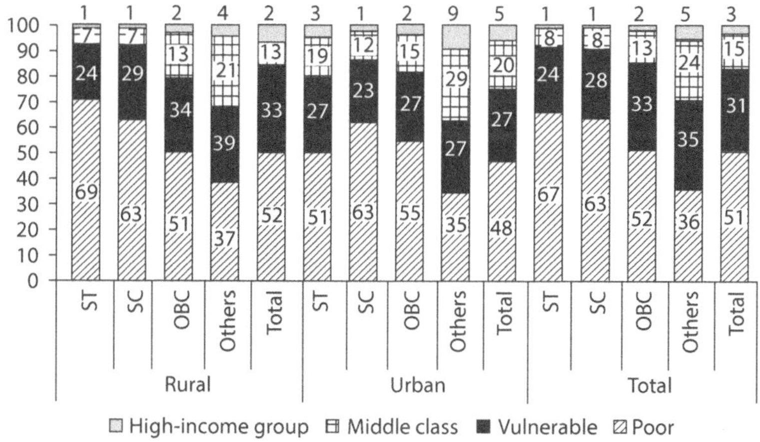

FIGURE 2.5 Percentage of Children by Social Groups and Income Categories
Source: Derived from NSS 2004–5.
Note: ST: Scheduled Tribe; SC: Scheduled Caste; OBC: Other Backward Class.

Children by Family Occupation

In occupations, there is significant overlap in households that are engaged in wage labour and that are poor. Expectedly, 73 per cent of children living in households engaged in agricultural labour in rural areas and 81 per cent of children living in households engaged in other labour in urban areas also live in conditions of poverty. In contrast, fewer children from households that are self-employed in non-agriculture—47 per cent and 51 per cent in rural and urban areas, respectively—live in conditions of poverty (Figure 2.6).

DEPRIVATIONS

In this section, the deprivations faced by children in six core areas[3] are discussed to provide a static (one point period) and descriptive analysis.

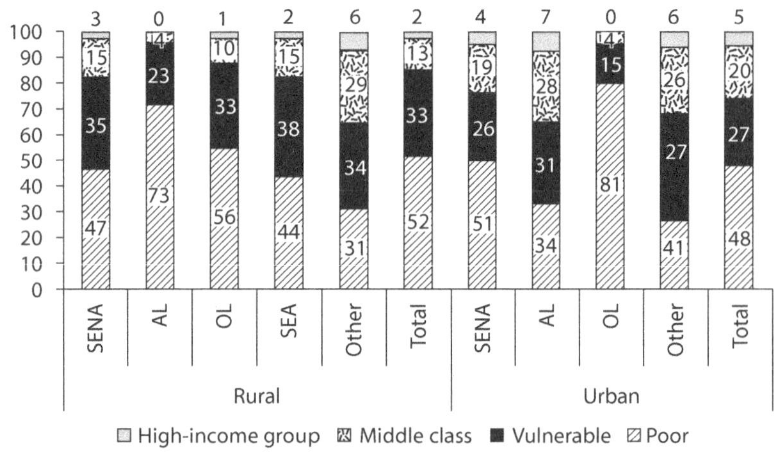

FIGURE 2.6 Percentage of Children Living in Poor Households, by Main Occupation

Source: Derived from NSS 2004–5.

Note: SENA: Self-employed in non-agriculture; AL: Agricultural labour; OL: Other labour; SEA: Self-employed in agriculture.

[3] A variation of the Bristol Approach for estimating child well-being is adopted for India. These indicators were modified to suit the Indian context and were based on the availability of relevant information from national secondary data sources. See Rustagi et al. (2012) for the Bristol Approach.

These deprivations relate to three child-specific and three household-specific ones. Are these deprivations associated with levels of poverty? In other words, do we find that there are more deprived children in states that have a higher proportion of children from poorer households? Does the pattern of individual and household-level deprivations vary or is there a confluence of all these deprivations? These questions are taken up in the discussion ahead.

Child-specific deprivations:

1. *Nutrition deprivation* (*a proxy of food*) is indicated when children (under five years) have heights or weights more than two standard deviations below the median of the international reference population for stunting, or wasting, or being underweight.
2. *Education deprivation* is indicated when children in the ages 6–17 years are not currently attending school (for the year 2004–5).
3. *Immunization deprivation* (*a proxy of health*) is indicated when children of 1–5 years (12–59 months) have not received full immunization, that is, all the basic specified vaccinations, such as BCG (Bacillus Calmette–Guérin) injections, DPT (diphtheria, pertussis, tetanus) and polio vaccines, and measles vaccine.

Household-specific deprivations:

1. *Water deprivation* is indicated when children are living in households that use surface water or where it takes 30 minutes or longer to collect water.
2. *Sanitation deprivation* is indicated when children are living in households with inadequate or no access to toilet facility. This includes no facility or using bush or field, composting toilet, or a dry toilet.
3. *Shelter deprivation* is indicated when children are living in dwellings with five or more people per room or with low quality and inadequate roof material (which includes natural and rudimentary roof materials, such as mud, thatch, palm leaf, grass mixture, plastic or polythene sheet, rustic mat, raw wood planks, and unburnt bricks).

Deprivations Faced by Individual Children

Based on the individual deprivations as defined above, more than one half of all children are deprived on account of nutrition status and full immunization cover (see Table 2.3). The rural areas uniformly

TABLE 2.3 Proportion of Children Deprived (Individual Deprivations)

	Nutrition	Immunization	Education
Total	62	54	31
Rural	65	59	33
Urban	53	41	24
Female	62	55	34
Male	61	53	24
SC	67	57	33
ST	70	65	44
OBC	63	57	31
Others	53	44	25

Source: Calculated using unit-level data from NFHS-3 2005–6.
Note: ST: Scheduled Tribe; SC: Scheduled Caste; OBC: Other Backward Class.

record worse outcomes compared with urban areas. In terms of social groups, ST have the highest deprivation levels, followed by SC. The gender differences are not very wide with regard to nutrition status and immunization cover, but are wider in levels of education. Let us consider each of these individual deprivations separately in the following paragraphs.

NUTRITION DEPRIVATION

UNICEF (2010) reports that, annually, nearly 1.83 million children die of preventable causes before completing their fifth year. Although all indicators of child mortality (neonatal, infant, and under-5) are declining (see Figure 2.7), the targets set by the Millennium Development Goals (MDG 4) for 2015 are not going to be achieved.

The critical window of opportunity for preventing under-nutrition begins with maternal health, care during pregnancy, and the newborn child's first two years of life. With 36 per cent of women recording a low level of body mass index (BMI) and more than one half of ever married women (15–49 years) being anaemic (55 per cent), the newborn child is exposed to grave risks of survival. These risks are exacerbated by the absence of quality reproductive and maternal care facilities. It is during the infancy years of children, up to 2 years, that nutritional interventions have proven to substantially improve the chances of children's survival as well as help them reach their optimal growth.

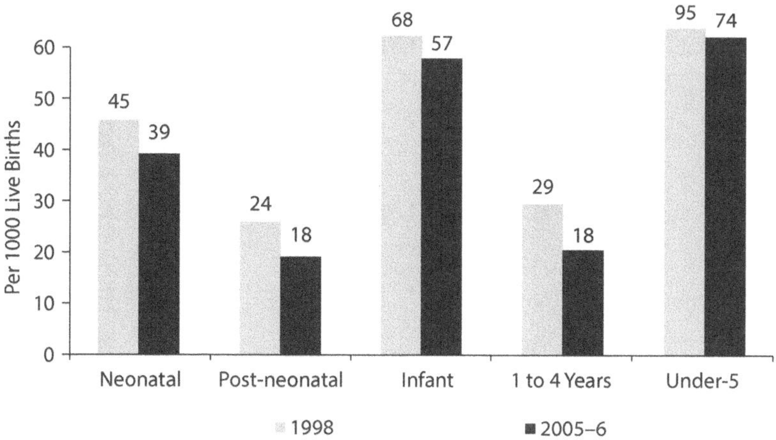

FIGURE 2.7 Mortality Rates among Children
Source: Derived from NFHS 1998–9 and NFHS 2005–6.

Poor and improper interventions in nutrition for and care of infants affect their survival; it also causes anaemia, ill-health, and stunting. From 1998–9 to 2005–6, incidence of stunting among children under the age of three years has declined from 51 per cent to 45 per cent. However, the proportion of children suffering from wasting has increased from 20 per cent in 1998–9 to 23 per cent in 2005–6 (see Figure 2.8). Under-nutrition is also known to impact cognitive development among children, their performance in school, and their physical development.

As per the NFHS-3 (2005–6), children under the age of five years affected by nutritional deprivation, that is, those who are stunted, wasted, or underweight, constitute a significantly large proportion of nearly 62 per cent. Children who suffer all three, that is, those who are stunted, wasted, and underweight, are severely undernourished and constitute 14 per cent.

The proportion of children facing deprivation on account of under-nutrition is highest in Madhya Pradesh, at 73 per cent, while the lowest is recorded in Kerala, at 40 per cent (see Table A2.2).

Even for Kerala, the rural–urban differences are nearly 10 points—with rural areas having 43 per cent of nutrition-deprived children. Figure 2.9 depicts the gaps across rural and urban areas. Rural areas in Uttarakhand, West Bengal, Jharkhand, Odisha, and Chhattisgarh

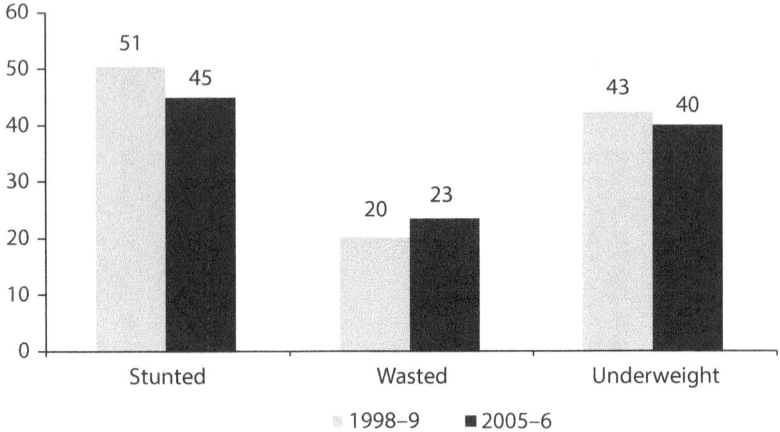

FIGURE **2.8** Nutrition Status of Children under 3 Years as per NFHS-2 and 3
Source: Derived from NFHS 1998–9 and NFHS 2005–6.

have more nutrition-deprived children compared with their urban counterparts.

DISTANCE FROM UNIVERSAL COVER OF FULL IMMUNIZATION

Every day, on an average, more than 26,000 children under the age of five years of age die around the world, mostly from preventable causes. Nearly all of them live in the developing world (UNICEF 2008). Basic vaccinations received by any child to be fully immunized are one dose of BCG injection to protect against tuberculosis, three doses each of DPT and polio vaccines, and one of measles vaccine, to be given during 12–23 months of age. Since, in India, even basic vaccinations are not received by many children, the goal of universal cover of full immunization needs to be achieved.

As per NFHS-3, more than one half of all children do not receive full immunization, that is, only 46 per cent of all children in India are reported to have received full immunization. Once again, it is barely two out of every five children in villages who receive all the vaccinations. Between boys and girls, the differences in full immunization cover are marginal. In urban areas, the situation is relatively better, almost the reverse of the rural scenario, with only two out of five children being deprived of full immunization (see Figure 2.10).

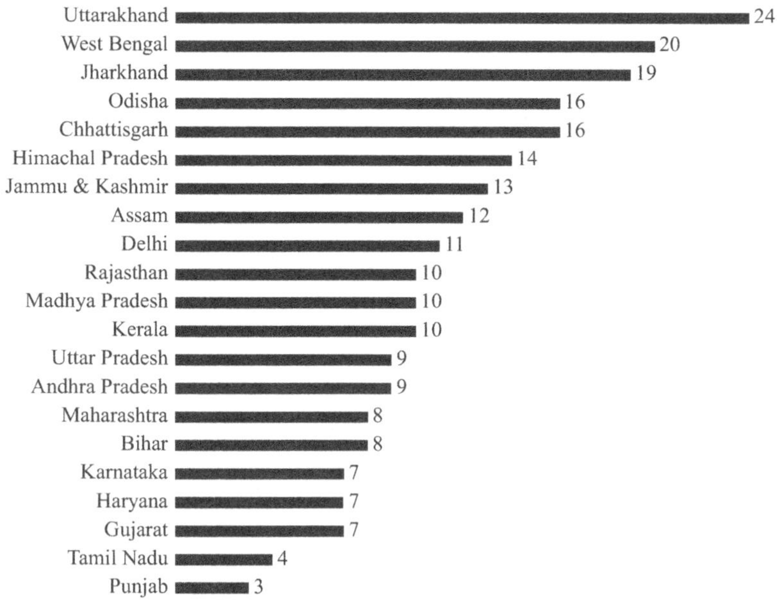

FIGURE 2.9 Rural–Urban Gap in Nutritional Deprivation
Source: Calculated using unit-level data from NFHS-3 2005–6.

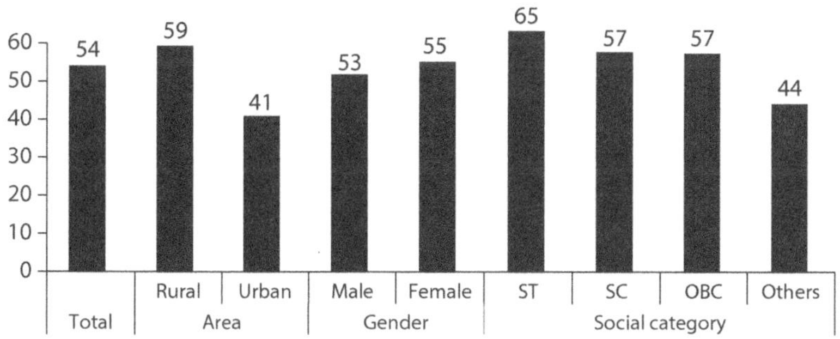

FIGURE 2.10 Percentage of Children (Ages 1–5) Not Receiving Full Immunization
Source: Derived from NFHS 2005–6.
Note: ST: Scheduled Tribe; SC: Scheduled Caste; OBC: Other Backward Class.

Analysis of immunization rates among the 1–2 year olds finds that compared with other vaccines, the immunization coverage of DPT-2 vaccine (at 33 per cent), DPT-3 vaccine (at 44 per cent), and measles vaccine (at 40 per cent) is relatively low compared with the other basic vaccinations in India.

More than one half of all children in the ages 1–5 years are deprived in terms of missing out on one or more vaccinations. The statistics reveal that 53 per cent of boys and 55 per cent of girls are deprived of full immunization. The female to male differences are more marked between rural girls, among whom only 40 per cent receive full immunization, and urban boys, among whom 60 per cent receive full immunization (see Table A2.3).

The distance to full immunization varies tremendously by social composition of children, with the maximum gap to universal cover noted among the ST children (65 per cent). This is followed by both SC and OBC children, with a distance of 57 per cent still to be traversed for attaining full cover.

The maximum distances to ensuring universal cover of full immunization are recorded from the states of Uttar Pradesh, Rajasthan, Assam, Bihar, and Jharkhand (see Table A2.3). Even at the other end, among the states with less of a distance in universal cover of full immunization, there are wide variations. Tamil Nadu has only 15 per cent children yet to be fully immunized, and this is followed by Himachal Pradesh and Kerala, each left with a little less than 20 per cent, while the gap to be met for Delhi is 32 per cent and for West Bengal it is 33 per cent.

Among the southern states, while Tamil Nadu and Kerala report a relatively better immunization cover, Karnataka and Andhra Pradesh report only one half of children as beneficiaries of full immunization cover. Urban Karnataka, in fact, is among the worst five states (in terms of the 21 major states included for analysis).

The relatively prosperous state of Haryana may be among the five least-deprived states on this count, both in rural and urban areas, but it still has a distance of 37 per cent in rural areas and 26 per cent in urban areas to ensure that all children are fully immunized. In other words, the point to be reiterated is that the differentials in immunization coverage across the states are partly due to the state-specific service delivery systems and its efficiency and therefore not explained by material poverty, although there might be some association or correlation between the two factors of income poverty and immunization cover.

Therefore, as seen in nutrition status, full immunization cover, too, does not seem to be a matter of wealth alone. Wealth category is also called quintiles in the NFHS. Figure 2.11 reveals the distance in terms

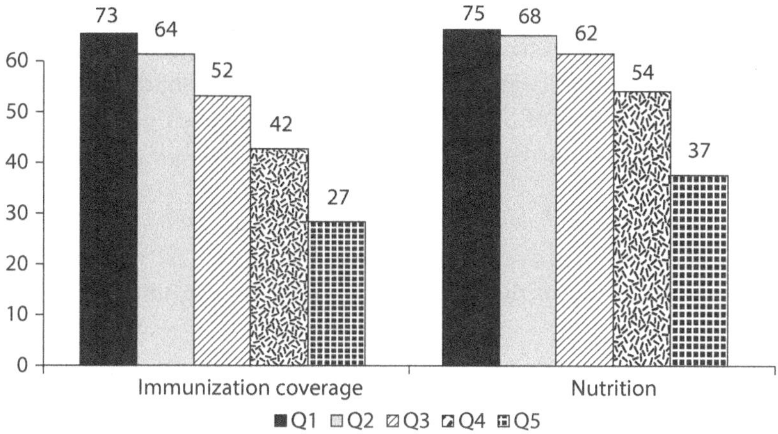

FIGURE 2.11 Deprivation in Immunization Coverage and Nutrition by Wealth Quintiles

Source: Calculated using unit-level data from NFHS-3 2005–6.

of percentages of children deprived across wealth index quintiles to reiterate the point, for even in the Q5—the highest wealth quintile, that is, relatively better-off sections of the population—children are nutrition deprived in 37 per cent of the cases and 27 per cent do not benefit from full immunization. Appropriate efforts to generate awareness on these issues and other health-related issues are essential, and education plays a great role in facilitating such awareness.

EDUCATION DEPRIVATION

In spite of India's considerable efforts towards achieving education for all, universalization of even elementary education is some distance from being achieved. The NFHS-3 data reports all children who did not attend school in 2004–5 as deprived of education. Thus, it reports less than one-third (31 per cent) of all children as deprived of education in India. However, children from villages (33 per cent) are the most deprived of education as compared with those in urban areas (24 per cent). Girls (34 per cent) have a higher risk of being out of school compared to boys (24 per cent).

Children in the school-going ages of 6–17 years who did not attend school in the year 2004–5 accounted for 31 per cent in the country as a whole. Older children (15–17 years) appeared to be more deprived (39 per cent) as compared to the 6–14 year olds (28 per cent). This is primarily due to the permissible legal age of entry into the labour market being 15 years in India. An illustration of the far higher proportion of ST children in the age bracket of 15–17 years being in the labour market compared with non-tribals is reflected in Figure 2.12.

Among the social groups, it is the ST children who are most deprived compared with all the others (see Figure 2.13). The gender differential noted for the children's population as a whole, with higher

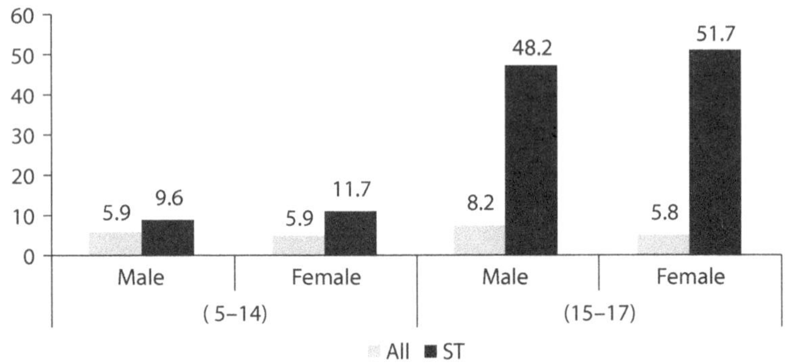

FIGURE 2.12 Working Children in Different Age Groups: 5–14 and 15–17 Years
Source: Calculated from Census of India 2001.
Note: ST: Scheduled Tribe.

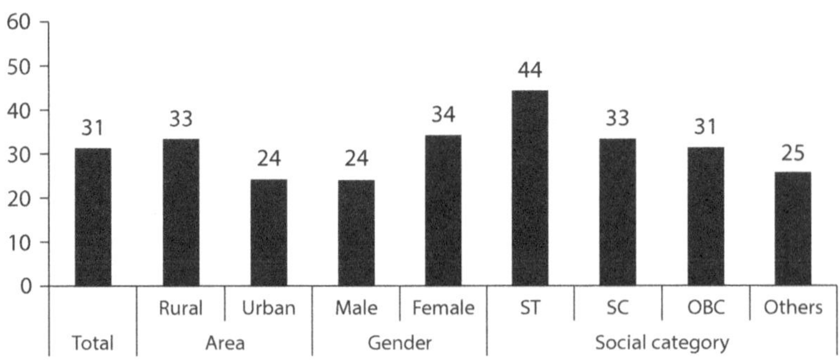

FIGURE 2.13 Education Deprivation (Percentage of Children)
Source: Calculated using unit-level data from NFHS-3 2005–6.
Notes: ST: Scheduled Tribe; SC: Scheduled Caste; OBC: Other Backward Class.

proportion of girls being deprived, implies that tribal girls must be the worst affected in the country.

The proportion of children enrolled for education in the year 2004–5 range from as low as less than half in Bihar to 92 per cent in Himachal Pradesh. With 69 per cent children in the age group of 6–17 years attending school during the year 2004–5, this report finds that more than one-third of the child population is left outside the ambit of schooling.

Clearly, there are wide inter-state variations in the distance still to be traversed towards universalization. Even a single variable-based indicator on the proportion of children attending school provides insights into this. The worst state among 21 major states is Bihar, at 51 per cent, followed by Jharkhand, Rajasthan, Uttar Pradesh, West Bengal; the least-deprived states are Himachal Pradesh (8 per cent), followed by Kerala (13 per cent), Uttarakhand (15 per cent), Tamil Nadu (16 per cent), and Maharashtra (22 per cent).

Rural–urban differences are high with differentials across states. There is close to 10 percentage point variation across locations on an average for the country as a whole. While rural areas generally report higher education deprivation levels across most of the states, with Chhattisgarh, Jharkhand, Odisha, Bihar, Rajasthan, and Madhya Pradesh being the worst in terms of the gaps between villages and urban areas, the states where urban education deprivation levels are higher than rural areas are Uttarakhand, Himachal Pradesh, Tamil Nadu, and Delhi.

Similar to the locational variations, there are variations in education deprivation levels across gender as well. The states with the highest gender disadvantage where girls are most education deprived in rural areas are Rajasthan, Jharkhand, Bihar, Uttar Pradesh, and Chhattisgarh (see Figure 2.14).

The mapping exercises stipulated in the Right of Children to Free and Compulsory Education Act of 2009 if undertaken with a mandate to identify specific regions, locations, or groups may assist the process of moving towards a more inclusive education for all children.

Household Deprivations Impacting Children

Inadequate shelter and sanitation facilities along with water deprivation impact the lives of children in multiple ways. Though water availability or access to sources of drinking water appears to be relatively better

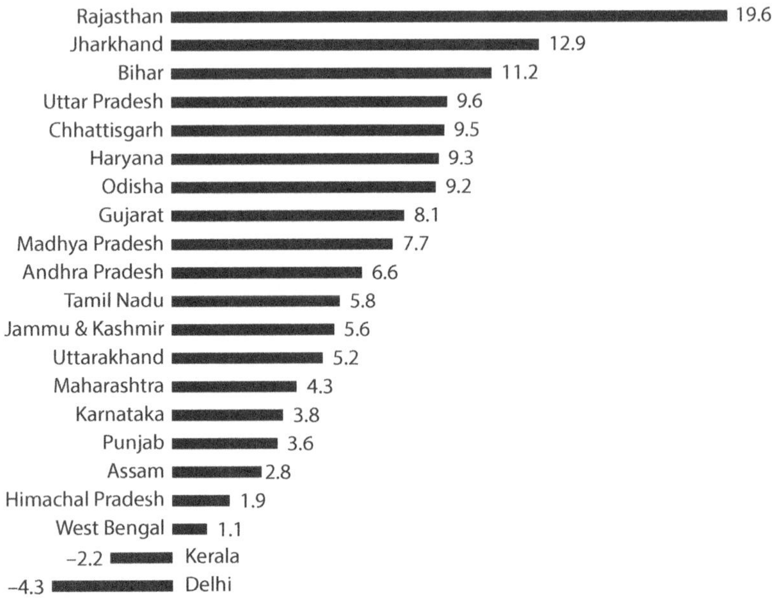

FIGURE 2.14 Gender Gap in Education Deprivation in Rural Areas
Source: Calculated using unit-level data from NFHS-3 2005–6.

than earlier (see Table 2.4), the quality of this water is not considered here. Again, though the safety of drinking water by source is the best way to consider this critical dimension, secondary data sources often do not allow for a more detailed or nuanced analysis.

Each of the three deprivations that pertain to the household level is considered in the following sections.

SANITATION DEPRIVATION

In the opening section on sanitation, the UNDP Human Development Report (2006) comments:

> [A]s a global community we face a vast deficit in sanitation—a deficit overwhelmingly concentrated in developing countries. Today, almost one in two people in the developing world lack access to improved sanitation…access to basic sanitation is a crucial human development goal in its own right: for millions of people not having a safe, private and convenient toilet facility is a daily source of indignity as well as a threat to well-being.

TABLE 2.4 Household Deprivations Affecting Children in India (in per cent)

	Sanitation	Shelter	Water
Total	63	49	14
Rural	78	52	16
Urban	22	39	8
SC	73	58	15
ST	85	54	30
OBC	69	50	14
Others	41	39	9

Source: Calculated from unit data of NFHS-3.
Note: ST: Scheduled Tribe; SC: Scheduled Caste; OBC: Other Backward Class.

More than half of the households (58 per cent) in India do not have any sanitation facility and three-fourths of these households belong to rural areas. It is even more disheartening to note that 55 per cent of households in India and 74 per cent of the villagers use bushes or fields for excretion. An analysis on the use of toilets by their type (flush, pit, or compost toilet) discloses that less than one-tenth (9 per cent) of the households in India have a flush to a piped sewer system and only one-fifth have a flush to a septic tank.

The states where proportions of children affected by sanitation deprivation are very high include Chhattisgarh (84 per cent), Odisha, Jharkhand, Madhya Pradesh, Rajasthan, and Bihar; Uttar Pradesh reports a 74 per cent sanitation deprivation. By and large, the situation across location highlights the poor sanitation facilities in these states.

Rural India is much more deprived in terms of basic sanitation facilities, with 78 per cent households being categorized as deprived compared with 22 per cent in urban areas. This distance in the levels of deprivation across location is noted for most of the states as well (see Table A2.5). However, irrespective of location, the states with relatively lower levels of sanitation deprivation are Kerala, Delhi, Assam, and Punjab, followed by Jammu and Kashmir, Uttarakhand, and West Bengal.

SHELTER DEPRIVATION

Over 640 million children in developing countries experience severe shelter deprivation (UNICEF 2005). Though the United Nations Conventions on the Rights of the Child (CRC) has recognized adequate and safe housing as the right of every child, about 40 per cent of households with children are deprived of shelter in India. Among children, 49 per cent are deprived of shelter in India. More children in rural areas (52 per cent) are affected by shelter deprivation than in urban areas (39 per cent). More than one half of Indians live in households with only one room for sleeping (55 per cent), and 32 per cent of households have two rooms for sleeping. Given the average family size, this reflects the extent of crowding.

Across the states of India, children are most affected by shelter deprivation in Bihar (64 per cent), then in Uttar Pradesh, Odisha, Rajasthan, and Andhra Pradesh (51 per cent). There is a very clear difference in the states reporting shelter deprivation in rural areas as opposed to urban areas. While Bihar, Uttar Pradesh, and Gujarat are deprived in both rural and urban areas; Rajasthan and Odisha are among the most deprived states in rural areas; Maharashtra, Andhra Pradesh, Madhya Pradesh, and Delhi in urban areas record levels of shelter deprivation that are higher than the all-India figures (see Table A2.6).

WATER DEPRIVATION

Only 24 per cent of all households in India had access to piped water. An even smaller proportion of only 13 per cent get their drinking water through pipes within their dwellings. The variations in access to water across rural–urban locations are very high. While one half of all households get piped water in urban areas, only a miniscule 12 per cent receive drinking water through pipes within their dwellings or plots in villages. The share of urban households which receive water within their premises is 32 per cent, while the situation in villages is very low with only 4 per cent of households having access to drinking water through pipes within their dwellings.

For the purposes of this study, water deprivation occurs when sources of drinking water are from rivers, dams, ponds, streams, canals, irrigation channels, or when it takes 30 minutes or more to collect water (walk to the water source, collect water, and return). Thus, two aspects have been considered for inclusion in the category of being water deprived. One, the source of drinking water, whether it is safe or unsafe, and secondly, the time taken to collect drinking water for the household. Since, in a large number of households, especially in rural India, children undertake the work of collecting water, this responsibility deprives them of time to study, develop, etc., and this becomes an added dimension of implicit concern.

The largest segment of households has access to drinking water from tube wells or boreholes (43 per cent). The proportion of rural households resorting to this source for their drinking water is higher (at 53 per cent) than that of urban households (at 21 per cent). Another 18 per cent of households depend on the public tap or standpipe (urban at 20 per cent, and rural at 16 per cent). Although dependence on tanker trucks and bottled water is marginal in terms of percentage of households, it is almost entirely an urban phenomenon. On the other hand, in rural areas, wells, springs, and various other unprotected water sources are used much more for drinking water than in urban areas.

As seen above, more than one half of all households (51 per cent) did have access to drinking water within their premises. Another 37 per cent manage to collect their drinking water within half an hour, while it takes more than 30 minutes but less than an hour to collect water for 11 per cent of the households. Thus, most households, as reported in the NFHS-3, manage to collect their water on an average within an hour. In all, as per the time-related dimension of water deprivation, 12 per cent of households are deprived.

Based on this definition, of the total number of households with children, 14 per cent of them are water deprived. The extent of water deprivation is expectedly higher in rural areas (with 16 per cent of the households in villages), while the proportion is lower at 8 per cent in urban areas.

Water deprivation is linked to the wealth index of households, with better-off households less likely to be water deprived as opposed to the lower wealth index segments. However, there are tremendous variations across rural and urban locations.

Households that are water deprived belong to the SC, ST, and OBC. Although not much, rural–urban difference is noticeable among the SC and OBC water-deprived households, ST households are deprived of water mainly in the rural areas.

Water deprivation is indicated as being relatively lower, since quality of water is not included. However, states with high levels of deprivation are Madhya Pradesh, Rajasthan, Jharkhand, Karnataka, Chhattisgarh, Odisha, Haryana, Jammu and Kashmir, Tamil Nadu, Uttarakhand, Andhra Pradesh, and Delhi (see Table 2.5).

Water deprivation is low in the states of Punjab (2 per cent), Kerala, Uttar Pradesh, Bihar, and Assam (7 per cent).

TABLE 2.5 States with Deprivation Levels Worse than All-India Level

Water	Shelter	Sanitation
Madhya Pradesh	Bihar	Chhattisgarh
Jharkhand	Uttar Pradesh	Odisha
Rajasthan	Odisha	Jharkhand
Karnataka	Rajasthan	Madhya Pradesh
Chhattisgarh	Andhra Pradesh	Rajasthan
Odisha	Gujarat	Bihar
Haryana		Uttar Pradesh
Uttarakhand		
Tamil Nadu		
Jammu and Kashmir		
Andhra Pradesh		

Source: Calculated using unit-level data from NFHS-3 2005–6.

The wealth-quintile-based analysis for all the deprivations displays the differences between individual and household-level deprivations. The households deprived of appropriate shelter, sanitation, and water facilities are often associated with wealth and income categories. The distinction in the proportion of children deprived in any of the household-level deprivations across quintile groups is much more pronounced than that for the individual deprivations (see Table 2.6). Although, the latter, too, displays some variations, the two health-related variables of nutrition and immunization clearly are not a matter of wealth alone. Does the picture alter while considering multiple deprivations, that is, children facing more than one deprivation up to those with five deprivations?

MULTIPLE DEPRIVATIONS

Less than only one-fifth of all the children in India are free of the core deprivations considered here—education, immunization, nutrition, shelter, sanitation, and water. In other words, four of every five children are affected by at least one of these six deprivations.

The different deprivations, which are considered together here to examine the incidence and characteristics of multiple deprivations, are affected by one shortcoming. While shelter, sanitation, and water are measured for all children as household deprivation, the individual

TABLE 2.6 Percentage of Children Deprived, by Wealth Categories

Area/quintile	Nutrition	Immunization	Education	Sanitation	Shelter	Water
Rural						
Q1	75	73	47	96	75	24
Q2	68	64	35	89	57	16
Q3	61	51	26	77	42	13
Q4	52	41	17	47	26	9
Q5	35	30	14	9	11	4
Urban						
Q1	77	70	55	92	83	23
Q2	71	66	42	75	69	19
Q3	65	53	35	47	56	15
Q4	57	43	25	14	43	8
Q5	38	26	14	1	18	3
Total						
Q1	75	73	48	96	75	24
Q2	68	64	36	47	58	16
Q3	62	52	28	71	45	14
Q4	54	42	21	32	33	9
Q5	37	27	14	3	17	3

Source: Calculated using unit-level data from NFHS-3 2005–6.

Note: Q1, Q2, Q3, Q4, Q5 denote wealth categories with Q1 including all households that fall in the bottom 20 per cent of the wealth distribution; Q2 the next 20 per cent, and so on.

deprivations of education, nutrition, and immunization refer to different age cohorts.

Education deprivation pertains to children of 6 to 17 years, while nutrition and immunization refer to children who are under 5 years only—thus, there can be no overlap between education and the other two individual deprivations.[4] For most of the discussions here, we limit the multiple deprivations to four only, since the incidence of five deprivations captures a lower proportion of children, and also because the indicators of nutrition and immunization pertain to only the children under 5 years.

One out of every seven children in India (14 per cent) suffers from any four of the six deprivations; less than two-fifths (38 per cent) are affected by any three deprivations; about three-fifths (62 per cent) face any two of the deprivations; and 8 out of 10 (83 per cent) are disadvantaged by at least one deprivation (see Figure 2.15). Deprivations among children are more common in rural areas, where about 9 out of 10 children suffer from at least one deprivation. The intensity is lower in urban areas, where about 6 out of 10 children suffer from at least one deprivation.

Are children living in poorer households necessarily deprived? An analysis of child deprivations across different wealth categories (quintiles) suggests that this may not be strictly true. It is true that children living in households at the bottom 20 per cent of the wealth distribution have greater deprivations than children living in the top 20 per cent, but the difference in deprivations of children living in households in the middle wealth quintiles is not very significant (as can be seen from Table 2.6).

Figure 2.16, depicting the incidence of multiple deprivations across children belonging to quintile one (Q1) households and quintile four (Q4)[5] households, portrays a clear picture. While the proportion of children belonging to quintile one households, that is, the relatively poorer households, is systematically increasing as one moves from one deprivation to four deprivations, exactly the reverse image is witnessed for those among quintile four.

[4] In other words, while measuring the incidence of multiple deprivations, there can only be a maximum of five deprivations, and for those individuals who are education deprived, only four deprivations can be included.

[5] Q4 is used to compare with Q1, the poorest segment, since Q5—the top-most segment—reports virtually no or negligible incidence of multiple deprivations.

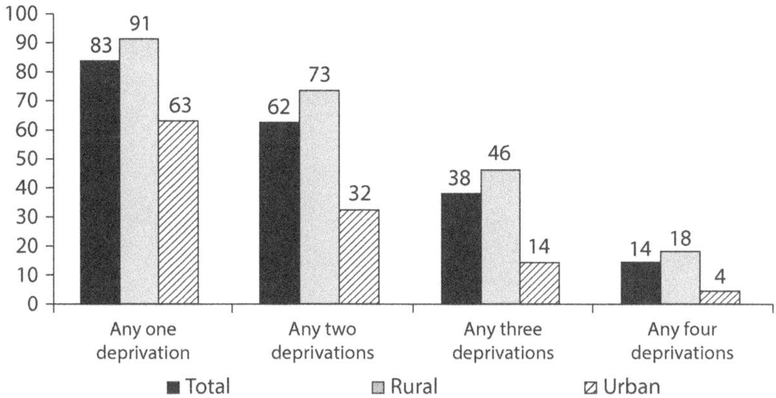

FIGURE 2.15 Multiple Deprivations among Children across Location
Source: Calculated using unit-level data from NFHS-3 2005–6.

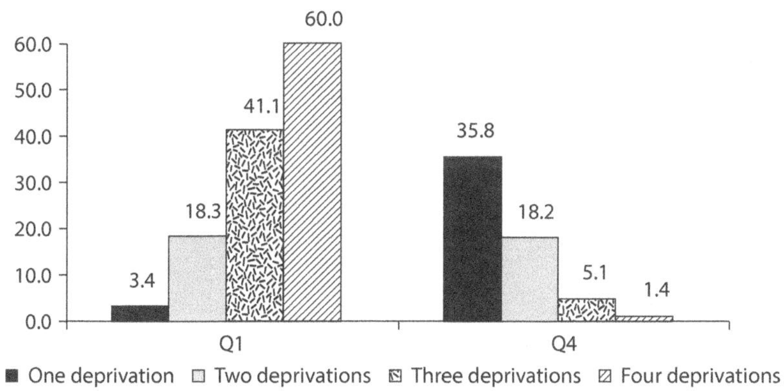

FIGURE 2.16 Percentage of Children with Mutiple Deprivations
Source: Calculated using unit-level data from NFHS-3 2005–6.

A look at the other variables such as the education level of the household head, family size, and social group of the children also presents an interesting pattern of the incidence of multiple deprivations.

The education level of the household head is associated with the incidence of multiple deprivations faced by children belonging to the household. This is especially so among the children affected by three or four deprivations (see Figure 2.17). The children of households, where the head of the family is illiterate, reported seven times more incidence of having four deprivations compared with those from households

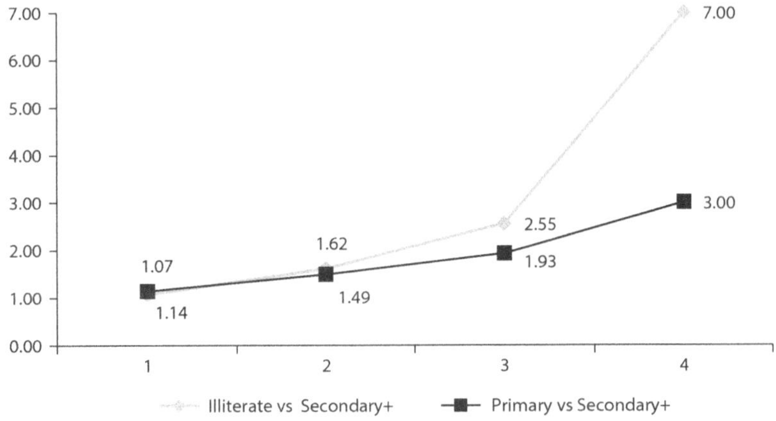

FIGURE 2.17 Multiple Deprivations by Education Level of Household Head
Source: Calculated using unit-level data from NFHS-3 2005–6.

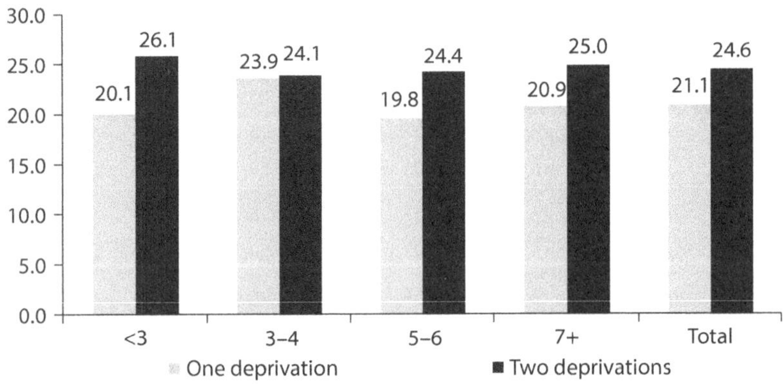

FIGURE 2.18 Children with One or Two Deprivations, by Family Size
Source: Calculated using unit-level data from NFHS-3 2005–6.

where the head of the family is educated up to or beyond secondary education levels. Children of households, where the head of the family has been educated up to only the primary level, have three times more incidence of multiple (four) deprivations as compared with children of households where the head of the family has been educated up to the secondary level or beyond.

The size of the family the child belongs to depicts the expected picture—the larger the size with more dependants, the higher the incidence of multiple deprivations (see Figure 2.18). The group of children belonging to households with less than three members could be families with single parents, orphans, or no adult members. In general, the vulnerability among these households is relatively higher unless both members are earning or the adult is in formal employment or other jobs with similar income profiles.

The single-deprivation analysis also shows that ST children are among the worst affected by most deprivations. Examining the social composition of the incidence of multiple deprivations, again, highlights the same phenomena, with ST children having the higher incidence of three and four deprivations, followed by SC children. It is only among the category of children deprived on account of one deprivation that the group not belonging to either ST, SC, or OBC reports the highest incidence (see Figure 2.19).

★ ★ ★

An examination of deprivations faced by children reveals the incidence and intensity of deprivations across locations, states, social groups, and gender. While there is certainly some association between material poverty and these core deprivations, the analysis also highlights the prevalence of non-material forms of child poverty as depicted through the incidence of certain other deprivations, such as health, immunization,

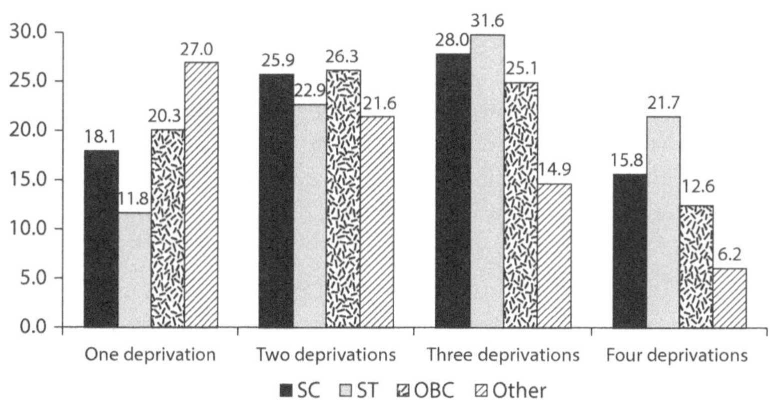

FIGURE 2.19 Multiple Deprivations across Social Groups
Source: Calculated using unit-level data from NFHS-3 2005–6.
Note: ST: Scheduled Tribe; SC: Scheduled Caste; OBC: Other Backward Class.

and nutrition, which are not a matter of wealth alone. This builds the case for exploring newer methods both for assessing and measuring child well-being that is different from the economic poverty approach.

This has implications for the perspectives adopted for addressing children's needs and ensuring inclusive development, because it requires catering to the disparate situations, as witnessed across the country. However, in order to undertake useful exploratory exercises that provide a comprehensive account of the status of child well-being and deprivations, reliable, systematic, and periodic information on children at the all-India level is required.

As for the policy approach, a judicious combination aimed at strengthening the economic status of families and providing quality services to their children is required. Given the diversity of the country both in terms of geography and social group and circumstance, there is a need to envisage universal policies in certain domains, while allowing for different approaches in other contexts.

Universal Approach

The wide spread of deprivations facing children across social groups suggests the need for adopting universal policies in certain non-negotiable domains such as elementary education, child labour, access to immunization, safe drinking water, acceptable sanitation facilities, and shelter. For many of these domains a non-discriminatory approach and equitable redistribution of services may be more desirable. Many chapters in this volume (especially this section) reaffirm the importance of universality as a principle of policy and resource investment for children and their families, based on the findings that reflect the deprivations that exist, albeit to a lesser degree, in even basic material needs among households in the wealthier quintiles.

Strong Rural Focus

Significantly higher levels of deprivations are faced by children living in rural areas. In comparison with urban areas, children in villages are affected by unacceptably lower nutrition levels, participation in schools, and immunization cover. It is not clear from this analysis whether higher deprivations in sanitation, water, and shelter in rural areas are due to economic poverty, lack of adequate state attention and investment into public provisioning, or apathy and poor governance. Since there are more children living in villages, it is imperative for any child-sensitive policy to have a strong rural focus.

Target Specific Groups of Children

However, given the fact that SC and ST children are affected the most by these core deprivations and the majority is located in rural areas too, just paying attention to area specificity may be inadequate, unless the historical inequalities and some of the insufficiencies of existing policies are addressed by targeting the social group. Substantial differences in human development outcomes across social groups, especially among ST and SC, are prevailing (IAMR 2011), in spite of efforts at rural development.

A similar situation prevails for gender differences too. Although gender gaps have reduced on some fronts, such as nutrition and immunization, more efforts are needed to ensure that girls attend schools until and beyond elementary education levels. Most states have reported gaps in schooling among girls much more than boys.

Target the Most Disadvantaged States

Variations across states are substantial. A major proportion of children are deprived in Bimarou states—Bihar, Jharkhand, Madhya Pradesh, Rajasthan, Odisha, and Uttar Pradesh. However, there are also other states identified, specifically in their rural and urban areas, for example, urban Delhi for nutrition deprivation, Gujarat for both nutrition and immunization, West Bengal for education, urban Karnataka for immunization, and so on.

However, states are large entities and it is therefore imperative to undertake similar analyses at the sub-state as well as sub-district levels to identify areas for targeting child-sensitive policies. This leads us to the issue of gaps in reliable data on children. Though the existing secondary data systems provide comprehensive data on certain issues, there are gaps in information. Carrying out data enumeration exercises for indicators relevant for children and their well-being on a regular, systematic basis can be very beneficial. This, together with the other points highlighted, is essential for ensuring the well-being of all children in India. Paying adequate attention to these concerns is a critical component of inclusive development.

APPENDIX A2

TABLE A2.1 Proportion of Children across Different Poverty Thresholds (in per cent)

States	Extremely poor	Poor	Marginal	POOR*	Vulnerable	Middle income group	High income group
							Total
Odisha	33.0	24.0	17.8	74.8	17.2	7.4	0.6
Chhattisgarh	24.9	30.2	19.3	74.4	17.9	6.6	1.2
Bihar	16.6	30.5	23.4	70.5	25.0	4.2	0.3
Madhya Pradesh	22.1	24.6	20.3	67.0	22.5	9.2	1.2
Jharkhand	14.3	29.9	22.5	66.7	24.8	7.5	1.0
Karnataka	10.0	23.8	22.8	56.6	30.1	11.1	2.2
Uttar Pradesh	11.5	22.7	21.4	55.7	30.7	11.6	2.0
All-India	**11.1**	**20.2**	**20.1**	**51.3**	**31.5**	**14.6**	**2.6**
Tamil Nadu	8.2	19.3	22.6	50.0	30.7	16.2	3.0
West Bengal	6.9	20.1	21.8	48.8	34.5	14.1	2.6
Maharashtra	10.9	18.4	18.5	47.8	30.7	17.5	3.9
Andhra Pradesh	8.8	18.2	19.0	46.0	34.6	17.0	2.4
Gujarat	5.5	14.5	21.1	41.0	34.6	21.7	2.6
Rajasthan	5.1	14.5	19.2	38.7	43.3	15.4	2.5
Assam	3.2	14.4	20.5	38.1	47.5	13.6	0.8
Uttarakhand	1.9	14.5	21.7	38.1	39.0	19.6	3.4
Delhi	1.7	7.0	17.0	25.6	36.0	29.3	9.1

Haryana	3.1	7.2	13.8	24.1	39.1	30.5	6.3
Himachal Pradesh	1.5	6.3	14.0	21.7	42.6	30.8	4.8
Punjab	1.0	7.2	13.2	21.3	38.9	32.2	7.6
Kerala	3.5	5.9	10.5	19.9	31.4	37.4	11.3
Jammu and Kashmir	1.9	3.0	9.7	14.5	45.7	34.3	5.5
Rural							
Chhattisgarh	24.5	31.6	20.8	76.9	17.7	4.8	0.6
Odisha	33.6	24.4	18.8	76.7	16.8	5.9	0.5
Bihar	15.5	30.9	24.0	70.3	25.6	3.9	0.2
Jharkhand	13.9	31.9	23.5	69.3	25.2	5.0	0.5
Madhya Pradesh	22.3	25.5	20.8	68.6	23.6	7.4	0.5
Karnataka	7.6	27.2	25.4	60.2	31.1	7.8	0.9
Uttar Pradesh	9.4	22.7	22.5	54.6	32.0	11.7	1.7
Maharashtra	11.5	20.9	20.1	52.5	31.5	13.6	2.4
All-India	**10.5**	**20.9**	**20.8**	**52.3**	**32.9**	**12.9**	**1.9**
Tamil Nadu	7.8	21.0	23.4	52.2	32.6	12.9	2.2
West Bengal	5.7	19.9	22.7	48.3	38.1	11.9	1.7
Andhra Pradesh	8.5	17.4	18.6	44.5	37.0	16.3	2.2
Gujarat	6.1	16.2	21.9	44.2	36.9	17.6	1.3
Assam	3.0	14.1	21.3	38.4	48.2	12.8	0.6
Uttarakhand	0.8	13.1	21.6	35.5	41.2	20.0	3.4
Rajasthan	3.1	13.2	19.0	35.3	47.2	15.5	2.0

(*Continued*)

TABLE A2.1 (*Continued*)

States	Extremely poor	Poor	Marginal	POOR*	Vulnerable	Middle income group	High income group
Himachal Pradesh	1.3	6.7	13.3	21.3	44.4	29.9	4.4
Haryana	1.4	6.2	12.1	19.7	41.7	32.1	6.6
Punjab	0.7	3.8	11.9	16.4	41.7	34.1	7.8
Kerala	2.3	4.7	9.4	16.4	32.2	39.5	12.0
Delhi	0.0	0.0	11.4	11.4	50.2	32.6	5.8
Jammu and Kashmir	0.8	2.9	7.5	11.1	47.6	35.1	6.2

Source: Calculated using unit-level data from NSS 2004–5.

Note: * Monthly per capita expenditure below 1.25 times the official poverty line (PL), that is, extremely poor, poor, and marginal, as per Sengupta et al. 2008.

Table A2.2 Nutritional Deprivation among Children under 5 Years

State ranked by total	% children total	State ranked by rural	% children rural	State ranked by urban	% children urban
Madhya Pradesh	72.6	Madhya Pradesh	74.9	Madhya Pradesh	65.2
Bihar	71.1	Jharkhand	73.9	Bihar	64.4
Jharkhand	70.3	Bihar	72.0	Gujarat	60.4
Uttar Pradesh	66.7	Uttar Pradesh	68.3	Uttar Pradesh	59.7
Chhattisgarh	65.6	Chhattisgarh	68.2	Jharkhand	55.1
Gujarat	65.0	Gujarat	67.8	Delhi	54.1
Odisha	59.4	Delhi	65.2	Maharashtra	53.8
Maharashtra	58.4	Uttarakhand	62.9	Haryana	52.9
Rajasthan	58.4	Maharashtra	62.1	Karnataka	52.3
Haryana	58.0	Odisha	61.7	Chhattisgarh	52.1
Uttarakhand	57.2	West Bengal	61.2	Rajasthan	50.7
West Bengal	57.1	Rajasthan	60.4	Tamil Nadu	48.3
Karnataka	57.0	Haryana	59.7	Andhra Pradesh	47.2
Assam	56.9	Karnataka	59.5	Assam	46.6
Delhi	55.3	Assam	58.2	Odisha	45.2
Andhra Pradesh	53.2	Andhra Pradesh	56.4	Punjab	41.4
Himachal Pradesh	52.6	Himachal Pradesh	53.9	West Bengal	40.9
Tamil Nadu	50.4	Tamil Nadu	52.2	Himachal Pradesh	40.2
Jammu and Kashmir	47.7	Jammu and Kashmir	50.2	Uttarakhand	38.6
Punjab	43.5	Punjab	44.7	Jammu and Kashmir	37.0
Kerala	39.8	Kerala	42.8	Kerala	33.2
All-India	**60.4**	**All-India**	**63.3**	**All-India**	**51.9**

Source: Calculated using unit-level data from NFHS-3 2005–6.

Table A2.3 Distance from Universal Coverage of Immunization for Children of Ages 1 to 5

State ranked by total	% children total	State ranked by rural	% children rural	State ranked by urban	% children urban
Uttar Pradesh	73.1	Rajasthan	78.5	Bihar	64.4
Rajasthan	72.5	Uttar Pradesh	75.7	Uttar Pradesh	62.7
Assam	68.8	Jharkhand	73.1	Assam	61.6
Bihar	68.4	Assam	69.8	Rajasthan	50.7
Jharkhand	67.0	Bihar	68.9	Karnataka	48.0
Madhya Pradesh	52.9	Madhya Pradesh	60.2	Odisha	47.0
Andhra Pradesh	51.9	Gujarat	56.7	Andhra Pradesh	46.7
Odisha	51.0	Andhra Pradesh	54.3	Jharkhand	42.3
Gujarat	50.7	Odisha	51.6	Gujarat	41.2
Karnataka	49.4	Karnataka	50.2	Punjab	31.5
Chhattisgarh	44.8	Chhattisgarh	48.6	Maharashtra	30.7
Maharashtra	37.9	Delhi	44.6	Uttarakhand	30.3
Uttarakhand	36.9	Maharashtra	44.4	Delhi	30.0
Punjab	36.8	Punjab	39.8	Jammu and Kashmir	29.6
Jammu and Kashmir	36.4	Uttarakhand	39.2	Madhya Pradesh	29.5
Haryana	34.2	Jammu and Kashmir	38.2	Chhattisgarh	26.4
West Bengal	33.1	Haryana	36.9	Haryana	25.9
Delhi	31.5	West Bengal	35.2	West Bengal	25.4
Kerala	19.7	Kerala	23.5	Himachal Pradesh	16.3
Himachal Pradesh	18.4	Himachal Pradesh	18.7	Tamil Nadu	15.5
Tamil Nadu	15.0	Tamil Nadu	14.6	Kerala	11.7
All-India	**54.1**	**All-India**	**59.0**	**All-India**	**40.5**

Source: Calculated using unit-level data from NFHS-3 2005–6.

Table A2.4 Educationally Deprived Children

State ranked by total	% children total	State ranked by rural	% children rural	State ranked by urban	% children urban
Bihar	50.6	Bihar	52.4	Bihar	40.9
Jharkhand	44.3	Jharkhand	47.9	Uttar Pradesh	32.6
Rajasthan	33.7	Rajasthan	36.1	Jharkhand	32.3
Uttar Pradesh	33.5	Chhattisgarh	35.7	West Bengal	27.4
West Bengal	32.9	Madhya Pradesh	34.8	Madhya Pradesh	26.2
Madhya Pradesh	32.8	West Bengal	34.7	Rajasthan	25.7
Chhattisgarh	32.4	Uttar Pradesh	33.8	Karnataka	24.4
Odisha	30.4	Odisha	32.6	Punjab	23.4
Karnataka	27.8	Karnataka	29.7	Delhi	22.9
Haryana	25.6	Gujarat	26.9	Haryana	22.8
Jammu and Kashmir	25.0	Haryana	26.6	Andhra Pradesh	21.7
Andhra Pradesh	24.6	Jammu and Kashmir	26.3	Jammu and Kashmir	20.3
Punjab	24.6	Andhra Pradesh	26.1	Chhattisgarh	19.5
Gujarat	23.7	Maharashtra	26.0	Odisha	19.1
Delhi	22.8	Punjab	25.1	Gujarat	18.7
Assam	22.6	Assam	23.4	Maharashtra	18.3
Maharashtra	22.4	Delhi	22.5	Uttarakhand	18.1
Tamil Nadu	15.8	Tamil Nadu	15.4	Assam	17.9
Uttarakhand	14.6	Uttarakhand	13.4	Tamil Nadu	16.4
Kerala	12.8	Kerala	13.3	Kerala	11.8
Himachal Pradesh	8.2	Himachal Pradesh	8.1	Himachal Pradesh	9.4
All-India	**30.7**	**All-India**	**33.1**	**All-India**	**24.4**

Source: Calculated using unit-level data from NFHS-3 2005–6.

Table A2.5 Children in Sanitation-deprived Households

State ranked by total	% children total	State ranked by rural	% children rural	State ranked by urban	% children urban
Chhattisgarh	83.5	Jharkhand	95.9	Odisha	44.5
Odisha	82.8	Chhattisgarh	95.0	Chhattisgarh	36.3
Jharkhand	81.7	Rajasthan	92.9	Madhya Pradesh	33.4
Madhya Pradesh	77.1	Madhya Pradesh	90.4	Bihar	32.2
Rajasthan	77.1	Odisha	89.9	Jharkhand	31.2
Bihar	76.6	Uttar Pradesh	87.5	Tamil Nadu	29.9
Uttar Pradesh	73.6	Tamil Nadu	84.4	Andhra Pradesh	29.4
Andhra Pradesh	60.7	Bihar	83.9	Uttar Pradesh	23.9
Karnataka	60.6	Karnataka	81.2	Karnataka	23.9
Tamil Nadu	60.6	Maharashtra	80.3	Rajasthan	21.8
Himachal Pradesh	59.6	Andhra Pradesh	76.1	Gujarat	17.8
Gujarat	53.3	Gujarat	75.5	Maharashtra	16.3
Haryana	52.8	Haryana	65.6	Jammu and Kashmir	15.5
Maharashtra	50.8	Himachal Pradesh	64.9	Haryana	15.0
West Bengal	48.4	Uttarakhand	60.5	West Bengal	13.6
Uttarakhand	46.8	West Bengal	58.9	Himachal Pradesh	10.7
Jammu and Kashmir	42.6	Jammu and Kashmir	50.3	Punjab	8.0
Punjab	33.2	Punjab	46.4	Delhi	7.9
Assam	25.9	Delhi	31.5	Uttarakhand	6.9
Delhi	10.2	Assam	29.4	Assam	3.0
Kerala	4.1	Kerala	5.2	Kerala	1.9
All-India	**62.8**	**All-India**	**77.9**	**All-India**	**21.9**

Source: Calculated using unit-level data from NFHS-3 2005–6.

TABLE A2.6 Children in Shelter-deprived Households

Stateranked by total	% children total	State ranked by rural	% children rural	State ranked by urban	% childrenUrban
Bihar	64.1	Bihar	67.1	Maharashtra	46.2
Uttar Pradesh	55.6	Uttar Pradesh	58.8	Bihar	46.0
Odisha	54.8	Rajasthan	58.7	Uttar Pradesh	44.1
Rajasthan	53.2	Odisha	58.1	Andhra Pradesh	43.8
Andhra Pradesh	50.8	Gujarat	55.0	Gujarat	42.4
Gujarat	50.2	Andhra Pradesh	54.2	Madhya Pradesh	39.4
Madhya Pradesh	48.4	Karnataka	53.8	Delhi	38.0
Karnataka	47.5	Tamil Nadu	52.9	Tamil Nadu	37.8
Maharashtra	47.3	Madhya Pradesh	51.2	Odisha	36.9
Tamil Nadu	46.3	Maharashtra	48.2	Karnataka	36.2
West Bengal	44.5	West Bengal	48.1	Rajasthan	33.8
Delhi	38.1	Haryana	40.1	Uttarakhand	33.4
Haryana	37.1	Assam	38.8	West Bengal	32.6
Assam	36.0	Delhi	38.6	Punjab	30.6
Uttarakhand	34.0	Jharkhand	34.5	Jharkhand	28.6
Jharkhand	33.2	Uttarakhand	34.1	Haryana	28.5
Punjab	32.0	Punjab	32.7	Chhattisgarh	24.2
Chhattisgarh	29.3	Jammu and Kashmir	32.6	Assam	18.0
Jammu and Kashmir	29.1	Chhattisgarh	30.5	Jammu and Kashmir	17.0
Himachal Pradesh	20.4	Himachal Pradesh	21.1	Himachal Pradesh	14.0
Kerala	13.5	Kerala	15.3	Kerala	9.8
All-India	**48.5**	**All-India**	**52.2**	**All-India**	**38.5**

Source: Calculated using unit-level data from NFHS-3 2005–6.

TABLE A2.7 Children in Water-deprived Households

State ranked by total	% children total	State ranked by rural	% children rural	State ranked by urban	% children urban
Madhya Pradesh	34.9	Madhya Pradesh	40.5	Karnataka	19.9
Jharkhand	27.4	Rajasthan	36.5	Madhya Pradesh	19.4
Rajasthan	27.3	Jharkhand	31.1	Jharkhand	15.8
Karnataka	21.9	Delhi	27.2	Tamil Nadu	12.2
Chhattisgarh	19.4	Karnataka	23.2	Delhi	12.2
Odisha	18.2	Haryana	22.2	Chhattisgarh	12.1
Haryana	16.8	Uttarakhand	21.7	Andhra Pradesh	11.2
Uttarakhand	16.4	Jammu and Kashmir	21.6	Odisha	11.2
Tamil Nadu	16.1	Chhattisgarh	21.4	West Bengal	7.6
Jammu and Kashmir	16.0	Odisha	19.6	Bihar	5.3
Andhra Pradesh	15.1	Tamil Nadu	19.4	Haryana	3.6
Delhi	13.4	Andhra Pradesh	17.1	Uttar Pradesh	3.6
Himachal Pradesh	10.5	Maharashtra	14.6	Gujarat	3.0
West Bengal	9.0	Gujarat	12.2	Maharashtra	2.8
Maharashtra	9.0	Himachal Pradesh	11.7	Assam	2.6
Gujarat	8.4	West Bengal	9.5	Uttarakhand	2.3
Assam	6.7	Assam	7.6	Kerala	2.2
Bihar	4.9	Uttar Pradesh	5.1	Rajasthan	1.9
Uttar Pradesh	4.8	Bihar	4.9	Himachal Pradesh	1.0
Kerala	3.3	Kerala	3.9	Punjab	1.0
Punjab	2.1	Punjab	2.8	Jammu and Kashmir	0.8
All-India	**13.9**	**All-India**	**16.6**	**All-India**	**8.1**

Source: Calculated using unit-level data from NFHS-3 2005–6.

REFERENCES

Institute of Applied Manpower Research (IAMR). 2011. *India Human Development Report 2011—Towards Social Inclusion*. New Delhi: Oxford University Press.

National Sample Survey Organisation (NSSO). 2005. Employment and Unemployment Survey, 2004–5 (61st Round), National Sample Survey Organisation, 2004–5, Central Statistical Organisation, Ministry of Statistics and Programme Implementation (MoSPI), Government of India.

Rees, Nicholas, Jingqing Chai, and David Anthony. 2012. 'Right in Principle and in Practice: A Review of the Social and Economic Returns to Investing in Children', UNICEF Social and Economic Policy Working Paper. New York: UNICEF.

Rustagi, Preet, Soumya Kapoor Mehta, Sunil Kumar Mishra, Balwant S. Mehta, and Ramya Subrahmanian. 2012. *Beyond Averages: Child Well-Being through an Equity Analysis*. New Delhi: IHD-UNICEF.

Saith, A. and R. Wazir. 2010. 'From Poverty to Well-Being: Alternative Approaches to the Recognition of Child Deprivation in India', IHD-UNICEF Working Paper Series on Children of India: Rights and Opportunities. New Delhi: UNICEF.

Sengupta, A., K.P. Kannan, and G. Raveendran. 2008. 'India's Common People: Who Are They, How Many Are They, How Do They Live?' *Economic and Political Weekly*, 43(11 and 15): 49–63.

United Nations Development Programme (UNDP). 2006. *Human Development Report 2006, Beyond Scarcity: Power, Poverty and the Global Water Crisis*. USA: Palgrave Macmillan.

UNICEF. 2005. *The State of the World's Children 2005—Childhood under Threat*. New York: UNICEF.

———. 2008. *The State of the World's Children 2008—Child Survival*. New York: UNICEF.

———. 2010. *The State of the World's Children 2010—Child Rights*. New York: UNICEF.

3 Economic Status and Child Deprivation

Findings from Village Surveys[1]

Madhura Swaminathan and Venkatesh Athreya

While India has experienced rapid economic growth, as measured by gross domestic product (GDP), the ground reality of mass deprivation has not been altered significantly over two decades of rapid economic growth. A particularly important social concern relates to the multiple deprivations suffered by children in rural India. While national surveys such as the National Sample Surveys (NSSs) and the National Family Health Surveys enable us to obtain indicators of deprivation—in terms of access to education, health care, drinking water, sanitation, and so on—these relate to high levels of aggregation, such as the state or the country as a whole. The average values of indicators that large-scale survey data provide are important, but need to be supplemented

[1] This work draws on papers written as part of the FAS–UNICEF Project Collaboration Agreement and specifically on village-level reports on *Child Well-Being, Schooling and Living Standards* for three villages of Andhra Pradesh and two villages of Uttar Pradesh. We are grateful to Koustav Dutta for help with the tables. All the data in the chapter comes from the archives of the Foundation for Agrarian Studies.

by insights from micro-level studies. Such studies, especially those that treat the village as the unit, can provide insights into processes and enable the exploration of relationships between deprivation at the household and individual level and between key variables, such as household assets or caste status. There are some interesting insights that emerge from this kind of analysis.

In this chapter, the focus is on selected dimensions of child deprivation, and variations in these across households in different asset quintiles are examined. The argument here is that household assets or wealth constitutes a key structural variable and is a good proxy for long-term economic status. Thus, this chapter explores variations in child deprivations across households with differing levels of asset ownership. This has been done with the help of data collected from village surveys conducted by the Foundation for Agrarian Studies (FAS). The data, from the Project on Agrarian Relations in India (PARI), are for five villages—three located in Andhra Pradesh and two in Uttar Pradesh.

THE VILLAGES[2]

In 2005–6, as part of PARI, in-depth census and sample surveys were conducted in two villages of Andhra Pradesh: Ananthavaram, a village in the paddy-growing region of Guntur district; and Bukkacherla, a village in the dry and drought-prone district of Anantapur. Kothapalle, a village in a groundwater-irrigated region of north Telangana (Karimnagar district) was also surveyed.[3] This was followed in June 2006 by census-type surveys in two villages of Uttar Pradesh: Harevli, located in the canal-irrigated, sugarcane-growing district of Bijnor; and Mahatwar, selected from eastern Uttar Pradesh. Mahatwar is in Ballia district and is located in a groundwater-irrigated, wheat paddy–growing belt. A brief description of the villages is given below.

1. **Ananthavaram** village, Kollur mandal, Guntur district, was chosen purposively: the village was one of the two surveyed by P. Sundarayya in 1974. A census survey of 2005 conducted by this study covered

[2] For an introduction to the FAS Project on Agrarian Relations in India, and details of the villages, see http://www.fas.org.in/pages.asp?menuid=16.

[3] For a socio-economic profile of these three villages, see Ramachandran et al. 2010.

667 households and 2,410 persons. Ananthavaram is a multicaste village with a significant Dalit population. Members of Dalit households constituted 45 per cent of the population, while members of Adivasi households formed 6.6 per cent of the population, and members of households of the Kamma caste (the dominant landholding caste) constituted 20 per cent of the population.

Ananthavaram was selected as being characteristic of a village from the paddy-dominated tracts of south coastal Andhra Pradesh. Ananthavaram is irrigated by river Krishna.

2. **Bukkacherla** village is located in Raptadu mandal, Anantapur district. A census survey of 2005 conducted by the PARI study covered 292 households and 1,228 persons. Members of households of the dominant, landholding Kapu caste constituted 40 per cent of the population, and members of Dalit households constituted 20 per cent of the population in Bukkacherla. People from the three caste groups—Kapu, Dalit, and Kuruba—constituted 71 per cent of the population.

   The important feature of land use in the village was that unirrigated land accounted for 89 per cent of the land under cultivation. Typically, therefore, there was a single agricultural season in the village, with cultivation occurring mainly in the kharif season (rainy season).

3. **Kothapalle** (P.N.) village is located in Thimmapur (Lower Maner Dam Colony) mandal, Karimnagar district. The nearest town is Karimnagar, which is 16 km away. The village is situated on the main Hyderabad to Karimnagar highway, a fact that has major consequences for the village economy. The village census survey covered 1,436 persons in 372 households. This is a multicaste village, and has an almost equal number of persons from the two major landholding castes, Reddy and Gouda. Members of Dalit households constituted 30 per cent of the population.

   There has been more than a fourfold increase in area under irrigation between 1991 and 2001 on account of the construction of the Lower Maner Dam. The two most important crops were maize and paddy. Tapping toddy from Palmyra palm trees was an important village occupation.

4. **Harevli** village is located in Najibabad block, Bijnor district, western Uttar Pradesh. There is no all-weather road to the village, and the main mode of transport from the village to Mandavli, the nearest

town, is by horse-drawn carts or bullock carts. Harevli is a small village in terms of population: the population was 668 persons at the Census of 2001. At the time of the PARI survey, 115 households and 674 persons were resident in the village. The dominant caste in the village was Tyagi. Dalit households constituted 38 per cent of all households.

Agriculture is the mainstay of the economy of Harevli. Sugarcane is the most important crop; wheat, paddy, and fodder crops are also cultivated.

5. **Mahatwar** village is in Rasra block, Ballia district, eastern Uttar Pradesh. Mahatwar is located near the highway linking Rasra to Mau, and there are bus and jeep transport services to nearby towns as well as cities, such as Varanasi. At the time of the PARI survey, there were 159 households and 1,114 persons residing in the village. Mahatwar is a multicaste village. Dalits constituted the majority in the village: 60 per cent of all households were Dalit.

   The major crops grown in Mahatwar were paddy during the kharif season and wheat (sometimes intercropped with mustard) during the rabi (winter) season. Non-agricultural occupations within and outside the village provided an important source of income to resident households.

To sum up, these five villages drawn from diverse agro-ecological regions of the country can provide an interesting cross-section picture of child well-being.

THE ASSET QUINTILES

For this analysis, we have classified all households in a village into five asset quintiles. Assets include land and water bodies, houses and buildings, trees, animals, other means of production, means of transport, domestic durable goods, and other assets such as grain stock and inventories. Assets do not include financial assets and gold. Assets are valued at present value reported by households. The details of absolute values of assets defining each quintile are shown separately for each of the five villages in Tables 3.2 to 3.6, while Table 3.1 gives the mean value of assets for each of the five villages. Following are some interesting points that emerge from Tables 3.1 to 3.6.

TABLE 3.1 Mean Value of Assets per Household, Five Villages, 2005–6 (in Rs)

Village	District	State	Mean
Ananthavaram	Guntur	Andhra Pradesh	447,739
Bukkacherla	Anantapur	Andhra Pradesh	296,483
Kothapalle	Karimnagar	Andhra Pradesh	299,696
Harevli	Bijnor	Uttar Pradesh	943,502
Mahatwar	Ballia	Uttar Pradesh	450,567

TABLE 3.2 Assets per Household by Asset Quintile, Ananthavaram, Andhra Pradesh, 2005 (in Rs)

Asset quintile	Minimum	Maximum	Median	Mean
Q1	120	16,140	7,158	7,913
Q2	16,170	40,150	24,100	26,060
Q3	40,490	90,350	61,580	63,191
Q4	90,850	340,860	164,620	180,363
Q5	344,975	40,455,400	896,850	1,967,646

TABLE 3.3 Assets per Household by Asset Quintile, Bukkacherla, Andhra Pradesh, 2005 (in Rs)

Asset quintile	Minimum	Maximum	Median	Mean
Q1	920	40,980	27,210	22,710
Q2	42,700	101,850	71,498	72,555
Q3	102,930	179,490	133,060	138,177
Q4	180,850	323,570	250,985	248,895
Q5	324,580	14,199,660	575,825	1,004,800

TABLE 3.4 Assets per Household by Asset Quintile, Kothapalle, Andhra Pradesh, 2005 (in Rs)

Asset quintile	Minimum	Maximum	Median	Mean
Q1	300	41,195	17,250	17,204
Q2	41,490	88,915	64,976	65,605
Q3	89,735	151,190	119,055	116,660
Q4	152,785	323,755	210,825	216,133
Q5	328,825	6,473,650	637,935	1,089,859

TABLE 3.5 Assets per Household by Asset Quintile, Harevli, Uttar Pradesh, 2006 (in Rs)

Asset quintile	Minimum	Maximum	Median	Mean
Q1	540	29,684	10,790	12,896
Q2	33,218	100,510	59,055	60,661
Q3	102,034	262,000	126,430	142,067
Q4	334,700	1,402,280	847,905	834,709
Q5	1,443,100	15,824,175	2,691,225	3,715,328

TABLE 3.6 Assets per Household by Asset Quintile, Mahatwar, Uttar Pradesh, 2006 (in Rs)

Asset quintile	Minimum	Maximum	Median	Mean
Q1	4,250	54,275	38,005	35,131
Q2	58,060	118,250	88,400	88,073
Q3	122,560	216,375	170,270	168,423
Q4	218,800	634,920	333,700	361,815
Q5	638,460	12,445,328	1,160,325	2,271,112

First, there is clearly huge intra-village inequality in the distribution of assets across households. To take an example, the ratio of the asset value of the household with the highest asset value and that of the one with the lowest asset value was 337,128 in Ananthavaram! The ratio was 15,434 in Bukkacherla, 21,579 in Kothapalle, 29,304 in Harevli, and 2,928 in Mahatwar. In each of the villages, a handful of households dominated the village economy, with their large asset (mainly land and buildings) holdings.

In almost all cases, the top asset quintile was heavily populated by other-caste Hindu households. Households belonging to other backward classes (OBCs), too, were present, but generally to a lesser extent. Scheduled Castes (SCs), Muslims, and Scheduled Tribes (STs) were present, if at all, only to a marginal extent. Details for each of the five villages, of the distribution of households of each social group across asset quintiles, and the distribution of households in each asset quintile across social groups are provided in Tables 3.7 to 3.11. These tables show that of all Dalit households, not more than 5 per cent belonged

TABLE 3.7 Distribution of Households by Social Group and Asset Quintile, Ananthavaram, 2005

Social group	As percentage of all households in asset quintile						As percentage of all households in caste group					
	Q1	Q2	Q3	Q4	Q5	All	Q1	Q2	Q3	Q4	Q5	All
SC	52.2	62.6	59.4	33.1	4.5	42.4	24.7	29.7	27.9	15.5	2.1	100.0
ST	19.4	10.5	2.3	0.8	0.0	6.6	59.1	31.8	6.8	2.3	0.0	100.0
BC	11.2	17.9	20.3	32.3	16.5	19.6	11.5	18.3	20.6	32.8	16.8	100.0
Other caste												
Hindu	11.2	6.0	15.8	31.6	78.2	28.5	7.9	4.2	11.1	22.1	54.7	100.0
Muslim	6.0	3.0	2.2	2.2	0.0	2.7	44.4	22.2	16.7	16.7	0.0	100.0
All	100.0	100.0	100.0	100	100.0	100.0	20.2	20.2	19.9	19.9	19.8	100.0

TABLE 3.8 Distribution of Households by Social Group and Asset Quintile, Bukkacherla, 2005

Social group	As percentage of all household in the asset quintile						As percentage of all households in caste group					
	Q1	Q2	Q3	Q4	Q5	All	Q1	Q2	Q3	Q4	Q5	All
SC	44.1	39.7	13.8	1.7	0.0	19.9	44.8	39.7	13.8	1.7	0	100.0
BC	33.9	31.0	39.7	50.0	12.1	33.6	20.4	18.4	23.5	29.6	7.1	100.0
Other caste												
Hindu	18.6	24.1	44.8	46.6	86.2	43.8	8.6	10.9	20.3	21.1	39.1	100.0
Muslim	3.4	5.2	1.7	1.7	1.7	2.7	25.0	37.5	12.5	12.5	12.5	100.0
All	100.0	100.0	100.0	100.0	100.0	100.0	20.4	19.9	19.9	19.9	19.9	100.0

TABLE 3.9 Distribution of Households by Social Group and Asset Quintile, Kothapalle, 2005

Social group	As percentage of all households in asset quintile						As percentage of all households in caste group					
	Q1	Q2	Q3	Q4	Q5	All	Q1	Q2	Q3	Q4	Q5	All
SC	37.3	53.3	39.2	23.0	5.4	31.8	23.7	33.9	24.6	14.4	3.4	100.0
ST	10.7	2.7	1.4	0.0	0.0	3.0	72.7	18.2	9.1	0.0	0.0	100.0
BC	33.3	36.0	48.5	59.5	24.3	40.4	16.7	18.0	24.0	29.3	12.0	100.0
Other caste												
Hindu	14.7	8.0	8.1	17.5	68.9	23.5	12.6	6.9	6.9	14.9	58.6	100.0
Muslim	4.0	0.0	1.4	0.0	1.4	1.3	60.0	0.0	20.0	0.0	20.0	100.0
All	100.0	100.0	100.0	100.0	100.0	100.0	20.2	20.2	19.8	19.9	19.9	100.0

TABLE 3.10 Distribution of Households by Social Group and Asset Quintile, Harevli, 2006

Social group	As percentage of all households in the asset quintile						As percentage of all households in the social group					
	Q1	Q2	Q3	Q4	Q5	All	Q1	Q2	Q3	Q4	Q5	All
SC	56.5	73.9	34.7	9.1	4.8	36.6	31.7	41.5	19.5	4.9	2.4	100
OBC	8.7	17.4	56.5	18.2	9.5	22.3	8.0	16.0	52.0	16.0	8.0	100
Other caste												
Hindu	4.4	0.0	4.4	54.6	85.7	28.6	3.1	0.0	3.1	37.5	56.3	100
Muslim	30.4	8.7	4.4	18.2	0.0	12.5	50.0	14.3	7.1	28.6	0.0	100
All	100.0	100.0	100.0	100.0	100.0	100.0	20.5	20.5	20.5	19.6	18.8	100

TABLE 3.11 Distribution of Households by Social Group and Asset Quintile, Mahatwar, 2006

Social group	As percentage of all households in the asset quintile						As percentage of all households in the group					
	Q1	Q2	Q3	Q4	Q5	All	Q1	Q2	Q3	Q4	Q5	All
SC	83.9	90.3	71.0	45.2	12.5	60.2	27.7	29.8	23.4	14.9	4.3	100.0
OBC	16.1	9.7	25.8	51.6	56.3	32.1	10.0	60.	16.0	32.0	36.0	100.0
Other castes	0.0	0.0	3.2	3.2	31.3	7.7	0.0	0.0	8.3	8.3	84.4	100.0
All	100.0	100.0	100.0	100.0	100.0	100.0	19.9	19.9	19.9	19.9	20.5	100.0

to the top asset quintile, Q5 (and the percentage was zero in two villages). The situation was worse among the Scheduled Tribes.

Second, there is considerable inter-village variation in both the average value of household asset holdings and the range of asset values. The mean value of asset ownership per household ranged from Rs 9.4 lakh in Harevli to Rs 2.9 lakh in Bukkacherla. Nevertheless, in each village, the median value was lower than the mean, indicating an unequal distribution of assets.

Third, in every village, the value of assets owned by households in the lowest three asset quintiles was relatively modest and hardly suggestive of a state of wealth or 'richness'. Thus, neither the median nor the mean value of assets per household in the third quintile exceeded two lakh rupees in any of the villages. The households in the bottom three asset quintiles, for the most part, appear to be non-rich, if not always poor.

Fourth, the top asset quintile is a class apart from other quintiles. In the first four quintiles, the median and mean values are close to each other for every village, suggesting a limited degree of inequality within the quintile. But the top quintile is characterized by the mean being much larger than the median asset value. There is clearly, in every village, a small part of the top quintile that is the most dominant in terms of assets and consequent economic—and almost always, political—power within each village. In Ananthavaram, for instance, the richest household has an asset value of more than Rs 40 million, while the minimum asset value for the top quintile in the village is a mere Rs 3.45 lakh, less than one-hundredth of the asset value of the richest household. The picture is similar in all the other villages, even if not as dramatic. The households in the top decile will be examined later, since they have distinctive features with respect to child well-being.

Interestingly, even children in the highest two asset quintiles are not entirely free of deprivation in relation to some indicators of deprivation.

Though this chapter will not be dealing with deprivation levels among children by caste or gender as a central concern, it needs to be pointed out that, as is well known, caste and gender are important axes of discrimination and deprivation in Indian society, especially so in rural India. Field data from the villages confirm the picture of a high degree of gender and caste inequality in relation to educational and health-related indicators.[4] As noted earlier, the tables in this chapter bring out the substantial overlap between asset deprivation and social group status. The focus on the relationship between household asset status and child deprivation is intended to show, without in any way understating the importance of caste and gender status as markers of child deprivation, the importance of the key structural economic parameter of household asset ownership in relation to deprivations that children experience.

SOME INDICATORS OF CHILD DEPRIVATION

In this section, certain specific aspects of deprivation that children experience are identified. The following variables are discussed in detail here:

1. School attendance
2. Incidence of child labour
3. Presence of educated/literate adults in households with children
4. Conditions of shelter
5. Sanitation (access to lavatories)

School Attendance

Table 3.12 shows the proportions of boys and girls attending school in different age groups in each of the five villages. In the youngest age group, 6–10 years, attendance rates were over 90 per cent in four of the five villages. In the age group of 11–14 years also, attendance rates were in the range of 80 to 90 per cent in most cases. Beyond the age of 14 years, attendance ratios fell sharply, for both boys and girls, in all the villages. For the age group of 6–18 years taken as a whole, female attendance ratios were lower than those for males in all five villages.

A striking feature is that Ananthavaram, a village with relatively high levels of paddy yields, and modernized agriculture, does more poorly in respect of school attendance not just in relation to the other Andhra Pradesh villages, but also in comparison with Mahatwar in

[4] These are the subject of a separate study: see Ramachandran et al. 2010 and Ramachandran and Swaminathan 2014.

TABLE 3.12 Percentage of Children Attending School, by Age Group and Sex, Five Villages, 2005–6

Age group	Ananthavaram		Bukkacherla		Kothapalle		Harevli		Mahatwar	
	Female	Male	Female	Male	Female	Male	Female	Male	Female	Male
6 to 10 years	81.1	86.9	96.2	96.2	90.4	95.8	91.5	90.7	96.8	98.8
11 to 14 years	71.1	83.9	89.7	88.1	95.2	92.7	86.5	75.8	94.4	94.6
15 to 18 years	36.0	39.8	49.0	43.7	52.2	68.8	27.6	58.8	55.9	79.0
6 to 18 years	61.5	69.6	78.9	83.3	79.5	87.4	73.5	77.7	84.5	91.5

Note: This is data on school attendance and not enrolment.

Uttar Pradesh.[5] Mahatwar, in fact, emerges as the village with better school attendance ratios than the other villages for the most part.[6]

While the observed rates of school attendance clearly indicate progress, nevertheless, schooling is not yet universal. This study did not find 100 per cent attendance, both in the age group of 6–10 years and in the age group of 11–14 years, in any of the villages.

How do attendance ratios vary across asset quintiles? The data are presented, separately for each village, in Tables 3.13 to 3.17.

The variation in attendance ratios across asset quintiles is relatively small for the age group of 6–14 years in all the villages, though the top two quintiles do marginally better on the whole. However, in the age group of 15–18 years, there is generally, though not invariably, a clear association between asset status and attendance ratios. Within each village, the top two asset quintiles tend to have a higher school attendance ratio than the bottom three quintiles.[7] The top asset quintile, in particular, is clearly a class apart.

While the attendance ratios by asset quintile for boys and girls are not shown separately, it is invariably the case that in every asset quintile, girls have a lower ratio than boys in the age group 6–18 years. Since the numbers in the age group of 15–18 years are quite small, it would be difficult to say much in this regard. However, what can be said is that females in the top asset quintile fare better than their counterparts in the lower quintiles.

One must note that, even in the top asset quintile, the attendance ratio in the age group of 15–18 years does not reach 100 per cent except in Harevli where the absolute numbers are small. This is a

[5] In fact, Ananthavaram does more poorly than Harevli also, except for boys in the age group of 11–14 years and girls in the age group of 15–18 years.

[6] The only exception is for females in the 11–14 age groups, where Kothapalle has a marginally higher ratio, but the difference is very small.

[7] The picture in Kothapalle seems to be different from the general picture. Here Q1 reports a much higher attendance ratio in the age group of 15 to 18 years than the next three quintiles. Also, Q4 does more poorly than Q2 and Q3. This has to do with differences in the number of children in the specified age group across asset quintiles. For instance, in Kothapalle, there are only 11 children in Q1, in the age group of 15 to 18 years, of whom eight are in school. On the other hand, there are 27 children in Q4 of whom 12 are in school.

TABLE 3.13 Children Attending School by Age Group and Asset Quintile, Ananthavaram, 2005

Age group	Q1		Q2		Q3		Q4		Q5	
	Number	Per cent	Number	Per cent	Number	Per cent	Number	Per cent	Number	Per cent
6 to 10 years	37	74.0	35	87.5	29	82.8	19	86.4	26	96.3
11 to 14 years	31	70.5	21	72.4	35	72.9	23	92.0	27	90.0
15 to 18 years	7	25.0	14	28.6	16	25.0	17	60.7	19	79.2
6 to 18 years	75	61.5	70	59.3	80	54.4	59	78.7	72	88.9

TABLE 3.14 Children Attending School by Age Group and Asset Quintile, Bukkacherla, 2005

Age group	Q1		Q2		Q3		Q4		Q5	
	Number	Per cent	Number	Per cent	Number	Per cent	Number	Per cent	Number	Per cent
6 to 10 years	23	95.8	19	100.0	21	91.3	15	100.0	23	95.8
11 to 14 years	16	88.9	15	88.2	28	82.4	31	96.9	14	87.5
15 to 18 years	3	37.5	7	38.9	19	65.5	16	57.1	17	70.8
6 to 18 years	42	84.0	41	75.9	68	79.1	62	82.7	54	84.4

Table 3.15 Children Attending School by Age Group and Asset Quintile, Kothapalle, 2005

Age group	Q1		Q2		Q3		Q4		Q5	
	Number	Per cent	Number	Per cent	Number	Per cent	Number	Per cent	Number	Per cent
6 to 10 years	25	86.2	30	93.8	32	97.0	29	96.7	28	90.3
11 to 14 years	14	82.4	18	90.0	24	92.3	29	100.0	26	100.0
15 to 18 years	8	72.7	19	51.4	10	55.6	12	44.4	20	83.3
6 to 18 years	47	82.5	67	75.3	66	85.7	70	81.4	74	91.4

Table 3.16 Children Attending School by Age Group and Asset Quintile, Harevli, 2006

Age group	Q1		Q2		Q3		Q4		Q5	
	Number	Per cent	Number	Per cent	Number	Per cent	Number	Per cent	Number	Per cent
6 to 10 years	21	87.5	17	81.0	22	95.7	8	88.9	24	100.0
11 to 14 years	7	87.5	10	76.9	15	68.2	9	81.8	16	100.0
15 to 18 years	1	50.0	6	37.5	3	15.8	8	50.0	10	100.0
6 to 18 years	29	85.3	33	66.0	40	62.5	25	69.4	50	100.0

TABLE 3.17 Children Attending School by Age Group and Asset Quintile, Mahatwar, 2006

Age group	Q1		Q2		Q3		Q4		Q5	
	Number	Per cent	Number	Per cent	Number	Per cent	Number	Per cent	Number	Per cent
6 to 10 years	42	97.7	36	94.7	35	100.0	27	100.0	33	97.1
11 to 14 years	16	80.0	23	95.8	24	100.0	16	100.0	25	96.2
15 to 18 years	7	25.9	13	61.9	14	58.3	19	82.6	29	85.3
6 to 18 years	65	79.3	72	86.7	73	88.0	62	93.9	87	92.6

feature that recurs in practically every indicator of interest and has implications for policy, which shall be discussed later.

While the gender disaggregated ratios are not presented here, it is the case that for all children as well as those in the age group of 15–18 years, female attendance ratios were generally lower than for males in every asset quintile. Similarly, the variation in attendance ratios across social groups generally, though not invariably, follows a hierarchy in which the highest ratios are among children from other caste Hindu families, followed by OBCs, SCs, and STs in that order. Muslims in some instances occupied the space between OBC and SC, and at other times, the space between SC and ST.[8]

Incidence of Child Labour

The previous section showed that in all five villages, a significant proportion of children of the ages 6–18 years were not attending school. It is possible that a fair proportion of such children are at work. It is also possible that several children attend school but are also engaged in some kind of work. In this chapter, a restricted definition of 'work' is used. Work is any activity that involves work on household operational holdings, work in household non-agricultural enterprises, except for work with animal resources and work for an employer, paid or unpaid, outside the household. This definition excludes work performed by young girls—and in some instances, young boys—at home, such as caring work or household chores. It also excludes work in animal tending, but in most of these five villages, this is not a very significant exclusion as far as child labour is concerned. Even with this restricted definition of work, this study finds that there is a significant proportion of working children in every village.

Table 3.18 presents the distribution of children of the ages 6–18 years by four categories across each of the five villages. This table should be read as follows. Taking row 1, in Ananthavaram village, 63 children were neither attending school nor working (often termed 'nowhere children'), 72 were not attending school and working (regular child labour), 334 were attending school and not working,

[8] The latter is true especially with respect to female attendance ratios, where SC sometimes did better than Muslims and OBCs.

TABLE 3.18 School Attendance among Children of Ages 6 to 18, by Work Status, and Village (number and per cent)

Villages	Not attending school		Attending school	
	Not working	Working	Not working	Working
Ananthavaram	63 (13.3)	72 (15.2)	334 (70.6)	4 (0.9)
Bukkacherla	23 (7.8)	18 (6.1)	250 (85.1)	3 (1.0)
Kothapalle	23 (6.4)	21 (5.9)	303 (84.9)	10 (2.8)
Harevli	30 (12.8)	27 (11.5)	157 (67.1)	20 (8.6)
Mahatwar	28 (6.9)	21 (5.2)	304 (74.4)	55 (13.5)

and 4 were attending school but also engaged in some work. The row total is the total number of children in the village in the age group 6–18 years, and the figures in parentheses are percentages of the row total. The former two categories, namely, nowhere children and regular child labour, are of most concern, as these children are out of school.

The proportion of children not attending school ranged from a low of 12 per cent in Mahatwar to a high of 28.5 per cent in Ananthavaram. In all five villages, this proportion was almost equally divided between working children and not working children. Taking the former only, the incidence of child workers ranged from a low of 6 per cent in Kothapalle to a high of 13 per cent in Harevli. Thus, the incidence of child labour among children of the ages 6–18 years is far from negligible. One must keep in mind that these proportions will be higher for girls and for socially disadvantaged sections, though these aspects will not be discussed here.

How do these percentages vary across asset quintiles? Table 3.19 shows the percentage of children in the age group of 6–18 years reported as not attending school and working (child labour) by asset quintile for each of the villages.

In general, the incidence of child workers was higher in the lower quintiles (Q1 to Q3) than in the higher quintiles, especially Q5, but these differences were neither very sharp nor clear-cut in all the villages. In Mahatwar, the number of child workers was highest in absolute and proportional terms in Q1. However, in Ananthavaram and Harevli, the incidence of child labour was highest in Q3.

TABLE 3.19 Number and Percentage of Children of Ages 6 to 18 Not Attending School and Working, by Village and Asset Quintile

Asset quintile	Ananthavaram	Bukkacherla	Kothapalle	Harevli	Mahatwar
Q1	23 (4.9)	3 (1.1)	2 (0.6)	1 (0.4)	9 (2.2)
Q2	16 (3.4)	4 (1.4)	9 (2.5)	8 (3.4)	6 (1.5)
Q3	32 (6.8)	4 (1.4)	2 (0.6)	13 (5.6)	3 (0.7)
Q4	1 (0.2)	4 (1.4)	5 (1.4)	5 (2.1)	1 (0.2)
Q5	0 (0.0)	3 (1.1)	3 (1.1)	0 (0.0)	2 (0.5)
All	72 (15.2)	18 (6.1)	21 (5.9)	27 (11.5)	21 (5.2)

Note: Figures in parentheses shows the per cent in relation to all children belonging to that age group.

There is a pattern that appears to be related to the degree of inequality in asset distribution and the degree of landlessness in a village. The highest incidence of child labour was in Ananthavaram (15 per cent), followed by Harevli (11.5 per cent), both canal-irrigated villages with productive agriculture and highly unequal income distributions (Swaminathan and Rawal 2011).

An interesting feature that emerges from the data is that the percentage of working children in Q1 tends to be less than that in Q2. This was so in Bukkacherla, Kothapalle, and Mahatwar. One reason could be that landless households tend to occupy Q1 to a greater extent and poor peasant households are found to a greater extent in Q2. The latter often have children working on the operational holding, while the former do not cultivate land. In Ananthavaram, tenants populate Q1 and so the proportion of working children is higher among Q1 than Q2.

These village studies show that child labour persists even in village economies where there is no specific demand for child workers (such as in match factories or carpet weaving). Also, child workers are found not only among the poorest households, but also spread out over the lower four quintiles. The picture is different for the top quintile, though even here occasional child workers can be found (though not in the top decile). When this is the case and when we see that even in the highest asset quintiles school attendance is not universal, there is clearly a case for universal public provisioning for education and for improving peasant incomes so that children do not have to work.

The Educational Environment

A child's educational achievement (even the fact of continuation in school) is clearly affected by the domestic environment and how supportive the environment is for education. In this regard, two indicators are examined. First, the presence or absence of educated adults in households with children is examined. Secondly, household amenities, such as conditions of shelter and provisions for drinking water and sanitation, which impact the pattern of time disposition of the children, their health and morbidity, and the physical environment for study and learning, are examined.

It is generally agreed that if there are literate and/or more educationally qualified adults in the household, this enhances the child's domestic learning environment. For instance, the likelihood of a child being sent to school improves if the mother is literate/educated. The same may be true if the father is literate/educated, even if the relationship is a little less strong. On the other hand, if a household has no literate adult, this makes for a less supportive educational environment at home.

Tables 3.20 to 3.24 present data on the proportion of households with children without (i) a literate adult female, (ii) a literate adult male, and (iii) a literate adult for each village and asset quintile.

Given the low levels of education of the ascendant generation, it is inevitable that children currently in school and those who are literate will have uneducated parents. Nevertheless, it is worth noting that in all five villages, more than one-fourth of all households with children did not have a single literate adult female in the household. One-fifth of all households did not have a literate adult male.

The second feature of note is the contrast between the villages of Andhra Pradesh and those of Uttar Pradesh. While the proportion of households with children without a literate adult female varied between one-fourth and three-tenths in the three villages of Andhra Pradesh, it was over five-eighths in Harevli and more than seven-tenths in Mahatwar. With regard to the proportion of households (with children) without a literate adult male, Harevli was the worst performer among the five villages (40 per cent). The proportion of households with children without any literate adult averaged around one-tenth for the villages of Andhra Pradesh and more than one-fourth for the two villages of Uttar Pradesh.

TABLE 3.20 Distribution of Households with Children by Absence of Adult Literates, by Asset Quintile, Ananthavaram, 2005

Asset quintile	Without literate adult female		Without literate adult male		Without a literate adult	
	Number	Percentage	Number	Percentage	Number	Percentage
Q1	26	35.6	25	34.3	10	13.7
Q2	24	32.9	22	30.1	12	16.4
Q3	31	42.5	22	30.1	13	17.8
Q4	10	13.7	11	15.1	5	6.9
Q5	2	2.8	4	5.6	0	0.0
All	93	25.6	84	23.1	40	11.0

TABLE 3.21 Distribution of Households with Children by Absence of Adult Literates, by Asset Quintile, Bukkacherla, 2005

Asset quintile	Without literate adult female		Without literate adult male		Without a literate adult	
	Number	Percentage	Number	Percentage	Number	Percentage
Q1	19	48.7	12	30.8	6	15.4
Q2	13	34.2	10	26.3	5	13.2
Q3	16	42.1	6	15.8	3	7.9
Q4	5	13.2	7	18.4	2	5.3
Q5	5	13.2	2	5.3	0	0.0
All	58	30.4	37	19.4	16	8.4

TABLE 3.22 Distribution of Households with Children by Absence of Adult Literates, by Asset Quintile, Kothapalle, 2005

Asset quintile	Without literate adult female		Without literate adult male		Without a literate adult	
	Number	Percentage	Number	Percentage	Number	Percentage
Q1	19	39.6	16	33.3	9	18.8
Q2	18	37.5	14	29.2	4	8.3
Q3	11	23.4	11	23.4	3	6.4
Q4	9	19.2	9	19.2	2	4.3
Q5	5	10.6	1	2.1	0	0.0
All	62	26.2	51	21.5	18	7.6

TABLE 3.23 Distribution of Households with Children by Absence of Adult Literates, by Asset Quintile, Harevli, 2006

Asset quintile	Without literate adult female		Without literate adult male		Without a literate adult	
	Number	Percentage	Number	Percentage	Number	Percentage
Q1	16	88.9	11	61.1	11	61.1
Q2	16	94.1	12	70.6	12	70.6
Q3	15	83.3	8	44.4	7	38.9
Q4	6	35.3	3	17.7	1	5.9
Q5	2	11.8	0	0.0	0	0.0
All	55	63.2	34	39.1	31	35.6

TABLE 3.24 Distribution of Households with Children by Absence of Adult Literates, by Asset Quintile, Mahatwar, 2006

Asset quintile	Without literate adult female		Without literate adult male		Without a literate adult	
	Number	Percentage	Number	Percentage	Number	Percentage
Q1	27	90.0	13	43.3	12	40.0
Q2	25	83.3	8	26.7	7	23.3
Q3	22	73.3	9	30.0	7	23.3
Q4	22	73.3	6	20.0	6	20.0
Q5	9	31.0	1	3.45	0	0.0
All	105	70.5	37	24.8	32	21.5

Turning to differences across asset quintiles, the top quintile, as one would expect, showed the lowest level of deprivation in this indicator in all villages. In all five villages, all households in this quintile had at least one literate adult. In terms of ensuring that a household had a literate adult female, even the top quintile performed poorly.

The performance on this indicator was clearly dismal for households in the bottom three asset quintiles and, for the most part, for those in the fourth quintile as well. As mentioned, the indicator fared worst in Harevli and Mahatwar. In general, the percentage of households without a literate adult female was much higher than that of households without a literate adult male in every quintile in every village. The only exceptions were the fourth quintile in both Ananthavaram and Bukkacherla, where the position was reversed, and the third and fourth quintiles in Kothapalle, where the two proportions were equal. In Harevli, the difference in the proportions, as between male and female adult literate, was very large in all but the top quintile. The worst performer with regard to the proportion of households without a literate adult female was Mahatwar, where the proportion was above 70 per cent in all quintiles, except the top one, and even in the top quintile, it was nearly one-third.

It is clear that the home environment for education, even in terms of a minimal measure like the presence of a literate adult, male or female, is very weak for children from a majority of households, particularly the poorest 60 per cent of households. It must also be underlined that the environment in this regard is not good even for the second highest asset quintile and less than ideal for the top asset quintile. This has implications for policy, as will be demonstrated further.

The inadequacy of the home environment for the education of children even in the higher asset quintiles becomes further evident when one looks at two positive indicators of adult educational achievement. Table 3.25 presents the number and percentage of households with children having at least one male graduate by asset quintile for all five villages. Table 3.26 presents the corresponding data relating to the presence of at least one female who has passed Class 10.

While the data bring out the dismal state of affairs with respect to the bottom three asset quintiles in all the villages, we can see that the position in the fourth quintile is also nothing to write home about. The top asset quintile does fare better than the other quintiles, but even here, the proportion of households with a male graduate exceeded 50 per cent only in Mahatwar, and was as low as 14 per cent in Ananthavaram.[9] Similarly, only about half of all the households in the top quintile met the even more modest requirement of having a female member of the household who has passed Class 10, except in Ananthavaram where the proportion was three-fifths.[10]

[9] In Ananthavaram, these data reflect the disparity even within the top quintile. This village has several engineers in the US but not all households in the top 20 per cent had a male graduate.

[10] In the top decile, there were five women with graduate degrees in Ananthavaram.

TABLE 3.25 Households with Children with at least One Male Graduate, by Village and Asset Quintile

Asset quintile	Ananthavaram		Bukkacherla		Kothapalle		Harevli		Mahatwar	
	Number	Per cent	Number	Per cent	Number	Per cent	Number	Per cent	Number	Per cent
Q1	3	4.1	0	0.0	0	0.0	0	0.0	2	6.7
Q2	4	5.5	1	2.6	0	0.0	0	0.0	1	3.3
Q3	0	0.0	4	10.5	0	0.0	1	5.6	7	23.3
Q4	6	8.2	3	7.9	3	6.4	1	5.9	3	10.0
Q5	10	13.9	13	34.2	11	23.4	7	41.2	15	51.7
All	23	6.3	21	11.0	14	5.9	9	10.3	28	18.8

TABLE 3.26 Households with Children with at least One Female 10th Pass, by Village and Asset Quintile

Asset quintile	Ananthavaram		Bukkacherla		Kothapalle		Harevli		Mahatwar	
	Number	Per cent	Number	Per cent	Number	Per cent	Number	Per cent	Number	Per cent
Q1	9	12.3	0	0.0	12	25.0	0	0.0	3	10.0
Q2	6	8.2	4	10.5	10	20.8	0	0.0	2	6.7
Q3	10	13.7	5	13.2	11	23.4	0	0.0	4	13.3
Q4	28	38.4	7	18.4	12	25.5	6	35.3	6	20.0
Q5	44	61.1	18	47.4	24	51.1	8	47.1	16	55.2
All	97	26.7	34	17.8	69	29.1	14	16.1	31	20.8

Conditions of Shelter

Conditions of housing, including the quality of shelter, access to electricity and safe drinking water, and access to lavatories are important aspects of an environment at home that is conducive to learning. In the discussion that follows, two features of housing, namely, the quality of shelter and access to lavatories, receive attention.

Table 3.27 presents data on the percentage of households with children living in non-*pucca* or non-permanent houses by asset quintile for all the five villages. Following the practice of the Census of India, we have classified houses into three categories: pucca (roof and wall of pucca or permanent material), semi-pucca (either roof or wall of pucca material) and *kutcha* (neither roof nor wall of permanent material).[11] Table 3.27 shows the aggregate of households living in either semi-pucca or kutcha structures, termed non-pucca structure.

In most villages, the proportion of households with non-pucca houses declines as we move from lower to higher asset quintiles. Bukkacherla is an exception for two reasons. On the one hand, there has been a housing programme for the landless (who populate the bottom quintiles heavily) that can explain a situation where the percentage of households living in non-pucca houses is lower for Q1 and Q2 than for Q3 and Q4 households. On the other hand, the traditional adobe and stone material used in most houses is classified as non-pucca

TABLE 3.27 Distribution of Households with Children Living in Non-pucca Houses, by Village and Asset Quintile

Asset quintile	Ananthavaram	Bukkacherla	Kothapalle	Harevli	Mahatwar
Q1	68.5	25.6	25.0	72.2	73.3
Q2	83.6	34.2	6.3	82.3	36.7
Q3	64.4	50.0	6.4	55.6	26.7
Q4	32.8	57.9	10.6	88.2	10.0
Q5	7.0	50.0	10.6	82.4	3.4
All	51.3	43.4	11.8	75.9	30.2

[11] The Census provides a list of materials that are to be considered as pucca/permanent.

by the Census of India definition, accounting for the low aggregate proportion of pucca houses.[12]

In all, the quality of shelter remains abysmal for most households in the bottom four quintiles in all villages except Kothapalle, where it is somewhat better, but still modest. Again, in Kothapalle, a large section of the village was resettled in new housing after building of the Lower Maner Dam. It is noteworthy that even households in the highest asset quintile fare very poorly in Harevli, but if we take the top decile, all households lived in pucca houses with latrines. This was true of Ananthavaram and Mahatwar also.

A second measure of the quality of housing is the number of rooms in a dwelling (allowing, for example, space for study). Table 3.28 presents the percentage of households with children living in single-room houses by asset quintile for the five villages. Ananthavaram is the worst performer, with one half of all households with children living in single-room houses. Mahatwar performs better, in relative terms.

In terms of variation across asset quintiles, in all villages except Mahatwar, at least one-fifth of households in the bottom three quintiles resided in single-room houses. The position was much worse in Ananthavaram. In all villages except Mahatwar, the poorest quintile fared very badly. Nearly three-fourths of such households in Ananthavaram and Harevli, two-thirds in Kothapalle, and nearly half in Bukkacherla lived in single-room houses. The top quintile did fare

TABLE 3.28 Percentage of Households with Children Living in Single-room Houses, by Village and Asset Quintile

Asset quintile	Ananthavaram	Bukkacherla	Kothapalle	Harevli	Mahatwar
Q1	72.6	46.2	66.7	72.2	26.7
Q2	68.5	31.6	35.4	70.6	16.7
Q3	56.2	23.7	21.3	33.3	13.3
Q4	38.4	23.7	10.6	5.9	20.0
Q5	9.7	0.0	12.8	0.0	0.0
All	49.2	25.1	29.5	36.8	15.4

[12] See discussion in Swaminathan and Singh 2014.

TABLE 3.29 Households with Children without Access to Lavatories, by Village and Asset Quintile

Asset quintile	Ananthavaram	Bukkacherla	Kothapalle	Harevli	Mahatwar
Q1	71.2	84.6	66.7	83.3	100.0
Q2	91.8	84.2	56.3	94.1	96.7
Q3	69.9	92.1	61.7	100.0	100.0
Q4	43.8	92.1	57.5	29.4	90.0
Q5	8.3	68.4	48.9	17.7	72.4
All	57.1	84.3	58.2	65.5	91.9

a lot better than the others, with not a single household living in a single-room house in three of the five villages.[13]

Finally, let us look at the state of sanitation. The indicator we use for this purpose is access to a lavatory (Table 3.29). Except for the top asset quintile in Ananthavaram, and to a lesser extent in Harevli, the position with respect to access to a lavatory was uniformly bad both across villages and across asset quintiles.[14] To put it differently, the status of sanitation was dismal in all five villages. With respect to sanitation, the ownership of assets does not appear to make much of a difference. Public provisioning, with assured water supply and a social mobilization effort to create adequate awareness about the benefits of proper sanitation, would appear to be critical.

POLICY IMPLICATIONS

Within each village, variations in selected indicators of child deprivation across asset quintiles were examined. The value of asset holdings of a household has been taken as a proxy for long-term economic status. While deprivations among children remain high on many scores and follow patterns already recognized (such as gender differences in school attendance and lower attendance at higher ages), there are some new insights that emerge from our study. The levels of deprivation were similar for households in the lowest three asset quintiles (Q1

[13] Six households in Kothapalle and seven in Ananthavaram from the top asset quintile lived in single-room houses.

[14] In both these villages, all households in the top decile lived in pucca houses with their own toilets.

to Q3). In most villages, children in Q5 households were distinctly better off than others (for example, in terms of attending school and not working, good quality housing, presence of adult literates in the households). Nevertheless, even children in Q5 were at times not in school, or living in single-room houses, or in families without adult literates. In villages with high level of asset and income inequality, such as Ananthavaram in coastal Andhra Pradesh and Harevli in western Uttar Pradesh,[15] the top decile rather than quintile was a class apart (indeed children from these households were often sent to boarding schools and then for higher education to the top educational institutes in the country or abroad).

The implications of these findings are, first, that we need a massive effort to address the observed deprivations among children in rural India. Overcoming educational deprivation of current school-age children not only requires provision of quality schooling, but also requires public provisioning of libraries and after-school and out-of-school extra-curricular study environments. This is essential given the limited educational attainments of parents. It is also important to invest in programmes of adult literacy, post-literacy, and continuing education that will specifically cater to rural residents.

Second, this effort has to target about 90 per cent of the population. Thus, there is a very strong case for child-related polices (in education, in health, in social mobilization for sanitation, etc.) to be universal in nature. Social policy for rural children needs to be designed in such a way as to ensure the inclusion of the lowest 90 per cent and not focus on exclusion of the wealthiest 10 per cent (such households can always have an option of self-selection).

Third, and concurrently, it is clear that households in Q1 to Q3—the bottom 60 per cent of the asset distribution—face acute deprivation, and therefore policy interventions must also be designed to ensure special attention to children from these groups. As we have shown, the lower quintiles have an over-representation of persons from SC, ST, and Muslims (as seen from Tables 3.7 to 3.11). So, the special attention towards the poorer 60 per cent of households encompasses special attention towards social groups that have faced deprivation and discrimination in the past. Similarly, special attention has to be paid to girls.

[15] See Swaminathan and Rawal 2011.

In the current context of social policy in India, these findings, though from only a handful of villages, bring out very clearly the need for policies pertaining to basic education, health, and shelter to be universal in scope with special attention and effort placed on more deprived households. It follows, then, that we must move away from policies designed specifically for 'below poverty line' (BPL) households, that is, policies of narrow targeting based on an arbitrary expenditure poverty line. As we have shown, the incidence of child labour is often higher among small landowning households than among landless labour households. So, ensuring all children are not working but attending school will require a focus on children that may belong officially to APL (Above Poverty Line) households. Similarly, we have seen that the problem of lack of space or absence of an educated woman in the family does not necessarily disappear with higher asset ownership.

In conclusion, we must move away from designing social policy based on a BPL/APL classification that is applied uniformly across different spheres. To quote Ramachandran et al. (2010):

> Poverty is multi-dimensional, that is, people can be poor with respect to some or all of a range of criteria—for instance, with respect to income, hunger, health, schooling and education, housing, access to the means of sanitary living, and so on. Why then should a single classification of poverty—whether based on criteria set by the MoRD (Ministry of Rural Development) or the Planning Commission or a combination of the two—be considered adequate to measure whether a person is income-poor, nutrition-poor, education-poor, housing-poor, and so on? The natural beneficiaries of a scheme that provides housing should be the population without adequate, safe and clean housing, just as the natural target group for a scheme to provide sanitary toilets is those who have no access to such facilities. Why should access to such schemes be determined by arbitrary reference to fictitious BPL categories? And why should State governments be forced to fit welfare policies to the Procrustean bed of the MoRD's current BPL measure?

REFERENCES

Foundation for Agrarian Studies. 2011a. *Child Wellbeing, Schooling and Living Standards: Report on Ananthavaram Village, Andhra Pradesh.*

———. 2011b. *Child Wellbeing, Schooling and Living Standards: Report on Bukkacherla Village, Andhra Pradesh.*

Foundation for Agrarian Studies. 2011c. *Child Wellbeing, Schooling and Living Standards: Report on Kothapalle Village, Andhra Pradesh.*

———. 2011d. *Child Wellbeing, Schooling and Living Standards: Report on Harevli Village, Uttar Pradesh.*

———. 2011e. *Child Wellbeing, Schooling and Living Standards: Report on Mahatwar Village, Uttar Pradesh.*

Ramachandran, V.K. and Madhura Swaminathan (eds). 2014. *Dalit Households in Village Economies.* New Delhi: Tulika Books.

Ramachandran, V.K., Vikas Rawal, and Madhura Swaminathan (eds). 2010. *Socio-Economic Survey of Three Villages in Andhra Pradesh: A Study of Agrarian Relations.* New Delhi: Tulika Books.

Ramachandran, V.K., Y. Usami, and B. Sarkar. 2010. 'Lessons from BPL Censuses', *The Hindu*, 21 April.

Swaminathan, Madhura and Vikas Rawal. 2011. 'Is India Really a Country of Low Income-Inequality?' *Review of Agrarian Studies*, 1(1): 1–22.

Swaminathan, Madhura and Shamsher Singh. 2014. 'Exclusion in Access to Basic Civic Amenities: Evidence from Fourteen Villages', in V.K. Ramachandran and Madhura Swaminathan (eds), *Dalit Households in Village Economies*, pp. 305–32. New Delhi: Tulika Books.

4 Demographic Transition, School Attendance, and Changing Activity Structure in Urban India

Amitabh Kundu and P.C. Mohanan

India has come to enjoy a distinct advantage in the labour market as compared with the most developed and also less developed countries owing to the fast-changing age distribution of its population. India is a late entrant into the process of demographic transition. Its population growth, which was maintained at a rate ranging between 2.1 and 2.2 per cent per annum during the first four decades since Independence in 1947, came down to below 2 per cent during the 1990s and then to about 1.6 per cent in the following decade. As a consequence, the country is witnessing a rapid decline in its percentage of population in the age group of 0–14 years. This is likely to go down further during the next two to three decades. Correspondingly, the figure for people in the economically active age group (15–59 years) would go up (particularly for women). It is predicted to touch 68 per cent in 2030, while that for China would go down from its current level of 70 per cent to 67 per cent (Figure 4.1). India is likely to overtake most of the East Asian countries including Thailand, the Philippines, and Malaysia, whose figures would be about 66 per cent only

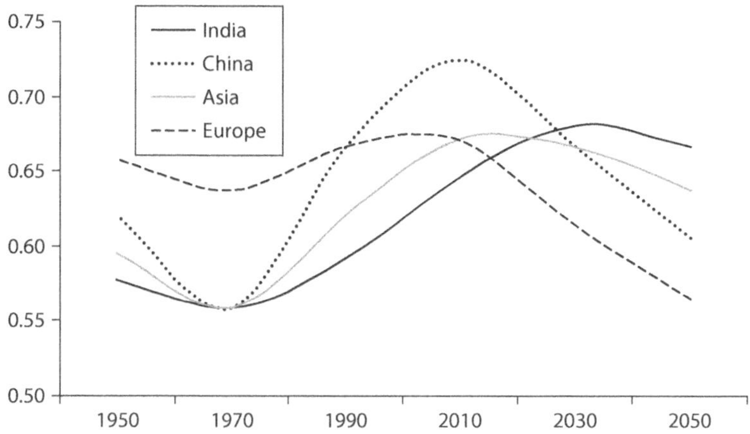

FIGURE 4.1 Projection of Percentage of Population of Ages 15 to 64 to Total Population

Note: Computed on the basis of the data obtained from World Population Prospects, 2004.

(EIAS 2006).[1] The decline in the natural rate of growth and the sluggish growth in the number of the aged in India would imply that India will have a relatively low dependency burden. All these predictions are being viewed as positive factors from the developmental perspective of the country.[2] India would thus enjoy a significant demographic dividend during the next few decades, because the process of fertility decline that has begun only recently would affect and alter the age structure favourably in coming years.

Many individual researchers and institutions have predicted that during the next two decades, a two-digit level sustained growth in national income will result in India's becoming the second largest economy in the

[1] This may be attributed to the fact that while the percentage of children in India would go down significantly, that of the aged population would not go up steeply.

[2] By 2050, the percentage of the economically active population in India would be much above that of all European and Asian countries. The three other countries that would have similar figures are Bangladesh, Nepal, and Cambodia.

world, next to only China. They have observed that the country would perform well in terms of not only achieving a high rate of economic growth, but also a reduction in its poverty, measured through monetary measures like per capita income or consumption expenditure. One of the reasons for this is the rapid decrease in the percentage of children, which is likely to continue during the next few decades—a decrease much more than that of other Asian and African countries.

Unfortunately, however, many of the targets under the Millennium Development Goals (MDGs) that have a bearing on equity and social upliftment would remain unfulfilled, the high economic growth and decline in poverty levels notwithstanding. Of particular concern is the well-being of children and young adults for whom the direct and indirect impact of the present growth dynamics has been predicted to be detrimental. Understandably, the shortfalls in meeting the MDG targets of universal primary education, reduction of gender inequality in schools and educational attainments, and increase in the share of women in non-agricultural employment have been predicted to be alarmingly high.

Given the conflicting visions of India's future development and the serious apprehension with regard to the well-being of children, it is important to analyse the changing age composition of the population, enrolment in schools at different levels, dropouts and incidence of child labour in the context of the goal of poverty reduction, and elimination of other forms of deprivation. It would also be important to assess their implications in the context of policy initiatives and judicial interventions that can be proposed to ameliorate the conditions of children and young adults in and outside the labour market.

Keeping the above objectives in view, the analysis in this chapter has been divided into five sections. The second section, which follows the present section, assesses the process of demographic transition in India and analyses its implications for future growth. The third section examines the usual disposition of boys and girls in the age group of 5–24 years, the thrust of analysis being on the pattern in urban areas. The changes in the percentage of children in educational institutions and in various work and non-work categories have also been assessed to determine the impact of demographic and economic growth on the well-being of children and young adults. The phenomenon of children dropping out of schools, assessed through alternate approaches, their engagement in work or non-work activities, and discrimination against girls in terms of not sending them to schools or their not being absorbed in the labour market has been analysed in the next section. The fifth section presents an overview of the trends and patterns of employment and unemployment among children and young adults since the 1980s, analysing the process of their withdrawal from educational institutions and absorption in different kinds of activities. The final section presents the major findings, discussing the implications of the changing demographic structure and absorption of children and young adults in various activities in the context of their social well-being.

DEMOGRAPHIC TRANSITION IN INDIA: A SPATIAL ANALYSIS

If the twentieth century was characterized by the 'population explosion', the twenty-first century would be noted for its stabilization at the global level and for many developing countries. Indeed, the International Institute for Applied Systems Analysis, Luxembourg, Austria, has predicted an 'end of world population growth' by the end of the present century. Understandably, the patterns and time phasing of demographic transition in Asian countries would be determined by their diverse socio-economic conditions. The population in China is likely to peak by about 2045, while for India, it would happen only by 2075.[3] The decline in population growth has been seen in India at the macro-level only during the 1990s, though a few states like Kerala and Tamil Nadu had reported this a couple of decades ago. Most of the states in the country are moving towards population transition at a slow but steady pace.

The smooth age pyramid of India bears no distinct trace of past demographic trauma or major policy intervention. Its age structure and the changes since Independence reflect a slow fertility decline at the national level. Its age pyramid has the typical shape of a country

[3] One of the dominant population discourses during the twenty-first century will be about *population ageing*, and this will not be limited to the 'developed' or 'advanced' countries including the EU-27, but will also include the Asia-26 countries covered in this study. The Asian population will be nearly ten times as large as that of the European Union by 2050.

with a young and fast-growing population. In 2009–10, about 64 per cent of its population was in the 15–64 year age group. With the decline in the natural growth of the population, the population in this age group is likely to go up significantly during the next couple of decades.

During the 1950s, India's average dependency ratio (non-workers to workers) was as high as 150 per cent, meaning that there were almost one and a half dependants for every worker. But sustained fertility reduction, whose impact was, to a certain extent, offset by reduction in the death rate and increased longevity, has resulted in a complete turnaround. The dependency ratio has been decreasing over the last four decades. Data from the National Sample Survey (NSS) for 2004–5 indicates that there has been an increase in work participation rates (WPRs), which will provide a further boost to labour supply. India is, thus, likely to enjoy an unprecedented period of demographic bonus that began in the 1990s and that will extend beyond 2050. Furthermore, the health expenditures for the aged, which are noted to be growing exponentially in many developed countries, may not shoot up in India, as the life expectancy in the high-age groups is not growing rapidly. This should make it possible for the government to make investments in water supply, sanitation, health, and other infrastructure facilities, thereby addressing various MDGs wherein the shortfalls are predicted to be high.[4]

The advantages of the demographic dividend in India should not be overestimated. The nature of economic growth does not guarantee that the growth in job opportunities will be equal to that of the working-age population or higher than that to wipe out the backlog of unemployment. If the 'jobless growth', witnessed in India during a part of the 1990s, recurs, as apprehended based on the data from the 66th Round of NSS for the year 2009–10, it may have adverse consequences on employment conditions and may reinforce social unrest.

[4] Europe has long enjoyed advantageous population structures as the child population there never exceeded one-quarter of the entire population, and the impact of increased longevity on age distributions was almost marginal. Unfortunately, this would no longer be so in the coming decades, as the share of the elderly would rise steeply.

The potential for further growth of human capital resources in India is estimated to be very high. There has been a significant increase in levels of not only literacy, but also in technological skills among the youth population, which has grown tremendously in recent years. The rapid advance in education among the younger generations is likely to improve the quality of labour and strengthen the country's position as a source of supply of educated persons for the global market. Researchers have predicted that this potential supply for the human-capital-intensive services sectors, which have been growing rapidly in recent decades, will enhance India's demographic dividend. The actual benefit may, however, turn out to be less than projected or expected, since it may not be possible to expand university and technical education to meet the country's intensified demand for human capital formation. The following section attempts to answer these concerns by analysing the work and non-work disposition of the population at young ages.

ENROLMENT AND WORK/NON-WORK DISPOSITION OF CHILDREN AND YOUNG ADULTS

Single-year and age-specific data, that classifies the population by their nature of work and non-work engagements, is available from various rounds of the NSS.[5] Tables 4.1 and 4.2 show the percentage of children and youth in the age group of 5–24 years, in different usual activity statuses in urban areas for boys and girls, as obtained from the 66th Round of the NSS for the reference period 2009–10. In the NSS, the activity profiles are recorded following different reference periods and approaches. For this study, the principal usual activity which is more suited for understanding the activities profiles has been followed.

In the context of the usual status disposition of children, the important activity status that needs to be seen in the two tables is attendance in educational institutions (91). It may be mentioned that those in

[5] The definition of usual principal status encompasses the concept of enduring status and, therefore, temporary absence from an activity would not matter. These categories are mutually exclusive, making simultaneous comparisons possible, with the sum total of the percentage figures across these being 100.

TABLE 4.1 Distribution of Urban Male Children and Youth of Ages 5 to 24 by Usual Activity Status

Age	Own account worker (11)	Employer (12)	Unpaid family worker (21)	Regular salaried worker (31)	Casual worker in public works (41)	Casual worker in other works (51)	Unemployed (81)	Student (91)	Engaged in household chores (92 & 93)
5								79.91	
6								93.50	0.07
7								96.65	
8								95.85	0.24
9							0.11	97.22	0.29
10			0.17	0.41		0.12		95.46	0.11
11			0.19			0.49	0.14	97.40	
12			0.37	0.64		0.45	0.12	94.10	0.38
13	0.26		0.70	0.97		0.70	0.34	94.05	0.31
14	0.13		1.24	2.71		2.46	0.70	89.04	0.34
15	1.29		2.44	2.99	0.10	3.45	1.45	83.59	0.60
16	1.24		4.02	4.25		7.60	2.14	77.21	0.65
17	1.33	0.01	4.26	6.49	0.06	5.89	3.31	75.04	0.41
18	4.11	0.01	6.52	10.54	0.19	11.00	5.09	59.61	1.24
19	4.30	0.02	5.72	11.93	0.27	11.19	5.11	58.32	1.12
20	6.30	0.08	9.29	17.64	0.38	12.64	4.80	46.99	0.89
21	7.00	0.32	8.53	21.22	0.41	12.82	8.28	39.32	0.42
22	9.90	0.18	11.30	26.38	0.40	13.46	7.02	28.59	0.37
23	12.73	0.11	10.03	33.83	0.33	14.38	9.00	18.29	0.44
24	13.13	0.17	11.79	36.60	0.35	15.11	6.27	14.11	1.26

Source: Data computed from unit-level data of NSS 66th Round 2009–10.

TABLE 4.2 Distribution of Urban Female Children and Youth of Ages 5 to 24 by Usual Activity Status

Age	Own account worker (11)	Employer (12)	Unpaid family worker (21)	Regular salaried (31)	Casual worker in public works (41)	Casual worker in other works (51)	Unemployed (81)	Student (91)	Engaged in household chores (92 & 93)
5								77.92	0.04
6								90.96	0.27
7							0.12	94.91	0.06
8								96.32	0.06
9				0.01		0.16		95.42	0.54
10								96.05	1.01
11	0.10		0.22					96.67	1.52
12	0.12		0.24	0.06		0.40	0.09	94.34	1.60
13	0.07		0.76	0.22		0.37	0.01	92.09	4.36
14	0.31		0.34	0.18		0.57	0.06	90.24	6.49
15	0.50		1.01	1.46	0.06	1.07	0.19	79.53	13.57
16	0.37		1.45	0.94		1.35	0.69	77.62	16.52
17	1.13		1.56	2.00		1.92	0.53	68.51	21.86
18	1.00		2.01	2.67		2.33	1.91	58.74	30.20
19	1.26		1.54	3.49		1.37	1.44	57.37	32.65
20	1.73		2.75	4.01	0.11	2.31	2.24	35.87	50.18
21	1.73		1.40	9.14		2.43	4.43	34.86	45.52
22	1.28	0.24	1.99	7.56	0.16	1.65	4.68	22.71	58.99
23	3.19		1.86	10.25		1.94	5.70	12.94	63.73
24	2.41		1.78	10.39	0.07	2.32	2.77	8.74	70.90

Source: Data computed from unit-level data of NSS 66th Round 2009–10.

category 91 are not necessarily in formal recognized schools. A large number of them, particularly at the age of 5 years, would be in nursery schools and other informal institutions. Information on own-account workers (11), employers (12), unpaid family workers (21), regular/salaried workers (31), casual workers in public works (41), and other casual workers (51) are presented in these tables and are discussed in some detail in a subsequent section. All these categories together constitute the total workforce. Two non-work categories included in the tables are: those attending domestic duties only (92) and those attending domestic duties besides being engaged in free collection of goods (vegetables, roots, firewood, cattle feed, etc.), sewing, tailoring, etc. (93). As expected, not many males are reported being engaged in these activities. Those available for work are the unemployed (81), and they are not insignificant among children and adolescents. Finally, for rentiers/retired persons (94), those not working owing to disability (95), beggars/prostitutes (96), and others (97), small values have been reported, which is why they have been excluded from the tables.

Slightly above three-quarters of the urban male children of 5 years of age are noted to have been in educational institutions in 2009–10 (Table 4.1).[6] This should roughly correspond to the actual number of persons who enrol, as there would be no dropouts at this age. The percentage figure increases to 93.5 at the age of 6 years and reaches 97.2 per cent at 9 years of age. The indicator attains its peak there and stays till 11 years of age.[7] After that, a sharp and monotonous decrease is seen in the figure, coming down to 77.2 per cent at the age of 16 years. This is the age when one generally completes secondary school. About 17 per cent of the boys aged 16 years are employed and, more importantly, 25 per cent of those working report regular wage employment. At the age of 18 years, about 60 per cent of the men are in educational institutions while one-third of them are in employment. For women at this age, the share of persons in educational institutions is almost the

[6] Data for all tables has been sourced from NSS 66th Round 2009–10, except where specified.

[7] In rural areas, the peak value of 94 per cent is reached in the age group of 9 to 11 years. The drop in the value for the age group of 10 years could be due to digit reporting preference (for age 10 years), which is likely to be higher among illiterate parents.

same, with only the number entering the labour market being much less, at approximately 10 per cent. The distribution of workers across categories has been analysed in detail in the fifth section.

For urban girls of 5 years of age, the percentage in educational institutions is 78. At the age of nine years, almost 95 per cent of these girls are in the schools (Table 4.2). These figures are similar to what was noted for boys. One would, therefore, argue that the gender difference in urban areas is not very prominent as far as the starting age for school attendance is concerned. (This is true for rural areas as well, as may be inferred from the NSS data of the 66th Round.) There are, however, large gender differences at the state levels that have been analysed elsewhere.

Among urban girls of 16 years of age, 78 per cent are in schools and only 4 per cent are in employment. This is in contrast to the figure of 17 per cent for boys in employment at this age, as noted above. As against that figure, 16 per cent of the girls are engaged in household chores and collection of free goods and, hence, do not get counted as being in the labour force. At the age of 18 years, their school attendance comes down to 59 per cent while the employment rate goes up to 8 per cent. The percentage of girls engaged in household chores and collection of free goods for use of the household is as high as 30 per cent.

Since the attendance keeps increasing till the age of 9 years for boys and 11 years for girls, it must be accepted that many children enrol at a higher age than the norm of 6 years for admission to Class I. Further, since the attendance drops after the age of 15 years for boys and 14 years for girls, which roughly corresponds to the completion of secondary level, if one joins Class I at the age of 6 years, it may be surmised that a large number of children do not go beyond the secondary stage. As many children join school at a later age, the rate of dropouts before the completion of secondary level education is very high.

Figure 4.2 shows the plotting of age and attendance for persons in the age group of 5–24 years. The innermost curve is for rural females, which is significantly below that for rural males at all ages, with the difference being very low at the lower ends. The urban female curve is also below that of urban males, but the gap is not very high at least up to 16 years of age. A steep fall in attendance is noticed around the age of 14 years for both the genders, with the fall being quite sharp

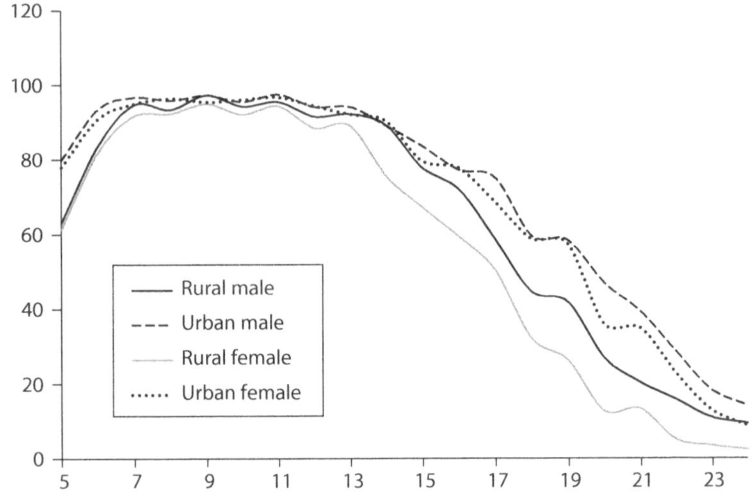

FIGURE 4.2 Percentage of Children and Youth Attending Educational Institutions

Source: Data computed from unit-level data of NSS 66th Round 2009–10.

in rural areas. For rural females, the fall starts at an earlier age and is steeper than the other categories.

If urban areas are compared with rural areas, it is interesting to observe that the children in the former move out of educational institutions to take up employment at a later age as compared with those in rural areas (the tables for rural areas are not given in this chapter). While for urban males and females, the attendance comes down to 75 per cent and 68 per cent respectively, at the age of 17 years, and in rural areas this happens at the age of 15 years.

The percentage of boys and girls reporting attendance in educational institutions for the ages of 18 years and above for the last five rounds starting from 1987–8 are presented in Table 4.3. There is significant increase in the figures, particularly during the second half of the last decade, which should be attributed to their pursuing higher education or a vocational stream. The increase, however, can be taken as spectacular for all the four categories that, in turn, can be attributed to increase in facilities for higher education or decline in employment opportunities in the urban informal sector, which is

TABLE 4.3 Percentage of Children of Ages 18, 19, and 20 Years Reporting Usual Status as Attending Educational Institutions

Round/Period	Rural boys	Rural girls	Urban boys	Urban girls
Aged 18 years				
1987–8	21.43	6.09	42.74	27.93
1993–4	25.57	9.50	46.12	38.09
1999–2000	29.03	14.05	46.38	39.47
2004–5	32.68	18.35	45.12	46.08
2009–10	44.7	32.1	59.61	58.74
Aged 19 years				
1987–8	17.86	5.65	41.49	27.55
1993–4	23.03	8.94	45.41	35.58
1999–2000	27.42	11.28	46.78	36.04
2004–5	30.17	15.88	50.80	45.23
2009–10	41.8	26.3	58.32	57.37
Aged 20 years				
1987–8	9.40	1.91	28.46	14.38
1993–4	11.59	2.85	31.39	19.87
1999–2000	14.95	4.78	32.30	24.21
2004–5	17.88	6.40	31.67	23.76
2009–10	27.0	12.8	46.99	35.87

Source: Data computed from unit-level data of NSS, various years.

responsible for a decline in the WPR during 2009–10, particularly for women. Table 4.4 shows that the WPR or the percentage of workers among illiterates has declined systematically, but that for persons with middle-school education, this has gone up, with the increase being significantly high for women. This reflects decline in demand for unskilled workers and an increase in demand for the semi-skilled. Surprisingly, while WPR for women with secondary or higher levels of education has gone down, for those with primary education, it has gone up. The rates for men with higher level of education have remained stable over the years. Unfortunately, however, no increase has been reported in the real wages for both casual as well as regular workers (Kundu and Sarangi 2007). One may hold that if the country wants to take advantage of globalization and create decent jobs for the youth, it must go in for capacity creation of a much higher order

TABLE 4.4 Education-level-specific Usual Status WPR for Persons of Ages 15 Years and Above in Urban Areas

Education level	1993–4		1999–2000		2004–5		2009–10	
	PS	PS + SS	PS	PS + SS	PS	PS + SS	PS	PS + SS
Urban males								
Illiterate	86.6	87	83.6	83.9	82.4	83.1	81.4	81.6
Literate up to primary	84.4	85	82.4	83	85.1	85.5	84.1	84.4
Middle	71.3	72.3	72.5	73.2	75	76	75.7	76
Secondary	66.3	67.7	66.1	66.8	66.2	67.3	66.4	66.7
Higher secondary	58.9	60.7	59.9	60.8	59.1	60.8	56.6	57.6
Diploma					77.2	79.8	71.9	73
Graduate and above	80.7	81.8	79.7	80.6	78.5	79.5	78.4	78.8
All	75.8	76.8	74.5	75.2	75.2	76.3	73.6	74
Urban females								
Illiterate	23.3	30	22.9	27.1	25	30.4	19.7	23.1
Literate up to primary	15	20.3	14.6	17.7	18.6	23.4	17.4	20.6
Middle	9.1	13.1	9.9	12.9	11.7	16.1	13.1	15.4
Secondary	10.8	13.4	10.4	12.4	9.5	12.3	8.2	9.7
Higher secondary	12.6	14.7	11.1	12.4	10.3	12.9	7.7	9.4
Diploma					42.3	48.6	36.5	39.3
Graduate and above	28.2	30.1	25.2	27.3	26.5	29	24.3	25.9
All	17.5	22.3	16.6	19.7	18.5	22.7	15.9	18.3

Source: Data computed from unit-level data of NSS, various years.

Note: PS: Principal Status, SS: Subsidiary Status. Principal status refers to the activity the person followed for major part of the reference year. This could be as employed, unemployed, or as not in labour force (such as students and housewives). Persons who are not employed in the principal status, but had employment for shorter duration exceeding a month, are referred to as being employed in a subsidiary status. These two together constitute the usually employed.

or in the technical field that can push up the real wages for different categories of workers.

Attendance rates in educational institutions for boys and girls in urban areas presently are about the same for those who are 18–19 years of age. The figure for women is slightly less than that of men at a higher age. The gender disparity in the figures is not very high in urban areas, with the combined percentage figure for the age group of 18–20 years for males being higher than the corresponding figure for females by about 3 percentage points. In rural areas, however, the figure for men is significantly higher than that of the women. Furthermore, the gender disparity was very high in the year 1987–8 in both urban and rural areas and can be noted as declining systematically over time.

SCHOOL DROPOUTS, 'NOWHERE' CHILDREN, AND GENDER DISCRIMINATION

One can compare the school attendance of 10-year-old children in 2004–5 and 15-year-old children in 2009–10 to obtain an idea of children dropping out of schools during the five-year period, assuming that there was no fresh enrolment for children of 10 years and above. In urban areas, 94.4 per cent of the male children aged 10 were attending different types of educational institutions in 2004–5, while only 81.3 per cent of those aged 15 were in these categories in 2009–10 (Tables 4.5 and 4.6). This implies that about 13 per cent of these children have dropped out of studies during the period. Making similar calculations, we obtain the figure 16 per cent as the decline in school attendance for girls during the same period. One would observe that there is a gender differential in this age group and that the dropout rate for girls works out to be larger than that for boys. The same holds true in rural areas as well.

The percentage of children below the age of 15 years reporting 'attended [school] in the past' is also a measure of dropping out of school. These children are unlikely to have completed secondary school, which is the basic level expected to have been completed. In 2004–5, the percentage of children reporting 'attended in the past' is 1.1 for urban boys aged 10 years and is 5.6 for boys aged 12 years. This steadily climbs to 8.1 per cent for boys aged 13 years and is as high as 21.5 per cent for 15-year-old boys. The corresponding percentage figures for urban girls for the above mentioned ages are strikingly similar. The figure for girls aged 15 years is 20.3 per cent—just 1.2 percentage points less than that of boys. It is important to note that the corresponding figures for the year 2009–10 obtained from the 66th Round are significantly less, indicating that there has been an

TABLE 4.5 Level of School Attendance for Children and Youth of Ages 5 to 24

Age	Never attended	Attended in the past	Attending non-formal	Pre-primary	Primary	Middle	Secondary and higher secondary	Graduate and above	All
Urban male									
5	25.3	0.8	0.4	29.4	43.9	0.3			100.0
6	9.1	0.3	0.5	11.9	77.9	0.4			100.0
7	4.9	1.2	0.4	4.6	87.5	1.4			100.0
8	6.7	0.7	0.2	3.3	87.6	1.5			100.0
9	4.2	0.8	0.2	1.0	85.1	8.7			100.0
10	4.6	1.1	0.4	0.6	61.6	31.7	0.1		100.0
11	2.4	3.4	0.1	0.0	26.8	66.8	0.5		100.0
12	4.9	5.6	0.1	0.5	18.5	62.1	8.3		100.0
13	3.5	8.1	0.1		6.3	50.6	31.3		100.0
14	5.1	11.2			3.5	27.2	53.0		100.0
15	6.5	21.5	0.1		2.2	12.0	56.9	0.8	100.0
16	5.6	25.1			0.8	6.7	59.5	2.3	100.0
17	5.7	31.1	0.0		1.2	2.1	48.4	11.5	100.0
18	7.2	47.8			0.1	0.8	23.9	20.2	100.0
19	4.5	45.4	0.1			0.1	14.3	35.5	100.0
20	9.1	58.3				0.4	5.6	26.5	100.0
21	5.4	62.4				0.2	2.1	29.8	100.0
22	8.8	71.1					1.1	18.9	100.0
23	9.1	74.2				0.0	1.5	15.2	100.0
24	7.3	80.8				0.3	0.6	10.9	100.0

Urban female									
5	26.0	0.9	0.6	30.8	41.6	0.1			100.0
6	11.0	0.8	0.1	11.0	76.6	0.5			100.0
7	6.6	0.3	0.7	4.6	86.2	1.6			100.0
8	6.9	1.8	0.4	1.1	87.1	2.6			100.0
9	4.2	0.8	0.2	2.8	81.2	10.8			100.0
10	6.2	1.7	0.1	1.4	56.0	34.6	0.1		100.0
11	5.2	2.0	0.0	0.1	28.8	63.3	0.6		100.0
12	4.8	6.1	0.3	0.0	14.4	62.5	11.9		100.0
13	5.9	7.1	0.0	0.6	6.9	44.6	34.5	0.3	100.0
14	6.4	12.7	0.0		3.5	24.9	52.5		100.0
15	8.7	20.3			0.6	10.6	58.6	1.1	100.0
16	10.4	25.5	0.1		0.3	4.5	55.2	4.0	100.0
17	7.3	33.8			0.4	2.7	43.6	12.2	100.0
18	11.5	43.1			0.7	0.7	17.5	26.5	100.0
19	11.6	43.6			0.0	0.7	9.3	34.7	100.0
20	17.0	58.4			0.2	0.5	3.4	20.6	100.0
21	10.9	63.5			0.2	0.0	3.1	22.3	100.0
22	16.7	71.3				0.0	0.3	11.5	100.0
23	11.9	76.9				0.0	0.4	10.8	100.0
24	12.1	79.8			0.2	0.0	0.1	7.8	100.0

Source: Data computed from unit-level data of NSS, 61st Round 2004–5.

Note: Some of the improbable entries in the cells are due to wrong coding or can be attributed to number preferences or specific situations like children attending special schools.

TABLE 4.6 Level of School Attendance for Children and Youth of Ages 5 to 24: 2004–5

Age	Never attended	Attended in the past	Attending non-formal	Pre-primary	Primary	Middle	Secondary and higher secondary	Graduate and above	Diploma and others
Urban male									
5	18.97	0.54	0.63	34.70	43.90				
6	6.36	1.03	0.29	11.37	79.71	0.68			
7	2.91	0.97	0.27	2.84	88.92	3.46			
8	2.90	1.44	0.26	2.55	87.24	4.21			
9	2.10	1.75	0.30	1.38	83.66	9.45			
10	2.74	2.17	0.00	0.34	61.63	31.72	0.24		
11	1.87	1.94	0.18	0.06	30.05	63.33	0.64		
12	2.78	3.63	0.11	0.34	12.16	67.73	10.74		
13	1.96	4.82	0.09	0.04	5.13	47.46	38.68		
14	4.32	7.59			2.05	22.62	61.25		0.25
15	4.35	12.25			1.63	10.65	68.18	0.15	0.74
16	3.87	19.36			0.59	4.35	67.16	1.67	1.23
17	3.69	21.96			0.12	0.70	56.88	10.68	3.81
18	5.42	35.23			0.17	1.10	23.15	25.61	7.54
19	3.66	36.34			0.16	0.31	15.79	31.00	10.82
20	5.29	46.22					6.48	32.41	8.69
21	4.43	53.36					3.41	25.67	12.27
22	6.75	62.51					2.22	19.76	8.35
23	3.77	73.43					0.35	12.14	10.13
24	5.23	79.76					0.43	9.22	5.27

Urban female

5	19.39	1.71	0.72	32.80	43.21				
6	9.73	0.52	0.70	9.29	76.89	2.65			
7	3.97	1.26	0.26	4.06	87.53	2.36			
8	3.25	0.89	0.16	1.51	87.80	5.35			
9	3.65	1.22		0.40	83.62	10.55			
10	3.13	1.23		1.05	56.71	35.85	0.07		
11	2.02	1.73		0.33	27.34	65.38	0.51		
12	3.09	2.92			13.25	67.37	12.29		
13	2.51	5.80		0.14	5.59	44.29	39.67		
14	4.30	5.71		0.28	2.24	20.45	65.02		
15	5.61	15.38			0.96	7.53	67.04	0.25	0.24
16	3.77	18.22			0.28	2.83	69.22	3.22	0.57
17	6.11	25.38			0.01	0.93	48.39	14.79	2.58
18	6.84	34.31			0.02	0.28	21.90	30.27	4.79
19	4.46	37.04			0.11		6.24	43.33	7.70
20	10.47	52.63			0.12	0.19	3.62	23.77	7.96
21	4.49	59.26					0.80	24.78	10.28
22	9.77	67.29					1.42	12.90	8.53
23	7.48	78.86					0.35	7.45	5.67
24	8.81	82.49					0.14	4.48	3.70

Source: Data computed from unit-level data of NSS, 66th Round 2009–10.

increase in retention in schools over the past five years. The improvement seems to be similar for boys and girls. A larger percentage of boys aged 10 years reporting 'attended school in the past' in 2009–10 compared with the figure of 2004–5 could be due to reporting or sampling error. Furthermore, one notes that the percentage of children reporting 'never attended school' and 'attended school in the past' has gone down in the intervening period of the two NSS rounds, both for boys and for girls. The fall, however, is higher for girls than the boys (9 points as opposed to 4 points for boys) at 14 years of age. Surprisingly, the pattern is just the opposite, if one considers the age of 15 years (Tables 4.6 and 4.7). This is understandably due to errors in single-year age reporting. One would, therefore, conclude that the percentage of girls not completing secondary education is similar to that of the boys which confirms the proposition that there exists no gender bias in urban areas up to the age of 14 years.[8]

Many of the children are noted to be neither employed nor attending any kind of educational institutions (Tables 4.1 and 4.2). These children have sometimes been described as 'nowhere' children.

TABLE 4.7 Percentage of Children Who Are Neither in Schools Nor Engaged in Economic Activities

Age	Rural boys	Rural girls	Urban boys	Urban girls
5	36.86	38.55	20.09	22.08
6	16.16	18.10	6.50	9.03
7	5.12	8.26	3.35	5.09
8	6.43	7.57	4.11	3.65
9	2.39	4.67	2.78	4.42
10	5.35	7.42	3.81	3.95
11	2.66	5.24	1.91	3.01
12	5.84	9.22	4.43	4.84
13	4.81	8.09	3.31	6.49
14	4.92	20.13	4.43	8.36

Source: Data computed from unit-level data of NSS, 66th Round 2009–10.

[8] The chance that 14-year-old children would have completed middle school is high in urban areas as compared with rural areas because of the early start of school attendance in the former.

The term may give an erroneous perception, suggesting uncertainty regarding the location of the person or his/her time-use disposition in the official statistical system. It is noted that a large number of boys and girls in the ages of five and six years, particularly girls, are included in this category owing to late enrolment in school. This definitely could not be a matter of serious concern, and they need not be included in the definition of 'nowhere' children, because many of them are simply preparing for admission into the formal schooling system. At higher age levels, several children, especially girls, are engaged in domestic work in their homes (Table 4.7). A large percentage of these children fall in categories such as attending domestic duties (codes 92 and 93).[9] Many would argue that these children are placed in the 'nowhere category' because of the inadequacy of the definition of workers in the NSS. However, the fact that 4 per cent of the male children and 8 per cent of the female children are not going to school, even though they are not a part of the labour force at the age of 14 years in urban areas in 2009–10, should be a matter of detailed investigation. Importantly, while the figures for such boys in urban areas are about the same as in rural areas, the corresponding urban figures for girls come to less than half (Table 4.7). The highest figures are reported among rural girls, as may be seen in Figure 4.3. The possibility that a section of urban children are street urchins, engaged in some unclassified work that compromises their safety and physical health or are being exploited in some other manner cannot be ruled out. However, it must be noted that in 2009–10, over 78 per cent of the so-called 'nowhere' urban girls at the age of 14 years were fully engaged in household duties, including collection of free goods, sewing, tailoring, etc. Describing them as 'nowhere' children sends out a wrong message to policymakers, civil society organizations, and researchers.

It has been noted above that there is no gender difference in children attending educational institutions up to the age of 14 years. The discrimination process begins only after that age and is reflected in a much sharper drop in the attendance rate for girls and, more significantly, their shifting towards non-work rather than work. The proposition is further confirmed from the information on

[9] Only a small fraction would be placed in the category of 'beggars, etc.' (code 96) or 'others' (code 97).

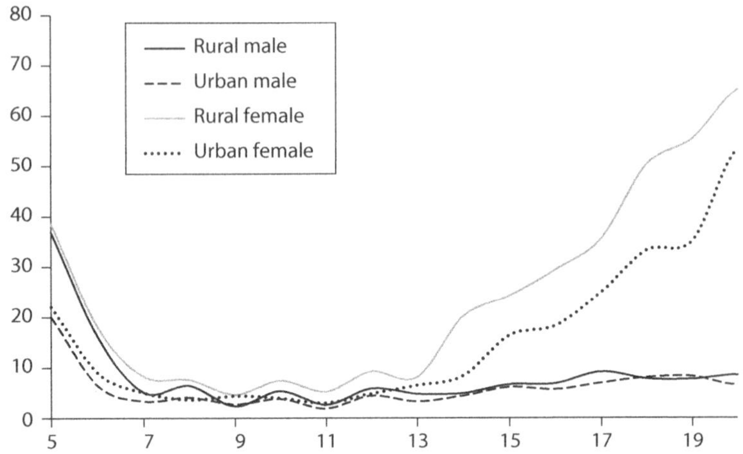

FIGURE 4.3 Perecentage of Children Not Attending Educational Institutions nor in Employment
Source: Data computed from unit-level data of NSS 66th Round 2009–10.

age-wise school (primary, secondary, and higher) attendance rates for the 61st and 66th Rounds, which are given in Tables 4.5 and 4.6. The percentage of male children not going to educational institutions in urban areas at the age of five years was as high as 25 in 2004–5, which went down to 19 in 2009–10. Correspondingly, the figure for children going to school at the pre-primary level has gone up from 29 to 35 per cent. The enrolment in primary school has, however, remained stationary at 44 per cent. The figures and trends for the attendance of female children in educational institutions are strikingly similar. This provides additional evidence that gender discrimination in sending the children to pre-primary and primary schools is low and has not got accentuated over time in urban areas.

Attendance rates among the six-year-olds reflect hardly any gender bias, because over three-fourths—both for boys and for girls in urban areas—were attending primary classes in 2004–5. The figures went up to over 79 per cent in 2009–10, and here, again, the gender gap can be noted to be marginal. Further, the percentages of boys and girls in pre-primary classes were 11.9 and 11.0, which came down to 11.4 and 9.3 per cent, respectively. One would infer that about 10 per cent of both boys and girls at the age of five years in urban areas are going for pre-primary education and another 80 per cent for primary education which has become stable over time.

The percentage of boys and girls attending pre-primary, primary, and middle school at the age of nine years was about 95 per cent in 2009–10, going up from 91 per cent in 2004–5. The rate now seems to have stabilized at that level as inferred from the data of the 66th NSS Round. For the ages of 17 and 18 years, the enrolment rates in secondary and graduation programmes for urban men have gone up significantly during 2004–9, but the increase for women was only slightly higher. This shows that gender disparity has gone down. That the gender gaps are very high for the ages of 19 years and above can be attributed to the fact that many of the women in this age group did not have the privilege of going to school earlier in their lives. The present deficit of women in secondary and graduation programmes at higher ages is, thus, largely a reflection of historical factors.

The percentages of male and female children who had never attended school were very high and came down significantly during the period 2004–5 for almost all ages between 5 and 24 years in urban areas. The male–female gap was very high except for a few specific ages like 5, 8, 9, and 12 years, but this too has declined over the given period (see column 2 in Tables 4.5 and 4.6). The decline is, however, more evident in the age groups between five and 14 years, of the child population. This is because the decline in gender discrimination, manifested in girls being sent to schools, is a recent phenomenon. This is manifested in the rates of children who 'never attended school', with there being little difference between the figures of boys and girls up to the age of 16 years. For the age groups ranging from 17 to 24 years, however, the gender disparity continues to be high, largely because of the discrimination that existed in the past and that resulted in females not being sent to school at earlier ages. Another important point is that the percentages of children who have attended but dropped out of educational institutions in 2009–10 are similar or slightly higher than the corresponding figures in 2004–5, particularly for boys in all ages up to 10 years. This could be due to relocation of the children from schools owing to higher mobility of households, as one would infer from higher mobility of family migration in recent years. For children above the age of 10 years, the figures are lower in 2009–10 compared with the earlier year, as can be seen in lower dropout rates that has taken place in recent years. However, the male/female differentials in the percentage figures is not very high at both points in time, as may be seen in column 3 in Tables 4.5 and 4.6. One can thus infer that the dropout rates for males and females were not and are not very different.

EMPLOYMENT AND ITS STRUCTURE FOR BOYS AND GIRLS DURING THEIR CHILDHOOD AND ADULTHOOD

Urban child employment is noticeable from the age of nine years onwards, for both boys and girls. This holds true in rural areas as well. At the age of 11 years, roughly two out of 100 male children (as against one for female) were working in urban areas in the year 2004–5 (Kundu and Mohanan 2010), with the figure in rural areas being the same for boys and slightly higher for girls. The employment rate for boys has come down particularly in urban areas as a result of the drive for universal education. The WPR is as high as 7 per cent for boys and 2 per cent for girls, at the age of 14 years in 2009–10. The corresponding figures for rural areas are only marginally higher.

It is heartening to note that there has been a decline in the incidence of child employment over the years. The percentages of children reporting employment in 1987–8 at different ages (Table 4.8), taken as a reference point, were significantly higher than those for 2009–10.

TABLE 4.8 Percentage of Children in Employment during 1987–8

Age	Rural boys	Rural girls	Urban boys	Urban girls
5	1.38	1.60	0.22	0.08
6	1.78	2.19	0.03	0.16
7	1.84	1.97	0.34	0.16
8	2.90	2.78	0.80	0.34
9	4.19	3.91	1.28	1.04
10	10.08	9.72	3.38	2.36
11	12.23	13.68	3.41	2.97
12	20.53	19.34	8.46	4.82
13	23.43	24.05	8.91	5.38
14	32.57	29.44	12.72	7.10

Source: Data computed from unit-level data of NSS 1987–8.

Understandably, the figures are significantly higher in rural as compared with urban areas. About 1.5 per cent of rural children were reported to be in employment even at the age of five years as compared with 0.15 per cent in urban areas in 1987–8. At 14 years of age, the percentages of boys and girls reporting employment were noted to be as high as 12.7 and 7.1, respectively. In rural areas, the figures are much higher—32.6 per cent for boys and 29.4 per cent for girls. There has been a substantial decline in the WPR of children over the past few years, as may be seen in Table 4.9. The increase in attendance in educational institutions is the key factor in this.

The uniform decline in WPR among children and adolescents (in the age group of 5–19 years) for both the genders during 1993–2009 in urban areas (Table 4.9) confirms the proposition that more and more of them are attending schools. This pattern is observed in rural areas as well (table not being given for sake of brevity) and here the decline is sharper than urban areas, both for boys and girls. This is possibly because of opening up of employment opportunities in urban areas within the household sector and various informal activities, which is not found as much in rural areas. The work opportunities for adult males in the age group of 20 to 59 years have improved distinctly in urban areas. The same cannot be said for opportunities for the women, as seen in the decline of their WPRs. The decline in the WPR for those 60 years or more may be considered to be a positive development as would be the decline in the WPRs of children and adolescents, discussed above.

While analysing the structure of employment (Tables 4.10 and 4.11), one notices that one-third of the urban boys reporting employment at the age of 16 years are in regular jobs, with the share of unpaid family workers and the self-employed being 22 and 15 per cent, respectively, in 2004–5. The share of regular wage employment for boys goes up from 31 per cent at the age of 14 years to 36 per cent at the age of 18 years and then to 40 per cent at the age of 24 years. Correspondingly, the percentage share of unpaid family workers goes down from 28.5 per cent at the age of 14 years to 18 per cent at the age of 24 years. The figure of self-employed or own-account workers, however, goes up from 13 per cent at the age of 14 years to 21 per cent at the age of 24 years. One may speculate that the male children on attaining adulthood move away from family work and take up regular jobs elsewhere

TABLE 4.9 Age-specific WPRs by Usual (Principal) Status in Urban Areas

Age group (years)	Men				Women			
	1993–4	1999–2000	2004–5	2009–10	1993–94	1999–2000	2004–5	2009–10
5–9	4	3	2	0	3	1	1	0
10–14	59	46	44	24	35	28	24	8
15–19	337	303	314	223	94	87	92	61
20–4	654	644	662	604	136	130	155	142
25–9	892	878	900	903	175	161	186	170
30–4	961	958	965	972	208	198	236	192
35–9	982	973	975	984	233	235	265	231
40–4	980	973	977	983	257	242	262	225
45–9	971	968	965	976	253	234	227	207
50–4	941	933	925	946	240	225	224	209
55–9	845	803	819	846	185	181	192	174
60+	429	386	355	335	91	82	86	61
All	513	513	541	539	121	117	135	119

Source: Data computed from unit-level data of NSS, various years.

or start working on their own. The other sector from which children withdraw as they grow older is casual work, though the withdrawal process takes place only at the age of 22 years. This is understandable as adults prefer to shift from less organized to more organized and better-defined activities.

Among the employed girls aged 18 in urban areas, 40 per cent are in regular jobs, which is marginally higher than that of boys, with

TABLE 4.10 Percentage Distribution of the Population Employed and Unemployment Rates for Selected Ages

Age	Own-account worker	Employer	Unpaid worker	Regular worker	Casual worker	Unemployment rate
Urban male						
14	1.94	0.00	18.93	41.48	37.64	9.69
15	12.57	0.00	23.73	29.11	34.58	12.39
16	7.22	0.00	23.51	24.85	44.43	11.09
17	7.36	0.05	23.65	35.98	32.97	15.49
18	12.70	0.02	20.14	32.57	34.57	13.58
19	12.87	0.05	17.11	35.68	34.30	13.27
20	13.60	0.17	20.06	38.07	28.10	9.39
21	13.92	0.63	16.96	42.19	26.30	14.14
22	16.07	0.29	18.34	42.81	22.49	10.23
23	17.83	0.16	14.04	47.36	20.61	11.19
24	17.01	0.22	15.28	47.44	20.04	7.51
Urban female						
14	21.88	0.00	24.57	12.64	40.90	4.12
15	12.12	0.00	24.59	35.67	27.62	4.37
16	8.90	0.00	35.31	22.78	33.00	14.36
17	17.13	0.00	23.64	30.26	28.97	7.45
18	12.47	0.00	25.13	33.33	29.07	19.24
19	16.43	0.00	20.15	45.51	17.91	15.79
20	15.80	0.09	25.18	36.73	22.20	17.02
21	11.76	0.00	9.49	61.95	16.80	23.09
22	9.90	1.89	15.44	58.70	14.08	26.63
23	18.52	0.00	10.81	59.41	11.26	24.83
24	14.20	0.00	10.47	61.23	14.09	14.02

Source: Data computed from unit-level data of NSS, 66th Round 2009–10.

TABLE 4.11 Percentage Distribution of the Population Employed and Unemployment Rate for Selected Ages in Urban Areas

Age	Own-account worker	Employer	Unpaid worker	Regular worker	Casual worker	Unemployment rate
Male						
14	12.74	0.00	28.46	31.12	27.69	11.21
16	15.13	0.00	22.29	32.90	29.68	17.77
18	12.83	0.53	24.03	36.24	26.37	13.45
20	17.06	0.50	18.45	36.91	27.08	13.09
22	18.74	0.43	18.86	41.01	20.96	11.83
24	21.25	0.91	18.05	40.25	19.54	11.15
Female						
14	13.10	0.00	46.15	25.57	15.18	13.49
16	10.79	0.00	33.50	30.87	24.84	16.02
18	21.77	0.08	23.25	39.52	15.37	15.66
20	15.77	0.00	26.27	40.50	17.46	23.04
22	15.25	0.00	21.54	51.00	12.21	27.09
24	17.41	0.42	16.88	51.28	14.01	21.24

Source: Data computed from unit-level data of NSS, 61st Round 2004–5.

the incidence of self-employed being about 23 per cent, similar to that of boys. The share of unpaid family workers, however, is higher for the girls. The percentage of regular workers for girls can be seen to be increasing continuously from a mere 25.6 per cent at the age of 14 years to 51 per cent at the age of 24 years. The share of self-employed persons also exhibits a similar increase with age. This trend is observed for men as well. The higher share of women regular workers in urban areas—higher than not only that of other categories of work, but also that for males—needs to be interpreted with caution. Many of the women are getting absorbed in various low-productive service activities, including domestic work, on a regular basis, wherein their earnings may not be much higher than that for casual workers. The most significant point from the gender perspective is that while the boys, after leaving schools, gravitate towards the left of Table 4.1—signifying a shift to employment-related activity status—the girls move to the right in Table 4.2—getting absorbed in different non-economic activities.

The unemployment rate, defined as the share of the unemployed in the labour force (Table 4.10), does not show any trend in the age group of 14 to 24 years for the urban boys. The rate is about 11 per cent at the age of 14 years, and goes up to 18 per cent at the age of 16 years, but subsequently falls to 13 per cent at the ages of 18–20 years and then to 11 per cent at the ages of 22–4 years. The important point to be noted here is that the unemployment rates in all these ages are much higher than that for the persons in 25–55 age group, with the average figure for urban males being only 4 per cent (Kundu and Sarangi 2007). The unemployment rate for women, however, shows a distinct increasing trend, going up from 13 per cent at the age of 14 years to 16 per cent at the age of 16 years, reaching the level of 27 per cent at the age of 22 years and then declining slightly to 21 per cent at 24 years of age. This would be considered alarmingly high, as the average figure for urban women is less than 7 per cent.

A comparison of the figures over time reveals that there has been a decline in self-employment and increase in paid employment, engaged on regular or casual basis, since 2004–5. Unemployment rates have gone up particularly for men in all ages.

Analysing the attendance in educational institutions across occupational categories, it is noted that casual labour households in urban areas report the lowest figure in both 2004–5 and 2009–10 (Tables 4.12 and 4.13). During this period the participation rates of children in education shows an increase in all types of households. The employment rate, however, is the highest among the self-employed households, wherein a large majority of the children fall in the unpaid family helper category. The incidence of child employment is the lowest in regular salaried households, because these are economically better off.

The increase in WPR in the age group of 15–19 and 20–4 years (by usual principal status) for urban male and women should be a matter of some concern. One would expect this figure to fall on account of an increase in the number of young boys and girls going to colleges and technical institutions for learning and training. While the figure in the first age group has exceeded the level of 1999–2000, for the second age group, the increase is phenomenal and has gone above that of 1993–4.

TABLE 4.12 Distribution of Children of Ages 5 to 14 by Principal Activity Status for Different Household Types in 2004–5

Household type	Broad principal status activity						
	Self-employment (11, 12, & 21)	Regular salaried (31)	Casual labour (41 & 51)	Unemployed (81)	Attending education (91)	Household chores (92 & 93)	Others (94–97)
Rural male							
Self-employed in agriculture	2.32	0.22	0.44	0.21	84.48	0.31	12.01
Self-employed in non-agriculture	0.95	0.22	2.79	0.18	76.43	0.59	18.83
Agricultural labour	1.11	0.33	1.35	0.3	81.23	0.49	15.19
Other labour	2.36	0.07	0.11	0.05	86.73	0.33	10.35
Others	0.12	0.06	0.07	0.04	91.78	0.22	7.71
Rural female							
Self-employed in agriculture	1.55	0.03	0.3	0.09	78.63	4.88	14.53
Self-employed in non-agriculture	0.86	0.08	2.95	0.1	69.14	7.19	19.67

Agricultural labour	0.78	0.31	1.06	0.09	75.5	5.89	16.37
Other labour	2.22	0.03	0.06	0.05	79.42	5.22	13.01
Others	0.44	0.02	0.13	0.02	87.17	2.74	9.48
Urban male							
Self-employed	1.55	0.39	0.42	0.32	89.19	0.24	7.89
Regular salaried	0.16	1.43	0.11	0.21	93.45	0.15	4.48
Casual labour	0.52	1.39	2.89	0.68	77.94	0.45	16.14
Others	0.11	0.05	0	0.01	94.74	0.05	5.03
Urban female							
Self-employed	1.26	0.21	0.05	0.02	87.92	3.12	7.41
Regular salaried	0.25	0.46	0.07	0.2	91.18	2.03	5.81
Casual labour	0.87	0.62	0.92	0.01	78.01	6.44	13.13
Others	0.23		0.03		93.01	1.67	5.05

Source: Data computed from unit-level data of NSS, 61st Round 2004–5.

Table 4.13 Distribution of Children of Ages 5 to 14 by Principal Activity Status for Different Household Types in 2009–10

Household type	Self-employment (11, 12, & 21)	Regular salaried (31)	Casual labour (41 & 51)	Unemployed (81)	Attending education (91)	House hold chores (92 & 93)	Others (94–97)
Rural male							
Self-employed in agriculture	0.82	0.07	0.38	0.21	90.45	0.18	7.89
Self-employed in non-agriculture	0.28	0.15	1.45	0.22	86.70	0.65	10.55
Agricultural labour	0.42	0.16	0.95	0.13	86.73	0.40	11.20
Other labour	1.29	0.06	0.11	0.06	91.13	0.25	7.10
Others	0.41	0.01	0.01	0.28	91.96	0.03	7.31
Rural female							
Self-employed in agriculture	0.74	0.02	0.06		88.43	2.29	8.45
Self-employed in non-agriculture	0.15	0.03	1.27	0.06	83.96	3.43	11.11
Agricultural labour	0.62	0.13	0.41	0.08	80.82	5.25	12.69

Other labour	1.29		0.01		87.39	2.59	8.73
Others	0.01	0.15	0.01	0.00	91.86	1.60	6.36
Urban male							
Self-employed	0.65	0.52	0.16	0.10	93.04	0.12	5.41
Regular salaried	0.01	0.63	0.24	0.05	95.81	0.12	3.13
Casual labour	0.21	0.34	1.41	0.45	87.81	0.56	9.22
Others	0.10		0.24		95.62	0.00	4.04
Urban female							
Self-employed	0.37	0.03	0.02	0.01	92.12	1.68	5.76
Regular salaried	0.02	0.05	0.06	0.00	96.24	1.14	2.50
Casual labour	0.33	0.10	0.71	0.11	86.05	2.84	9.85
Others	0.06		0.01	0.10	95.99	0.51	3.33

Source: Data computed from unit-level data of NSS, 66th Round 2009–10.

★ ★ ★

This chapter analyses the data from various rounds of the NSS to understand the activity profiles of children and young adults in urban areas, including their attendance in the education institutions, their exit from them at different ages, and the implications of the latter.

The process of demographic transition in India indicates that the country would enjoy demographic dividend over the next few decades. The actual benefit may, however, turn out to be less than projected because it may not be possible to expand university and technical education to meet the increased demand for a skilled workforce. In order to take advantage of the process of globalization and create decent jobs for the youth, the country must opt for skill formation on a massive scale, which would help in increasing the real wages for the rapidly growing unorganized workforce and reduce the differences with those in the organized sector.

The most disturbing conclusion emerging from the above analysis is that the dropout rates among children are alarmingly high after the age of 11 years. There is, therefore, a substantial dropout after five or six years of schooling. The rate becomes very high at the age of 15 years, for both boys and girls. Despite a sharp rise in the enrolment of children in regular primary schools at the age of 6 years in recent years, it is unfortunate that many of them do not go beyond the secondary level. More significantly, over the years, the proportion of children going in for higher studies has not increased in comparison with the increase in enrolment in primary and middle schools.

As far as the percentage of children attending pre-primary and primary schools is concerned, there is not much gender difference. The shares of boys and girls who do not complete their secondary schooling, too, are similar, which confirms the proposition that presently, there is not much difference in their dropout rates. Indeed, there is not much gender bias in urban areas, as far as primary education is concerned. The decline in gender discrimination is, however, a recent phenomenon. Understandably, the percentages of children, who have 'never attended school' among both boys and girls up to the age of 14 years are not very different. For the age groups ranging from 17 to 24 years, however, the current gender disparity works out to be very high. This is due to the discrimination that existed in the past, resulting in female children not being sent to primary and secondary schools.

It is heartening to note that there has been a decline in the incidence of child employment over recent years. The percentages of children reporting employment in 1987–8 at different ages were significantly higher than those for 2009–10. There is no reporting of child labour till the age of 10 years. The smaller decline in the incidence of employment for urban children above the age of 10 years, compared with the rural counterpart, is partly due to emerging employment opportunities within the household sector and various informal activities. An important point from the gender perspective is that, while the boys after dropping out from schools gravitate towards employment-related activities, the girls get absorbed in different non-economic activities, mostly within the household.

The share of regular wage employment for boys goes up systematically from the age of 14 years to 24 years. The percentage share of unpaid family workers, on the other hand, goes down. The figure of self-employed or own-account workers, however, goes up. One would observe that the male children, on attaining adulthood, move away from family work and take up regular jobs elsewhere or start working on their own. The children also withdraw as they grow older from casual work, although this withdrawal takes place only at higher ages. These can be attributed to adults shifting from less organized to more organized jobs.

The lowest attendance in educational institutions, for both boys and girls, is reported among casual labour households. The self-employed households, however, record the highest employment rate, as a large majority of children here get engaged as unpaid family workers. The incidence of child employment is the lowest in regular salaried households, because these are economically better off and have affordability for out-of-pocket expenditure for education, which is growing alarmingly.

The high rates of employment for males in the age groups of 15 to 24 years in urban areas should be a matter of serious concern. Much of the employment in these age groups is in the form of unpaid family work or self-employment in household enterprises. This reflects an inadequate level of skill formation, which is preventing the country from reaping the benefits of globalization through the creation of decent jobs. Also, very high levels of unemployment for these age groups suggest the need for generating work through wage and self-employment programmes. There is tremendous pressure on these children and young adults from their families to enter the labour force as part of the strategy of the family for survival. If this section of people have to be covered under skill-formation programmes, it would be important to make provision for appropriate economic support for the individual and his/her family. Until such time, they must find employment in productive sectors of the economy with reasonable wages. This seems to be the only way to avoid the problems of growing frustration and resentment among the young adults that are reflected in mass protests, rallies, and group violence that can lead to major socio-political instability in the country.

REFERENCES

European Institute for Asian Studies (EIAS). 2006. 'Stocktaking Study on the Implications for Europe of Asia's Demographic Changes', The Guilmoto-van der Geest Report for the European Commission, Brussels.

Kundu, A. and N. Sarangi. 2007. 'Migration, Employment Status and Poverty: An Analysis across Urban Centres', *Economic and Political Weekly*, (42)4: 299–306.

Kundu, A. and P.C. Mohanan. 2010. 'Demographic Transition, Employment Structure and MDG Goals: Focus on Child Population in Urban India', IHD-UNICEF Working Paper Series. New Delhi: Institute for Human Development and UNICEF India.

Part II

Macro Context and Policy Spaces

5 Achievements and Challenges in Legal Protection for Child Rights

Asha Bajpai

It was only during the twentieth century that the concept of children's rights emerged. This shift in focus from the 'needs and welfare' approach to the 'rights and development' approach is significant. Earlier the child was considered a beneficiary and a recipient of services. Today the child is a participant and partner in his or her own development and decisions that affect his or her life. The rights approach is primarily concerned with issues of social justice, non-discrimination, equity, and empowerment. It is embodied in the United Nations Convention on the Rights of the Child (UNCRC, henceforth referred to as CRC), 1989, which is a landmark in the international human rights legislation. India ratified the CRC in December 1992 and is bound to make laws in conformity with the Convention. The rights-based approach includes children as rights holders and states as primary duty bearers.

Children constitute over 400 million of the one billion-plus population of India. The twenty-first century has heralded a number of important policy and legislative initiatives as well as significant court interventions, and there are many important Bills which are pending before the Parliament of India to make the laws more child friendly.

The Constitution of India is the basic law of the country, which includes the Fundamental Rights[1] and Directive Principles[2] for every citizen. The Constitution encompasses most rights included in the CRC as Fundamental Rights and Directive Principles of State Policy. It is significant to note that the Constitution mandates special protection of children by adopting positive discrimination through special provisions for them.[3]

INDIAN LAW AND THE DEFINITION OF 'CHILD'

The trouble with child rights begins with the very definition of a child by law. There are several grey areas in the law here (Bajpai 2007). Age limits are a formal reflection of society's assessment of the evolution of children's capacities and responsibilities. Almost everywhere, age limits formally regulate children's activities: when they can leave school; when they can marry; when they can vote; when they can be treated as adults by the criminal justice system; when they can join the armed forces; and when they can work. But age limits differ from activity to activity and from country to country and in India from legislation to legislation.

According to Article 1 of the CRC, 1989, 'a child means every human being below the age of 18 years unless, under the law applicable to the child, majority is attained earlier'. The Article thus grants discretion to individual countries to determine by law whether childhood should cease at 12, 14, 16, or whatever age they find appropriate (Bajpai 2007).

The word 'child' in Indian laws has been used in various legislations as a term denoting relationship; as a term indicating capacity; and as a

[1] Fundamental Rights, if violated, can be brought before the courts. A writ petition can be filed in the Supreme Court and High Courts.

[2] The Directive Principles lay down the guidelines the governments have to follow. If they are violated, they cannot be taken before the courts, but because of judicial interpretation, many of the Directive Principles relating to children have now become enforceable through legal actions brought before courts. Articles 39(e) and (f) direct the state policies towards ensuring that the tender age of children is not abused.

[3] Constitution of India, Article 15(3).

term of special protection. Underlying these alternative specifications are very different concepts about the child.

For purposes of criminal responsibility, the age limit is 7 years and 12 years under the Indian Penal Code (IPC), 1860. For purposes of protection against kidnapping, abduction, and related offences, the age is fixed at 16 years for boys and 18 years for girls. However, the IPC, while defining rape in Section 375, exempts a person from the charge of rape if he has forcible sexual intercourse with his wife who is above 15 years of age.

The Criminal Law (Amendment) Act, 2013 passed by the Lok Sabha on 19 March 2013, and by the Rajya Sabha on 21 March 2013, provides for amendment of IPC, Indian Evidence Act, and Code of Criminal Procedure, 1973 on laws related to sexual offences. The most important change that has been made is the change in definition of rape under IPC. Although the Ordinance sought to change the word rape to sexual assault, in the Act the word 'rape' has been retained in Section 375, and was extended to include acts in addition to vaginal penetration. The definition is broadly worded with acts such as the penetration of penis, or any object, or any part of the body, to any extent, into the vagina, mouth, urethra, or anus of another person; or the act of making another person do so; or the application of mouth or touching of private parts. Such acts constitute the offence of sexual assault. The section has also clarified that penetration means 'penetration to any extent', and lack of physical resistance is immaterial for constituting an offence. Except in certain aggravated situations the punishment will be imprisonment of not less than seven years but which may extend to imprisonment for life, and the accused will also be liable to a fine. In aggravated situations, punishment will be rigorous imprisonment for a term which will not be less than ten years but which may extend to imprisonment for life, and the accused will also be liable to a fine.

Under this Act, a new section, 376A, has been added, stating that if a person committing the offence of sexual assault, who 'inflicts an injury which causes the death of the person or causes the person to be in a persistent vegetative state, shall be punished with rigorous imprisonment for a term which shall not be less than twenty years, but which may extend to imprisonment for life, which shall mean the remainder of that person's natural life, or with death'. In case of 'gang rape', persons involved regardless of their gender would be punished with rigorous imprisonment for a term which will not be less than 20 years, but which may extend to life, and they will pay compensation to the victim, which will be reasonable to meet the medical expenses and rehabilitation of the victim. The age of consent in India has been increased to 18 years, which means any sexual activity irrespective of presence of consent with a woman below the age of 18 will constitute statutory rape.

Certain changes have been introduced in the Code of Criminal Procedure (CrPC) and Evidence Act, such as the process of recording the statement of the victim has been made more victim friendly and easy. Two critical changes are: (i) the 'character of the victim' is now rendered totally irrelevant, and (ii) there is now a presumption of 'no consent' in a case where sexual intercourse is proved and the victim states in the court that she did not consent.

Under the Immoral Traffic (Prevention) Act, 1986, a child means a person who has not completed 16 years of age and a minor means a person who has completed 16 years of age and not completed 18 years.

Under the Child Labour Prohibition and Regulation Act, 1986, a child means a person who has not completed his fourteenth year of age. By prohibiting child labour in hazardous occupations, the law implies that a child below 14 years of age can work in non-hazardous occupations or processes. An area of concern is that no minimum age for child labour has been specified. For purposes of special treatment under the Juvenile (Care and Protection of Children) Justice Act (JJA), 2000, the age is 18 for both boys and girls, and The Protection of Women from Domestic Violence Act, 2005, defines a child as any person below the age of 18 years including any adopted, step, or foster child. Under the Plantation Labour Act, 1951, a child means a person who has not completed his fourteenth year of age.

The absence of a comprehensive and common definition of the term 'child' is problematic. Though one may like to have a uniform age limit legally prescribed for the status of childhood, it may not be possible. Nevertheless, a degree of rationalization is possible or some norms can be laid down, since some of the age limits in the laws appear to be arbitrary or based only on socio-cultural perceptions. If the best interest of the child is the consideration, one could perhaps err on the side of having a higher age limit for protective care and a lower age limit in respect of civil and cultural matters. The question of reviewing the definition of the term 'child', in the light of Article 1 of the CRC has been referred to the Law Commission of India, which will consider this matter while undertaking a comprehensive review of the Code of Criminal Procedure, the Indian Evidence Act, and the Indian Penal Code.

Competency of Child Witnesses

The courts have held that the evidence of a child witness, if found competent and reliable to depose to the facts, could form the basis for a conviction. In other words, even in the absence of an oath, the evidence of a child witness can be considered under Section 118 of the Evidence Act, provided that such witness is able to understand the answers. Therefore, the evidence of a child witness and its credibility would depend upon the circumstances of each case. The only precaution that the court should bear in mind while assessing the evidence of a child witness is that the witness must be a reliable one and his or her demeanour must be like that of any other competent witness, with no likelihood of the child being tutored.

Further, Section 118 of the Indian Evidence Act holds that all persons shall be competent to testify, unless the court considers that they are unable to understand the questions put to them or give rational answers to these questions, because of tender years, extreme old age, disease—whether of mind or any other cause of the same kind. However, a child of tender age can be allowed to testify if he or she has the intellectual capacity to understand questions and give rational answers. For example, the Mumbai High Court upheld the testimony of a 12-year-old in a murder case. The lone eyewitness account of a 12-year-old grandson helped to indict two persons accused of murder. The court held that the 'child witness was a witness of truth'. The court reiterated that depositions by children who have the capacity to understand things and their consequences cannot be discarded as evidence in a criminal trial. In this case, the child's testimony was corroborated by the physical evidence of strangulations marks and injuries on the victims.

While the law recognizes the child as a competent witness, the court does not rely on the sole testimony of a child unless it can be substantiated by other corroborative evidence, particularly if the child is at a tender age, say of 6 years, and is unable to form a proper opinion about the nature of the incident because of immaturity of understanding. The evidence of the child is required to be evaluated carefully because he or she is an easy prey to tutoring. Therefore, the court looks for adequate validation from other evidence to his testimony.

CHILDREN IN THE JUVENILE JUSTICE SYSTEM

Children encounter the juvenile justice system as offenders or as victims. The JJA, enacted in 2000 and amended in 2006 and 2011, deals with two categories of children—juveniles in conflict with law and children 'in need of care and protection'. Its objective is to provide for proper care, protection, and treatment by catering to their development needs and by adopting a child-friendly approach that is in the best interest of children and conducive for their ultimate rehabilitation. The JJA, 2000, is a legislation that conforms to the CRC and the United Nations Minimum Standards for Administration of Justice to Children (Beijing Rules). The CRC has laid down the basic principles of decision making to promote the best interests of children, and all decisions relating to children need to be guided by this consideration. The Beijing Rules direct that institutions should be used only as a last resort and only after community measures are not available for children. As JJA, 2000, was specifically made to implement India's obligations under these and other international instruments, it is incumbent upon the authorities implementing this legislation to ensure protection and promotion of these principles that are embodied in this Act. The Act also provides that a report in any newspaper, magazine, news-sheet, or visual media of any inquiry, regarding a juvenile in conflict with law or a child in need of care and protection under this Act, would not disclose the name, address of the school, or any other particulars that can lead to the identification of the juvenile or child nor any picture of any such juvenile or child can be published. The authority holding the inquiry may permit such disclosure in exceptional cases, if, in its opinion, such disclosure is in the interest of the juvenile or the child. In spite of these specific provisions, many well-known publications even today, reveal the identity of the child.

In this Act, 'juvenile' or 'child' means a person who has not completed the eighteenth year of age, mainly to bring juvenile legislation in conformity with the CRC. Both boys and girls below the age of 18 years enjoy the protection of juvenile legislation

Children in Conflict with Law

The definition of juvenile in conflict with law was amended in 2006, and it is clear today that this refers to a juvenile who is alleged to have committed an offence and has not completed the eighteenth year of age as on the date of commission of such an offence. Violent juvenile crimes are a global phenomenon and are on the increase at an alarming rate in India. The National Crime Records Bureau (NCRB) says that 83.7 per cent of crimes committed by juveniles in 2006 came under the IPC. While Maharashtra reported the highest number of IPC crimes among juveniles in 2006, Madhya Pradesh registered the highest number of crimes such as murder, rape, kidnapping, and abduction (Ministry of Home Affairs 2006). The news of teenagers being used to smuggle marijuana makes almost regular headlines.

The legal definition of a child will also affect how the courts deal with offenders. A person who is a minor or a child cannot be convicted in the same manner as an adult. Children have to be dealt with under the juvenile justice system and not the adult criminal justice system. Children can never be given imprisonment or a death sentence. If a juvenile is accused of an offence under the provisions of the Narcotics Drugs and Psychotropic Substances Act, or Prevention of Terrorist Act, he or she is unequivocally entitled to the necessary benefits under the JJA, 2000. While different high courts took different positions on the applicability of JJA, 2000, to cases where the accused is a child, the Supreme Court has clearly held that JJA, 2000, will universally apply to children alleged to have committed offences under those special penal legislations.[4]

Claim of Juvenility

Whenever a claim that a person is a juvenile or below 18 years is raised before any court or a court is of the opinion that an accused person produced before was a juvenile on the date of commission of

[4] *Madan Singh vs State of Rajasthan* [2005] SC DOJ 2.4.05; *Raj Singh vs State of Haryana* [2000] 6 SCC 759.

the offence, the court shall make an inquiry, take such evidence as may be necessary (but not evidence of age on an affidavit) to determine the age of such person, and then the court will record a finding whether the person is a juvenile or not, stating his age as nearly as it may be. Later, if the court finds that the person was below 18 years on the date when the offence was committed, the court must send the juvenile to the Juvenile Justice Board (JJB). It is only the JJB that may pass any order. An important provision is that a claim of juvenility or that the accused was a juvenile may be raised before any court, and it shall be recognized at any stage even after disposal of the case. In India, there are millions of children, especially in villages, who do not have birth certificates. If the court finds a person to be juvenile on the date of commission of the offence, it shall forward the juvenile to the Board. It has been observed that in many instances, if the police who take a child 'in custody' find a child well built, he is considered to be an 'adult' and denied the beneficial provisions of the juvenile justice system. A mention must be made of a 'Baba Room' in one of the well-known prisons, where children whose ages have not been confirmed or could not be confirmed are huddled up waiting for their age verification.

Age determination of children in conflict with law is a very complex issue. The largest number of cases that come before the high courts and the Supreme Court under this legislation and its predecessors has been for determination of age. In the absence of a birth certificate, a child may easily be excluded from the operation of the JJA and denied its care and protection (Kumari 2007). Ameena, a minor girl from Hyderabad, who was married to a 60-year-old Arab, and who was rescued by airhostess Amrita Ahluwalia, remained in an observation home in Delhi for over seven months before being sent back to Hyderabad. But her age was never properly determined and different courts kept referring to her as 10, 11, or 12 years old. In the case of Ramdeo Chauhan,[5] the Supreme Court refused to determine the age of the accused on the basis of entries in the school register or medical evidence, both of which indicated him to be a child on the date of the offence, and the Supreme Court confirmed the death penalty for the offence of murder even though one judge expressed doubt

[5] [2001] 5 SCC 714 & 2000 II AD [Cr] SC (801).

that the boy was an adult on the date of commission of the offence. The Governor later commuted his sentence to life imprisonment on the recommendation of the National Human Rights Commission (Kumari 2007). There have been several judgements on this issue. The Supreme Court has held that on the point of proof of age, a school-leaving certificate is the best form of evidence, and as far as the medical certificate is concerned, the same is based on an estimate and the possibility of error cannot be ruled out. The Supreme Court has held that the entry relating to date of birth entered in the mark sheet is one of the valid proofs of evidence for determination of age of an accused person. The school-leaving certificate is also a valid proof in determining the age of the accused person.[6]

Only in the absence of matriculation or equivalent certificates, date of birth certificate from the school (other than a play school) first attended, and the birth certificate given by a corporation or a municipal authority or a panchayat, a medical opinion would be sought from a duly constituted medical board to declare the age of the juvenile or the child.[7]

The Juvenile Justice (Care and Protection of Children) Bill, 2014 has been passed by the cabinet to replace and repeal the JJA 2000. It is, as of now,[8] before the standing committee. The 2014 Bill aims to introduce some special provisions in law, aiming at children's rights and incorporating various international obligations and covenants into the legal framework. Corporal punishment and ragging have been made specific offences in this Bill. A highly controversial provision in the Bill that needs to be repealed is that the JJB has been given powers to decide if a juvenile above 16 years, who has committed serious offences such as rape and murder or any other serious offence entailing a punishment of more than seven years imprisonment for adults, could be transferred to the adult criminal justice system. The scientific findings and studies about the development of the brain and its functioning at adolescence have now been recognised and used by the American Supreme Court for abolition of death penalty and

[6] *Shah Nawaz vs State of UP & Anr* (2011) 13 SCC 751.

[7] *Hari Ram vs State of Rajasthan* (2009) 13 SCC 211.

[8] At the time of writing the chapter (January 2015).

life imprisonment without parole. Even the Indian Supreme Court refers to such studies and findings. The Verma Committee report also was against trying 16–18 year olds for heinous crimes as adults. But regardless of this, the 2014 Bill prescribes transfer of children, of 16–18 years of age, to adult system for trial for serious offences, which is not acceptable. This seems to be a knee jerk and short-sighted reaction to the campaign after the gang-rape in New Delhi in which a 17-year-old boy is alleged to have taken part. The object of juvenile legislation is rehabilitation and reformation, and not retribution and punishment. Juvenile legislation does not punish a child according to the seriousness of the offence committed, but treats the circumstances which resulted in the child offending. Trial by regular court would go against the very spirit of the principles of juvenile justice. There is a thin line between child in need of care and protection and a child in conflict with law. Neglect leads to delinquency and vice versa. The long-term consequences of sending them to prisons have not been considered in the proposed Bill. It also fails to spell out the ways to achieve the rehabilitation and social re-integration. Each of these children in conflict with law who are under 18 years of age must be subjected to a well-planned, short-term and long-term rehabilitation and reintegration programme. The length of rehabilitation must be based on a case-to-case basis till the person is rehabilitated. An initial assessment must be done on child's physical, medical, educational, training, and mental needs. This process must be based on a holistic, individualized care plan prepared by a team of multidisciplinary team of experts like mental health, educators, counsellors, and social workers, life-skills trainers, occupational therapists, vocational trainers, and medical doctors based on each child's abilities, background, circumstances, needs, and wishes. It must be periodically reviewed and changed if required. It is hoped the standing committee to whom the 2014 Bill is referred to takes all the above factors into consideration and reviews and repeals this provision of transferring children, between 16 and 18 years of age, to adult criminal justice system.

Some of the other provisions in the proposed 2014 Bill that need review include revamping of the after-care system, making courts the final authority to give the child in adoption, strengthening the families of children in conflict with law, reviewing the basic principle of presumption of innocence, and laying down criteria for identifying place of safety. At present, the JJBs which are the backbone of the system are part-time, honorary structures appointed in many cases on political considerations. They need an on-going structured institutionalized training. We need full-time committed personnel for this important role. The definition of child labour must not be restricted to only the Child Labour Prohibition and Regulation Act, establishing clear and uniform procedures relating to age determination for all states and making non-institutional services a reality. A child-friendly Juvenile Procedure Code must be developed rather than the ideologically different criminal procedure code.

The implementation of the Juvenile Justice laws in India has been a history of hopes unrealized and promises unfulfilled. Under the current JJA, that is JJA 2000, all children in conflict with law, irrespective of the nature of offence, are dealt by the JJBs. It is a central legislation, but the implementation is left to the state governments. The states have not achieved the objectives of the juvenile justice in our country. The entire system has failed the children of our country.

In practice, the spirit of the Act has been completely lost in the administration and implementation by the states. Ad hoc distribution of homes in regions based on political considerations and not on needs or interest of children; insensitive and untrained staff; violation of right to education, health, and nutrition; no proper vocational training; no regular or proper monitoring and inspection; exploitation and abuse of children; and corruption are common features of this system. The special homes do not reform, rehabilitate, or reintegrate the children in conflict with law, as stated in the preamble. The after-care homes, which could have played an important role in further rehabilitating and reintegrating them after they are above 18 years of age are a farce. They have become mismanaged and serve simply as badly maintained hostels or places for basic shelter. Also, such after-care homes are very few in number. The trouble begins with the licencing process itself. Many homes are run not by child rights professionals but by 'politicians' and vested interest groups who have 'managed' to get licences.

A child in conflict with law, who is already a victim of his circumstances—such as poverty, poor schooling, family crisis, unemployment, and harsh discipline—when he or she comes in conflict with the juvenile justice system, is subjected to secondary, in fact multiple, victimization. The detention, investigation, trial, and institutionalization processes further contribute to his victimization. The delays in the system at every stage further add to the trauma of the child. There are many children who are asked to plead guilty by their lawyers or by the JJB. A number of such children who plead guilty do so not because they have committed the offence but because they can be let off and allowed to carry on with their life. They cannot be called repeat offenders, if caught again. The insensitivity has led to the children being scared of the system. A terrified child generally stands before JJB; not knowing what is happening or going to happen. Children cannot be reformed in such an abusive, corrupt, and exploitative system.

Children in Need of Care and Protection

Children in need of care and protection include vulnerable children who are victims of their circumstances—for example, street children; orphaned, abandoned, abused, and destitute children; working children; child labourers; trafficked children; mentally ill children; and HIV-/AIDS-affected children—and children who are victims of conflict and disaster situations. Some other categories of children who need special assistance are migrants and those affected by armed conflict and natural calamities like floods or cyclones. They are children in especially difficult circumstances and need to be protected from all kinds of abuse, neglect, and exploitation.

An area of concern that recently came up is the issue of vulnerability of mentally challenged children in institutions. Children with mental and other developmental disabilities in institutions become targets for neglect, sexual abuse, and assault, which can be seen in the alarming number of cases of abuse, starvation, and even deaths. Sexual assault on differently-abled children, often by their 'caretakers' in the institutions, is a severe, heinous breach of trust and faith, particularly since the children see the institution as a 'place of refuge'. It is a collective failure of the structures and system.

On 23 August 2010, *Mumbai Mirror* reported that five children had died of malnourishment in an orphanage in Thane, a suburb of Mumbai. Some were sexually abused and more would have died had they not been shifted elsewhere in response to the report. The report disclosed the unsanitary conditions in which the children had been housed and the lack of basic facilities. The high court of Mumbai took *suo motu* cognizance of this article and a public interest litigation was initiated (PIL 182/2010). The court stated that

> [T]he case highlights the plight of children desperately in need of care and protection. Their needs have been ignored in years of neglect. Their right to life under the Constitution has been brazenly infringed... We write in great anguish over the deprivations faced by our young and the disabled but in the determined hope that judicial review can activate a democratic deficit of governance.

The matter is before the high court of Mumbai and important directions are being given. Some of the directions for mentally challenged children who are in institutions (Mentally Deficient Children's [MDC] homes) are:

- The Department of Women and Child Development (DWCD) revised its licencing norms.
- All MDC homes in the state are to be taken over by the Social Justice department.
- The state issued a government resolution asking all MDC homes to develop Individual Care Plans for each child in their care.
- The Directorate of Health Services got involved to provide regular health check-ups for children in MDC homes across the state.
- Security arrangements at MDC Home, Mankhurd have improved. Fencing and gates have been put up through the Public Works Department.
- Norms have been laid out for participation of mentally challenged, and hearing and speech impaired children in criminal trials.
- State rules for the JJA (amended in 2006) are notified.
- Moratorium on opening of new homes in the state's new licencing policy.
- Education under RTE assured for disabled children till the age of 18 years instead of 14 years.

Non-institutional Services under the JJA, 2000

The JJA, 2000, provides for the rehabilitation and social reintegration of children in conflict with law as well as children in need of care and protection.

The process of children's rehabilitation and social reintegration has to begin in the children's home or special home.[9] Non-institutional services are based on Articles 20[10] and 21 of the CRC. The Act provides for non-institutional services like adoption,[11] foster care,[12] and sponsorship.[13] The court may allow a child to be given in adoption to a person irrespective of the person's marital status or sex of the child to be adopted. In-country adoption is the first option as per the Hague Convention which India has ratified.

CHILD VICTIMS OF ABUSE AND CRIME

Child abuse and exploitation can be physical, sexual, and emotional. In India, 6–7 lakh children are victims of sexual abuse (Save the Children 2007). When a child is used for sexual gratification of an adolescent or adult, it constitutes child sexual abuse. Trafficking of children for marriage or sexual exploitation and rising corporal punishment are the main concerns of judicial interventions.

A paedophile is an adult who is sexually attracted to children. In 1996, following the conviction of Freddy Peats, a paedophile who sexually violated and trafficked children under the guise of running

[9] Section 40, JJA, 2000.

[10] As per Article 20 of CRC, children deprived of family environment should be provided with alternative family care or institutional placement.

[11] Adoption means the process through which the adopted child is permanently separated from his biological parents and becomes the legitimate child of his adoptive parents with all rights, privileges, and responsibilities that are attached to the relationship, as per Section 2(a) of JJA, 2000. Adoption is considered as the best service for the orphaned, abandoned, destitute child, since it provides permanent substitute care in a family environment. In India, adoption laws are religion based. There is an adoption law for Hindus called the Hindu Adoption and Maintenance Act, 1956. There is a legal vacuum regarding adoption laws of other communities in India.

[12] Foster care provides temporary substitute care for children whose parents are unable to care for them owing to illness, death, desertion of one parent, or any other crisis situation.

[13] Providing financial support to families to meet the medical, nutritional, and educational needs of children and improve general quality of life.

a shelter in Goa, there were different perceptions of the problem of travelling sex offenders. It was believed that the Peats case represented the tip of the iceberg. Later, in the Anchorage case in India, two Britons, Duncan Grant and Allan Waters, ran the Anchorage Shelter Home in Colaba, Mumbai, where they sexually abused children for years. In 2001, after the facts became public, the two British nationals absconded but were made to face trial after a lengthy extradition process. After taking all the facts, evidence and witness accounts, the sessions court convicted them under sections 120B, 107, 373, and 377 of IPC and sentenced Grant and Waters to six years imprisonment and a fine of 20,000 pounds each. However, they challenged this in the Mumbai High Court and, in a shocking judgement, were acquitted of all charges. Finally, the case went to the Supreme Court, which overturned the High Court's judgement and restored the original sentence, thereby convicting the paedophiles. The judges, while passing the judgement, rightly said:[14]

> A deterrent punishment is being imposed in order to help wipe out the name of India from the map of sex tourism. Let paedophiles all over the world know that India should not be their destination in future. Children are the greatest gift to humanity. The sexual abuse of children is one of the most heinous crimes.

An area of grave concern in India is the unregulated surrogacy scenario in the country. A disturbing report of an Israeli paedophile, who served a year and a half in jail for sexually abusing children, having managed to adopt a four-year-old girl through an arrangement with a surrogate mother in India, further highlighted this gap.[15] There are guidelines by the Indian Council of Medical Research on surrogacy that have not been turned into a law so far and there is no registry for surrogacy in India. Currently it is seen as a private contract that two parties enter into for personal services. There is no agency to check the background of foreigners or Indians keen on renting a womb here.

[14] *Childline India Foundation and Anr vs Allan John Waters and Ors* (Decided on 18.03.2011) MANU/SC/0254/2011).

[15] http://www.dnaindia.com/india/report-indias-shame-story-israeli-paedophile-adopts-girl-through-surrogate-mother-1845195.

Physical Abuse

Incidents of brutal corporal punishments in schools are on the rise. There is no national prohibition of corporal punishment in schools by law. The government has issued instruction to states to stop corporal punishments in schools and the National Policy on Education (1986, modified 1992) states in Section 5.6 that 'corporal punishment will be firmly excluded from the educational systems'. The Right of Children to Free and Compulsory Education Act, 2009, or simply the Right to Education (RTE) Act, prohibits corporal punishment in schools for all children between the ages of 6 to 14 years.

Some states have prohibited corporal punishment in schools. Children have limited protection from physical violence and abuse under the Indian Penal Code (IPC), 1860, and the JJA, 2000, though the IPC states that corporal punishment is unlawful under the JJA, 2000, which prohibits torture and other cruel, inhuman, or degrading treatment or punishment. Using the provisions of the JJA, 2000, and the IPC, the law must effectively bring to book the violators. The National Commission on the Protection of Child Rights has introduced guidelines for the protection of children against corporal punishment. The Protection of Women from Domestic Violence Act, 2005, also covers children below the age of 18 years and includes adopted, step, or foster children who are the subjects of physical, mental, or economic torture. Any person can file a complaint on behalf of a child.

Sexual Abuse and Exploitation

Child sexual abuse and exploitation is not new; children are sold, rented out, and sexually abused by adults worldwide (Bajpai 2006). When a third party benefits from child sexual abuse for profit, it becomes exploitation. Commercial sexual exploitation of children commonly refers to using a child for sexual purposes in exchange for cash or in kind favours between the client/customer and intermediary or agent who profits from such trade in children. Those who profit from such trade in children include a wide range of persons (predominantly men, but also women), including parents, family members, agents, and community members. Exploitation includes child prostitution, through trafficking, child sex tourism, and child pornography.

Laws Relating to Child Sexual Abuse

Until 2012, there was no comprehensive law on child sexual abuse. The laws dealing with sexual offences do not specifically address child sexual abuse. The IPC, 1860, does not recognize child abuse. Only rape and sodomy could lead to criminal conviction. Anything other than rape as defined by the law amounts to 'outraging the modesty'. After several years of campaigning for a separate law on child sexual abuse (CSA), the Protection of Children from Sexual Offences Bill, 2012, (POCSO) was passed by the Lok Sabha on 22 May 2012.

The highlights of the new law are:

1. It defines CSA as a gender-neutral crime.
2. It defines acts that constitute CSA comprehensively by including penetrative, non-penetrative, and non-touch forms of abuse.
3. It grades the quantum of punishment on the basis of regular and aggravated offences that take into account custodial forms of CSA.
4. It sets up a detailed procedural mechanism, including the establishment of special courts with child-friendly methods of recording evidence and conducting trials.
5. It has provisions enabling reporting of cases by a child and squarely imposes burden of proof on the accused.

Since many CSA cases are not reported to the police, the law must include support services to such child victims as well. Secondly, an issue of concern is that the age of sexual consent is raised to 18 years. This provision of criminalizing consensual sexual behaviour may be misused by the police or even parents in some cases. In April 2012, Additional Sessions Judge, Kamini Lau, while deciding a case in a Delhi court, observed:

> The legal system cannot be used to punish youngsters in love who are on the verge of attaining majority and this court cannot ruin their lives by taking a hyper-technical view, especially so when the age gap between these youngsters is within acceptable limits and does not reflect an exploitative coercive situation.

Child Marriage

Child marriages can also be regarded as a form of sexual abuse of children. In Rajasthan, on Akshya Tritiya day, which is popularly known as the Akha Teej, hundreds of child marriages are openly conducted. Akha Teej is regarded as the most auspicious day for celebrating marriages. On this day, even infants who have just been born or children who are only a few years old are given in marriage.

Under the Child Marriage Act, 2006, the following are some of the shortcomings:

- Marriage can be considered void only in cases of compulsion and trafficking.
- Onus of declaring is void only if child or guardians file legal proceedings a marriage.
- Traditional marriages are implicitly acknowledged.
- There is no punishment listed for officials.
- There is no provision for incentives for traditional communities.

The Supreme Court of India on 14 February 2006, made it mandatory for all marriages to be registered and directed authorities across the country to amend rules so that its order could be implemented within three months.[16] This judgement could have a significant effect on child marriages. The Court was of the view that one way of curbing the practice of child marriages was to make it legally mandatory for everyone to register their marriages to ensure that people record their ages at the time of marriage. The Supreme Court directed the central government to publicize this order. The central and state governments will have to incorporate appropriate provisions for the consequences of non-registration as well as false documentation during the registration of marriages. The Court also made it clear that the rules should specifically contain a provision for the appointment of an officer for this purpose. A petition was filed in the Supreme Court, challenging the fact that child marriages continued despite there being a legislation in force that prohibited child marriages. The PIL sought that errant government officials, village officials and policemen be held responsible for abetting child marriages, and also seeks compensation and other relief for the victimized girl child.[17]

[16] *Smt. Seema vs Ashwani Kumar* MANU/SC/0996/2006.

[17] *Forum for Fact Finding and Documentation vs Union of India* W.P. (Civ.) No. 212/2003, dated 25 April 2003). Read more on http://hrln.org/hrln/child-rights/pils-a-cases/3-forum-for-fact-finding-and-documentation-vsunion-of-india-child-marriages-in-india.html.

Child Trafficking and Child Prostitution

Child trafficking means the procurement, recruitment, transportation, transfer, harbouring or receipt of persons, legally or illegally, within or across borders, by means of threat or use of force or other forms of coercion, of abduction, of fraud, of deception, of the abuse of power or of a position of vulnerability, or of giving or receiving payments or benefits to achieve the consent of a person, or of having control over another person, for monetary gain or otherwise.

Under the JJA, 2000, victims of child trafficking are treated as children in need of care and protection. In the IPC, there are provisions for dealing with children who are trafficked; the Immoral Traffic (Prevention) Act (ITPA), 1986, was enacted for the prevention of immoral traffic. All persons who are exploited sexually for commercial purposes, whether males or females, fall under the purview of the ITPA. Offences against children are dealt with more severely than other offences by increasing the period of imprisonment. The ITPA does not criminalize prostitution or prostitutes per se, but mostly punishes acts by third parties facilitating prostitution like brothel keeping, living off earnings, trafficking and soliciting or seducing for the purposes of prostitution, which are all punishable offences. The ITPA provides more severe penalties for trafficking of women and for child prostitution.

The age of rescued trafficked victims is an important factor in law enforcement and justice delivery. A person under 18 years is a child under the JJA, 2000, and cannot be sent to a jail, but has to be looked after in a home and treated as per the provisions of the Act. There are several anomalies relating to the issue of age verification of trafficked minor girls after rescue. The IPC, 1860, states that sexual intercourse with a girl child under 16 years, even with her consent, is an offence of rape under Section 375 IPC; procurement of a minor girl under 18 years of age is an offence under Section 366(A); importation of girls less than 21 years of age from the state of Jammu and Kashmir to any other state or from any foreign country to anywhere in India is an offence under Section 366(B); and selling/buying of minor girls under 18 years of age for purposes of prostitution is an offence under Sections 372 and 373 IPC.

The ITPA does not define trafficking; traffickers and brothel owners, enter the age of minors as 18 years or above in their records, which absolves them, if apprehended, under the ITPA, and the rescued minors return to their effective confinement and exploitative conditions.

There is a need to ensure accountability of the doctors who carry out age verification and also of the police officers who record the age immediately after rescue. The age verification/medical examination reports usually place the victims in an age bracket. There are enough police records showing the age of girls as: 'appears to be of 18–19 years of age'. The Supreme Court has held that when the expert's opinion is given on the age bracket, the lower age in the bracket should be taken into consideration, so that the benefit of the doubt favours the victim. Thus, a girl reported to be in the age bracket of 17–19 years, has to be considered as being 17 years old and not 19 years or even 18 years, for the purposes of law enforcement.

Child Pornography and Child Sex Tourism

Child pornography can be dealt with under the provisions of the Information Technology Act, 2000.

Under this Act, as also under the IPC, the publishing of obscene information in electronic form is punishable. Child sex tourism is a frighteningly well-organized operation, and police enforcement in India has been notoriously lax. A decade or so ago, the Interpol had listed Goa as an organized hub of such activities, and other states, too, have been known to attract such offenders.

Some Important Judicial Responses to Child Sexual Abuse and Exploitation

Regarding child prostitution in the light of traditional practices involving *devadasis* and *jogins*,[18] the Supreme Court asked governments to set up advisory committees to make suggestions for the eradication of child prostitution and to evolve schemes for the rehabilitation of child prostitutes.[19]

[18] Traditionally devadasis were young girls 'married' to a deity and dedicated to the worship of the deity. Now, the devadasi tradition has been banned because of its controversial link to prostitution and exploitation. Devadasis are known by various names, for example, in Andhra Pradesh they are known as jogins.

[19] *Vishal Jeet vs Union of India* 1990 (3) SCC 318.

The Delhi High Court initiated several proactive steps by delegating the task of ensuring effective rescue, rehabilitation, and reintegration of trafficked/exploited children to NGOs and government officers. Emphasis was laid on accountability of officers, empowerment of the survivors, and preventing prospects of their being re-trafficked.[20]

The High Court of Mumbai has directed:[21]

- medical examination of rescued girls to determine their age and to check if they are suffering from any medical ailment;
- counselling and aftercare;
- treatment of children rescued from brothels as 'children in need of care and protection' under the JJA, 2000; and
- represented of victims by a lawyer who is not representing the accused.

It has now been well established that all judicial proceedings relating to victims of sexual abuse must be conducted in an 'in camera' trial.[22] The Delhi High Court allowed the evidence of victims of trafficking who had been rehabilitated in their home states to be recorded through video conferencing, in consonance with the judgement of the Supreme Court in the *State of Maharashtra vs Dr Praful Desai*.[23] This is the first instance of a court allowing evidence to be recorded through video conferencing in a case of trafficking.

In the leading case of *Sakshi vs Union of India*,[24] the court gave the following directions: In holding trial of child sex abuse or rape:

1. a screen or some such arrangements may be made where the victim or witnesses (who may be equally vulnerable like the victim) do not see the body or face of the accused;
2. the questions put forth for cross-examination on behalf of the accused, in so far as they relate directly to the incident should be

[20] *Court on its own motion vs UOI* (Crl. M. No. 862/01) in a PIL: Crl.W. No. 532/92 filed in Delhi HC for implementation of ITPA.

[21] *Public at large vs State of Maharashtra* Writ Petition No. 112/92.

[22] *State of Punjab vs Gurmit Singh* 1996 SCC (CR) 316.

[23] AIR 2003 SC 2053.

[24] (1999) 6 SCC 591.

given in writing to the presiding officer of the court who may put them to the victim or witnesses in a language which is clear and is not embarrassing; and

3. the victim of child abuse or rape, while giving testimony in court, should be allowed sufficient breaks as and when required.

Victim and Witnesses of Trafficking for Commercial Sexual Abuse and Exploitation

Incidents of violence against women and children (including trafficking) have considerably increased in the last decade in South Asia, though only few cases are reported to the law enforcement agencies and even fewer reach the trial stage. A small percentage of the accused are convicted. Most cases result in acquittals. The reason is the reluctance of victims to come forward in filing complaints against those who have violated their rights or to testify in court. There is a need to have a law on victim/witness protection. A draft protocol called the Regional Victim/Witness Protection Protocol to Combat Trafficking, Commercial Sexual Exploitation and Sexual Abuse of Women and Children in South Asia[25] recommends basic guidelines on standards of prosecution of offenders and specific measures to be taken collaboratively by state and civil society. It deals with protection of victims, repatriation, rehabilitation and reintegration, and extradition of such victims and witnesses of trafficking.

The SAARC Convention on Preventing and Combating Trafficking in Women and Children for Prostitution was signed on 5 January 2002 and ratified on 2 September 2003. The SAARC Convention on Regional Arrangements for the Promotion of Child Welfare in South Asia was also signed on 5 January 2002 and ratified on 2 September 2003. At the international level, Optional Protocol on the Sale of Children, Child Prostitution and Child Pornography was ratified on 15 November 2004. More multilateral and bilateral efforts are required to control this offence which has now taken the form of organized crime.

[25] Final Protocol drafted by Asha Bajpai, prepared for Sariq (South Asia Regional Initiative/Equity Support Program), India (Bajpai n.d.).

CHILD SEX RATIO AND THE RIGHT TO LIFE

The child sex ratio has deteriorated across the country over the last decade. In the Indian context there is a strong preference for sons. The girl child's very existence is threatened. Female foeticide and infanticide reflect the prevalence of preference for a male child. The IPC deals with these offences,[26] but there is hardly any prosecution or convictions under the IPC. The Pre-natal Diagnostic Techniques (Regulation and Prevention of Misuse) Act, 1994, now stands renamed as The Pre-conception and Pre-natal Diagnostic Techniques (Prohibition of Sex Selection) Act, 2003 (PC-PNDT). The PC-PNDT Act provides for the prohibition of sex selection before or after conception and regulates the use of prenatal diagnostic techniques for the purpose of detecting genetic abnormalities or other sex-linked disorders in the foetus. According to the PC-PNDT Act, no person should conduct or cause to be conducted any prenatal diagnostic techniques including ultrasonography for the purpose of determining the sex of a foetus. Several offences and penalties have been included in the PC-PNDT Act. Every offence under this Act is cognizable, non-bailable, and non-compoundable.

In order to implement the provisions of the PC-PNDT Act more rigorously, the Supreme Court, in a landmark judgement,[27] has issued a number of guidelines for the central government, the central supervisory board, and the state governments.

ECONOMIC EXPLOITATION OF CHILDREN: CHILD LABOUR

Another vulnerable group of children subjected to abuse and exploitation are the child labourers. In almost all societies, children work in some way, though the types of work they do and the forms of their involvement vary. But many millions of children work under abusive and exploitative conditions that are clearly dangerous to them. The census survey of 1991 indicated that 60 million child labourers were

[26] IPC, Sections 312–18.

[27] *Centre for Enquiry into Health and Allied Themes and Ors vs Union of India and Ors* AIR 2003 SC 3309.

working in various sectors, and this figure excluded the large number of children employed in the unorganized sector and agriculture.

Child actors performing in television entertainment programmes is another form of child labour. Balancing both work and school and the stress associated with it is an abuse of their tender age that affects their healthy development. Though what constitutes 'hazardous' is not clearly defined under the Child Labour Prohibition and Regulation Act, 1986, any labour can be regarded as hazardous that hinders the education of the child.

A landmark judgement was delivered in the case of *M.C. Mehta vs State of Tamil Nadu and Ors*,[28] and some of the important rulings of the case are given below:

1. Offending employer must be asked to pay compensation of a sum of Rs 20,000 for every child employed in contravention of the provisions of the Child Labour Prohibition and Regulation Act.
2. Inspectors appointed under Section 17 of the Child Labour Prohibition and Regulation Act should be made responsible to see that for each child employed in violation of the provisions of the Act, the concerned employer pays Rs 20,000, which is to be deposited in the Child Labour Rehabilitation-cum-Welfare Fund. The income of the fund so generated should be used only for the concerned child.
3. The state should see that an adult member of the family, whose child is in employment in a factory or a mine or in other hazardous work gets a job anywhere in lieu of the child.
4. In those cases where alternative employment is not made available, the parent/guardian will be paid the income, which would be earned on the 'corpus', and which would be a sum of Rs 5,000 for each child per month.
5. The employment given or payment made would cease to be operative, if the child is not sent to school for education by the parent or guardian.
6. Regarding non-hazardous jobs, the inspector should see that working hours of the child are not more than four to six hours a day,

[28] AIR 1997 SC 699.

and the child receives education for at least two hours each day at the cost of the employer.

The implementation of this judgement along with the right to education will go a long way in reducing child labour.

Enforcement of the Child Labour Prohibition and Regulation Act

The enforcement of Child Labour Prohibition and Regulation Act (CLPRA), 1986 is poor owing to several factors, such as lack of willing witnesses, corruption, age determination, certain lacunae in the law, and insensitivity of civil society. The CLPRA does not cover a major section of the workforce in India employed in the unorganized sector, including the majority of child labourers in this sector. Children working in the agricultural sector and in home-based industries have been also left out. The law covers only the child workforce in the formal, industrial sector in occupations identified as 'hazardous' under the law and those working in plantations.

What constitutes 'hazardous' work is not clearly defined in this Act, and, therefore, several hazardous industries have been excluded. The physical and psychological implications for children working in hazardous occupations also have to be taken into consideration. The 1986 Act is silent on the educational needs of the child, which is a key strategy for the elimination of child labour. The CLPRA should integrate rehabilitation in its purview and work in coordination with other related legislations.

There is an increasing trend of migration and trafficking of children for labour in different parts of the country. Compelled by the socio-economic conditions, a large number of children are migrating from economically backward areas to big cities for work. In many of these cases, these children are being trafficked by middle men and agents, who bring them to employers in the city by extending meagre advances to the parents and giving false assurances of lucrative jobs and good job prospects. These children work under highly exploitative situations, such as very long working hours, paltry wages, and unhygienic and most difficult working conditions. Such children mostly work in industries such as *zari* (gold-thread embroidery) making, jewellery units, domestic helps, dhabas (street-food stalls), and tea stalls. Very often, they are kept within the confines of the work-places and, therefore, lack any kind of freedom and are vulnerable to abuse. State governments have authorized raids in these workplaces to rescue such children from the clutches of unscrupulous employers. On being rescued, they are, in most cases, kept in temporary shelters before being repatriated to their native places.

A disturbing trend which has not been considered at all in the CLPRA is that there are instances of migration or trafficking of children for labour from neighbouring countries, such as Nepal and Bangladesh. These children are being brought to big cities in India in search of labour and they end up working in very difficult conditions, mostly in dhabas and tea stalls, or as domestic servants. Being so far away from their families, these children are highly vulnerable to all kinds of abuses, including physical and sexual abuse. Issues related to repatriation and rehabilitation of children who are victims of cross-border trafficking becomes even more complex and difficult, as it involves coordination with the countries the children come from. There needs to be a mechanism for smooth and safe repatriation of such children.

There are several laws that need to be combined for the protection of children, such as the Juvenile Justice Act, the Bonded Labour Act, and Contract Labour Act.

There is a need to ratify the 182 ILO Convention on Hazardous Occupations that has provisions for the prohibition of employment of children below 18 years in hazardous occupations.

INSTITUTIONAL STRUCTURES RELATING TO PROTECTION OF CHILDREN

Institutions and structures under the various laws have been provided to protect the rights of the child. The institutions and structures under the JJA are: observation homes, special homes, children's homes, shelter homes, juvenile justice boards, child welfare committees, special juvenile police units, child protection units, and aftercare organizations. In addition there are family courts established under the Family Courts Act, 1984, and the National Commission for Protection of Child Rights Act, 2005.

Management of Institutions

Though the JJA has rightly increased the age of children, keeping in conformity with the CRC, the infrastructure as well as human resources under the Act was not upgraded and is grossly inadequate. The education, training, and recreation for children have not been provided for. Besides, basic or school education and higher education and training of these children have to be considered. The educational and vocational facilities in the institutions need modernization. There needs to be shift in training from outdated non-marketable vocations to job-oriented training in areas such as computer education, and certified courses on dress designing, etc. Open school and Open University education should be made accessible to the children. Trained duty counsels have to be appointed by the state legal services authority to represent the children in the courts (some states, such as Maharashtra, have appointed duty counsels in the juvenile justice boards). The institutional staff and the law enforcers including the police and judiciary need training so that the spirit of the Act can be followed. The law enforcers have to be made aware that children have a right to legal aid and other constitutional rights, such as right to counsel, right to speedy trial, right to speedy disposal of cases, and right to child friendly proceedings. The rules of the JJA, 2000, and the Orphanages and Charitable Homes Act, 1960, have to be synthesized.

Family Courts

The main objective of the family courts must be such as to stabilize the marriage, to preserve the family, and where a marriage has been broken down irretrievably, to dissolve it with maximum fairness and minimum bitterness, distress, and humiliation. The family courts are supposed to be specialized courts where sensitive, delicate matters have to be expedited in connection with the parties to marriage, their children, and their property and in a manner to reduce expensive legal and technical procedures. The Family Courts Act, 1984, emphasizes conciliation, counselling, and concern for an individualized approach based on initiative and innovative procedural modifications (Bajpai 2006).

Children's issues that are dealt by the family court include custody, guardianship, and maintenance cases. It is clear that rulings granting custody are affected by issues such as poverty, adultery, immorality, religion, sex, age, abandonment, remarriage, wishes of parents and children, and nearness of kin (Bajpai 2006). These are the factors that are taken into account by the courts while determining the best interests of the child.

There have been some important judgements on the issue of custody, guardianship, and maintenance of children.

The Family Courts Act, 1984, is a legislation that relies significantly on networking among a large number of professionals concerned with the complex dimensions of families in India. The networking envisages the working of judges, social workers, counsellors, case workers, psychiatrists, psychologists, police, and NGOs. The concept of networking underscores the need to share roles in a dispute to get a shared and multidisciplinary understanding of the situation. Some of the family courts, especially in big cities, such as Mumbai, Nagpur, and Pune, have introduced services within the court premises, such as child guidance clinics, a children's complex where the parents can get access to their children, inquiry cells, drug-addiction centres, and counselling and stress-management centres, which perform psychological screening and testing and diagnostic and counselling therapy for all litigants wherein psychological problems are detected during either the litigation or pre-litigation stage. In cases relating to custody, guardianship, and maintenance of children, the courts have to adopt the best-interest-of-the-child principle.

Decisions in family courts cannot simply be decided on the basis of 'proven' or 'not proven'. In family courts, the principles of law, the conscience of the community, personal relationships, and sociological and psychological factors work in conjunction.

By and large, the spirit and the objectives of the Act have been forgotten and many family courts are working, in practice, like civil courts. There is thus a need to document the best practices of integrating support services in family courts, and after suitable adaptation, replicating it in others that do not have them. The counsellors play a very important role in family courts, but in the absence of proper infrastructure and uniform rules with regard to remuneration, of the counsellors, skilled counsellors are either not available or are engaged for very low fees, which demoralizes and demotivates many of them and deters them from giving quality time or attention to the cases.

National Commission for the Protection of Child Rights

The initiative taken by the Government of India to enact The Commissions for Protection of Child Rights Act, 2005 is an important milestone in translating commitments into action. The National Commission for Protection of Child Rights (NCPCR) is a statutory body of the Government of India, set up in March 2007, to protect, promote, and defend child rights in the country.

Some significant tasks done by the National Commission were to issue guidelines against corporal punishment in schools, facilitate investigation into complaints on corporal punishments and child labour, and review laws relating to juvenile justice and child labour. The Commission's role has raised hopes among activists as being a positive initiative towards protecting the rights of the child. However, the Commission's powers and resources need to be enhanced and be given independence from political pressures to work and act to realize its primary goals.

★ ★ ★

This decade has seen a spurt of legislative initiatives on the issue of child rights. The right to protection includes freedom from all forms of exploitation, violence, abuse, and inhuman or degrading treatment. There are about 250 legislations in India that directly or indirectly deal with children. Some major strides forward have been witnessed recently, including the landmark Right to Education.

Laws on trafficking, corporal punishment, surrogacy and reproductive tourism, adoption, cybercrimes against children, education, and child labour, have to be reformed and formulated.

Child labour is assuming new forms as seen in the number of child artistes and migrant child labour. Enacting a child friendly legislation demands a convergence of laws on education and child labour, not just to link education to a reduced prevalence of child labour, but also to ensure education of equitable quality to every child in India.

There are links between missing children, forced labour, and trafficking. There is no national data base or uniform tracking procedure existing in India today that deals with missing children across the country. It is an issue of serious concern following the Nithari[29] killings in Noida, Uttar Pradesh, where out of 38 missing children, many of them were later found to have been killed. The missing children issue can no longer be dealt through knee-jerk reactions as in the recent Nithari killings. On an average over 40,000 children in India are reported missing every year (HAQ 2005).

India is moving towards the standards set by international laws. Monitoring and enforcing the laws is the next important step. It is also necessary for lawmakers, law enforcers, and civil society to appreciate the spirit of the laws, so that children get justice and these laws do not simply remain on paper, for child rights are non-negotiable. Children must be considered citizens entitled to rights guaranteed to them under the Constitution of India and under international laws. The major significance of the CRC and other international instruments ratified by India is that it represents a commitment to improving the situation of children in India.

A convergence of laws and collaborative efforts of ministries dealing with child well-being issues must form a strategic part of ensuring child protection and care. For instance, close links between education and the prevalence of child labour demand a convergence of laws on education and child labour. Today, there are a number of fragmented laws on various issues relating to children. While laws on child labour speak about penalizing employers who employ child labour, child labour laws do not speak of education, except as found in the *M.C. Mehta*

[29] Noida and the surrounding areas were for long haunted by incidents of kidnapping. Parents approached police officials for help but were always denied support. The incidents of kidnapping of little children, mostly girls, continued unchecked. On 29 December 2006, when police were investigating the kidnapping of a teenaged girl, electronic surveillance brought them to an unoccupied house owned by a Moninder Pandher. The electronic surveillance traced the cell phone of the kidnapped girl, who was later found to have been sexually assualted and killed, to this house. As police investigations progressed, skeletal remains of many more children were found in sacks in the drain that was situated behind the house. This was when the case of serial killings came to light. When the skeletal remains and the objects found in the sacks were tested, it was found that they belonged to the children who had gone missing.

vs Tamil Nadu case.[30] But, both require significant commitment and engagement from state governments and civil society.

Prosecution and conviction rates in cases relating to contravention of the laws relating to children are low, pointing to the poor implementation of the law, administrative lapses, and lacunae in the laws. There is an urgent need for law reforms. Policies and legislations for children have suffered from weak implementation owing to scant attention to issues of child protection, and this, in turn, has resulted in scarce resources, minimal infrastructure, and inadequate services to address child protection problems. Laws are made with good intentions, but implementation and enforcement are not ideal. Laws relating to children are difficult to enforce, because the victims themselves are weak and vulnerable. It must be understood that strict enforcement of the laws should in itself act as a deterrent to the violators. When new laws are being drafted or when law reform is being undertaken, this must be incorporated. The seriousness of a child-related offence must be conveyed to the law enforcers and interpreters. For instance, under the Child Labour Prohibition and Regulation Act, imprisonment as well as fine is given for violations. But, it has been observed that this discretion is generally in favour of the employers, as the courts penalize the employers with fines instead of imprisonment. The process of change in laws must involve civil society, and their recommendations must be seriously considered. A child friendly judiciary trained in child rights is also required.

The psychological conditions of rescued and victimized children are not considered in Indian laws and in judgements. In legislations concerning children and their rights, mental health considerations must become an important component of law, and therapists must be included in the legal framework, both for an appreciation of evidence and for the future benefit of the child as a long-term remedy (Sharma 2005). The lawmakers, the medical doctors, and judges must take the mental health concerns of the child in the laws, medical reports, and judgements relating to children. There must be a move towards therapeutic jurisprudence.

Alternate dispute resolution techniques need to be developed for dealing with children-related issues. Children's involvement must be there in conciliation and mediation services and in litigated/contested/

[30] AIR 1997 SC 699.

defended court proceedings concerning their care arrangements or guardianship issues.

Moreover, to achieve the Millennium Development Goals a comprehensive approach to child protection is required. All budgets for child protection schemes and programmes should be in the plan category and not in the non-plan category (HAQ 2005). In this context, the concluding observations of the UN Committee on Child Rights are very significant:

> Make every effort to increase the proportion of the budget allocated to the realization of children's rights to the maximum extent of available resources... Develop ways to assess the impact of budgetary allocations on the implementation of children's rights...[31]

Awareness of the rights and laws by various stakeholders, including children, is essential to recognize the extent of the problem, tackle it politically, legally, and socially with significant commitment from the state and civil society. The effects and processes of globalization, privatization, and liberalization on children must be seriously considered and addressed. The negative linkage of globalization and privatization on rights of children in several countries across the world needs to be examined. India cannot become a world economic power with its children being abused, exploited, and trafficked and their rights violated.

REFERENCES

Bajpai, Asha. 2006. *Child Rights in India—Law, Policy and Practice*. New Delhi: Oxford University Press.

———. 2007. 'Who Is a Child? *InfoChange News & Features*. Pune: Centre for Communication & Development Studies.

———. n.d. 'Regional Victim/Witness Protection Protocol to Combat Trafficking, Commercial Exploitation and Sexual Abuse of Women and Children in South Asia', Document 1339, South Asia Regional Initiative/ Equity Support Program (SARI/Equity). http://lastradainternational.org/doc-center/1339/regional-victim-witness-protection-protocol-to-combat-trafficking-commercial-exploitation-and-sexual-abuse-of-women-and-children-in-south-asia, last accessed on 10 October 2014.

[31] Thirty-fifth session vide letter No CRC/C/15 /Add 228 dated 30 January 2004.

HAQ: Centre for Child Rights. 2005. *Report on Child Rights*. New Delhi.

———. 2013. *Budget for Children*. New Delhi: HAQ.

Kumari, Ved. 2007. *InfoChange News & Features*, June.

Ministry of Home Affairs. 2006. 'Crime in India'. New Delhi: Government of India.

Save the Children. 2007. 'VOICES and ACTIONS of Girls and Boys to End Violence against Children in South and Central Asia', Discussion Paper by Save the Children Sweden. http://resourcecentre.savethechildren.se/sites/default/files/documents/1525.pdf, last accessed on 10 October 2014.

Sharma, Parul. 2005. 'Point of View', *JIACAM*, 1(4): Article 6.

6 Rising Food Prices and the Global Financial Crisis

Tracking Impacts on Women and Children

S. Mahendra Dev

There has been a significant increase in global food prices due to several structural and cyclical factors in the last few years. India has experienced high food inflation in the last few years. Apart from the problem of rise in food prices, India has also been facing the adverse impact of the global financial crisis since the third quarter of 2008. India has largely avoided the impact on its banking system, though the crisis has had an adverse impact on the liquidity situation and economic growth. The European sovereign debt problem, particularly in Portugal, Italy, Ireland, Greece, and Spain in 2010–11, has led to additional problems for India.

Poor people typically spend 60 to 70 per cent of their income on food, and they have little capacity to adapt as prices rise, because wages may not adjust accordingly. This, in turn, can have an adverse effect on the poor and on the food security of the country.

Although the underlying causes for the rise in food prices and financial crisis are different, they are interconnected through their implications on financial stability, food security, and political security (von Braun 2008). At the global level, capital was diverted from the collapsing housing market to speculation in agricultural futures. Speculative activities were partly responsible for the rise in global food prices. The food crisis increased general inflation and the impact on macroeconomic policies. Similarly, the financial crisis can have an impact on employment, poverty, agricultural investment, and social sector expenditures. Therefore, both the food crisis and the financial crisis may have an adverse impact on the food and nutritional security of India and undermine the poverty-reduction efforts and the gains over the last several years, if large sections of the population cannot cope with the rise in prices. These two crises can potentially exacerbate and further deepen existing vulnerabilities in India for the poor and disadvantaged groups including women and children. The coping strategies due to these crises could have an adverse impact on the food security and human development of women and children.

The objective of this study is to examine analytical issues that would identify the pathways of the effects of the rising food prices and financial crisis on households, particularly on women and children. It also outlines desirable macro, sectoral, and social protection policies and measures that would mitigate the negative effects and that would have the strongest effect on protecting levels of living of the households, in particular levels of nutrition, health, education, and thus enhance child protection.

FOOD INFLATION AND IMPACT OF THE FINANCIAL CRISIS ON THE MACROECONOMY

Food Inflation

It may be noted that increase in food prices has been a significant negative feature of India's economic environment in recent years. It has had a tremendous impact on the quality of life, for people struggle to maintain nutritional standards that they had previously achieved or they give up some other forms of consumption in order to do so.

As shown in Table 6.1, food prices were very high in the years preceeding 2011 before declining moderately in the first quarter of the financial year 2011–12. The inflation for food articles rose from about 7 per cent in 2006–7 to about 9 per cent in 2008–9, and then to about 15 per cent in 2009–10 and 2010–11 before declining to around 9 per cent in the first quarter of 2011–12.

In recent years, there has been a diversification in dietary consumption patterns in India. The predominance of cereals in the typical household diets has given way to greater balance than earlier and

TABLE 6.1 Food Inflation for Major Groups and Subgroups: 2007–8 to 1st Quarter of 2011–12 (year on year changes)

Food group/subgroup	2007–8	2008–9	2009–10	2010–11	2011–12 (average of April–July)
All commodities	4.7	8.0	3.8	9.6	9.5
Primary articles	8.3	11.1	12.7	17.7	12.9
Food articles	7.0	9.1	15.3	15.6	8.9
Foodgrains	6.9	11.0	14.5	4.8	2.3
Cereals	9.5	11.9	12.6	5.3	5.0
Rice	11.02	14.8	12.3	5.9	2.6
Wheat	7.3	9.9	12.8	3.0	0.4
Maize	6.3	6.8	10.2	10.1	1.9
Pulses	−2.8	7.5	22.4	3.2	−8.18
Urad	−16.5	0.0	43.0	19.0	−9.23
Arhar	16.4	14.4	48.8	−4.5	−16.3
Moong	−11.9	6.1	55.4	19.9	−21.4
Fruits & vegetables	11.5	8.2	9.7	16.4	16.0
Milk	5.1	7.6	18.8	20.1	8.0
Eggs, meat, and fish	3.2	7.7	20.8	25.5	9.1

Source: Office of the Economic Advisor, Department of Industrial Policy & Promotion, Ministry of Commerce and Industry, Government of India.

a consequent increase in the demand for proteins, such as, pulses, milk, meat, fish, and eggs, and also for vegetables and fruit. The demand for proteins has increased significantly, and it is no surprise that these items have been the primary cause of food inflation in the recent period. Table 6.1 shows that inflation for three major pulses (urad, arhar and moong) was nearly 50 per cent, it showed negative inflation in later months. Similarly, inflation for milk, eggs, meat, fish, fruits, and vegetables was very high. However, in December 2011, food inflation was negative, and there were signs of decline in food inflation.

The trends in food prices by groups/subgroups (changes in wholesale price index [WPI]) from April 2005 to April 2011 are given in Figures 6.1 to 6.6. The trends in prices in food articles in Figure 6.1 show that inflation was the highest during December 2009 to July 2010. Of course, the period of high inflation differs across subgroups and crops.

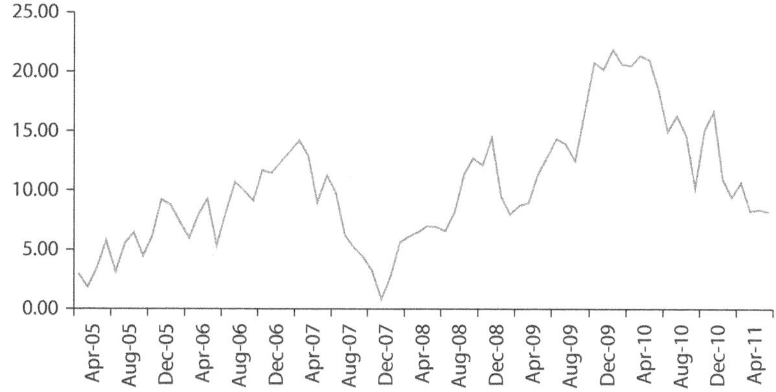

FIGURE 6.1 Year to Year Changes in WPI: Food Articles

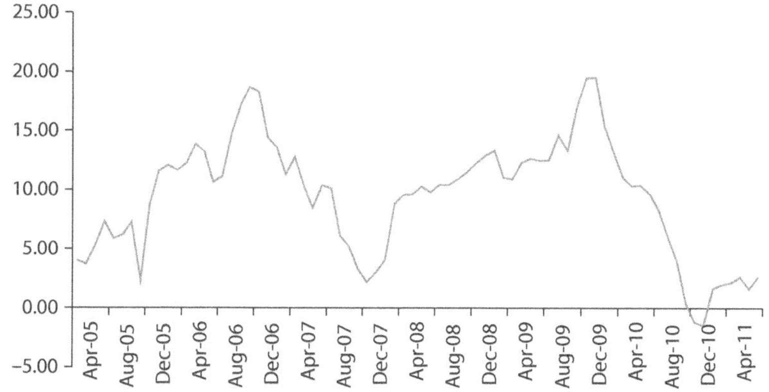

FIGURE 6.2 Year to Year Changes in WPI: Foodgrains

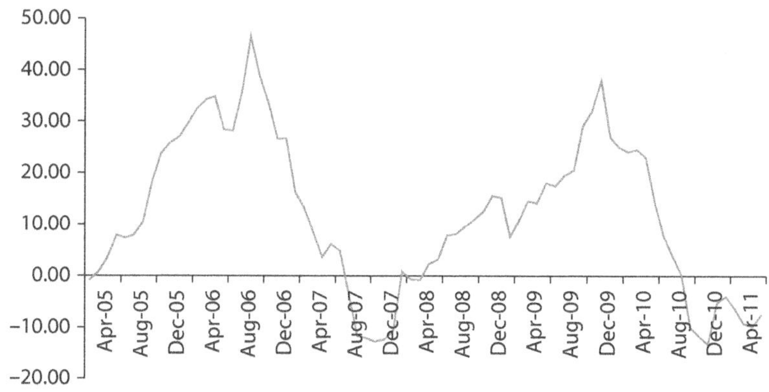

FIGURE 6.3 Year to Year Changes in WPI: Pulses

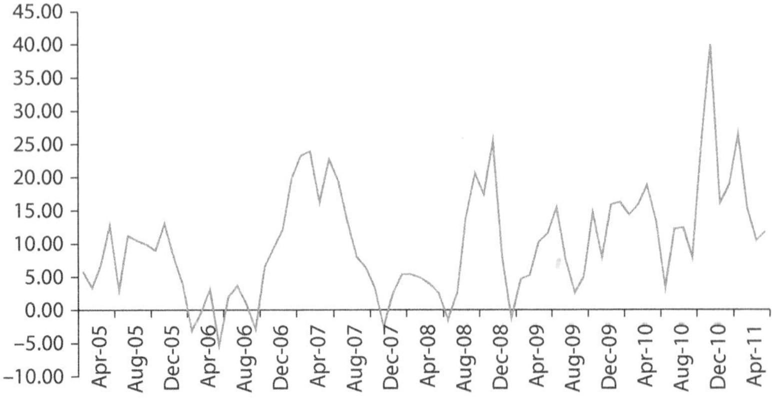

FIGURE 6.4 Year to Year Changes in WPI: Fruits and Vegetables

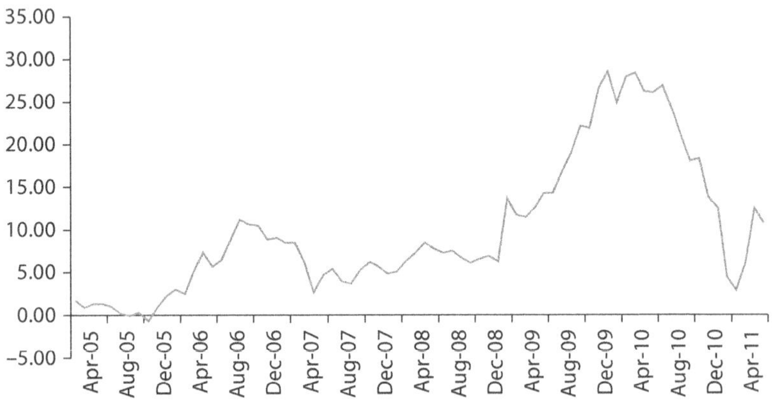

FIGURE 6.5 Year to Year Changes in WPI: Milk

What have been the drivers of higher food inflation in India in the last two and a half years? Both global factors and domestic factors are responsible, but domestic factors like supply shortages play a greater role than global factors (RBI 2011). Food inflation does not seem to be a transitory phenomenon, and it seems to be more of a structural problem now, especially the protein (pulses, milk, eggs, meat, and fish) inflation (RBI 2011).

Impact on the Macroeconomy

The global financial crisis has had an adverse impact on economic growth, balance of payments, capital flows, exchange rate, etc.

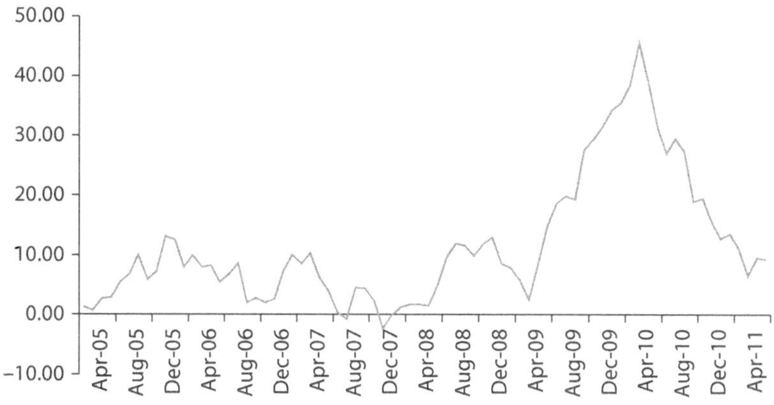

FIGURE 6.6 Year to Year Changes in WPI: Eggs, Meat, and Fish

On account of monetary tightening, investment demand was affected, although consumption demand was less affected. This, along with rising interest rates, high inflation, and global uncertainty, has had an adverse impact on growth. In spite of high agricultural growth, total growth was about 8.5 per cent in 2010–11 and is likely to show further decline in 2011–12. The first quarter GDP growth in 2011–12 was 7.7 per cent compared with 8.8 per cent in 2010–11 during the same quarter. The second quarter GDP growth in 2012 declined to 6.9 per cent, but the RBI's view is that in the short term, there would be a trade-off between growth and inflation. In the medium term, there would be low inflation with high growth.

Trade deficit was higher in recent years, as export growth could not match the growth of imports. Portfolio inflows were also affected because of the European sovereign debt problem. Further, the current account deficit is nearing 3 per cent of GDP. The rupee also depreciated against the US dollar by 17 per cent since August 2011. The budget estimate of the centre's fiscal deficit of 4.8 per cent of GDP is likely to increase to more than 5.5 per cent of GDP in 2011–12.

All these macro-developments due to the global financial crisis in the US and Europe were projected to have an adverse impact on the Indian economy, which, in turn, would have consequences on the lives of women and children.

TABLE 6.2 Economic Growth: Past Performance and Projections (in per cent)

Sectors	2006–7	2007–8	2008–9	2009–10 (QE)	2010–11 (Rev)	2012	
						Quarter 1	Quarter 2
GDP at factor cost	9.6	9.3	6.8	8.0	8.5	7.7	6.9
Agriculture & allied	4.2	5.8	-0.1	0.4	6.6	3.9	3.2
Industry	12.2	9.7	4.4	8.0	7.9	5.1	3.2
Manufacturing	14.3	10.3	4.2	8.8	8.3	7.2	2.7
Services	10.1	10.3	10.1	10.1	9.4	10.0	9.3

Source: Ministry of Finance 2011.

PATHWAYS THAT LEAD TO POOR OUTCOMES FOR WOMEN AND CHILDREN

Both the food and financial crises affect the conditions of women and children. In this section we discuss the pathways leading to poor outcomes for vulnerable groups.

Pathways Created by Food Prices and Nutrition

There are four main pathways in the context of rising food prices that lead to poor outcomes in nutrition, health, and education of children. These are pathways that (i) have an impact on poverty levels; (ii) have a macroeconomic impact, which affects employment and the social sector; (iii) have an impact on nutrition and social protection programmes; and (iv) have an impact on women's well-being and intra-household decision making.

IMPACT ON POVERTY

A recent study in eight countries estimates that the rise in food prices between 2005 and 2007 increased poverty by 3 percentage points on an average. Extrapolating these results globally suggests that as a result of the rise in food prices, the total world population in poverty may have increased by 73–105 million people (World Bank 2008).

High food prices have different effects on net sellers and net buyers. However, in India, net buyers are large in number and include all urban poor and a majority of rural poor. The 59th Round data of National Sample Survey (NSS) indicates that only about a quarter of all rural households and only 44 per cent of farming households were net sellers of main crops, such as rice, wheat, maize, and other cereals (Viswanathan and Serajuddin 2010). And while it is true that net sellers are likely to benefit from rising food prices, the constraints on agriculture may prevent farmers responding positively to the crisis in the short run. Some of the small producers with a marketable surplus could in fact become worse off with higher prices. This is because a small producer typically sells the surplus immediately in the post-harvest season when prices are low and buys food when prices are high.

In India, rising food prices would have an adverse impact on the poor, because (i) the poor have a large share of expenditures on food, and (ii) most poor households are net buyers of staple food rather than net sellers. The impact on poverty would have four damaging effects on the poor, through (i) impaired nutrition status of pregnant and lactating women and of preschool children; (ii) impaired health status of women and children; (iii) an increase in child labour and withdrawal of children from school; and (iv) the distress sale of productive assets (see Viswanathan and Serajuddin 2010).

MACROECONOMIC IMPACT AND THE EFFECT ON EMPLOYMENT AND THE SOCIAL SERVICE SECTOR

Rising food, commodity, and oil prices have increased general inflation. Apart from the food price rise, an increase in general inflation would also hurt the poor and vulnerable sectors of the population.

Reduced economic activity due to rise in food prices and general inflation would affect the social sector, especially education and health. At the macro-level, reduction in economic growth would lead to a reduction in the tax/GDP ratio. This would have an adverse impact on employment and social sector expenditures. Even if growth does not decline, an increase in food prices would occasion an increase in subsidies, tax concessions, and so forth, reducing government's ability to increase social sector expenditures. This may adversely affect women and children in terms of nutrition and health outcomes (see Dev and Mooij 2004).

IMPACT ON NUTRITION AND SOCIAL PROTECTION PROGRAMMES

A rise in food prices could worsen nutrition, especially among infants (0–24 months), pregnant women, and lactating mothers. Children suffer long-term consequences from short-term shocks. The countries hit by the food crisis already have the highest pre-existing rates of malnutrition. The malnutrition situation would worsen with an increase in food prices.

The food price rise would affect the total food consumption of households, which, in turn, would reduce food consumption by women and children. Also, households may spend more on cheaper high-calorie staples and less on foods rich in protein and vitamins, such as meat, fish, dairy, fruit, and vegetables, thereby reducing the quality of their diet. This will have significant negative consequences for nutrition.

Bouis (2008, p. 1) cites four basic factors supporting this conclusion:

1. Expenditures on non-staple foods by poor consumers comprise 40–60 per cent of total expenditures on food.
2. Demand for food staples (rice, wheat, maize, etc., depending on the geographical region and culture) is highly inelastic. Income and price elasticities for food staples in the aggregate are low.
3. In diets, minerals and vitamins are concentrated in non-staple foods; energy is concentrated in staple foods.
4. Current intakes of vitamins and minerals are already very low, which results in high prevalence rates of micronutrient deficiencies. Modest decrease in current intakes of minerals and vitamins will drive these prevalence rates significantly higher, with severe consequences for the nutritional status of the poor and for public health.

Increased micronutrient malnutrition is one likely health consequence of high food prices. According to Klotz et al. (2008), increased staple food prices around the world are forcing households to reduce their consumption of micronutrient-rich foods, which will have a range of health consequences depending on the pre-existing nutritional status of a given population.

A rise in food prices would affect social protection programmes, particularly the food-based schemes. For example, India has food supplementation programmes as found in the Integrated Child Development Services (ICDS) and the mid-day meal programme for primary school children. In the Mid-Day Meal Scheme (MDMS), the Government of India provides subsidized food grains that are used, along with pulses, oil, and vegetables, to prepare hot meals for children, the cost of which is borne by the government. The cost of these programmes would increase with higher food inflation.

WOMEN'S WELL-BEING AND INTRA-HOUSEHOLD DECISION MAKING

High food prices have differing impacts on women consumers and producers. The rise of food prices could increase incentives for producers.

However, owing to constraints on input supplies and other factors, past evidence suggests that higher prices may not necessarily stimulate production by female farmers (Quisumbing 2008). At the household level, a rise in food prices affects the household budget, and women reduce expenditures on food, or they become constrained for time when they find employment to counteract rising prices, or they do both, which adversely affect children's nutrition and the time needed for childcare. Intra-household dynamics are key to determining the impact on children because of a rise in food prices. The intra-household allocation of resources to children depends on several factors, including women's empowerment and education, the household wealth and asset base, and social protection measures reaching the household (Plan and ODI 2008). Thus, household-coping mechanisms relate to decisions about children's activities. In some cases, children may be withdrawn from school to take up paid work activities. In other cases, children may have less study and leisure time because of their increased involvement in paid or unpaid economic activities.

Pathways That Lead to Poor Outcomes due to Financial Crisis

The financial turmoil that started in the US financial system and the present European sovereign debt problem has blown into an unprecedented financial crisis all over the world.

The indirect impact of the crisis, transmitted through capital flows, financial markets, and trade (real sector), has affected India. The foreign exchange reserves have declined in India and have created a liquidity crisis as well as a premature tightening of monetary policy. The exports from India would also be affected. Lower growth may affect employment prospects. It may also have an adverse impact on social sector expenditures as tax/GDP ratio may go down with lower growth.

More importantly, the impact of the financial crisis is likely to have negative effects on the agricultural sector and food security. The pathways through which the agricultural markets will be affected are on both demand and supply sides (FAO 2008). The slowing down of economic growth would affect demand for agricultural commodities. Prevailing uncertainty and consequent negative market expectations could further dampen demand.

On the supply side, agricultural production also would be affected. Increase in oil and fertilizer prices would affect the supply of agricultural commodities. The financial crisis is likely to have a negative impact on agricultural credit, which is widely regarded as a major constraint to agriculture in developing countries. Farmers who took advantage of rising agricultural prices to invest in raising production may find themselves unable to pay off their debts because of falling output prices subsequently.

The combination of fluctuating agricultural prices and reduction in agricultural investment and access to credit may have a negative effect on agricultural production. It would then have serious implications for food security. Poverty-reduction efforts may be stalled because of low employment and volatility in food prices. The negative impact on household income would affect the well-being of women and children.

Vulnerabilities and Impact on Children

The vulnerabilities have short-term and long-term impacts on children. Decline in food consumption and expenditures on health would have an impact on nutrition and health indicators of children. As mentioned earlier, other such adverse effects are: reduction of expenditure on non-food items, such as health and education; distress selling of productive assets by families; withdrawal of children from school; increased use of child labour; falling into debt, etc.

A study on Andhra Pradesh shows that the impact of risk responses increased indebtedness. The extent of borrowing from moneylenders and the rich farmers is quite high (nearly 90 per cent) (SERP 2001). Looking at the responses for the different groups, some scheduled castes, scheduled tribes, and other backward classes had to revert to attached/bonded labour. Also, migration has affected their children's education and health.

RISING FOOD PRICES AND HOUSEHOLD RESPONSES

A Rapid Price Impact Survey, 2008, in Bangladesh was conducted by the World Bank to know household responses to price rise (Viswanath 2008). Members from about 1,200 rural and 800 urban households were interviewed in this survey. The results of the survey are given

TABLE 6.3 Household Responses to the Food Price Increase: Bangladesh (in per cent)

Response type	Urban	Rural	Total
Reduce quantity of food intake	72.3	77.9	75.7
Switch to lower quality food	86.9	87.8	87.5
Reduce non-food expenditures	86.0	86.5	86.3
Spend savings/sell belongings	43.5	46.5	45.3
Take out loans	46.3	59.9	54.5
Gift/help from community members	0.9	9.3	6.0
Take children out of school	6.5	8.8	7.9
Decrease education expenses	32.5	43.2	39.0
Work more/increase production	24.6	39.8	33.8
Stop loan payment	3.1	6.1	4.9

Source: Viswanath 2008.

in Table 6.3. It shows that about 43 per cent of households in rural areas reduced their expenses on education while 9 per cent of rural households have taken children out of school.

HUNGER INDEX IN INDIA

The vulnerabilities across states in India can be examined by looking at the hunger index of International Food Policy Research Institute (IFPRI). The hunger index shows that relatively developed states, such as Gujarat, Maharashtra, and Karnataka, rank higher in the hunger index than states such as Uttar Pradesh and Rajasthan and are closer in rank to states such as Orissa and Chhattisgarh (Table 6.4). It shows that poverty and hunger are not strictly correlated and vulnerability of children is high in developed states like Gujarat, Maharashtra, and Karnataka also.

It may be noted that social disparities overwhelm regional disparities regarding poverty and vulnerability and incidence of malnutrition. For example, the numbers in Table 6.5 show that scheduled caste/scheduled tribe and Muslims are suffering from more poverty and vulnerability as compared with other backward classes and other castes. The incidence of malnutrition (chronic energy deficiency) among women is the highest for scheduled castes/scheduled tribes, followed by other backward classes and Muslims. This is true of all the states in India.

Table 6.4 Hunger Index and Components in India: States

State	Prevalence of calorie under-nourishment	Proportion of underweight among children <5 years	Under-5 mortality rate, reported as deaths per hundred	India state hunger index score	India hunger index ranking
India	**20.0**	**42.5**	**7.4**	**23.31**	**NA**
Andhra Pradesh	19.6	32.7	6.3	19.54	3
Assam	14.6	36.4	8.5	19.85	4
Bihar	17.3	56.1	8.5	27.30	15
Chhattisgarh	23.3	47.6	9.0	26.65	14
Gujarat	23.3	44.7	6.1	24.69	13
Haryana	15.1	39.7	5.2	20.01	5
Jharkhand	19.6	57.1	9.3	28.67	16
Karnataka	28.1	37.6	5.5	23.74	11
Kerala	28.6	22.7	1.6	17.66	2
Madhya Pradesh	23.4	59.8	9.4	30.90	17
Maharashtra	27.0	36.7	4.7	22.81	10
Orissa	21.4	40.9	9.1	23.79	12
Punjab	11.1	24.6	5.2	13.64	1
Rajasthan	14.0	40.4	8.5	20.99	7
Tamil Nadu	29.1	30.0	3.5	20.88	6
Uttar Pradesh	14.5	42.3	9.6	22.17	9
West Bengal	18.5	38.5	5.9	21.00	8

Source: IFPRI 2008.

TABLE 6.5 Incidence of Malnutrition among Women (Chronic Energy Deficiency): 2005–6

State	Total population	SC/ST population	OBC population	Muslim population	Others
India	**35.6**	**42.7**	**36.0**	**35.1**	**27.5**
Andhra Pradesh	33.5	38.4	37.0	27.6	22.2
Assam	36.5	34.5	30.4	46.0	31.4
Bihar	45.1	58.4	43.3	49.6	31.4
Chhattisgarh	43.4	46.6	44.8	28.9	26.2
Gujarat	36.3	48.0	40.5	37.0	22.9
Haryana	31.3	36.4	33.1	49.0	26.6
Jharkhand	43.0	44.6	45.3	47.3	26.5
Karnataka	35.5	41.8	34.9	26.9	31.7
Kerala	18.0	24.1	18.6	15.6	18.0
Madhya Pradesh	41.7	48.7	42.2	37.4	27.7
Maharashtra	36.2	43.6	36.1	23.8	34.5
Orissa	41.4	50.6	39.6	63.5	30.7
Punjab	18.9	26.7	18.0	22.5	14.4
Rajasthan	36.7	44.1	33.3	36.1	32.3
Tamil Nadu	28.4	36.1	26.8	20.7	8.3
Uttar Pradesh	36.4	43.6	35.4	36.4	28.3
West Bengal	39.1	45.2	39.2	37.4	31.5

Source: Compiled from Kannan 2008. The data is from NFHS-3 data.
Note: SC: Scheduled Caste; ST: Scheduled Tribe; OBC: Other Backward Class.

POSSIBLE WAYS OF TACKLING THE ADVERSE IMPACTS ON CHILDREN

In this section, we discuss policies at the macro and sectoral level and the social protection measures needed to mitigate the effects of the food and financial crises, which, in turn, would improve the well-being of children. In this context, it is important to ensure that there are measures that combine policies aimed at alleviating household poverty along with specific child-focused policies.

Macro-policies

The macro-policies should follow pro-poor and people-centric policies. Growth and equity objectives should be pursued simultaneously rather than 'growth first and equity next' approach. Here we are concerned with policies that mitigate household poverty in order to reduce the negative impacts on women and children and improve their well-being.

Several governments internationally have responded in varying degrees to contain the rise in prices as well as to mitigate the adverse effects on the poor. The Indian government has used several policies to contain prices. So far the policies of the government in the first round were aimed at stabilizing food prices. It has used instruments such as trade bans, administrative controls on private trade, import tariffs, subsidies, etc., to contain food prices. However, the medium- to longer-term agenda should be to improve agricultural productivity and improve the functioning of social protection programmes.

In order to reduce the impact of the financial crisis, India has taken several monetary and fiscal measures.

The monetary and fiscal measures announced by the RBI (Reserve Bank of India) and the government in 2008–9 were in the right direction, which was to improve liquidity and investor confidence in the economy. When inflation increased in 2010 and 2011, the RBI increased interest rates 13 times from March 2010 to reduce demand. This affected the investment demand much more than consumption demand. The growth rate of 2011–12 declined to 6.5 per cent.

There are, however, different views on the policies that need to be adopted to come out of the financial crisis. One view is that demand should be increased through direct fiscal action by the government. The objective of larger government spending must be to reverse the squeeze on the living standards of the people. 'In short, the new paradigm must entail inter alia a foodgrain-led growth strategy (on the basis of peasant, not corporate, agriculture), sustained through larger government spending, which simultaneously rids the world of both depression and financial and food crises' (Patnaik 2008). In other words, a stimulus package needs to be given to the agricultural sector and primary food producers.

Another view is the one by the National Commission for Enterprises in the Unorganized Sector (NCEUS). According to the NCEUS (2008), immediate attention has to be given to protect the livelihood security, employment, and income of the vast majority of the people who are either poor or vulnerable. This will also stimulate economic growth. The higher growth of the Indian economy in the last 20 years, however, has bypassed 77 per cent of the people. Most of them continue to be illiterate or have only primary-level education and suffer from malnutrition and ill-health. Most of them are unemployed or belong to the working poor, or are self-employed unorganized workers. Among the farmers, 84 per cent are marginal and small farmers having not more than two hectares of land. The total number of agricultural labourers, who constitute the bottom layer of the occupational structure and who include a majority of workers from the scheduled caste and scheduled tribe communities, is about 89 million. The smallest segment of the unorganized sector (with investment below Rs 5 lakh in Plant and Machinery) gets less than 2 per cent of net bank credit while investment below Rs 25 lakh gets 4.3 per cent of formal sector credit.

NCEUS is of the view that given the global financial meltdown and the repercussions on the Indian economy and particularly on the unorganized workers, a major response is urgently required. It advocates a major fiscal stimulus comprising: (i) programmes to boost pro-poor public investments in physical and social infrastructure; (ii) programmes/schemes which protect and promote incomes of the poor; (iii) expansion in scope and coverage of social security schemes of the unorganized workers.

The macro pro-poor policies are expected to help increase the incomes of poor households and reduce the negative effects of higher food prices and the financial crisis. Improvements in household incomes can thus have positive effects on the well-being of women and children.

Sectoral Policies

To counter the rise in food prices and tackle the financial crisis, growth in agriculture and the rural non-farm sector is important along with formulating sectoral-level policies on health and nutrition and women's empowerment.

RAISING AGRICULTURE GROWTH

With the onset of the financial crisis, economic growth has slowed, which is likely to have second-round effects for investment and productivity with a direct impact on food prices and food security (von Braun 2008).

IFPRI projections from 2005 to 2020 compare a scenario of continued high economic growth (as a baseline scenario) with two recession scenarios at the global level (von Braun 2008).

Scenario 1: Economic growth is reduced by 2 to 3 percentage points depending on world regions, and agricultural productivity and investments are maintained by wise policy choices.

Scenario 2: Economic growth is reduced as in scenario 1, and agricultural investment and productivity also decline, in line with the reduced economic growth.

Food prices would increase significantly under Scenario 2. Poor people are likely to consume fewer calories because of recession. Globally, 16 million more children will be malnourished in 2020 compared with the baseline scenario. However, if, developing countries can maintain agricultural productivity and investments under a recession (Scenario 1), the negative effects of the financial crisis can be avoided. Under this scenario, rise in cereal prices and malnourishment will be lower and per capita calorie consumption will be much higher by 2020.

The analysis by IFPRI indicates the importance of agriculture on the food security of households, women, and children. Therefore, India has to focus more on the agriculture sector.

There are several challenges for India to achieve 4 per cent growth and equity in agriculture. The supply- and demand-side constraints have to be removed to raise growth.

There are basically six factors which need to be focused on in the short and medium term. These are: (i) infrastructure; (ii) land and water management; (iii) research and extension; (iv) inputs including credit; (v) marketing including price policy; and (vi) diversification and development of rural non-farm sector.

RURAL NON-FARM SECTOR

Poverty cannot be removed when 55 per cent of workers are in the agricultural sector. There is a need to promote rural non-farm sector. India currently produces about 50 million tonnes of fruits and 90 million tonnes of vegetables. Only 2 per cent of these fruits and vegetables are processed as against 23 per cent of agricultural produce processed by China, 78 per cent by the Phillippines, and 83 per cent by Malaysia. Half of the workers engaged in agriculture are still illiterate, and just 5 per cent have completed higher secondary education. Even in 2011–12, about 56 per cent of rural male workers and 78 per cent of rural female workers were either illiterate or were educated only up to the primary level. In other words, there is a high correlation between education and skills, which can act as a constraint towards poverty reduction.

India can learn from China about effecting rural transformation. China experienced a structural transformation in the last three decades, because the state's role has been decisive in building up the physical and social infrastructure (including land reforms). India can benefit from models used in China for reforms in agriculture, rural non-farm employment, public investment, and human development. The impact of growth on poverty reduction is quite significant (Rao 2005).

SECTORAL INTERVENTION ON NUTRITION AND HEALTH

Economic growth alone cannot address the problems of nutrition and health of women and children. Sector-specific interventions are required in order to improve nutrition and health outcomes. For example, a package consisting of expanded child and maternal benefits such as immunization, antenatal care coverage, nutritional supplementation (including promotion of exclusive breastfeeding), and home-based neonatal services (including treatment of pneumonia) is likely to bring about significant reduction in both infant mortality and child malnutrition (Deolalikar 2004). There is also a need for synergy across sectors—between the processes directed at improving drinking water facilities, sanitation, and public hygiene, access to elementary education, nutrition, and poverty alleviation and the processes that improve access to public health and medical services.

WOMEN'S EMPOWERMENT AND IMPACT ON CHILD WELL-BEING

Advancement in the status of women and their well-being would have a positive spillover impact on child well-being. A comprehensive review of the linkages between women's empowerment and child well-being brought out clearly that there are four mechanisms for transmitting the effects of women's empowerment to child well-being (Jones et al. 2007). They include education, economic empowerment, intra-household decision-making power, and community-level empowerment. Educating the mother is positively associated with better education for children and better health and nutrition outcomes. Greater economic resources may translate into better outcomes for children, because mothers are likely to advocate the interest of their children in intra-household bargaining and to be taken seriously by their male partners.

Social Protection Measures

Comprehensive social protection programmes are required to address the negative effects due to the food price crisis and financial crisis.

Relinquishing economic growth to market forces without social protection buffers would substantially increase risk exposure (health risks, labour market risks) and inequality for large sections of people. The presence of social protection measures can maintain an acceptable minimum floor for social cohesion and can prevent irreversible losses of human capital in hard times. The recent theory and evidence 'offers a new perspective on social protection policies in poor countries, suggesting that there is scope for using these policies to compensate for the market failures that perpetuate poverty, particularly in high-inequality settings' (Ravallion 2003).

India has many social protection programmes. The present major schemes for the poor in India fall into four broad categories: (i) food transfer as in the Public Distribution System (PDS) and supplementary nutrition; (ii) self-employment; (iii) wage employment; and (iv) social security programmes for unorganized workers. There are also many direct programmes for women (see Economic Survey 2004–5). Some of the social protection schemes have to be scaled up and their effectiveness improved.

SOCIAL SECURITY PROGRAMMES FOR UNORGANIZED WORKERS

It is well known that only organized workers, constituting less than 10 per cent of the total workers in India, get all social security benefits. In other words, more than 90 per cent of Indian workers who belong to the unorganized sector do not have contingent social security benefits.

The social security problems of the unorganized workers can be divided into two sets of problems. The first one is 'capability deprivation', understood in terms of inadequate employment, low earnings, low health, and educational status, and which is related to general deprivation of poorer sections of the population. The second one is 'adversity' in the sense of absence of adequate fallback mechanisms to meet contingencies such as ill health, accident, death, and old age (NCEUS 2006).

At present, the central government, state governments, and NGOs provide social security benefits to some unorganized workers. But, these initiatives are for less than 10 per cent of the unorganized workers. The NCEUS has proposed a universal but minimum level of social security for the unorganized workers. It consists of schemes covering (i) sickness and maternity health; (ii) disability and death; and (iii) old age security in the form of a national pension for those belonging to Below Poverty Line (BPL) households and a contributory provident fund for those belonging to Above Poverty Line (APL) households. The NCEUS proposal is estimated to cost the government only half a per cent of GDP for all the unorganized workers.

MEASURES OF FISCAL STIMULUS AND SOCIAL PROTECTION TO REDUCE NEGATIVE EFFECTS OF THE FINANCIAL CRISIS

The NCEUS has proposed several urgent measures and fiscal stimulus to protect the informal economy. These measures are given below.

1. *Enhance pro-poor public investment*: This includes expansion of rural infrastructure, such as roads providing connectivity, housing, drinking water, sanitation, and rural production infrastructure.
2. *Strengthen and expand Mahatma Gandhi National Rural Employment Guarantee Act (MGNREGA)*: With few exceptions, the employment generated under MGNREGA is often less than the legally guaranteed hundred days of employment. The commission provides suggestions for strengthening and expanding the MGNREGA.
3. *Introduce an urban employment guarantee programme*: In order to complement the MGNREGA, an urban employment guarantee programme has to be introduced. The activities can include low-cost housing especially for slum dwellers, electrification, water supply, slum improvement, low-cost waste management, etc.

4. *Strengthen and expand self-employment programmes*: A number of measures have to be taken to graduate micro-finance to livelihood finance. The measures can assist both farm and non-farm workers who are likely to face reduced prospects of employment in the wage market.
5. *Special programme for marginal and small farmers*: Institutional credit for small and marginal farmers has to be improved. Special programmes, such as land improvement, minor irrigation, capacity-building, and training, can be provided for these farmers.
6. *Enhancing access to credit to micro-enterprises*: In times of financial crisis, the small producers will be pushed out of the credit market. Steps have to be taken to increase credit to the unorganized sector of micro-enterprises.
7. *Create a national fund for the unorganized sector*: A national fund for the unorganized sector has to be established in order to step up credit and developmental effort for this sector.
8. *Programme for skill development in the informal economy*: The government has provided measures to expand skill training. But they remain mostly for the organized workers. There is a need to have programmes for giving on-the-job training in unorganized enterprises. This scheme aims at workers who have primary but less than secondary-level education.
9. *A national minimum social security for informal workers*: As mentioned above, the commission has proposed a universal but minimum level of social security for all the unorganized workers in the country.
10. *Strengthen and expand investment in human development of the poor and vulnerable*: The families and children in the informal economy suffer capability deprivation. Given the conditions of poverty and vulnerability and low human capabilities, there is a need to strengthen and expand programmes that improve human development of members of vulnerable households and communities. Here the programmes such as Sarva Shikshan Abhiyan, National Rural Health Mission (NRHM), Public Distribution System (PDS), and Integrated Child Development Services should be expanded and strengthened for the benefit of the unorganized workers.

In order to save the informal sector from collapse, the NCEUS has sought a special package of Rs 58,000 crore to implement all the above programmes. If implemented, these programmes would create about 57 million additional jobs over the next five years.

These recommendations were given in 2008. However, the government had less financial leeway in 2012, as the fiscal deficit was expected to be more than 5.5 per cent of GDP.

INVESTING IN SOCIAL PROTECTION PROGRAMMES

The social protection programmes discussed in this section can help families to cope with the double crises of rise in food prices and the financial meltdown. These programmes also include child-specific policies, such as ensuring adequate nutrition, school-children feeding programmes, health, and education for children.

At the international level, there are many examples of good social protection programmes. Cash transfers are preferred to food or other in-kind transfers, because cash increases the purchasing power of the households (see Rashid 2008). Conditional cash transfers that have worked well include the food-for-education programme in Bangladesh, Mexico's PROGRESA programme, and the Bolsa Escola in Brazil.

GOVERNANCE

The focus of reforms can now be shifted to more efficient delivery systems of public services. It has been recognized that good governance is very important for equitable development. This is imperative for better implementation of sectoral policies and social protection programmes. Social mobilization, community participation, and a decentralized approach are needed as well. It may be noted, however, that governance has to be contextualized in relation to the socio-economic environment. Appropriate institutions are needed for better implementation of policies and programmes. For example, rural institutions to manage land, water, marketing of agricultural and non-agricultural products, credit, technology, and infrastructure are needed for improved governance. Similarly, people-centric programmes and institutions are needed for effective implementation of social protection schemes. Finally, the rights-based approach plays an important role in improving implementation of development programmes. Right to food, right to health, right to education, right to employment, and right to information, etc., put pressure on governments to deliver services to citizens. Also, there is a need for convergence of departments at the macro- and micro-level to improve all indicators of well-being, with special emphasis on malnutrition among children.[1]

★ ★ ★

It may be noted that social inequality is high in India across all the states. Poverty and vulnerability are high for the SCs, STs, and Muslims as compared with OBCs and other castes. This is true of almost all the states. Similarly, malnutrition among women is high among the SCs, STs, OBCs, and Muslims as compared with other castes. Thus, social inequality is as important as or more important than regional inequality.

India has many social protection programmes, which have to be scaled up and effectiveness improved in order to reduce the negative effects of food price rise and financial crisis. Child-specific programmes also need to be scaled up and effectively implemented.

Policymakers and implementers need to be made aware of the effectiveness of convergence of programmes, because results may be achieved at a faster pace than has been achieved during the last 65 years. Ultimately, success depends on political commitment. Commitment at the Centre can contribute significantly to improve the well-being of women and children. State-level experiences also show that political commitment at the state level can play an important role in the successful implementation of programmes and policies, the Tamil Nadu experience being a case in point.

REFERENCES

Bouis, Howarth. 2008. *Rising Food Prices will Result in Severe Declines in Mineral and Vitamin Intakes of the Poor.* Harvestplus, Washington, DC: IFPRI.

von Braun, Joachim. 2008. 'Food and Financial Crisis: Implications for Agriculture and the Poor'. Washington, DC: IFPRI.

Deolalikar, A. 2004. *Attaining Millennium Development Goals in India: Roles of Public Policy and Service Delivery.* Washington, DC: World Bank.

[1] For more on convergence, see Dev 2012.

Dev, S. Mahendra. 2012. 'Agriculture and Nutrition Linkages and Policies in India', Paper submitted to IFPRI, New Delhi.

Dev, S. Mahendra and Jos Mooij. 2004. 'Social Sector Priorities: An Analysis of Budgets and Expenditures in India in the 1990s', *Development Policy Review*, January, 22(1). UK: Blackwell Publishing.

Food and Agriculture Organization of the United Nations (FAO). 2008. 'Agricultural Commodity Markets and the Financial Crisis', Food Outlook, November. Rome: FAO.

Government of India. 2005. 'Economic Survey 2004–05'. Ministry of Finance, Government of India.

International Food Policy Research Institute (IFPRI). 2008. 'The India State Hunger Index: Comparisons of Hunger Across States', Purnima Menon, Anil Deolalikar, Anjor Bhaskar, 14 October. New Delhi: IFPRI.

Jones, Nikola, Madhuri Mukherjee, and S. Galab. 2007. 'Ripple Effects or Deliberate Intentions? Assessing Linkages between Women's Empowerment and Childhood Poverty', UNICEF, Young Lives Social Policy Paper 002, May.

Kannan, K.P. 2008. 'Dualism, Informality and Social Inequality: An Informal Economy Perspective of the Challenge of Inclusive Development in India', Presidential Address, 50th Annual Conference of the Indian Society of Labour Economics, 13–15 December, Giri Institute of Development Studies, Lucknow.

Klotz, C., Saskia de Pee, A. Thorne-Lyman, K. Kraemer, and M. Bloem. 2008. 'Nutrition in the Perfect Storm: Why Micronutrient Malnutrition Will Be a Widespread Health Consequence of High Food Prices', *Sight and Life*, 2: 6–13.

Ministry of Finance. 2011. 'Economic Outlook 2011–12', Economic Advisory Council the Prime Minister, July 2011, Government of India; Mid-term review. New Delhi: Ministry of Finance, Government of India.

National Commission for Enterprises in the Unorganized Sector (NCEUS). 2006. 'Report on Social Security for Unorganized Sector'. Delhi: NCEUS.

———. 2008. 'The Global Economic Crisis and the Informal Economy in India: Need for Urgent Measures and Fiscal Stimulus to Protect the Informal Economy', Note submitted to the Prime Minister of India by NCEUS, Delhi.

Patnaik, Prabhat. 2008. 'The Present Crisis and the Way Forward', *The Hindu*, 14 November.

Plan and ODI. 2008. 'Understanding the Impact of Food Prices on Children'. London: Plan UK.

Quisumbing, A., Ruth Meinzen-Dick, and Lucy Bassett. 2008. 'Helping Women Respond to the Global Food Price Crisis', IFPRI Policy Brief 7, Washington, DC.

Rao, C.H.H. 2005. *Agriculture, Food Security, Poverty and Environment*. New Delhi: Oxford University Press.

Rashid, Mansoora. 2008. 'Safety Nets: South Asia and Worldwide: Addressing Chronic Poverty and Coping with Shocks', Presentation at the conference on food price crisis in South Asia, jointly sponsored by the World Bank Insitute, South Asia Region of the World Bank, and the Bangladesh Power and Participation Research Centre (PPRC), 15–16 November 2008, Dhaka.

Ravallion, M. 2003. 'The Debate on Globalization, Poverty & Inequality: Why Measurement Matters', World Bank Policy Research Working Paper 3038. Washington, DC: World Bank.

Reserve Bank of India (RBI). 2011. 'Annual Report, 2010–11'. Mumbai: RBI.

Society for Elimination of Rural Poverty (SERP). 2001. 'Livelihood Assessment Report', Society for Elimination of Rural Poverty, Hyderabad.

Viswanath, Tara. 2008. 'Impact of Rising Food Prices on Poverty: South Asia Region', Powerpoint Presentation at the Conference on 'South Asia Regional Conference on Managing Food Price Inflation' organized by the World Bank, 15–16 November, Dhaka, Bangladesh.

Viswanath, Tara and Umar Serajuddin. 2010. 'Welfare Impacts of Rising Food Prices in South Asian Countries', in Sadiq Ahmed and Hans G.P. Jansen (eds), *Managing Food Inflation in South Asia*, pp. 45–84. Dhaka: The University Press Limited.

World Bank. 2008. 'Double Jeopardy: Responding to High food and Fuel prices', G8 Hokkaido-Tokyo Summit.

7 The Tryst Compromised

India's Fiscal Policy and Its Impact on Children

Praveen Jha and Subrat Das*

> Long years ago we made a tryst with destiny, and now the time comes when we shall redeem our pledge, not wholly or in full measure, but very substantially... The service of India means, the service of the millions who suffer. It means the ending of poverty and ignorance and disease and inequality of opportunity. The ambition of the greatest man of our generation has been to wipe every tear from every eye.
>
> —Pandit Jawaharlal Nehru, on the eve of India's Independence

Pandit Nehru's stirring speech on the eve of Independence may be considered as having the most inspirational vision and agenda for the citizens of any country in the modern era. It had promised freedom from a whole range of deprivations within a foreseeable future. Sixty-seven years down the road, revisiting that speech, the authors find that India has fallen short of fulfilling the most basic promises to some of the country's most disadvantaged sections of population, in particular the children of such sections.

*This chapter draws significantly from the research on a number of themes being pursued at Centre for Budget and Governance Accountability (CBGA), New Delhi.

A large proportion of India's children are highly vulnerable, as they are exposed to a range of deprivations and difficult circumstances, some of the alarming manifestations of which are a relatively high rate of infant mortality, a very high proportion of children under the age of three years being underweight, a large number of children being out of school, the educational attainments of children enrolled in schools being very modest, and the prevalence of child labour in almost all states in the country. The central government and state governments have undertaken a number of interventions through development programmes/schemes focusing on children; however, the outcomes of many such government interventions are believed to have been far from satisfactory. While on the one hand, acute shortage of financial resources has often been cited as a major constraint for many such child-focused government interventions, on the other, ineffective implementation of the programmes and schemes has been seen as a common problem in this domain. In this context, the present chapter attempts to map the fiscal policy space available to the government in India for making public investments in children.

The first section of the chapter discusses the need for stepping up prioritization in India's Union Budget and state budgets of the social sectors, in general, and child-focused interventions, in particular. It sketches the problem of acute shortage of resources for social sectors in the country and highlights, in that context, the need for an expansion of the fiscal policy space available to the government in India. In the second section, the chapter briefly discusses the gradual shrinking of the fiscal policy space in the country over the last one and a half decades. The third section then focuses on the need for and the feasibility of improving the country's tax–GDP ratio, which would enable the Indian government to provide more resources for development spending in crucial sectors.

BUDGETARY RESOURCES FOR SOCIAL SECTORS AND INVESTMENTS FOCUSED ON CHILDREN

With regard to state intervention for the development of any of the disadvantaged sections of the population, the policy priorities underlying public investments by the government have considerable significance. The policy priorities of any government in power are reflected in the trends and patterns of its public expenditure. The structures and processes pertaining to the Union Budget of India and the state budgets need to be taken into account in any substantive analysis of the country's fiscal policy and public expenditure.

As per the budgetary classification being followed in the country, government's functions can be divided into three distinct categories, namely, social services, economic services, and general services. Social services or social sectors include a range of sectors where government interventions are expected to have a direct influence on human development, such as education, health and family welfare, water supply and sanitation, social security and welfare, and nutrition. Economic services include a host of sectors, such as agriculture and allied activities, roads and transportation, power, and telecommunications, where government interventions are likely to have a direct impact on income-generation activities in the country. All those sectors that are left out of both social and economic services, such as defence, police, running of different organs of the state, and interest payments and pension, are clubbed under general services.

While the adequacy and quality of public expenditure in general can be expected to benefit all sections of the population, including children, most of the direct government interventions for children (such as those pertaining to children's education, health, early childhood care and nutrition, and protection of children in difficult circumstances) fall under social services or social sectors. Hence, it would be pertinent to examine the priorities for social sectors within India's public expenditure over the last decade.

Inadequacy of India's Total Public Spending on Social Sectors

India's total public spending every year on social sectors (that is, combined budgetary spending by centre and states on sectors such as education, health, water and sanitation, and nutrition) continues to be less than 7 per cent of the country's Gross Domestic Product (GDP), while most of the developed countries have been investing much greater magnitudes of public resources on such sectors for decades now. The average level of budgetary spending on social sectors in the Organisation for Economic Cooperation and Development (OECD) countries in 2006 (excluding their social security payments) was 14 per cent of GDP, nearly double the level of budgetary spending on social sectors in India.

In OECD countries, apart from the conventional social sectors, such as education, health, and housing and community amenities, their budgets apportion a large share of expenditure towards social protection. Table 7.1 presents relevant data on OECD countries' budgetary spending on social sectors (including expenditure on social protection), as a proportion of the total budget, as of 2011. As shown in this table, the priority accorded to social sectors (including social protection) in the budgets of the 31 OECD countries was as high as two-thirds (66 per cent) of the budget on an average. While this information pertains to the most recent time period for which the relevant data are available, it is well known that many of the developed countries have been investing relatively high magnitudes of public resources on social sectors for decades now.

However, the priority for social sectors in India's budgets has been much lower. Table 7.2 shows that India's budgetary expenditure (by Centre and states combined) on social sectors has accounted for less than 25 per cent of the total budget for most of the years over the last decade, with this proportion rising to 25 per cent or higher only in the most recent years. If we look at India's budgetary expenditure on social sectors in comparison to the size of the country's economy, that is, as proportions to India's GDP, the scenario looks even more disturbing.

The D.S. Kothari Commission had recommended in 1966 that India's total budgetary expenditure on education should be raised to 6 per cent of the Gross National Product (GNP) by 1986. Subsequently, a slightly modified version of this policy prescription, that is, raising the country's total budgetary expenditure on education to 6 per cent of the GDP, became popular and was reiterated in the promises made by a number of national political parties over the last few decades. A worthwhile reference in this regard would be to the National Common Minimum Programme (NCMP) of the United Progressive Alliance (UPA) government at the Centre in 2004, which talked about increasing the total public spending on education in India to 6 per cent of GDP by 2008–9. The same NCMP of the UPA had also acknowledged the need for increasing the country's total public spending on health to 2–3 per cent of GDP by 2008–9. However, even in 2010–11, India's

Table 7.1 OECD Countries' Budgetary Spending on Social Sectors (including Expenditure on Social Protection) as a Percentage of the Total Budget (as of 2011)

Country	Expenditure as a percentage of total budget					
	Housing and communities amenities	Health	Recreation, culture and religion	Education	Social security payments/social protection	Total social sectors (including social security payments)
OECD average (average for 31 OECD countries*)	1.9	14.7	2.7	13.1	33.5	65.9

Source: Compiled from the data provided in OECD 2011.

Note: * The 31 countries in OECD, whose budgetary expenditures have been taken into account here, are: Australia, Austria, Belgium, Canada, Czech Republic, Denmark, Estonia, Finland, France, Germany, Greece, Hungary, Iceland, Ireland, Israel, Italy, Japan, Korea, Luxembourg, Netherlands, New Zealand, Norway, Poland, Portugal, Slovak Republic, Slovenia, Spain, Sweden, Switzerland, UK, and US.

TABLE 7.2 India's Budgetary Expenditure (by Centre and States Combined)* on Social Services

Year	Total budgetary expenditure (by Centre and states) as % of GDP	Social services expenditure (by Centre and states) as % of GDP	Total Expenditure on social services as % of total budget
2004–5	25.4	5.3	20.9
2005–6	25.3	5.5	21.7
2006–7	25.3	5.8	22.9
2007–8	24.9	5.8	23.3
2008–9	27.2	6.6	24.3
2009–10 (RE)	28.0	7.1	25.4
2010–11 (BE)	25.7	6.7	26.1

Source: Compiled from the data provided in GoI 2011.
Note: RE: Revised Estimates; BE: Budget Estimates.
* This refers to the total expenditure from Union Budget of India and state budgets combined; without any double counting of the inter-governmental transfers like central grants and loans to the states.

total public spending on all social sectors combined (that is, education, health, water and sanitation, nutrition, and social security and welfare, among others) hovered over a very low magnitude of 6.7 per cent of GDP; the total public spending on education was about 3.5 per cent of GDP, while that on health was about 1 per cent of GDP. There can be little doubt about the inadequacy of India's total public spending on social sectors as compared with the size of its economy and the low priority accorded to social sectors in the country's budgets.

Budgetary Resources vis-à-vis Poor Implementation

Over the last few years, several policymakers and development policy analysts have observed that the central government has increased the magnitude of budgetary support for social sectors quite significantly since 2004–5, and the problem now is not of shortage of resources but of poor implementation or utilization of these resources in the social sectors. However, this is a misleading hypothesis that does not take into account some of the key aspects of the federal fiscal architecture in India and the causal factors underlying the phenomenon of poor utilization of funds in social sector programmes and schemes.

As we discuss further, the total budgetary spending on social sectors in India continues to be far below the desired levels. The availability of resources has improved only in specific programmes and schemes launched by the central government ministries in some of the social sectors, and the problem of underutilization of available budgetary resources, too, is prevalent mainly in such central programmes and schemes. Also, the inability of the state governments to fully utilize the available funds in the central schemes is rooted in the fact that some aspects of the fiscal policy adopted over the last decade have resulted in systemic weaknesses in the government apparatus in social sectors across many states; and also because of the rigidity in the norms, guidelines, and unit costs governing the central schemes and the lack of fiscal decentralization from Centre to state governments as well as from state governments to local governments in most of the states.

Over the last one and a half decades, the direct contribution by the central government to India's total public spending on social sectors has been only about 30 per cent, which has been less than 2 per cent of GDP every year. Hence, the gradual increases in social sector spending from the Union Budget witnessed over the last eight years (that is, since 2004–5) have not translated into any visible increase in total public spending on these sectors in the country, as most of the state governments have not made any significant increase in their budgetary spending on these sectors.

As shown in Table 7.3, the direct contribution from the Union Budget for social sector spending in India has gone up from a meager 1.2 per cent of GDP in 2004–5 to 2 per cent of GDP in 2010–11; however, as we had observed with reference to Table 7.2 earlier, the total magnitude of budgetary spending (by centre and states combined) has increased from 5.3 per cent of GDP in 2004–5 to 6.7 per cent of GDP in 2010–11. Given that most of the developed countries and some of the developing countries have been spending much higher magnitudes of their public resources for social sectors since many decades now, and that the deficits in social sectors in India can be expected to have aggravated over time because of the persistence of the problem of resource shortage, the present level of total public spending on social sectors in India cannot be considered adequate. The poor quality of infrastructure (for example, schools, hospitals/health care centres, and *anganwadi* centres) in these sectors, the shortage of qualified and trained human resources for delivery of services (for example, teachers, doctors, paramedical personnel, and anganwadi workers), the shortage of human resources for management of the programmes (for example, staff for monitoring and supervision and also for finance and accounts), and the unacceptably low levels of unit costs for provisioning of various services in these sectors are all manifestations of the acute shortage of public resources in social sectors in India.

However, as observed earlier, the underutilization of available budgetary resources in some of the states has been cited by many observers and policymakers as the key problem in social sectors in the country at present. We need to note in this context that the problem of underutilization of available budgetary resources is prevalent mainly in the central programmes and schemes in the social sectors and not in the general budgetary resources provided mostly by the state governments for these sectors.

TABLE 7.3 Priority for Social Services in the Union Budgets of India

Year	Expenditure from the union budget on social services* (in Rs crore)	Expenditure from the union budget on social services*	
		As % of total expenditure from the union budget	As % of GDP
2004–5	39,123	7.9	1.2
2005–6	49,535	9.8	1.3
2006–7	55,246	9.5	1.3
2007–8	78,818	11.1	1.6
2008–9	110,542	12.5	2.0
2009–10	122,345	11.9	1.9
2010–11	151,013	12.6	2.0
2011–12 (RE)	162,277	12.3	1.8
2012–13 (BE)	194,442	13.0	1.9

Source: CBGA 2012.

Notes: RE: Revised Estimates; BE: Budget Estimates.

* This figure does not include non-Plan capital expenditure from the Union Budget on Social Services, if any. Non-plan capital expenditure on Social Services is sporadic and usually of a very small magnitude. Hence, the figure presented here captures almost the entire magnitude of expenditure on Social Services from the Union Budget. Non-plan expenditure is explained in the next section.

Public expenditure in India is usually divided into two categories, namely, Plan expenditure, which refers to all kinds of public expenditure incurred on the programmes and schemes laid out in the ongoing Five-Year Plan (simply referred to as Plan), such as expenditure incurred on Sarva Shiksha Abhiyan, Mid-Day Meal Scheme (MDMS), and Integrated Child Development Services (ICDS) I, among others, and non-Plan expenditure, which refers to all kinds of public expenditure that is outside the purview of the Five-Year Plan, such as expenditure on defence services, interest payments, organs of the state, and on the running of existing government institutions in different sectors, among others. In the case of non-Plan expenditure, a very large part of this category of expenditure in the states is meant for the salaries of staff working for the government. Since such payments are in the nature of 'entitlements', it would be much easier for government departments to disburse the funds meant for such payments when the concerned staff members are already in place. Hence, the ability of the state governments to utilize their non-Plan budget outlays is not in question. With regard to the Plan expenditure, however, several states have shown noticeable levels of underutilization of Plan budget outlays, especially in the social sectors.

The findings of a series of studies conducted by the CBGA, New Delhi (*Budgeting for Change* series, CBGA and UNICEF, 2012) throws light on a set of institutional and procedural constraints, which need to be removed in order to enable the states to effectively utilize greater magnitudes of Plan outlays in the social sectors. This series has analysed the implementation of major Plan schemes for children, such as Sarva Shiksha Abhiyan, Mid-Day Meal, Reproductive and Child Health Programme (RCH), Universal Immunization Programme, ICDS, National Child Labour Project, and Total Sanitation Campaign at the district level in selected states. With regard to the selected Plan programmes and schemes for children, the study finds that a number of problems have been observed across various states over the last few years, particularly in the backward states. These are:

1. Low capacity of some of the states to increase spending in the Plan schemes, which is evident from the noticeable levels of unspent budget outlays left with some of the states and low levels of actual spending as compared with approved budgets for the schemes in many states; and

2. Poor quality of spending and fund utilization in the Plan schemes, because, first, the fund utilization levels are skewed across the four quarters in a fiscal year (typically, a large share of spending getting crowded in the last two quarters), second, fund utilization levels are skewed across different components in a scheme (spending on those components increases quickly where it is easier to disburse money as compared with some other components that require greater efforts from the implementing agencies), and, third, fund utilization levels are skewed across different regions.

Some of the main reasons for such underutilization of Plan outlays by the states in the child-focused schemes can be traced to the institutional and procedural bottlenecks in the process of implementation of Plan programmes and schemes and deficiencies in the planning process being followed at the district level.

The above-mentioned series identifies a number of factors that could be responsible for the identified problems in the levels and quality of fund utilization in Plan schemes for children, which can be broadly divided into the following categories:

1. The first set of factors pertains to the deficiencies in decentralized planning of most of the schemes that is caused by a shortage of staff to carry out planning activities, lack of emphasis on training and capacity building of staff and community leaders for decentralized planning, and inadequate emphasis on community participation in the planning process.
2. The second set of factors pertains to bottlenecks in budgetary processes in the schemes, such as delay in the flow of funds, delay in sending sanction orders for spending, decision-making being centralized within the states, low delegation of financial powers to the district and sub-district-level authorities, uniform norms of centrally sponsored schemes for all states, incomprehensibility of guidelines of some of the centrally sponsored schemes, very low unit costs that are in reality unrealistic, and weak monitoring and supervision of programme implementation activities.
3. The third set of factors relates to systemic weaknesses in the government apparatus in the states, particularly the less developed states. A shortage of trained, regular staff for various important roles like management, finance and accounts, and frontline service provision has weakened the capacity of the government apparatus

to implement Plan schemes. Weak infrastructural facilities within the government apparatus, too, have had an adverse impact. Moreover, too many Plan schemes are being implemented in most of the states, without adequate convergence and integration across them.

As regards the last set of factors mentioned above, that is, the systemic weaknesses in the government apparatus in the states, it can be argued that non-Plan expenditure by the state plays an important role in improving the capacity of the government apparatus. Non Plan expenditure shapes, to a significant extent, the strength of the state government apparatus, in terms of the availability of regular qualified staff and adequacy of the government infrastructure, for implementing Plan programmes and schemes. However, over the last decade, non-Plan expenditure in social services has been checked by many states owing to the emphasis of the prevailing fiscal policy on the reduction of deficits through the curtailment of public expenditure. As a result, the capacity of the government apparatus to implement Plan programmes and schemes has been adversely affected. Thus, the country needs to have a fiscal policy that enables the state governments to increase non-Plan spending in the development sectors. The institutional and procedural bottlenecks in planning, fund flow, and fund utilization processes need to be removed through concerted efforts by both the Centre and the states. Moreover, there is also a need for imparting some flexibility to the states vis-à-vis the norms, guidelines, and unit costs in the central schemes.

Low Priority for Child-focused Investments from Budgets and Neglect of Critical Areas of Child Well-being

The inadequacy of the total public spending on social sectors and the poor quality of utilization of available funds in some of the social sector programmes/schemes are factors that would necessarily have had an adverse impact on government interventions in India for the well-being of children. However, the availability of budgetary resources for government programmes/schemes focused on children and the composition of such resources merit further scrutiny. Over the last decade, some of the civil society organizations in the country (like HAQ: Centre for Child Rights and CGBA, amongst others) have been tracking the quantum of public investments from the Union Budget and budgets of different states that are meant for child-specific schemes (that is, development programmes or schemes which are meant largely for the benefit of children).

Studies done by these organizations have revealed some trends and patterns that are worth taking into account here. For instance, the CBGA–UNICEF (2012) series show that:

1. With regard to state budgets (like those of Uttar Pradesh, Madhya Pradesh, Rajasthan, Odisha, Bihar, and Chhattisgarh during the years 2004–5 to 2007–8), the budgetary resources allocated for educational services for children (that is, all kinds of educational facilities up to higher secondary level) account for a very large share (about 90 per cent) of the total resources from the state budget that are allocated for child-specific programmes and schemes.
2. Government interventions pertaining to early childhood care and nutrition, child health, and protection of children in difficult circumstances are financed by the remaining 10 per cent of the total resources from the state budget allocated for child-specific programmes and schemes; hence, the problem of shortage of resources/under-funded government interventions is much more acute in these three areas than it would be in child education.
3. In these three areas of child well-being, namely, early childhood care and nutrition, child health, and protection of children in difficult circumstances, most of the states are dependent largely on central programmes and schemes and hence allocations for such schemes from the Union Budget.
4. The priority accorded to the quantum of resources earmarked for the child-specific government interventions has not been high in any of the state budgets examined; resources vary from 13 per cent to 18 per cent of the total state budget, depending significantly on the priority for education within the state budget in a year. For instance, in 2006–7 BE, the total budgetary resources allocated for child-specific schemes accounted for 15.2 per cent of the state budget for Rajasthan, 14.8 per cent for Uttar Pradesh, and 14.4 per cent for Madhya Pradesh.

With this backdrop, it would be worthwhile to look at the trends and patterns emerging from such analyses of the Union Budgets in a little more detail. Figure 7.1 shows the priority accorded to child-specific schemes in the Union Budgets of India (that is, the combined allocation from the Union Budget for all central schemes that are meant largely for children) during the five years from 2007–8 to 2012–13. It can be seen that the total budgetary resources for child-specific schemes accounted for only 4 per cent of the total Union Budget (RE) in 2007–8, which increased to 4.8 per cent of the Union Budget in 2012–13 (BE). Even at the level of 4.8 per cent of the total expenditure from the Union Budget, the priority accorded to child-specific schemes appears to be very low when we take into account the fact that children (that is, all persons up to the age of 18 years) constitute more than 41 per cent of the country's population and that a large proportion of India's children are highly vulnerable, as they are exposed to a range of deprivations and difficult circumstances. Thus, the central government and state governments in India need to significantly step up the quantum of public investments on interventions targeted at children.

Figure 7.2 shows the sector-wise prioritization of the total outlay for child-specific schemes in the Union Budget continues to be highly

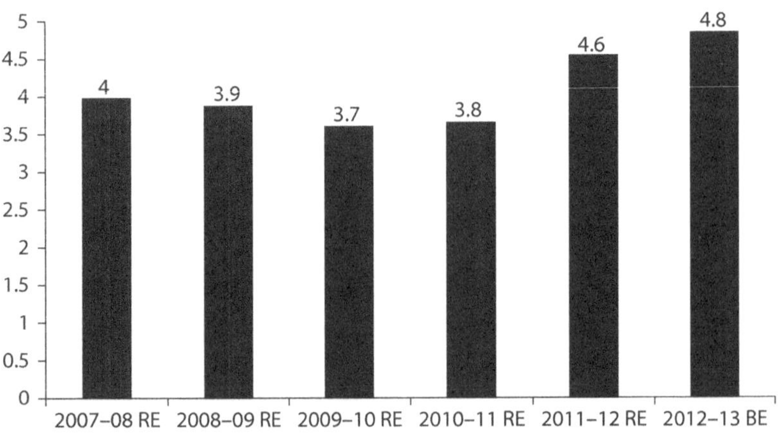

FIGURE 7.1 Outlays for Child-specific Schemes as a Proportion of the Total Union Budget (in per cent)

Source: CBGA 2012.

Note: RE: Revised Estimates; BE: Budget Estimates.

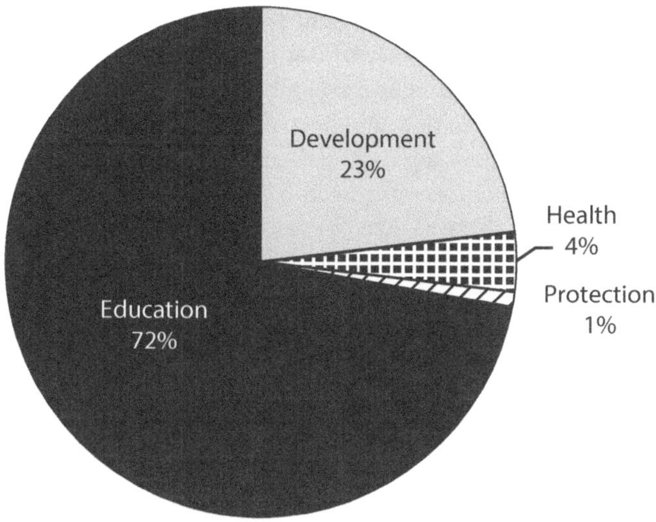

FIGURE 7.2 Sector-wise Composition of the Total Outlay for Child-specific Schemes in Union Budget 2012–13 (BE)
Source: CBGA 2012.

skewed in favour of child education (which includes funds for Sarva Shiksha Abhiyan, MDMS, Rashtriya Madhyamik Shiksha Abhiyan, Kendriya Vidyalayas, Navodaya Vidyalayas, etc.) and child development (which includes funds for schemes like ICDS, National Crèche Scheme, etc.), whereas child health (which includes funds for schemes, such as Immunization Programmes, RCH programme, and Children's Hospital) and child protection (which includes National Child Labour Project and Integrated Child Protection Scheme, among others) are neglected. Hence, the investments from the Union Budget and state budgets need to be stepped up particularly for interventions in the hitherto neglected sectors of child health and protection of children in difficult circumstances.

The foregoing discussion clearly indicates the need for enhancing prioritization in India's Union Budget and state budgets for social sectors, in general, and child-focused interventions, in particular. But, a reprioritization of the government budgets alone will not address the problem of acute shortage of resources in these sectors, and, also, it could be very difficult for the government to reduce the budgetary allocations being provided to any sector (for generating additional budgetary resources for social sectors) at present. Hence, a substantive and lasting remedy of this problem of acute shortage of resources for social sectors would be possible only through an expansion of the total fiscal policy space available to the government in India. However, over the last one and a half decades, there has been a gradual shrinking of the fiscal policy space in the country, as discussed briefly in the subsequent section.

FISCAL POLICY SPACE IN INDIA

In any country, the space for fiscal policy available to the government is reflected in the magnitude of its total expenditure, that is, the magnitude of the government budget. A comparison of the magnitude of total government expenditure (compared to the size of the country's economy) in different countries for various years between 1997 and 2002, as presented in Figure 7.3, reveals that the magnitude of total public expenditure in India has been significantly smaller than that in several developed countries as well as in some of the developing countries. Thus, the total fiscal policy space available in India for public investments towards the socio-economic development of the country appears to be limited in comparison to that of several other countries.

Table 7.4 depicts the trend in the magnitude of total public expenditure in India over the last one and a half decades. On the whole, this shows that the combined budgetary expenditure by centre and states has shown a decline from 26.5 per cent of GDP at the end of the 1990s to 25 per cent of GDP by the end of the last decade. This shrinking magnitude of the combined budgetary expenditure by centre and states indicates the nature of the fiscal policy adhered to by the successive governments at the centre since the late 1990s.

The fiscal policy adopted by successive governments at the centre over the last one and a half decades has been marked by 'fiscal conservatism', which advocated strongly for reducing the magnitude of deficits in the government's budget so that the size of public debt could be kept under check. The implications of government borrowing for the Indian economy, which, according to several economists, had been demand-constrained over the last decade, and the question

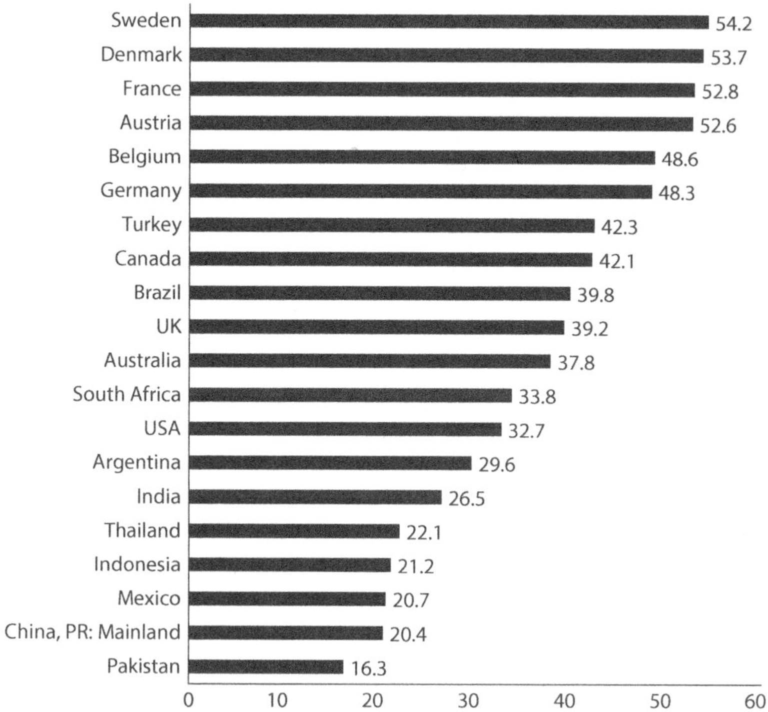

FIGURE 7.3 Total Public Expenditure across Different Countries (as % of GDP)

Source: Based on the data provided in Lorie 2003.

of sustainability of public debt in India have been intensely debated among economists of different schools of thought. However, the policymakers at the centre have consistently adhered to fiscal conservatism since the 1990s, with the exception of just a couple of years during 2008–9 and 2009–10 when the country was witnessing the adverse impact of the global economic recession, and the central government responded to the same with an economic stimulus package strongly backed by an expansionary fiscal policy. As soon as the Indian economy was perceived to have overcome the recessionary impact, the centre revived its fiscal orthodoxy in 2010–11, and the combined budgetary expenditure by centre and states fell from 28 per cent of GDP in 2009–10 (RE) to 25.1 per cent of GDP in 2010–11 (BE).

TABLE 7.4 Total Public Expenditure in India

Year	GDP at market prices (at current prices, in Rs crore)	Total public expenditure in India* (in Rs crore)	Total public expenditure as % of GDP
1990–1	569,624	155,142	27.2
1998–9	1,751,199	445,980	25.5
1999–2000	1,952,035	517,056	26.5
2000–1	2,102,314	552,125	26.3
2001–2	2,278,952	613,591	26.9
2002–3	2,454,561	661,664	27.0
2003–4	2,754,621	762,765	27.7
2004–5	3,242,209	824,480	25.4
2005–6	3,692,485	933,642	25.3
2006–7	4,293,672	1,086,592	25.3
2007–8	4,986,426	1,243,598	24.9
2008–9	5,582,623	1,519,081	27.2
2009–10 (RE)	6,550,271	1,833,730	28.0
2010–11 (BE)	7,877,947	1,973,762	25.1

Source: Compiled from the data provided in GoI 2008 and 2011.
* This figure presents the combined (centre + states) expenditure, incurred from the Union Budget and budgets of all the states and UTs (at current prices).

Table 7.5 depicts the trend in the magnitude of the central government's total expenditure over the last decade. The total expenditure by the centre has shown a decline from 15 per cent of GDP at the beginning of the last decade to 14 per cent of GDP by the end of the decade. This declining trend in the magnitude of total expenditure by the centre, as compared with the size of the country's economy, reiterates the fact that successive governments at the centre have made a conscious effort to check the fiscal policy space utilized by the government over the last decade. This, as mentioned earlier, was seen as necessary for reducing the magnitude of borrowing by the government.

Even if one does not question the economic rationale for the government's efforts to reduce the size of the public debt, the means through which it is pursued does raise serious concerns. As we discuss in the next section, India's performance in increasing the magnitude of public revenue collected through taxes has been quite unsatisfactory.

TABLE 7.5 Central Government's Total Expenditure

Year	Central government's total expenditure# (in Rs crore)	Central government's total expenditure as % of GDP
1990–1	1,00,884	17.7
2000–1	3,13,011	14.9
2002–3	3,67,227	15.0
2003–4	3,59,839*	13.1*
2004–5	4,02,550*	12.4*
2005–6	4,96,614*	13.4*
2006–7	5,64,934	13.2
2007–8	7,01,985	14.1
2008–9	8,74,831	15.7
2009–10 (RE)	10,24,497	15.6
2010–11 (BE)	11,00,692	14.0

Source: Compiled from the data provided in GoI 2008 and 2011.

Notes: # This figure presents the Total Expenditure incurred from the Union Budget (at current prices).

* The figures for central government's total expenditure for the years 2003–4, 2004–5, and 2005–6 as reported in this table (based on the *Indian Public Finance Statistics 2010–11*), are lower than the figures reported in the Union Budget documents. This is on account of the difference in treatment of the 'repayment of loans' by states to centre, the concurrent 'repayment of loans' by the centre to the National Small Savings Fund (NSSF), and the issue of fresh loans (at a lower interest rate than before) by the NSSF to states—under the Debt Swap Scheme, which was carried out during 2003–4 to 2005–6. In the authors' view, the figures reported by the *Indian Public Finance Statistics 2010–11* are a more accurate depiction of the total expenditure by the central government during those three years.

Instead of trying to improve the tax–GDP ratio for the country, the path adopted for checking the size of public debt has been that of expenditure compression. Besides reducing the magnitude of total expenditure from the Union Budget (as compared to the GDP), the centre has also advocated strongly for a check on public spending by the states over the last one and a half decades.

In order to expand the fiscal policy space for public investments in social sectors, the magnitude of total public expenditure in India needs to be increased. Therefore, it would be pertinent to discuss the scope for a significant increase in the magnitude of tax revenue mobilized in the country, which is taken up in the next section.

EXPANDING THE FISCAL POLICY SPACE THROUGH TAX REVENUE

The magnitude of public resources available to the government in India has been grossly inadequate in comparison with several other countries, mainly owing to the low magnitude of tax revenue collected in the country. A comparison of the magnitude of total tax revenue mobilized by the government (as compared with the size of the country's economy) in different countries for various years between 1998 and 2002, as presented in Figure 7.4, shows that the amount of tax revenue collected in India has been significantly lower than that in several developed countries as well as in some of the developing countries. The total tax revenue collected by centre and states (combined) has fallen from the already low level of 17.4 per cent of GDP in 2007–8 to 14.7 per cent of GDP in 2010–11 (BE) (GoI 2011). Even in the

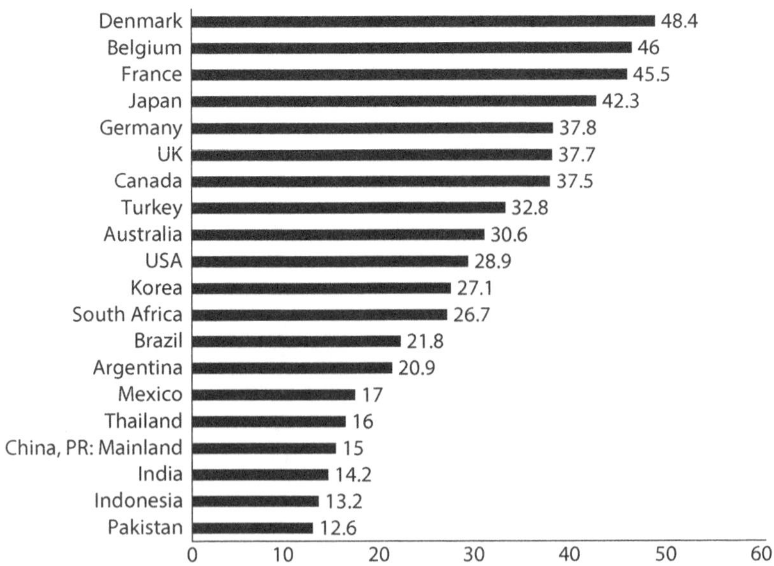

FIGURE 7.4 Total Tax Revenue across Different Countries (as % of GDP)
Source: Based on the data provided in Lorie 2003.

TABLE 7.6 Tax–GDP Ratios for Selected Countries

Developed countries	Developing countries
Sweden: 50.1	Brazil: 34.2
Denmark: 49.1	Turkey: 32.5
France: 44.7	Russia: 32.3
Netherlands: 39.5	South Africa: 31.2
UK: 37.4	Ghana: 22.4
USA: 27.3	China: 16.6

Source: IMF 2011.

Note: The tax revenue figures (used for computing the tax–GDP ratios) include social security contributions, if any.

most recent years, India's tax–GDP ratio compares poorly against those of several other countries (see Table 7.6).

Hence, it is critical to emphasize the need for and the feasibility of increasing the country's tax–GDP ratio, which would enable the Indian government to provide more resources for development spending in crucial sectors. Moreover, of the total tax revenue of the country at 14.73 per cent of GDP (in 2010–11), while indirect taxes account for 9.25 per cent of GDP, direct taxes account for only 5.48 per cent of GDP (GoI 2011). Thus, India's tax system, which collects almost two-thirds of the revenue from indirect taxes and only one-third from direct taxes, is regressive as compared with the tax system of many other countries that collect a much higher proportion of tax revenue from direct taxes. If India is to move towards a more progressive tax system, the government should rely more on direct taxes (such as, corporation tax, personal income tax, and wealth tax).

India's total revenue collection from wealth taxes (which include wealth tax, inheritance tax, and gift tax) was just about Rs 1,000 crore in 2011–12; and it is projected to be Rs 1,244 crore in 2012–13 (that is, a meagre 0.0001 per cent of the country's GDP). However, several developed countries collect sizable amounts of revenue from wealth taxes, as is indicated in Table 7.7. Hence, the present system of a flat rate of 1 per cent wealth tax being levied on specified assets needs to be overhauled.

With regard to the serious concern of India's low tax–GDP ratio, the rationale for increasing the rate of securities transaction tax (STT)

Table 7.7 Revenue Collected from Property Taxes in Selected Countries (as per cent of GDP)

Country	Total tax revenue as % of GDP	Collections from different kinds of taxes on property					Total taxes on property (as % of GDP)
		Recurrent taxes on immovable property (as % of GDP)	Estate, inheritance, and gift taxes (as % of GDP)	Recurrent taxes on net wealth (as % of GDP)	Non-recurrent taxes (as % of GDP)	Other recurrent taxes on property (as % of GDP)	
Japan	17.6	2.03	0.31	2.03	–	–	4.37
UK	35.7	3.27	0.23	–	–	–	3.50
Canada	32.2	2.77	–	0.15	0.21	–	3.14
US	26.9	2.90	0.24	–	–	–	3.13
France	43.1	2.19	0.41	0.22	–	–	2.81
Iceland	36.0	1.67	0.08	–	–	–	1.75
Italy	43.2	0.64	0.03	0.64	0.01	0.08	1.39
Germany	36.4	0.43	0.19	0.00	–	–	0.63
Korea	26.6	0.10	0.03	–	–	–	0.12

Source: Compiled by CBGA from OECD 2008.

is plausible. The principle underlying STT is to 'curb purely short-term speculation by big operators, FIIs [foreign institutional investors] and fund managers without significantly affecting the long-term investors' (Singh 2001). Short-term trading is considered to be one of the major factors responsible for market volatility and the STT ensures stability in the financial markets. It had been estimated (more than a decade ago) that a 0.25 per cent rate of STT would generate tax revenue of Rs 37.5 crore every day and Rs 9,375 crore every year (Singh 2001). But the rate of STT was reduced in the latest Union Budget (2012–13) from an already low level of 0.125 per cent to 0.1 per cent.

The total magnitude of tax revenue forgone owing to exemptions/deductions/incentives in the central government tax system is estimated (by the Union Ministry of Finance) to be Rs 529,432 crore in 2011–12. What it implies is: the estimated amount of additional tax revenue that could have been collected by the central government in 2011–12, if all exemptions/deductions/incentives (both in direct and indirect taxes in the central government tax system) had been eliminated, is a staggering 6 per cent of GDP (see Table 7.8).

At present, on an average, the statutory tax rate for corporations is 33 per cent, but the effective tax rate paid by them is only around 24 per cent. As per Annex 15 of Receipts Budget in the Union Budget 2012–13 (GoI 2012), companies with the largest share in total profits paid an effective tax rate below 20 per cent while companies with the lowest share in total profits paid the highest effective tax rate of 33.21 per cent or higher. This implies that major concessions and exemptions

TABLE 7.8 Tax Revenue Forgone Owing to Exemptions in the Central Government Tax System

	Corporate income tax	Personal income tax	Excise duty	Customs duty	Total
Revenue forgone in 2009–10 as % of GDP	1.1	0.7	2.6	3.0	7.4
Revenue forgone in 2010–11 as % of GDP	0.8	0.5	2.5	2.3	6.0
Projected revenue forgone in 2011–12 as % of GDP	0.6	0.5	2.4	2.5	5.9

Source: Compiled by CBGA from the data provided in GoI 2012.

in the central government tax system are favouring bigger companies rather than smaller ones. Revenue forgone in the central government tax system on account of deduction of export profits for Software Technology Parks of India units (software technology industries), export-oriented units, free trade zones, and accelerated depreciation are substantial; particularly the depreciation allowance/accelerated depreciation is a dominant factor underlying the forgone tax revenue.

With regard to tax exemptions, the 49th Report of the Parliamentary Standing Committee on Finance has emphasized that each exemption should serve an economic purpose. It added that an annual or periodical review of each of the exemptions is also crucial in assessing the fulfilment of their economic purposes. It has also opined that exemptions should not be for a very long period. Hence, tax exemptions need to be minimized, carefully designed, and justified with sound social and economic reasons. Even if half of the tax revenue, forgone presently because of the plethora of exemptions in the central government tax system, gets collected, it would generate additional tax revenue worth 3 per cent of GDP.

Thus, it is feasible for the government in India to increase the tax–GDP ratio for the country sizably, so that the total fiscal policy space available gets expanded, which in turn would enable the government to increase significantly the budgetary resources provided to social sectors and interventions pertaining to children.

★ ★ ★

We have noted that the public resources available in India for making investments towards socio-economic development appear insufficient in comparison to those in several other countries. In this context, it has been observed that the implementation of strong and progressive policy measures by the government in the domain of taxation can play a significant role in expansion of the total fiscal space available for public investments in the country. There is clearly a need for moving away from a conservative to a progressive fiscal policy for the whole country.

In terms of the expenditure priorities, from the point of view of influencing development outcomes relating to children, the quantum of public investment on important social sectors, such as education, health, water supply and sanitation, nutrition, and social security and welfare, needs to be stepped up significantly. Moreover, the central government and state governments also need to significantly enhance the quantum of public investments on interventions targeted towards children. Investments via the Union Budget and state budgets need to be increased, particularly for interventions in the hitherto neglected sectors of child health and protection of children in difficult circumstances. Finally, with regard to the factors constraining the effective utilization of budget outlays, it was observed that the state governments should be enabled to increase non-Plan spending in the development sectors; the centre and states should make concerted efforts to remove institutional and procedural bottlenecks in planning, fund flow, and fund utilization processes; and the states should be given flexibility vis-à-vis the norms, guidelines and unit costs in the central schemes.

REFERENCES

Centre for Budget and Governance Accountability (CBGA). 2012. 'Unfulfilled Promises?—Response to Union Budget 2012–13'. New Delhi: CBGA.

Centre for Budget and Governance Accountability (CBGA) and United Nations Children's Fund (UNICEF). 2011. 'Budgeting for Change—Tracking India's Commitments to Children'. New Delhi: CBGA.

Government of India (GoI). 2008. 'Indian Public Finance Statistics 2007–8'. New Delhi: Ministry of Finance, GoI.

———. 2011. 'Indian Public Finance Statistics 2010–11'. New Delhi: Ministry of Finance, GoI.

———. 2012. 'Statement of Revenue Foregone' in *Union Budget 2012–13*. New Delhi: Ministry of Finance, GoI.

International Monetary Fund (IMF). 2011. 'Revenue Mobilization in Developing Countries'. Washington, DC: IMF.

Lorie, H. 2003. 'Priorities for Further Fiscal Reforms in the Commonwealth of Independent States', IMF Working Paper, IMF. http://www. imf.org/external/pubs/ft/wp/2003/wp03209.pdf, last accessed on 14 January 2013.

Organisation for Economic Cooperation and Development (OECD). 2011. 'Government at a Glance 2011'. Paris: OECD.

———. 2008. 'Revenue Statistics 2008'. Paris: OECD.

Singh, Kavaljit. 2001. 'Tax Financial Speculation—The Case for a Securities Transaction Tax in India', Asia-Europe Dialogue Project, Public Interest Research Centre.

Part III

Gender, Family, and Marriage

8 Adverse Child Sex Ratios and Gender Discrimination

Challenges for Law and Policy

Mary E. John

When the population results of Census 2011 were first announced, newspaper headlines were quite unambiguous in capturing the nation's priorities; first and foremost were the 'positives'—decline in the growth rate of the population, including in the state of Uttar Pradesh (though less than expected for some commentators); a rise in literacy rates; and a rise in the overall sex ratio of the number of women per 1,000 men. The problem was the child sex ratio (CSR, measuring those in the age group of 0–6 years) which dropped from 927 in 2001 to an all-time low of 918 in 2011. The Secretary to the Home Ministry appeared on the evening news saying that on the matter of the girl child, the government must re-examine its policies.

How should we approach the whole question of sex ratios and the counting of girls? Gender has become both naturalized and a critical instrument in the undisputed aim to control the population, while not allowing the number of females to drop unduly. Even references to gender discrimination are too often subsumed within this larger concern over the role that women play through their fertility patterns in the governance of the population. The inclusion of information on literacy and the 'positive' figure of increased literacy among girls and women are part and parcel of this drive towards ensuring fewer births. At the same time, there are significant relationships between adverse child sex ratios and gender discrimination that need to be addressed. It therefore becomes an even greater challenge to look more closely at questions relating to law and policies—those that the government has been promoting specifically to combat the skewed sex ratio—and also other issues, whose effects on the life chances of girls may not be so obvious, but are nonetheless critical. But first, what has been the story so far and what can we learn from Census 2011?

CHILD SEX RATIOS IN INDIA SINCE 1991

In order to begin a discussion of India's child sex ratio patterns, a table (see Table 8.1) has been prepared that draws from both earlier census figures and the final figures for 2011 now available. The difference in successive decades has also been included for easy reference. The break-up of the country into the regions of the north-west, north-central, west, east, and south offers a quick overview of broad patterns in the last two decades. (We might keep in the back of our minds that this period happens to not just correspond to the so-called era of neo-liberalism, but also that it spans roughly a generation.) At the national level, the decline of 18 points in the CSR in 2001 has now been followed by a further decline of 9 points. As more families are having fewer children (registered by the reduced fertility rates), there is, therefore, an ongoing gendering in their sex composition. To put it briefly, practices leading to fewer girls in the 0–6 years' age group have been spreading more thinly during the last decade over a much larger proportion of the country.

The figures from 1991 have been included in order to recall why the Census 2001 made such headlines over a decade ago. This was when the CSR first dropped below that of the overall sex ratio. While the CSR fell from 943 in 1991 to 927 in 2001, the overall sex ratio rose from 927 to 933 in the same period (a clear sign that life expectancy among women was increasing significantly). It was in 2001 that several states in north-west India witnessed plunges in their CSRs—with Punjab leading the way by dropping below the 800 mark, while other states, such as Himachal Pradesh, experienced huge declines for the first time. Secondly, 2001 made history (especially at the district level)

TABLE 8.1 Child Sex Ratios (0–6 Years) in Select States: 1991–2011 (females per 1,000 males)

State	1991	2001	Difference 2011 – 2001	2011	Difference 2011 – 2001
India	945	927	−18	918	−9
North-west					
Himachal Pradesh	951	896	−53	909	13
Punjab	875	798	−77	846	48
Haryana	879	819	−40	834	15
Chandigarh	899	845	−46	880	35
Delhi	915	868	−47	871	3
North-central					
Uttar Pradesh	928	916	−12	902	−14
Madhya Pradesh	952	932	−20	918	−14
West					
Gujarat	928	883	−45	890	7
Rajasthan	916	909	−7	888	−21
Maharashtra	946	913	−33	894	−19
Goa	964	938	−26	942	4
East					
Bihar	959	942	−17	935	−7
Jharkhand	NA	965		948	−17
West Bengal	967	960	−7	956	−4
Nagaland	993	964	−29	943	−21
Odisha	967	953	−14	941	−12
South					
Andhra Pradesh	975	961	−14	939	−22
Karnataka	960	946	−14	948	2
Tamil Nadu	948	942	−6	943	1
Kerala	958	960	2	964	4

Source: Census of India 2011: Total Population, Provisional Figures; Census of India, 2001, series-I, India: Primary Census Abstract, Total Population: Table A-5; Census of India, 1991, Series-I, India, Part IV A-C Series, Socio-Cultural Tables, Vols I and II.

because of evidence of CSRs falling below the 950 mark (taken as the general norm the world over) in other parts of the country outside the north-west, such as Goa, urban Odisha, and even pockets in the north-east. In the north-west these patterns were put down to the intensification of practices of sex selection before birth in regions with known prior histories of female infanticide and higher female mortality; elsewhere, a smaller proportion of families was now resorting to similar practices probably for the first time.

Moving on to Census 2011, we find that the state figures point to a clear difference between the north-west and the rest of India. It would appear that there has been a peaking (or plateauing) of the practice of sex selection in states like Gujarat, Haryana, Delhi, and Himachal Pradesh, with small improvements from very low levels in Chandigarh and Punjab (notice that none of the north-western states have fallen further, though they have by no means come back to 1991 levels, which were themselves well below the 950 mark). Punjab's rise from 798 to 846 (48 points) according to 2011 figures makes its CSR similar to that of its neighbours, but only a district-wise analysis would reveal where the real changes are. In Punjab, the severity of the practice has thus eased slightly. In states like Delhi and Gujarat, roughly the same proportion of families is resorting to sex selection as was true a decade ago (since this is a comparison of the number of girl children born and alive between 1996–2001 and 2006–11). According to district-level data for the state of Haryana, the district of Kurukshetra (which had the worst CSR of 771 in 2001) now has a CSR of 817, similar to the trend for Punjab. However, many more districts (Jhajjar, Mahendragarh, Rewari, Bhiwani, and Faridabad among others) have worse CSRs than in 2001.

Whatever be the improvements in north-west India, CSRs are falling in large parts of western, central and eastern India, including Maharashtra, Rajasthan, Madhya Pradesh, and Uttar Pradesh; even Andhra Pradesh has joined the ranks from among the southern states. (Of course, the state of Tamil Nadu is well known for its history of female infanticide and sex selection in districts like Salem and Dharmapuri—so it remains to be seen what a more disaggregated picture of that state would reveal.) In other words, the state-wise figures demonstrate a widening of the circle well beyond the so-called prosperity belt of north-west India, to the poorer states. A recent news report on Uttar Pradesh, for instance, highlights the spread of sex selection to eastern towns and districts where it was hardly known before. Reports from Maharashtra also indicate huge declines in several districts, with the backward district of Beed in the lead recording a massive drop from 894 to 801 between 2001 and 2011. (The only state whose figures are so strange that there is every reason to doubt them is Jammu and Kashmir, where the Census was undertaken after a gap in 1991, in 2001, and 2011. According to the provisional figures, the CSR has plummeted from 941 to 862, a drop of 79 points; along with this, Jammu and Kashmir is the only state in the whole country to have registered a positive increase in its fertility during this period. Whatever the form that the ongoing conflict is taking, such figures are hard to make sense of, and require further investigation.)

It is likely that the improvements in the north-west are related to efforts at monitoring the use of sex determination testing, in contrast with its spread elsewhere. Therefore it would be premature to simply equate an improvement in the sex ratio with a lesser gender discrimination (or vice versa), since the picture is more complex than that. The very fact that the CSRs are falling in such a wide variety of states—from poor states like Rajasthan and Madhya Pradesh, and a heterogeneous state like Maharashtra, to pushing southwards into Andhra Pradesh—makes it absolutely necessary to wait for the time when a more contextual micro-level understanding can be undertaken.

An example of such contextual analysis during the previous decade is a study that was conducted by a group of researchers (John et al. 2008) from 2003–5 in five of the lowest CSR districts of north-west India. It became evident that within this broad belt where CSRs had dropped severely, local contexts were nonetheless extremely significant. Thus, for instance, while Fatehgar Sahib in Punjab demonstrated the presence of families with just one son (especially among Jat Sikhs and urban upper castes) and families in Kangra and Rohtak strived for two children (but very few with only girls), in the districts of Dholpur and Morena, forms of child neglect leading to significant rates of mortality among girls in larger families went hand in hand with the growing practice of sex selection. This chapter will be directly concerned with the practice of sex selection as distinct from female infanticide or excess female mortality, because it appears to be the most prominent reason for adverse CSRs. The practice of eliminating the female foetus has been spreading alarmingly, even though efforts have been underway since several decades to combat it.

THE DEBATE TODAY

In order to get a better perspective on adverse sex ratios, let us recall the decade of the 1980s when practices of amniocentesis[1] for sex selection became the subject of the first campaigns by women's groups and health activists in Maharashtra, Delhi, and Punjab. At that time, this issue garnered little public support; indeed, it was not even clear to most people what the problem was. Today we might be in the opposite situation, where the sex ratio has become symbolic of gender discrimination as such, and few are interested in anything beyond balancing the numbers. One must underscore the extent of activism and analysis, both in India and abroad, and the range of organizations from local groups, the state, religious organizations, international bodies, and so on, who are closely monitoring these figures.

The results of the Census 2011 have therefore been highly awaited, if from varying perspectives. Some scholars have offered predictions of likely patterns, drawing from the National Family Health Surveys (the most recent being NFHS-3, 2005–6), as well as the Sample Registration at Births made available every year. Significant differences have also been crystallizing. Has there been too great or too little a focus on the law to curb the practice of sex selection? Counter-intuitively, could there be reduced son preference even though the numbers are more skewed than ever before in India's history? Is the problem one of 'mind-sets' out of synch with modern values of equality, or, does modernity itself have a lot to do with what is happening? On the one hand, some advocates have been demanding that the main focus must continue to be the effective criminalization of unscrupulous medical practitioners, while others are warning that the very campaigns against sex selection

[1] Amniocentesis was the first technique introduced into the country during the 1970s and the 1980s to check for foetal abnormalities during pregnancy and involves testing the amniotic fluid of the pregnant mother. This technique came to be 'misused' by using the genetic information to determine the sex of the foetus. This method has, since the 1990s, been widely supplanted by ultrasound as a method of prenatal sex determination.

have turned into a problematic, if inadvertent, campaign against abortions per se. While some have predicted heightened practices of 'female genocide', others see signs of a turnaround.

There is something curious about much of this debate and the positions that have been taken. On what basis would we, after all, expect change to happen? Planning the number and sex composition of one's children is surely at the confluence of a range of processes, from stretching limited resources, wanting the 'best' for one's children with the effect of heightening the burden of having them, extreme socio-economic volatility, varying individual morality, the kinds of technologies available, and the nature of gender disparities across classes and groups in contemporary society. A lot has been said about signs of reduced son preference as more and more families say that they want a boy and a girl. But what if this preference actually translates into a willingness to have 'at least one boy, and at most one girl'? Moreover, what kind of structural changes are we witnessing such that expectations of a turnaround could have a genuine basis?

As already mentioned, the secretary to the Home Ministry went on record to say that, in the face of further decline in the child sex ratio, the state should re-examine its policies. Let us, then, look more closely at what these policies have been. At present, on the legal front, there is the Pre-conception and Pre-natal Diagnostic Techniques Act (PC-PNDT), a law explicitly meant to prevent sex selection and most recently revised in 2003. There are also a series of schemes, which have taken the form of conditional cash transfer schemes to families in several states, meant to ease the burden of having a girl child. Whether it is the PC-PNDT Act or the schemes, it would appear that these have been far from satisfactory.

SEX SELECTION AND THE LAW

A brief review of the history of the PC-PNDT Act would be instructive in order to gain a better perspective of the difficulties besetting this legislation. It was in the 1980s that women's organizations and health activists discovered that a new technology, amniocentesis testing for foetal abnormalities, was being misused for determining the sex of the foetus, which was followed up with decisions to abort should the foetus be female. The campaigns by the Forum against Sex Determination and Sex Pre-selection (formed in Bombay [now Mumbai] in 1985) resulted in an Act by the State of Maharashtra in 1988 to ban sex determination testing in all government establishments and oversee its regulation in the private domain. The first central legislation took the form of the Pre-natal Diagnostic Techniques (Prohibition of Sex Selection) (PNDT) Act of 1994, subsequently revised as the PC-PNDT Act of 2003. However, legislation by no means had the result that was expected—the practice continued and has been spreading even when it is illegal.

In terms of the legal campaign, it is particularly important to recall that its primary locus has been on the technologies involved in sex determination testing, that is, amniocentesis, specialized pre-selection methods, and ultrasound, and not on the subsequent act of having an abortion (which in any event would not obtain in the rare cases of pre-selection). This point is often missed, given that the campaign is against what is variously termed female foeticide or sex-selective abortions and becomes particularly confusing given all the media focus on foetal images or on sensational cases involving the discovery of aborted foetuses. Indeed, till date, there has been no amendment to the Medical Termination of Pregnancy (MTP) Act of 1971 and the conditions under which abortions can be performed. Obviously it is the processes whereby the female foetus is eliminated or is not selected that results in 'missing girls' and a skewed sex ratio; but the law, as it stands, is designed to stem this tide at the first stage of sex determination or pre-selection.[2] As its title suggests, the PC-PNDT

[2] Nivedita Menon has challenged the campaign against sex selection by arguing that the very effort to obtain justice from the law is doomed to failure. It is simply philosophically incoherent to argue in favour of abortion 'in terms of the right of women to control their bodies and, at the same time, demanding that women be restricted by law from choosing specifically to abort female fetuses' (Menon 2004, p. 72). Abortion in other parts of the world already encountered problems when deploying the language of rights because of the ways in which foetal rights were then placed in opposition to those of the mother. In our context, Menon asks how the law can be 'selective', that is to say, distinguish between a general right to abortion, on the one hand, and the specific abrogation of that right in the case of sex selection. However, as indicated in this discussion, the law itself is not focused on abortion per se, but rather on the prior process of sex determination.

Act is an attempt at regulation—naming the techniques, determining where prenatal diagnostics can be conducted, who can conduct them, procedural aspects of registration, record maintenance, and, finally, provisions for inspection by state-appointed bodies. It is when a breach in such procedures is revealed by the state-monitoring body that a conviction should result, the most significant breach being that the test being conducted is for purposes of sex determination and that the sex of the foetus is disclosed to the pregnant woman (punishment includes a jail sentence of up to three years and a fine of Rs 10,000. For details, see Jaising 2004).

In their subsequent examination of the legislative history and context of the PC-PNDT Act, Indira Jaising, C. Sathyamala, and Asmita Basu begin by pointing out the first problem with the 1994 legislation—next to nothing was done in terms of its implementation (Jaising et al. 2007). A Public Interest Litigation (PIL) led by Sabu George, CEHAT, and MASUM seeking directions was therefore filed in the Supreme Court in 1998. At this point in time, technological advances available in India included highly expensive and complex possibilities of pre-selection through certain sperm sorting techniques in combination with Assisted Reproductive Technologies (ARTs) to 'choose' the sex of a child at the time of conception through in-vitro fertilization. In flagrant violation of the PNDT Act even 'home kits' for knowing the sex of a baby have frequently been advertised over the internet from countries like the US and Canada.

But as Jaising et al. state with great emphasis, it is with the ubiquity of standard ultrasound, prescribed for all pregnancies, that the limits of the law have become most obvious. The law had to be 'prohibitive' in the case of specialized pre-selection practices, but could only be 'regulatory' against the 'misuse' of something like ultrasound, now an integral part of the burgeoning medical business involved in all pregnancy monitoring. Somehow, this regulation had to prevent the communication of the sex of the foetus 'behind closed doors', which, as they point out, could really only be ensured if a legal authority were physically present. In any event, the law had originally been drafted with genetic testing units in mind, not general ultrasound check-ups (Jaising et al. 2007, pp. 3–9). In other words, the very law meant to curb a specific medical practice has encountered its biggest stumbling block in the fact that what had started out as a particular medical technique to detect foetal abnormalities via specialized genetic centres was now part of the generalized 'normal' practice of antenatal medical care via ultrasound.

Unlike other forms of neglect or even female infanticide, what makes sex selection unique is that it requires the active intervention by medical personnel and their misuse of medical technology. Medical personnel, moreover, occupy positions of social power and influence, and also legitimacy. While doctors are themselves products of a gender-biased society and may well feel the pressure of vulnerable women who come to them for help in eliminating an unwanted girl, there is no getting away from the fact that, 'unlike women, they are not the victims of societal structures. With the power to use medical technology also comes the responsibility to prevent its abuse' (Oommen and Ganatra 2004, p. 186). Moreover, they have played their part in the active advertising and spread of the technology of sex selection before it was criminalized. Hence, one of the biggest failures of the PNDT Act has been the immunity of medical practitioners for the most part. While it is a commonplace to look for the failure of all our social policies in the realm of implementation (so much so that the language of rights is becoming more and more rhetorical), as far as the PNDT Act is concerned, absolutely nothing was done for several years after the law was first passed in 1994 to put the monitoring bodies in place, leaving no scope for implementation.

It should come as no surprise, then, that extreme measures such as sting operations by news channels with decoy patients have been resorted to in efforts to catch erring doctors. According to Brinda Karat and Sabu George (2012), there is a strong nexus connecting medical personnel, politicians, and bureaucrats, which has made a mockery of the law:

> Since 1994 when the Pre-conception and Prenatal Diagnostic Techniques (Prohibition of Sex Selection) law was enacted there have been only 93 convictions. Of the 1,036 ongoing cases, only a small per cent, possibly 10 per cent, relate to charges of communication of the sex of the foetus. A majority of the cases are for non-maintenance of records and non-registration of ultra-sound machines. Even in cases following widely publicised sting operations of sex determination, no action has been taken against the doctors concerned. For over a decade, the Medical Council of India refused to change its rules to include sex selection

as a ground to delicense doctors. In Rajasthan when the licenses of 25 or so doctors were suspended in 2006, following a state-wide campaign, the Secretary of the Medical Council, who was held responsible for the suspension of the licences by the medical fraternity was removed and the suspensions rescinded. The DM of Hyderabad was physically assaulted by leading members of the Hyderabad Medical Association because of his efforts to implement the law.

It would appear, then, that it is not enough to keep saying that there is nothing wrong with the law (which must certainly be included in any comprehensive policy now under consideration) when its implementation has been either non-existent or so flawed. Moreover, there are other aspects to the law that need more attention. The context in which the first PNDT Act was enacted was the introduction of amniocentesis techniques in India meant for the detection of foetal abnormalities. Even though there was some initial discussion among women's organizations about the advisability of demanding a complete ban on any amniocentesis testing, the basic form taken by the law was to make a distinction between 'legitimate' grounds and their 'misuse'. In other words, while checking that certain genetic abnormalities in a foetus are medically and socially acceptable grounds for aborting such a foetus should there be a positive diagnosis, sex determination testing followed by an abortion is a crime. In recent years, disability activists have questioned this taken-for-granted problem of the disabled foetus. Why, they have pertinently asked, should there be such an automatic assumption against bringing a potentially disabled child into the world? What, they go on to suggest, does this tell us about the absence of any effective rights for the disabled and especially of society's responsibilities towards children with disabilities? It is thanks to the efforts of the disability movement that there is at least some awareness of the complexity that surrounds any simple assumptions about 'abnormality'. Politicizing the 'social' bias against girls cannot be advanced without also politicizing the 'naturalised' bias towards disability. By comparing the two—disability and gender—it is therefore apparent that more discussion and advocacy are needed at the interface of both these movements (Ghai 2008; Ghai and Johri 2008).

So far this chapter has focused on the major impasses that have been encountered in both creating and implementing the law against sex selection. This does not mean that nothing has or can be achieved through this law. A recent effort has been made to estimate the positive effect of the law by arguing that in its absence the CSR would have been even more skewed (Nandi and Deolalikar 2011). The efforts of the Collector at Hyderabad, Arvind Kumar, during his tenure there (following the Census results of 2001), in ensuring regular and effective monitoring have been frequently cited as an example of what committed implementation can achieve by way of curbing the practice of sex determination testing. (The city of Hyderabad showed a vastly improved CSR in comparison to neighbouring districts.) Though bureaucrats and politicians have frequently turned to the idea and practice of pregnancy tracking and monitoring as a way forward, it is hugely problematic. This shifts the focus not only from the doctor to the pregnant woman, but also to any decision to undergo an abortion, thus bringing within its ambit abortions that were not preceded by sex determination. Punjab has been using this method of tracking pregnancies by Auxiliary Nurse Midwives (ANMs), especially among women who have had one or two daughters, according to Bijoyalaxmi Nanda (unpublished report). She goes on to say that the improved CSR in Punjab according to Census 2011 has both made the government complacent about any further implementation of the Act and resulted in the withdrawal of donor support to local campaigns, which were quite vibrant a decade ago. The latest effort in the state of Maharashtra has been to introduce a tracking device within ultrasound machines called the 'silent observer', whose purpose is to 'silently' keep an account of all ultrasounds and thereby aid the state in the monitoring sex determination. Without any prior studies to test its efficacy, it remains to be seen whether this technology will identify erring doctors or display the same problems that accompany the tracking of a pregnancy.

A more positive development in the State of Maharashtra has been the new formation of a coalition of organizations and individuals, the Forum against Sex Selection (FASS), in the wake of Census 2011. This advocacy group has been particularly vigilant in making clear distinctions between sex determination and sex-selective abortion, demanding that the state focus on the former. At the time of writing this chapter, in August 2012, the Maharashtra government announced that it would treat female foeticide on par with murder, and FASS has been quick to oppose such a move.

POPULATION POLICIES, GOVERNMENT SCHEMES, AND THE GIRL CHILD

This chapter began by pointing out the ongoing centrality of governing populations through reducing numbers, and how this compulsion has also affected state action and policies towards combating the adverse child sex ratio. This is glaringly evident when we look at the conditional cash transfer schemes for the girl child being variously promoted by a number of state governments.

At the back of most of these schemes is an aspect of population policy that enjoys widespread consent, namely the two-child norm. Though the National Population Policy (2000) contains no such provisions and though India has been a signatory to the International Conference of Population and Development (IPCD), which entails a commitment to reproductive rights, recent Supreme Court rulings as well as population policies promulgated by several states, including Haryana, Rajasthan, Madhya Pradesh, Chhattisgarh, Odisha, and Andhra Pradesh, seek to penalize and disbar those who have more than two children from accessing various government programmes. First and foremost, such a policy constitutes a violation of human rights, especially, as the National Human Rights Commission noted in 2003, those of 'the marginalised and vulnerable sections of society, including women' (NHRC 2003, p. 1). As Mohan Rao has argued, the 'imposition of the two-child norm, and the disincentives proposed (including disbarment to stand for elections right from the level of local government), would mean that the majority of the deprived population would bear the brunt of the state's withdrawal of ameliorative measures, pitiably inadequate as they are' (Rao 2008, p. 301). But, what is less well recognized, in the context of the present focus on adverse CSRs, is that a 'vigorous pursuit of the two-child norm is an invitation to female sex selective abortion' (Rao 2008, p. 303). Indeed, among the more common rationalizations offered by doctors who agree to perform sex determination and SSAs is precisely their belief that they are helping to bring down population growth. This means that if the State is indeed serious about questioning its policies in the wake of the ongoing decline in the CSR, widespread support for population policies such as the two-child norm, including the introduction of coercive disincentives, must be reviewed if not discontinued.

T.V. Sekher's chapter in this volume (Chapter 12) provides a detailed desk-based overview of many of the current schemes being promoted in several states. These schemes are all variations of the Girl Child Protection Scheme first launched by the Tamil Nadu government in 1992 in the face of the discovery of female infanticide in certain districts during the 1980s. A sum of Rs 100 was put into a state fund for each baby girl enrolled in the scheme, followed by further amounts in step with completing various stages of schooling, until finally, at the age of 21, if still unmarried, she would receive a lump sum of Rs 20,000. As Rajeswari Sunder Rajan, among others, has been quick to point out, however, this scheme was further saddled with various eligibility criteria—no sons, indeed, subsequent sterilization of the mother to ensure no further births, and BPL income levels for a family that wished to enrol (Sunder Rajan 2003). While the amounts of money have increased in the interim, if anything, the conditionalities and eligibility criteria for the various schemes on offer today, as discussed by Sekher, have multiplied. Moreover, the scrambling of population control with protecting the girl child is particularly problematic. Poverty has also been turned into an eligibility criterion when it is well known that planning the gender of one's children is at its most acute among the non-poor, that is, among those striving for upward mobility with limited resources. Many have critiqued such schemes for effectively providing a lump sum as dowry to a family—and in northwest India the '*ladli*' scheme is locally called '*dahej*' (dowry) scheme. It is to be hoped therefore that these schemes will be subjected to a much-needed review.

DOWRY AND BEYOND

In the early years of sex determination testing, when medical practitioners openly advertised their services, a common slogan found on roadsides and in suburban trains was 'spend Rs 500 now and save Rs 50,000 later'. This invitation to rationalize supply and demand through a simple financial calculation—pay doctors a fraction for a girl's elimination before birth and be spared her dowry—is surely crass. Yet, it clearly touched and continues to touch a nerve—indeed, the battle against dowry is one of the oldest struggles of the women's movement. According to historians like Veena Talwar Oldenburg, the rise in dowry (over bride price) during the nineteenth century among several castes in colonial Punjab, which was a consequence of changes in British revenue policy, resulted in a parallel spurt in female infanticide. She sees an ongoing parallel today with dowry deaths and sex selection (Talwar Oldenburg 2002). Even Sabu George and Brinda Karat in their recent discussion on the need for a comprehensive policy to target the declining sex ratio, state at the outset that the government must act against the menace of dowry being driven by the consumerist policies of the country. As they put it: 'Like a black shadow in the wake of dowry demands, is the spread of sex selection' (Karat and George 2012). It is perhaps not accidental, then, that the National Commission for Women at the time of writing is engaged in reviewing the Dowry Prohibition Act, another one of our laws that has been supremely lacking in the capacity for implementation.

There are a number of important issues here that we must look at, as we turn now to the 'demand' side with more and more families seeking recourse to sex selection. Dowry represents the payments in cash and kind that have come to accompany the marriage of a daughter, and there is considerable evidence that it has been spreading and increasing over time. (The obverse, which is often not openly mentioned, is that having a son also means expectations of receiving a hefty dowry at the time of his marriage.) The first point being made here, given that this chapter is appearing in a volume on children, is the somewhat transient place that a child occupies in the course of a given life. When parents are attempting to actually plan the number and sex composition of their children, it is not childhood that is on their horizon. They are planning to have or not have a daughter or a son who will have to be brought up into adulthood, 'settled', and whose future relationship will be shaped by the inter-generational transfer of resources. This is also why the image of the 'girl child' who must be 'saved' (as in '*Beti bachao*' campaigns) may not actually name the problem that is driving the changing nature of son preference and daughter aversion today. Growing daughter aversion is about wishing to be spared the burden of bringing up a girl into an adult woman, with all the attendant costs involved.

Secondly, while dowry no doubt has its place, the new levels reached by adverse CSRs require a correspondingly multidimensional level of analysis and cannot simply rest content with dowry as a one-size-fits-all phenomenon symbolizing gender discrimination. No single factor—be it available technologies on the supply side or heightened demands for dowry—can stand in for the combination of factors that are at work. Technologies may well be closing the gap between demand and supply; but are not, an independent causal factor, since the southern states, with the longest histories of medicalization of pregnancies, have not become leaders in sex selection. There is no question that a decline in fertility has set in and is spreading across the country, aided by population policies as well as by more voluntary 'choices' to have fewer children, when it comes to the non-poor. Contemporary India is witnessing a highly gendered version of this choice—in north-west India, according to the findings of the study already cited earlier (John et al. 2008), this veers from one to three children. It is worth underscoring that this marks an unprecedented shift in son preference as well and that extra sons are no longer wanted either. Now family planning means planning for one or two sons and allowing for the birth of at most one daughter. It would surely be worth exploring whether this dynamic has now moved beyond north-west India into the swathe of the country that has seen a downward spiral over the last decade.

What kind of broader analyses are therefore required? While much has been said about the north-west being the most prosperous region of the country, this prosperity, especially post the Green Revolution, requires a much more nuanced analysis. A huge disenchantment with agriculture characterizes this region, supplemented by highly volatile socio-economic forms of development. At the same time, modern changes are palpable, such as increases in educational levels and rises in the ages of marriage.

> These unintended consequences of contemporary social processes, when combined with parental fears of the unattached sexuality of adult daughters in a context of a highly competitive and differentiated marriage market, are compounding the sense of burden represented by the birth of a daughter. She now requires many more years at home with higher investments in nutrition, health and education... Sons, on the other hand, embody a range of ritual and economic roles. If the current climate of economic volatility and masculine anomie makes them often fall short of expectations, nonetheless at least one is essential for the future of the family. It is this conjuncture that is producing the falling child sex ratio? (John et al. 2008, p. 86)

There has been far too much focus on the need to restore the 'balance' to the skewed numbers and on quick-fix solutions. What is forgotten is that, in a growing population like ours with its hypergamous marriage market, male privilege has benefited over the course of the last century from an excess of marriageable women in any given cohort. In other words, there has been an invisible structural imbalance at work in most parts of the country outside the north-west, but which was never considered to be a problem to be 'corrected'. (The peculiar case of Kerala with its positive sex ratio but highly discriminatory practices against women is a case in point.) Furthermore, in most of the discussions on fertility and sex ratios, little attention is given to what is arguably the most critical indicator of the status of gender in our country. According to Indrani Mazumdar and N. Neetha, the 64th Round of the National Sample Survey (2007–8) has the stunning revelation that, after twenty years of unprecedented economic growth, the total proportion of women in any kind of paid work is no more than 15 per cent. Another way of putting this would be to say that 85 per cent of all women are destined to find their future through structural forms of dependency, namely, marriage. This does not even begin to discuss the nature of the work that constitutes the 15 per cent (Mazumdar and Neetha 2011).

This means that beyond the practice of dowry, a larger canvas is discernable, which begins with the social, educational, and sexual burdens experienced in bringing up a daughter. This does not simply conclude with the compulsory nature of marriage that takes her away, since it may not represent the end of parental responsibilities for her. While it is commonplace to think of these as aspects of contemporary culture with longer traditional roots in India's history, we cannot neglect to notice how well this fits in with the pattern of economic growth that we have been witnessing, one that is generating a revolution in modes of consumption, but presents precious few opportunities of economic security for women in the new labour market.

If indeed the government is serious about reconsidering its policies in the wake of the declining CSR, then it must recognize the range of policies that are shaping the futures of today's girls and boys. Surely, the government has to show greater political will in exposing the nexus between medical practitioners and the political machinery, if the law against sex selection is to have any chance of making sex selection a crime. But, unless both government and society acknowledge how 'choices' for having a girl are at the confluence of policies relating to access to health, education, sexual safety, and economic viability, it is unlikely that we will see any lasting impact on the sex ratio, much less curtail its further spread.

REFERENCES

Ghai, Anita. 2008. 'A Disabled Feminism?' in Mary E. John (ed.), *Women's Studies in India*. New Delhi: Penguin.

Ghai, Anita and Rachna Johri. 2008. 'Prenatal Diagnosis: Where Do We Draw the Line?', *Indian Journal of Gender Studies*, 15(2): 291–316.

Jaising, Indira (ed.). 2004. *Pre-conception and Pre-natal Diagnostic Techniques Act: A Users Guide to the Law*. New Delhi: Universal Law Publishing Co.

Jaising, Indira, C. Sathyamala, and Asmita Basu. 2007. *From the Abnormal to the Normal: Preventing Sex Selective Abortions through the Law*. New Delhi: Lawyers Collective.

John, Mary E., Ravinder Kaur, Rajni Palriwala, Saraswati Raju, and Alpana Sagar. 2008. *Planning Families, Planning Gender: The Adverse Child Sex Ratio in Selected Districts of Punjab, Haryana, Himachal Pradesh, Rajasthan and Madhya Pradesh*. Bangalore: Books for Change.

Karat, Brinda and Sabu George. 2012. 'Don't Trash This Law—The Problem Lies in Implementation', *The Hindu*, 4 February.

Mazumdar, Indrani and N. Neetha. 2011. 'Gender Dimensions: Employment Trends in India, 1993–94 to 2009–10', *Economic and Political Weekly*, 46(43): 118–26.

Nanda, Bijoyalaxmi. (n.d.). 'The Girl Child Counts—Census and Other Stories', Unpublished Report.

Nandi, Arindam and Anil B. Deolalikar. 2011. 'Does a Legal Ban on Sex Selective Abortions Improve Child Sex Ratios? Evidence from a Policy Change in India', April. Washington, DC: Centre for Disease Dynamics, Economics and Policy.

National Human Rights Commission. 2003. *Declaration*. New Delhi: National Colloquiuum on Population Policies.

Oommen, Nandini and Bela R. Ganatra. 2004. 'Sex Selection: The Systematic Elimination of Girls', *Reproductive Health Matters*, 10(19): 185–9.

Rao, Mohan. 2008. 'Population Policy and the Two Child Norm', in Mary E. John (ed.), *Women's Studies in India*, pp. 297–304. New Delhi: Penguin.

Sunder Rajan, Rajeswari. 2003. 'Children of the State? Unwanted Girls in Tamil Nadu', in *The Scandal of the State: Women, Law and Citizenship in Postcolonial India*. Delhi: Permanent Black.

Talwar Oldenburg, Veena. 2002. *Dowry Murder: The Imperial Origins of a Cultural Crime*. New Delhi: Oxford University Press.

9 Delaying Age of Marriage

Social Norms and Policies

Priya Nanda and Sonvi A. Khanna

The practice of child marriage has been historically prevalent in several societies across the world. Though child marriage of boys is not uncommon, the practice is far more acute with regard to girls. In many predominantly patriarchal societies, girls are married off early, sometimes even before they have attained puberty. Early marriage reduces the risk of girls' losing their virginity before marriage and thereby protects family honour. The consequences of marrying girls early, often before the legally allowed ages of 16 or 18 years, have been well documented (UNICEF 2011). Early marriage of girls not only restricts their opportunities for personal and physical development, but also prematurely burdens them with the responsibilities of being a wife, mother, and householder. It also places a disproportionate health burden on them by subjecting them to high risks of early childbirth and repeated pregnancies.

More than a third of the world's marriages of girls under the age of 18 take place in India (UNICEF 2009). Between 2000 and 2009, almost 47 per cent of Indian women of the ages 20–24 years were either married or in union by the age of 18. Though early marriage in India is not restricted to girls, only 5 per cent of boys as compared with 30 per cent of girls in the ages 15–19 are either married or are in union (UNICEF 2011).

In the absence of sexual and reproductive health information as well as the power to negotiate and make informed decisions, young women find that an early marriage into traditional patriarchal families often puts pressure on them to prove their fertility. Son preference in many parts of India also translates into pressure to produce a son, which might mean repeated births and/or repeated sex-selective abortions to ensure birth of the desired number of sons. This has serious consequences for a country like India where almost 56 per cent of girls in the ages 15–19 are anaemic and therefore run a higher risk of maternal death from repeated or underage pregnancies. Maternal mortality in 2008 stood at 230 maternal deaths per 100,000 live births (UNICEF 2011), which far exceeds the country's target of 109 for 2015 in compliance with the Millennium Development Goals (MDGs). Besides mortality, early and repeated pregnancies also cause debilitation and nutritional deficiencies in the young mother, which continue through her life and get passed on to the next generation (UNICEF 2011).

While India has achieved almost 100 per cent gender parity in primary school enrolment (at 0.98), gender parity is lower (at 0.86) for secondary school enrolment. The prevalence of early marriage is highly correlated with dropout rates from secondary schooling (UNICEF 2011). Once girls seem to be of 'marriageable' age, it is common for families to stop enrolling their girls in schools for secondary education. Even among those who are enrolled, dropping out is common after marriage or *gauna* (ceremony of sending girl to her marital home). Curtailing girls' schooling restricts their opportunities for personal growth as well as their earning potential.

Despite these wide-ranging consequences of marrying girls early, the global response to this issue gained momentum only in the last few decades, following the 'Cairo International Conference on Population and Development', 1994, which brought attention to adolescent reproductive health, and the UN 'International Conference on Women' in Beijing in 1995, which championed the cause of human rights of women and girls. While some countries like India had issued legislations to set a minimum legal age for marriage long before these international events, the momentum created by the latter led to the expansion of programmes focusing on the rights of women and girls, as well as emphasizing the need for systematic evaluations of these programmes. More recently, concerns raised over poor achievement of

MDG targets by various developing countries, including India, have identified child marriage of girls as a critical impediment to achieving many of these goals; thereby reinstating the need for a serious evaluation and scaling up of efforts to ensure that the age of marriage for girls is raised. As a result, donors, national governments, international and national non-governmental organizations (NGOs), stepped up their efforts to address the issue.

While India is one of the countries that launched a range of policy and programmatic interventions to raise the age of marriage, in the last two decades, research conducted by ICRW documented a critical need to rigorously evaluate and improve these efforts to make them effective (Das Gupta et al. 2008; Malhotra et al. 2011).

This report provides a broad overview of India's policy and programmatic efforts to address child marriage of girls, with a categorization and analysis of these initiatives. It aims to assess the potential of these different approaches for addressing the issue of early marriage. The report additionally uses recent evidence from a qualitative study conducted by ICRW in Bihar and Rajasthan to understand the long-standing norms governing early marriage and any positive shifts in the same (Nanda et al. 2011). It concludes with key recommendations to improve government efforts to address early marriage of girls in India.

PATRIARCHAL STRUCTURES: THE ROOT OF EARLY MARRIAGE OF GIRLS IN INDIA

Several pervasive traditions lead to girls being married very young in India. The practice of dowry is one of them. Families perceive the birth of a daughter as an economic burden that only ends with her marriage, because marriage shifts her responsibility from her natal to marital home. Marriage of an older girl is costlier than that of a younger girl, because the amount of dowry increases in proportion to the girl's age and education. Her potential groom would have to be older, more educated, or have a higher earning potential than the girl, and he would therefore command a higher price (Nanda et al. 2011). Other economic factors, such as the expense of conducting the marriage ceremony, may also lead to the early marriage of girls. In Rajasthan, it is not rare for several girls of a family to be married off in one marriage ceremony to save expenses. Often, only one of the girls may be of legal age to marry while the other sisters or cousins might be underage (Nanda et al. 2011).

Another factor that contributes to early marriage in many patriarchal societies in India is the perception that the marriage of children is one of the most important responsibilities a family has towards its children. In fact, families consider marrying off their daughter as their final responsibility towards her as she is thereafter considered *paraya dhan* (someone else's property). On the other hand, it is the girl's responsibility to protect her natal family's honour and learn to efficiently execute domestic tasks, even at a young age, in order to attract a good match and prove her good upbringing in her marital house.

A natal family's honour is often considered synonymous with the girl's chastity before marriage and is given great importance in patriarchal societies. Girls reach the 'appropriate' age of marriage at the first signs of their physical maturity, which is often much earlier than the legal age of marriage. Marriage later than the 'appropriate' age or the age of physical maturity may become an issue of shame for the family, particularly as chastity may be at risk. As a result, many restrictions are imposed on a girl's mobility as soon as she attains puberty.

In parts of Rajasthan, however, tradition allows families to marry children (boys and girls) even at birth, though the girl is not sent to her marital house (gauna) until after puberty. Even though the gauna is delayed, early marriage *ipso facto* restricts a girl's opportunities for personal growth, since decision-making about her education or future aspirations often shifts to her marital family.

Emerging Role of Education

Despite this predominant mindset, many parents in the sites studied in Rajasthan and Bihar aspired to provide education to their daughters so that they are capable of earning an income. In the drought and poverty-stricken Tonk district of Rajasthan, a mother expressed her desire to educate her daughter enough to have some degree of literacy and to do basic calculations. This would at least offer her daughter options other than agriculture (such as starting a small tea stall) and would protect her from poverty by expanding her choices (Nanda et al. 2011). However, these aspirations can only be realized by having a functional public education system even in these rural areas. Presently, however, the schools are in a dismal state in most of these areas. Both the quality of teaching and the school facilities are substandard. Teacher absenteeism and indiscriminate corporal punishments are common in government schools, which undermine students' motivation to attend school and also hamper their learning process. Girls are also forced to discontinue school when they attain puberty, because of lack of proper toilets for girls in schools. To add to this, not all villages have schools beyond Class 5. Girls often need to travel long distances to attend high school, which, in the absence of proper and subsidized travelling facilities, discourages most parents from sending their girls to school. As a result, most girls drop out after Class 5 or 6, making them an easy target for early marriage.

Without functional and accessible schools to provide an alternative to early marriage, vocational training options are also important for girls who drop out of school because of disinterest in formal education or other reasons. Though government initiatives such as the Kishori Shakti Yojna and Mahila Samakhya are supposed to provide vocational training to adolescent girls (UNFPA 2003), not much evidence of these interventions was seen in the study sites of Rajasthan and Bihar. In the absence of these options, dropping out from school pushes girls back into the domestic space, and thus makes them easily available for marriage (Nanda et al. 2011).

EARLY MARRIAGE OF GIRLS: AN INDIA-WIDE PROBLEM

The prevalence of early marriage of girls is not consistent across the country. In 2005–6, eight states were marked as high prevalence with more than 50 per cent of girls of the ages 20–24, married before the age of 18 years. Mainly concentrated in the northern belt, with the exception of Andhra Pradesh, these states were: Uttar Pradesh, Bihar, Rajasthan, Madhya Pradesh, West Bengal, Chhattisgarh, and Jharkhand (Kishor and Gupta 2009). Despite the high prevalence, statistics recorded some decline in early marriage of girls in most states in the country. Only Punjab and Gujarat have shown no improvement between 1992 and 2006, whereas Madhya Pradesh, Maharashtra, and Haryana recorded a 15 per cent decline. Across the board, state-level statistics mask the sharp differences between rural and urban areas. In 2005–6, more than 50 per cent of girls in the ages 20–24 who resided in rural areas married before the age of 18 compared with 29 per cent of girls living in urban areas across the country (NFHS 1 and 3, cited in Das Gupta et al. 2008).

THE RESPONSE TO EARLY MARRIAGE IN INDIA

Over the last decade, there have been several key governmental and non governmental initiatives and programmes to address the issue of early marriage in India. International Center for Research on Women (ICRW) conducted a systematic review in 2008 to identify programmatic interventions and policy strategies that had documented and measured a shift in age of marriage as well as change in knowledge and behaviours or attitudes towards early marriage (Nanda et al. 2011). Sources used for this review included both published and unpublished reviews—from academic journals, programme reports to project visits and interviews with key stakeholders. Finally, the study narrowed the list down to 58 programmes that had actually measured and documented change in behaviours or attitudes and knowledge regarding age of marriage.

The review conducted by ICRW between 2005 and 2008 suggests that these initiatives are largely concentrated in the high-prevalence states of Rajasthan, Bihar, Uttar Pradesh, and Madhya Pradesh. Majority of these efforts are led by non-government organizations rather than by the national and state governments (Das Gupta et al. 2008). However, these NGO programmes are mostly concentrated in small pockets of these states only. Government efforts, on the other hand, are much wider in geographic spread and scale. So far, government efforts to delay marriage for girls have mainly focused on cash incentive schemes as well as on the strengthening of the Prohibition of Child Marriage Act, 2006. According to ICRW's review, the government's large-scale reach and investment, such as in schooling, leaves much to be desired and needs to be effectively tapped for delaying marriage of girls (Das Gupta et al. 2008).

Governmental and non-governmental interventions to delay marriage of girls in India have adopted a variety of direct and indirect measures. Adapted from the ICRW review, 2008, Figure 9.1 provides a

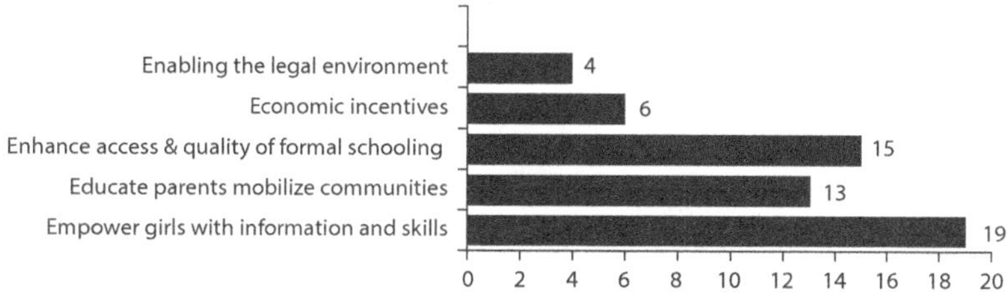

FIGURE 9.1 Types of Approaches Used in Programmes to Delay Age of Marriage for Girls Reviewed (frequency of occurrence)

picture of the types of strategies deployed and the number of interventions that have adopted these strategies to address the issue.

Evidently, most interventions are aimed at building various life skills for girls and educating them on reproductive health issues with the purpose of increasing their knowledge and developing soft skills for negotiating opportunities for themselves. A large number of interventions (not shown) have also attempted to delay marriage by providing girls with knowledge and skills on livelihoods to help them explore new opportunities. By providing girls with information to know themselves and their world better, the programmes build their capacity to reduce their economic and social isolation and improve their well-being. In addition, 15 out of the 58 interventions promoted formal schooling for girls. Evidence from evaluative studies and qualitative research also show a strong correlation between girls' education and increase in the age of marriage (Das Gupta et al. 2008; Malhotra et al. 2011; Nanda et al. 2011). Women with secondary or higher education are 70 per cent less likely to be married as children than women with low or no literacy (Das Gupta et al. 2008). Research conducted by ICRW in Bihar and Rajasthan also demonstrated that alternative models of education prove most effective in keeping girls in school, often empowering them to voice their opinions and envision alternatives to marriage for themselves (Nanda et al. 2011). By improving their human and social capital, these interventions equip girls to assert their independence and to seek and gain appropriate skills for educational or economic opportunities as an alternative or complement to marriage.

A few interventions also recognize the role of family and community and therefore target them through programmes on community awareness and legal awareness. This is portrayed in Figure 9.2, which demonstrates that a few programmes also target key stakeholders including legislators, health workers, and community members in general. These programmes can help increase social acceptance of delayed marriage as well as help parents and community members expand their aspirations for girls to include girls' personal growth and achievement in addition to a secure marriage.

It was identified that interventions that give financial incentives, such as conditional cash transfer schemes, were the least common. However the latter has evoked considerable policy interest, because the government is increasingly considering cash transfer schemes as a key instrument of social change.

Interestingly, of the 58 initiatives reviewed only one exclusively targeted adolescent boys (Figure 9.2). Young boys can be catalysts of change in norms on early marriage. In our previous study we found that boys who migrate to cities for work witness the advancement of girls in cities and often become supporters of or advocates for higher education and delayed marriage of their sisters (Nanda et al. 2011). Some also realize the advantages of marrying girls who have deferred marriage for personal development since they would have the

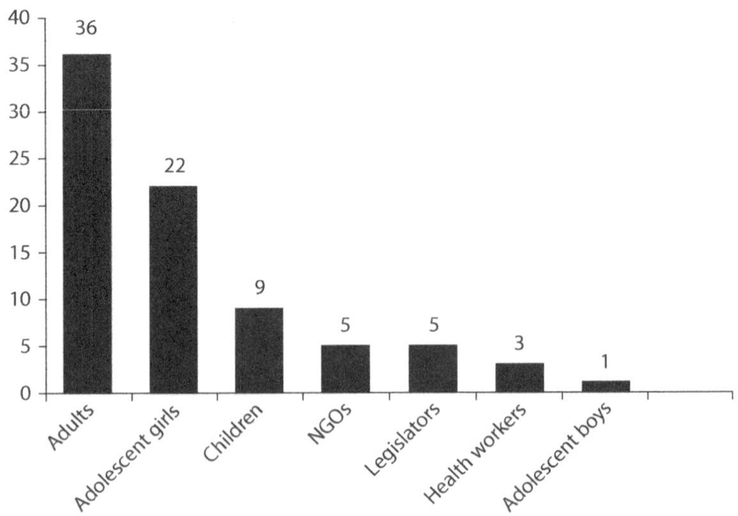

FIGURE 9.2 Key Target Groups Selected for Promoting Community Awareness and Legal Awareness (in per cent)

maturity to better handle the responsibilities of marriage. In regions like Rajasthan, where even boys are married as children, young boys articulate how marriage interferes with their personal development and affects their future earning potential. While migrant boys are earning and have greater agency within their family, initiatives are required to enable other boys to effectively voice their opinion on the issue of early marriage as well as to promote these game-changing ideas among their peers (Nanda et al. 2011).

While NGO-led interventions to address early marriage in India are greater in number and considered more innovative in approach than government interventions, few of these are rigorously evaluated and thus cannot be taken to scale. On the other hand, government interventions are often introduced with built-in scale, but do not seem to have a significant impact or, at least, the impact is unknown because of lack of evaluation of its programmes (Das Gupta et al. 2008). The section below offers a closer look at India's policy response to early marriage in order to determine the factors that prevent policy interventions from achieving their potential.

THE POLICY RESPONSE: A CLOSER LOOK

Poor indicators for girls, such as the prevalence of anaemia, underage pregnancy, low literacy levels as well as a persistent decline in female sex ratios at birth and early childhood, have prompted the government to pay increased attention to the target group of girls. The undervaluation of girls by their natal families has been articulated as the root cause of most of these problems. Policy attempts made to address this root cause in the last decade have focused mainly on two manifestations of girls' undervaluation by their own family: prenatal elimination of the female foetus and child marriage for girls.

Since 2001, the central and state governments have introduced multiple interventions to delay marriage of girls, which can be broadly categorized as follows: introduction of punitive laws that prohibit child marriage; conditional cash transfer schemes to incentivize families to delay marriage of their girls; and interventions that promote education/schooling as an alternative to marriage. Another ICRW study conducted in 2008–9 reviewed policies and programmes that address gender-based discrimination against daughters (hereby daughter discrimination). The study systematically screened 61 policies of which 10 were selected for an in-depth review of their potential to address daughter discrimination. The review looked at how policies are conceptualized, articulated, and implemented, and it was able to draw insights into the merits and demerits of various types of policy interventions made to address daughter discrimination. Drawing both from this review and the previously cited study in Rajasthan and Bihar, the analysis below evaluates the contributions and drawbacks of the three types of efforts made by the Indian government to delay marriage of girls in the country.

Punitive Legislation

India's first law against early marriage, the Sarada Act, was enacted in 1929 setting a minimum age for marriage of both boys and girls. The law was strengthened through multiple revisions, with the latest version enacted in 2006. The Prohibition of Child Marriage Act, 2006, prohibits marriages in which either or both individuals are minors. The law sets the legal age for marriage as 18 years for girls and 21 years for boys. It enforces punitive measures against all who perform, permit, or promote child marriage. These measures include rigorous imprisonment of up to two years or a fine of up to 100,000 rupees. It also provides for nullification of a child marriage, if either of the married individuals files a petition requesting the same. It gives a separated female the right to maintenance and residence from her husband or in-laws, until she is remarried. Any children born from a child marriage are deemed legitimate. In the case of separation, either party can claim custody, which will be allotted as considered best for the children. Finally, the law provides for recruitment of a special officer, the Child Marriage Prohibition Officer (CMPO), to undertake enforcement of the law (Nanda et al. 2011).

While the current Act is much stronger than its predecessors, not many cases have been filed under this Act so far. Limited awareness and weak implementation processes undermine the potential effectiveness of the law. Stakeholders in Bihar and Rajasthan noted that though most community members were aware of the existence of the law, knowledge of the penalties and punishment was minimal. While people are aware of the legal age of marriage, they do not perceive a serious threat of being convicted or punished on violation of the law. This only leads to underage marriages being conducted, but covertly. Very few people interviewed during the study were aware of who could be convicted under the law and the associated penalties. Despite the fact that the current provisions of the Act are stronger, its weak enforcement shows how ineffective it is in communities where the practice needs to be most discouraged (Nanda et al. 2011).

Gaps in enforcement have impeded the successful implementation of this law. The position of the CMPO often lies vacant and the responsibility of this office is clubbed with that of the District Magistrate or the SDO (Sub-Divisional Officer) (Nanda et al. 2011). In addition, neither the issue nor the law is taken very seriously by the law implementers. Higher officials tend to only focus on issues for which targets need to be achieved. Another critical impediment is that in the absence of any sensitization, the various developmental and health workers share the same views and attitudes of the communities to which they belong and thus may not have much sympathy for enforcing this law. According to a government official in Patna, ground-level implementers, such as the *anganwadi* workers,[1] lack conviction in the law and the responsibility it entrusts them with. Often, these workers are also afraid of challenging social norms within their own communities, and support from agencies like the police is almost negligible. High levels of corruption allow underage marriages to take place in the presence of police officials, which invalidates the purpose of such a law, as the law enforcement agency itself blatantly allows its violation. Clearly, all agencies involved in law enforcement have not been sensitized to the serious consequences of violation of this law, which, in turn, undermines its enforcement (Nanda et al. 2011).

[1] The role of ICDS programme is to combat child hunger and malnutrition. An anganwadi worker is a voluntary frontline health worker at the village level, employed by the ICDS programme. She needs to provide care for newborn babies as well as ensure that all children below the age of 6 are immunized or, in other words, have received vaccinations. They are also expected to provide antenatal care for pregnant women and ensuring that they are immunized against tetanus. In addition to this they must also provide postnatal care to nursing mothers.

Conditional Cash Transfers

The second type of policy intervention is the conditional cash transfer (CCT) schemes. The success of CCTs as catalysts of social and behavioural change is yet to be established. However, this instrument has received strong political backing in the last decade. There seems to be a policy inclination towards CCTs as a single lever that can bring about transformative shifts in attitudes and behaviours that have otherwise been slow or resistant to change. An interview with the Child Development Project Officer (CDPO) in Nawada, Bihar reaffirmed the government's faith in this policy intervention. According to the CDPO, economic benefits would be more effective in delaying marriage of girls than the punitive threat of law. The CDPO was convinced that if benefits of the existing Mukhyamantri Kanya Suraksha Yojna were made conditional on marriage after the legal age, it would prove to be a more effective tool to delay marriage than the law (Nanda et al. 2011). However, such faith in the effectiveness of CCTs is belied by the ambiguities and gaps in their implementation.

There are mainly two kinds of CCTs that target early marriage of girls. Some are long term like the Apni Beti Apna Dhan Haryana scheme, which incentivizes parents who keep girls unmarried until they have reached the age of 18 (more recent adaptations also have conditions related to timely immunization and school enrolment of girls). This variety of CCTs offers a protracted benefit to its participants, because girls are enrolled at birth and can only encash these benefits if they remain unmarried at 18, which implies that their natal families do understand the need to look after them till they turn 18 and that the benefit is a promised amount in the future. The next type of CCTs' targeting early marriage promises more immediate benefits to families with young girls. They offer families financial help to meet their daughters' marriage expenses, provided the couple to be married is of the legal age of marriage. Both the Mukhyamantri Kanya Vivah Yojna in Bihar and the Sahyog scheme in Rajasthan are examples of such CCTs. These schemes offer Rs 5,000 as incentive to families to marry their girls after they have turned 18 (Nanda et al. 2011).

ICRW's study in Bihar and Rajasthan found that short-term CCTs were not very popular among people, despite their more attractive and immediate benefits. The reason for this was poor public awareness of these schemes. People interviewed during this study complained that members of the panchayat do not keep villagers informed about such schemes. In some study sites, the panchayat falsified beneficiary lists to favour their supporters rather than the rightful eligible beneficiaries. In other cases, fake birth certificates were accepted, which proved beneficiaries to be older than actual age. This, in turn, allowed girls to be married before the legal age and still provided them the benefits of these CCTs (Nanda et al. 2011). Even for those who are aware of these schemes, corruption, accessibility, and the payment process deter them from benefiting from these CCTs. Application forms are not always available at the local levels, and there is lack of clarity about who should be approached in such a situation. Middlemen, who are often used to facilitate this access and to apply on behalf of the family, also demand a cut of the incentives, which sometimes reduces the already paltry amount by half. In addition, there are delays of even up to six months in receiving the money, though government officials state that payments are disbursed on time to beneficiaries (Nanda et al. 2011).

The official articulation of these CCTs suggests that the economic benefits offered could be used to pay off the girl's marriage expenses or dowry. As a result, CCTs meant to address the undervaluation of girls become popularly understood as the dowry scheme (a practice abolished by the Dowry Prohibition Act of 1961) thereby reinforcing the very practice responsible for girls' devaluation in their family (personal interview with a key government stakeholder in 2010).

The government officials tend to enrol the requisite number of beneficiaries into these CCTs, though not much effort is made to see if these are being availed by the right people. Devising effective tracking and monitoring systems is important to ensure that CCTs reach the intended beneficiaries and provide them the complete benefits of the scheme. The critical question is whether the positive impact of CCTs remains restricted to short-term behavioural changes or extends to shifting long-standing attitudes on early marriage as well. Encashing the scheme may be followed by immediate marriage of the girl, which suggests that marriage is delayed only to meet the conditions of the scheme and not due to any positive shift in parents' beliefs on the issue. But this does not prove that the CCTs are completely unsuccessful. It only points to the fact that CCTs need to be accompanied by other efforts such as campaigns or stronger enforcement of laws that empower women to claim their rights. Simply relying on CCTs may not be sufficient to shift long-standing attitudes on the issue of early marriage.

Promoting Education as an Alternative to Marriage

Efforts to modify society's gender expectations of young girls need to create feasible alternatives to marriage. One such clear alternative is to invest in girls' education. While this is a strategy that the government has stated to have used for decades, its success is questionable because the state of public education is still dismal. Our research on the ground suggests that parents are increasingly aspiring to educate their girls. While many of these parents wish to educate girls as an end in itself or to improve their chances in the marriage market, some also do so to facilitate their girls' employability in the future. However, the government education system is unable to capitalize on these changing aspirations and use them to foster higher education as an alternative to early marriage.

The poor quality of education combined with the scarcity of secondary schools in rural areas isolates girls from the benefits of higher education. A high school typically caters to several villages and thus is not in close proximity to many communities. In the absence of cheap public transport, girls have to walk long distances to and from school daily. This increases the perceived risk of young girls to sexual harassment and deters parents from sending their girls to high school. Parents in rural Bihar and Rajasthan also spoke of the need for more all-girls secondary schools as these would reassure parents of their girls' safety and would encourage them to send their daughters for higher studies. The lack of female teachers at the secondary level of schooling acts as yet another deterrent. Finally, secondary schools often lack basic facilities such as separate and clean toilets for girls, which, in turn, forces girls to remain home during menstruation.

While the basic fee for secondary schooling is covered by the government, additional costs of education increase during these years. Families with limited resources often make strict cost–benefit calculations and invest their small resources in boys in the hope of returns once the boys start earning. While the government offers scholarships to meritorious female students, it does not cover the larger population that is unable to afford the cost of secondary education.

Clearly, efforts aiming to keep girls in school beyond the primary level need to be aware of their unique needs, especially those of physical safety and menstrual hygiene. The central government's Kasturba Gandhi Balika Vidyalaya (KGBV) offers a model for imparting education that comes close to addressing most of these needs. The KGBV is a residential schooling programme that was initiated by the central government in 2004. The programme focuses on the Educationally Backward Blocks (EBB) of the country where the levels of female literacy and gender parity in literacy are lower than the national average. These schools target girls who had dropped out between Classes 5 and 8 and provide them formal education up to the eighth class so that they can join regular school from Class 9 and onwards.

These remedial school options seem to be successful in controlling secondary school dropouts among girls in both Bihar and Rajasthan,[2] and they provide girls with other skills in addition to formal education (Nanda et al. 2011).

The KGBV programme is one example of a strategy that does not just succeed in providing girls the skills to explore alternatives to early marriage, but also challenges the restrictive gender stereotypes and expectations of communities that prescribe marriage as the only option for young girls. ICRW's ground research also found that many parents, especially in Bihar, preferred vocational training for their girls, because this was more directly related to a potential source of income in addition to formal education. However, the study team found that there were no known government initiatives for imparting vocational skills to girls. Although vocational training was being given by NGOs

[2] The KGBV in Bikaner holds *Bal Melas* each year to invite parents of students and potential students to visit the school campus and check the facilities for themselves. The school also holds regular parent–teacher meetings to keep parents informed and interested in their daughter's performance. Finally, the quality of education imparted in the KGBVs separates them from the other government education models. Before being admitted into the school, students have to pass an entrance test. The aim of the test is to ensure that girls are admitted to classes corresponding to the levels of their knowledge. Separate classes are held for each class between Classes 6 and 8, following the formal education syllabus. Tuitions or extra classes are also organized during after-school hours on a need basis.

(Naari Gunjan in Bihar, Urmul in Rajasthan) and as an extra activity for KGBV students, trainees found it hard to translate learnt skills into income-generating activities. The investment needed for raw materials and tools was one of the impeding factors. Lack of access to a proper market was another deterrent (Nanda et al. 2011). While issues of resources and scale hinder NGOs from addressing these gaps, it may be possible for vocational training institutes to be run through the government in order to foster effective linkages between employment and markets.

Although the government articulates girls' education as a high-priority policy agenda, efforts to improve access to quality education are piecemeal. The government needs to further scale up successful models like the KGBVs, expand them to cover education beyond Class 8 as well as invest in more and better day-schools for secondary and higher education of girls. Additionally, having successful vocation skill programmes is not so easy, and they need clear expertise and linkages, which may not fall within the bandwidth of one organization but can be provided through larger government structures.

DISCUSSION

India's governmental policies address the issue of early marriage at various levels. First are efforts to catalyse change at the structural level through promotion of schooling and education. Next are interventions aimed to bring about change at the behavioural level through conditional cash incentives. Finally, the government seeks to deter child marriage of girls through punitive legal measures. While these different strategies have contributed to addressing the issue to some extent, the desired impact is yet to be achieved.

Misplaced political commitment to targets rather than the issue, mishandling of funds, and the erratic monitoring and evaluation of these strategies stymie their potential to delay marriage for girls in India. However, perfecting the government's own strategies alone is far from what is required to address child marriage in India. Many of the innovative and evaluated efforts that have been successful in addressing child marriage of girls have been implemented by NGOs. And the government's role also includes taking these successful models to scale.

Further, the prioritization of certain type of policy efforts to prevent early marriage of girls needs to be based on evidence, including that produced from social science research. Both quantifiable results and qualitative studies provide unique insights into changing aspirations that could be tapped to catalyse social change. Government's efforts need to draw insights from the available external studies before formulating new policy efforts and expanding existing ones while also investing in systematic evaluations of its various efforts on the issue. Social science research provides clues to how behaviour change may be taking place and what are some of the more resistant norms that need to be tackled through multipronged approaches with effective linkages between strategies.

None of the policy efforts to address early marriage, be it laws or schemes, is accompanied by strong communication and dissemination mechanisms to inform people about their provisions and benefits. Public dissemination of these efforts needs to reach farther and wider, and through a variety of media. It should provide a simple to understand yet comprehensive, detailed explanation of the eligibility criteria, benefits, conditions, and reporting system of a policy intervention. Not only would this enhance public participation in government efforts but also enable people to check and report misuse of government schemes by local authorities.

★ ★ ★

The number and variety of policy initiatives launched by the Indian government in the last two decades testify that policymakers recognize the seriousness of the problem of early marriage, especially for girls. Though these policies are clearly conceptualized and directly address the issues of concern, gaps in their design and implementation need to be further assessed and addressed in order to make existing efforts more effective.

This report has provided a review of the types of efforts made by the central and state governments in India in the last decade to delay marriage of girls. It gives a conceptual framework to these government interventions, specifying the level of the problem addressed by each type of effort and the strategy deployed by it. Some efforts intervene at the structural level to challenge gender expectations by creating alternatives to early marriage for young girls. Another category of interventions hopes to change families' behaviour towards their daughters by offering conditional cash incentives. The third category seeks to address the issue through punitive action against violators. While the government's multipronged approach for addressing the issue has potential, it has not yet achieved the desired impact. Attention needs to be paid to removing loopholes in the government machinery, which can prevent the best interventions from achieving the desired impact. The government also needs to identify successful NGO models that may have contributed to preventing or delaying marriage for girls and take them to scale.

Implementation of government efforts can be drastically improved through a sound tracking and monitoring system. Not only would this curtail access of government efforts by ineligible people, but would also provide tracking records that are fundamental to evaluating the impact of government efforts on the issue. Involvement of panchayats and women leaders at this level would also be critical to ensure that more effective targeting of schemes and messages is occurring.

Implementation of government efforts would also improve tremendously through sensitization of its personnel at all levels. The roles of personnel need to be differentiated and defined on the basis of levels of implementation of programmes. Creating a synergistic system is essential to prevent overburdening of personnel so that government initiatives can have the optimum impact. Coordinators of programmes need to define not only the role of each level of implementers, but also how to deal with community resistance where it occurs. Finally, it needs to convince the implementers that while social change is a slow process, their efforts can have a catalytic effect. Political efforts to address early marriage must aim for transformation in behaviour and attitudes, and not strive to achieve targets alone.

REFERENCES

Das Gupta, S., S. Mukherjee, S. Singh, R. Pande, and S. Basu. 2008. 'Knot Ready: Lessons from India on Delaying Marriage for Girls'. New Delhi: ICRW.

Department of Women and Child Development, Delhi. 2009. 'Delhi Ladli Scheme'. Government of the NCT of Delhi. http://wcddel.in/eligibility.html, last accessed on 30 January 2012.

Department of Women and Child Development, Delhi. 2005. 'Rules of New Girls Child Scheme "Ladli"', Government of Haryana. http://wcdhry.gov.in/WOMEN/ladli%20-rules(english).pdf, last accessed on 30 January 2012.

Kishor, S. and K. Gupta. 2009. 'National Family Health Survey (NFHS-3) India 2005–06: Gender Equality and Women's Empowerment in India', Ministry of Health and Family Welfare, Government of India. http://www.nfhsindia.org/a_subject_report_gender_for_website.pdf, last accessed on 30 January 2012.

Malhotra, A., A. Warner, A. McGonagle, and S. Lee-Rife. 2011. 'Solutions to End Child Marriage: What the Evidence Shows'. Washington, DC: ICRW.

Nanda, P., S. Kapoor, S. Mukherjee, M. Hersh, S. Basu, and R. Bhargava. 2011. 'Delaying Marriage for Girls in India: A Formative Research to Design Interventions for Changing Norms'. New Delhi: UNICEF.

United Nations Population Fund (UNFPA). 2003. 'Adolescents in India: A Profile', UNFPA for UN System in India. http://whoindia.org/LinkFiles/Adolescent_Health_and_Development_(AHD)_UNFPA_Country_Report.pdf, last accessed on 28 March 2012.

UNICEF. 2009. 'World's One-third Child Brides Live in India', *Daily News and Analysis,* 7 October. http://www.dnaindia.com/world/report_world-s-one-third-child-brides-live-in-india-unicef_1295834, last accessed on 30 January 2012.

———. 2011. *The State of the World's Children Report: Adolescence—An Age of Opportunity*. http://www.unicef.org/sowc2011/pdfs/SOWC-2011-Main-Report_EN_02092011.pdf, last accessed on 30 January 2012.

10 Parent–Child Communication and Sexual and Reproductive Health Matters[1]

Shireen J. Jejeebhoy and K.G. Santhya

Parents are in a unique position to protect their adolescent children's sexual and reproductive health and enable them to make a safe transition to sexual life (WHO 2007). A growing body of research conducted on young people in developing country contexts has confirmed that parents can influence the timing of sexual initiation and safe sex practices of their adolescent children (see, for example, Bettinger et al. 2004; Blum and Mmari 2005; Kumi-Kyereme et al. 2007; Li et al. 2000; Mohammadi et al. 2007; Ngom et al. 2003; Roche et al. 2008;

[1] We are grateful to the Population Council for permission to reproduce parts of the report, *Parent Child Communication on Sexual and Reproductive Health Matters: Perspectives of Mothers and Fathers of Youth in India* (Jejeebhoy and Santhya 2011), prepared using data from the *Youth in India: Situation and Needs*, a study conducted jointly by the International Institute for Population Sciences, Mumbai, and the Population Council. We acknowledge with thanks the financial support for the study from the John D. and Catherine T. MacArthur Foundation and the David and Lucile Packard Foundation; and for this analysis, from the Ford Foundation. We are grateful to Nicole Haberland and Pertti J. Pelto for comments and suggestions, and M.A. Jose, Shilpi Rampal, and Komal Saxena for research assistance.

Zhang et al. 2007). These findings are consistent with a considerably larger body of evidence from the US that has found that parent–child connectedness and communication play an important role in delaying sexual initiation, reducing multiple-partner relations, and increasing condom use (Aspy et al. 2007; Hollander 2007; Kirby 2007; Lederman et al. 2004; Meschke et al. 2000; Miller et al. 1998; Ryan et al. 2007; Whitaker et al. 1999).

Further, several studies in developing countries that have focused on the nature and influence of parent–child communication on sexual and reproductive matters have concluded that such communication rarely takes place (Biddlecom et al. 2009; Cui et al. 2001; Joint United Nations Programme on HIV/AIDS [UNAIDS] 2008; Kiragu et al. 2007). When discussions do take place, messages that parents convey to their children are usually ambiguous; for example, 'do not play with boys' (Luwaga 2004).

In India, there is scant evidence on parent–child interaction and communication on sensitive matters, such as the physical changes associated with puberty and matters relating to sex, pregnancy, and sexually transmitted infections/HIV. Evidence that is currently available comes largely from the perspectives of young people rather than parents themselves and suggests that communication on sensitive personal matters between parents and children tends to be limited (see, for example, Abraham and Kumar 1999; Alexander et al. 2006; IIPS and Population Council 2010; Mehra et al. 2002; Shekhar et al. 2007), and that strong cultural taboos inhibit discussions on sex (Lambert and Wood 2005).

Evidence on parent–child communication on sexual and reproductive matters from the perspectives of parents comes from a few small and unrepresentative studies (Garda and Alexander 2009; Mahajan and Sharma 2005; Shetty et al. n.d.; Soletti et al. 2009). These studies confirm that communication is limited and they highlight a range of obstacles that may inhibit parents' ability or skill in communicating with their children on the physical changes associated with puberty and sexual matters more generally. For example, studies have identified parents' own lack of awareness about sexual matters (Garda and Alexander 2009; Soletti et al. 2009) and their perception, sometimes unfounded, that their children would never be at risk of HIV as key factors limiting communication (Soletti et al. 2009); other studies have documented parental discomfort and perceptions that informing their children about sexual matters would lead them to engage in sex (Garda and Alexander 2009; Mahajan and Sharma 2005; Shetty et al. n.d.).

For the first time, data is available from several states of India that sheds light on socialization and parent–youth interaction patterns from the perspectives of parents of young men and women as well as from the perspective of young people themselves. The data allows us to explore the interaction between youth and their parents on sensitive sexual and reproductive matters.

In this chapter, we probe, from the perspective of parents, the extent and nature of communication with their children on matters of sexual and reproductive health (SRH) and the factors that inhibit parents from discussing these matters with their children. SRH matters encompassed in this chapter cover the physical changes associated with puberty and matters relating to sex, pregnancy, and sexually transmitted infections/HIV. Perspectives of the youth have been described in an earlier work (IIPS and Population Council 2010) and will be compared with the parents' perspectives presented in this chapter to draw attention to the extent to which both parents and young people underscored limited communication between parents and children.

POLICY CONTEXT

In India, a number of policies have articulated the need to raise young people's awareness of SRH matters and to actively engage parents in enabling adolescents to make safe and healthy transitions to adulthood. Prominent among these are policies formulated by the Ministry of Health and Family Welfare (MoHFW) and the Ministry of Youth Affairs and Sports (MoYAS). Specifically, the National Population Policy, 2000, has recommended the need to ensure that adolescents have access to sexual and reproductive health information as well as counselling and services that are affordable and accessible (MoHFW 2000). The National AIDS Prevention and Control Policy, 2002, has stressed the need to promote an understanding of HIV infection and safe sex practices among the young and has advocated the provision of HIV/AIDS education in schools and colleges through curricular and extra-curricular activities (NACO 2002). The National Health

Policy has recognized the need to raise awareness among school and college students about health-promoting behaviours (MoHFW 2002). The National Youth Policy, 2014, has advocated developing education and training materials that integrate information and skill-based approaches that are expected to enable young people to adopt appropriate changes in their behaviours and actions. It has also advocated establishing linkages with agencies dealing with health issues and building the capacity of community-based organizations to create awareness about HIV-related matters (MoYAS 2014).

Policies formulated by several other ministries, including the Ministry of Human Resource Development (MHRD) and Ministry of Women and Child Development (MWCD) have also acknowledged these needs. For example, the National Policy on Education has emphasized that educational programmes should actively motivate and inform the youth about family planning and responsible parenthood (MHRD 1998). The National Curriculum Framework, 2005, has also articulated the need for integrating adolescence education within the school curriculum (NCERT 2005). The National Plan of Action for Children, 2005, has recognized the special needs of adolescents up to the age of 18 and has argued for strategies to build awareness on sexual and reproductive matters (MWCD 2005). It has also stressed the need to enhance the capabilities of both the parents to look after the multiple needs of children through effective parenting programmes. It stresses the need to impart life-skills education to youth in partnership with parents, families, educators, and health care providers.

While these policy commitments have been commendable, their impact in the lives of young people has been far from impressive. Programmatically, efforts to create a supportive environment for young people have been limited, including efforts on the ground to sensitize different gatekeepers, notably parents. While the Implementation Guide for State and District Programme Managers, under the National Adolescent Reproductive and Sexual Health Strategy, has included parents in the target audience, the guide contains no discussion of the specific measures to be taken to involve parents or the special messages to be imparted to them (MoHFW 2006). The 2009 Rajya Sabha Report on the Adolescence Education Programme in which even the nation's political leadership displayed a reluctance to support the provision of SRH-related information to school-going adolescents in Classes 9 and 11 highlights, moreover, the absence of a supportive environment for young people to learn about SRH matters.

STUDY SETTING AND DESIGN

Data for our analysis has been drawn from the *Youth in India: Situation and Needs* study, a sub-nationally representative study of key transitions experienced by young people, undertaken for the first time in India (IIPS and Population Council 2010). The study was conducted both in rural and urban settings of six states (Andhra Pradesh,[2] Bihar, Jharkhand, Maharashtra, Rajasthan, and Tamil Nadu), which were purposively selected to represent the different geographic and socio-cultural regions within the country. Together, these six states are home to almost two-fifths of India's population (Office of the Registrar General and Census Commissioner 2001). Distributions of the youth population in these states taken together by age, level of literacy, religion, caste, and marital status were similar to those of the youth population nationally. Nonetheless, the six states lie at the extremes of the socio-economic and cultural spectrum of the country, reflecting, for the most part, the well-known regional diversity within the country in social, economic, and demographic characteristics. Andhra Pradesh, Maharashtra, and Tamil Nadu are among the more economically progressive states in the country, each accounting for 7–13 per cent of the national gross domestic product (GDP), while Bihar, Jharkhand, and Rajasthan are among the lesser developed states, each accounting for 2–4 per cent of the GDP (MoSPI 2008). Maharashtra and Tamil Nadu are among the most urbanized states, with close to one-half of their populations living in urban areas. In contrast, Bihar, Jharkhand, and Rajasthan are characterized by large rural populations, with just one-tenth to one-quarter of their populations living in urban areas (Office of the Registrar General and Census Commissioner 2011). Finally, differences are also evident in terms of kinship structure and gender relations: the three northern states represent settings in which family systems are particularly age- and

[2] The state of Andhra Pradesh was not bifurcated when the study, data from which is presented in this chapter, was conducted; the state-level data presented in this chapter, therefore, refers to the undivided Andhra Pradesh.

gender-stratified, and women's agency particularly restricted, while Maharashtra and the two southern states represent settings in which relations are relatively more egalitarian and women have relatively more agency (Altekar 1962).

The Youth Study comprised three phases: a pre-survey qualitative phase that included in-depth interviews with parents, a survey of youth, and post-survey in-depth interviews with selected survey respondents. Data presented in this chapter is drawn from in-depth interviews with parents of youth in all six states.

Interviews with parents aimed to obtain the perspectives of this key, but poorly studied, gatekeeper group. Within each state, study sites were purposively selected to correspond with villages and urban wards selected for the Youth Survey. For the selection of rural sites, one or two villages were selected from each of the geographic divisions into which each state was divided. Further, the selected villages were required to be located at a distance of approximately 10 km from a village selected for the Youth Survey, so that parental perspectives would be drawn from roughly the same socio-cultural areas as youth perspectives and yet would not affect the implementation of the Youth Survey in any way. For the selection of urban sites, one ward was selected from each of the three largest urban areas of the state, with the focus on low-income wards to ensure that the selected ward was similar to the one selected for the Youth Survey in terms of socio-economic conditions. In this way, five to six rural and three urban settings were selected in each state.

In each village or urban ward, the aim was to interview a total of eight parents (four mothers and four fathers): a mother of an unmarried young woman (between 15 and 24 years), a father of an unmarried young woman (between 15 and 24 years), a mother of a married young woman (between 15 and 24 years), a father of a married young woman (between 15 and 24 years), a mother of an unmarried young man (between 15 and 24 years), a father of an unmarried young man (between 15 and 24 years), and lastly, a mother of a married young man (between 15 and 29 years) and a father of a married young man (between 15 and 29 years).

Interviews focused on parental experiences from the perspective of mothers or from the perspective of fathers of all their children in these age groups, enabling comparisons on the socialization of sons versus daughters. A snowball sampling method was used to identify eligible respondents. Parents were selected purposively, through key influentials (*sarpanch* or panchayat member, health care provider, school teacher or *anganwadi* worker, or a representative of a non-governmental organization [NGO] working in the area) in each study village or urban ward. Only one parent from a selected household was eligible for interview. In each state, between 60 and 72 mothers and fathers were interviewed in-depth, making for a total of 412 interviews across the six states, including 209 mothers and 203 fathers.

In-depth interviews with parents focused on three aspects of communication. Parents were first asked about communication with their children on general topics, followed by what the main topics of discussion were, and, last, how free and open the parent–child communication style was. They were also asked specifically about whether they had talked to their children about sexual and reproductive matters, such as the physical changes associated with puberty and issues relating to sex, pregnancy, and sexually transmitted infections/HIV; the discussion focused not only on whether these topics had been discussed but also what aspects were discussed, and if communication was limited, the perceived reasons. We note that, in general, more parents were willing to elaborate on their communication with their children on matters relating to physical changes associated with puberty rather than on matters relating to sex, pregnancy, or sexually transmitted infections/HIV.

ANALYSIS

A coding scheme was developed and transcripts were coded in ATLAS.ti,[3] using this code list. The coded blocks of text related to specific themes, for example, communication with children on the physical changes associated with puberty and matters relating to sex, pregnancy, and sexually transmitted infections/HIV, reasons for non-communication, and so on. These blocks were analysed to capture typical patterns.

In order to give an idea of the extent to which typical patterns were observed, the researchers have provided counts of various response

[3] ATLAS.ti is a computer programme used in qualitative data analysis that helps researchers uncover and systematically analyze complex phenomena hidden in unstructured data.

categories along with textual evidence. In addition, in view of the large numbers of in-depth interviews conducted in this study, we have opted to provide percentages throughout the chapter. These percentages enable gender differences to become more clearly evident. However, we advise readers that percentages presented in this chapter may not be representative of the population at large and should be interpreted cautiously. Finally, because, as discussed above, the focus of parents' narratives lay more in the area of the physical changes associated with puberty rather than on other aspects of sexual and reproductive health, our analysis discusses communication relating to the physical changes associated with puberty and communication relating to sex, pregnancy, or sexually transmitted infections/HIV separately.

RESULTS

A profile of the socio-demographic characteristics of mothers and fathers who participated in the study shows that, typically, mothers were of the ages 40–45 and fathers, 45–55. As expected, fathers were, for the most part, more likely than the mothers to have ever attended school, and mothers from the two southern states were considerably more likely than those from the northern states to have done so. Almost all mothers in Bihar and Jharkhand (31 each) reported that they were not engaged in wage-earning activities at the time of the interview compared with considerably fewer mothers in the remaining four states (13–23). Most fathers were engaged in cultivation or agricultural labour (10–16 in five states, and three in Tamil Nadu) or in service, business, or professional activities (7–11 in five states, and 13 in Tamil Nadu). Reflecting well-known disparities in fertility levels, mothers and fathers from the three northern states had about one child more on average than did their counterparts in the western and southern states (4.3–4.5 versus 3.0–3.5). Household size ranged from four to six among mothers and fathers in Tamil Nadu to six to eight among those in the three northern states.

Communication about Sexual and Reproductive Health: Perspectives of Young People and Parents

Interaction between parents and their adolescent children about sexual and reproductive matters was limited, as reported both by young people in the survey and by parents, irrespective of the sex of the parent, urban–rural residence, or state (see Table 10.1).

Survey findings highlighted, from the perspective of youth, the limited communication between parents and children on sexual and reproductive matters. Findings presented in Table 10.1 show that few youth had discussed the physical changes associated with puberty with their father (4–7 per cent). While few young men had discussed these issues with their mother (6 per cent), far more young women had done so (77 per cent)—presumably reflecting the discussion between mothers and daughters on menstruation (IIPS and Population Council 2010). A largely similar picture emerged when young men and women

TABLE 10.1 Parent–child Interaction, Reports of Youth of Ages 15–24

Interaction level	Young women (N=29,616)	Young men (N=13,708)
A. Communication with parents		
Had discussed adolescent body changes with mother	76.9	6.4
Had discussed adolescent body changes with father	4.2	6.6
Had discussed reproductive processes with mother	5.5	0.4
Had discussed reproductive processes with father	0.6	0.3
B. Parent as confidante on hypothetical situations		
Mother as leading confidante in case of boy–girl relationship issues	12.1	0.3
Father as leading confidante in case of boy–girl relationship issues	0.5	0.4
Mother as leading confidante in case of concerns about menstrual problems/ nocturnal emission*	72.3	0.7
Father as leading confidante in case of concerns about menstrual problems/ nocturnal emission	0.2	1.6

Source: IIPS and Population Council 2010.

Note: * Young women were asked about menstrual problems and young men were asked about nocturnal emission.

were asked in whom they would confide if they experienced concerns about boy–girl relationships, on the one hand, and menstrual problems or nocturnal emission, on the other. Hardly any young men reported that they would confide in a parent for either of these matters (1–2 per cent). While hardly any young women would confide in their father, 12 per cent, and 72 per cent reported that they would confide in their mother about boy–girl relationship issues and menstrual problems, respectively.

In-depth interviews with parents by and large corroborate young people's reports about communication on the physical changes associated with puberty. Discussion on the physical changes associated with puberty, as reported by parents, was gendered, both in terms of communication with daughters versus sons and in terms of communication by the mother versus the father (Table 10.2). Communication with daughters about the physical changes associated with puberty was largely the domain of mothers and was rarely reported by fathers. Indeed, 99 of the 104 fathers who addressed the topic (95 per cent) said that they had not discussed these matters with their daughter. While more mothers had communicated on these issues with their daughter, the content of this communication was limited to menstruation. Of the 145 mothers whose narratives covered whether or not they had discussed matters relating to the physical changes associated with puberty with their daughter, 86 (59 per cent) said that they had talked about menstruation. Even so, many mothers (41 of 145, 28 per cent) specifically noted that girls were not provided with information about menstruation until it happened, and, as a result, many described their daughter's fears and bewilderment about it when it occurred:

> She said, 'See mother. What is this red mark that has come on my clothes?' I told her that she has started menstruating. I also taught her to use folded cloth with the help of a cloth-string during menstruation. (Mother, Jharkhand, rural, age 40 years, education level not available.)

Narratives suggest that communication about menstruation was largely restricted to how to protect oneself ('how to use the cloth') and keep clean during menstruation, on the one hand, and the dos and don'ts relating to behaviour during menstruation, on the other, as a result of her new status as a mature person. As such, communication covered, for example, staying out of the kitchen, staying away

Table 10.2 Extent of Communication between Parents and Daughters and Sons about Sexual and Reproductive Health

Communication type	Mother	Father
A. COMMUNICATION ON PHYSICAL CHANGES ASSOCIATED WITH PUBERTY		
1. With daughters		
Total whose narratives addressed whether they had discussed the physical changes associated with puberty with their daughters	**145**	**104**
Discussed the physical changes associated with puberty	86	5
Yes, no elaboration	45	5
Explained when menstruation happened	41	–
Explained everything without hesitation	14	–
Did not discuss the physical changes associated with puberty	59	99
No (not elaborated)	38	34
No, she told someone else/adult female relative	21	2
No, likely discussed with respondent's spouse	–	65
2. With sons		
Total whose narratives addressed whether they had discussed the physical changes associated with puberty with their sons	**93**	**81**
Discussed the physical changes associated with puberty	7	12
Yes, no elaboration	7	12
Did not discuss the physical changes associated with puberty	86	69
No (how can he talk, knows on his own)	62	61
No, not even with respondent's spouse; may have told someone else	20	1
No, maybe with respondent's spouse	6	9
B. COMMUNICATION ON MATTERS RELATED TO SEX, PREGNANCY, AND SEXUALLY TRANSMITTED INFECTIONS/HIV		
Total whose narratives addressed whether they had discussed matters related to sex, pregnancy, and sexually transmitted infections/HIV with their daughters/sons	**164**	**137**
Discussed these matters	12	13
Did not discuss these matters	152	124

Source: In-depth interviews with parents.

from boys, not speaking freely in general, and not going outside of the home, if avoidable, rather than the meaning of menstruation and the menstrual cycle and its links with pregnancy:

> Yes. I told her about menstruation time and the use of cloth; what she should do when she has her period; how to dress up and everything regarding that. (Mother, Rajasthan, urban, age 35 years, education level up to Class 6.)

> Yes. When she first had her period, I explained to her that she should not enter the kitchen or touch the food or water... I told her about all this, and asked her not to worry but stay away from the kitchen for four days. (Mother, Rajasthan, urban, age 45 years, education level up to Class 5.)

> We told her how she should sit, what she should and should not eat; [that she] should sit in a corner and not come out in the presence of boys... She should not show herself to boys for a week or ten days and should not touch anything. (Mother, Andhra Pradesh, urban, age 50 years, no education.)

Others reported discomfort stemming from shyness and shame or embarrassment about discussing even menstruation with their daughters, many leaving it to other women in the family, most often grandmothers and aunts, to convey information to children.

Communication with sons about the physical changes associated with puberty was even more limited than with daughters, and this was so among both mothers and fathers. In total, just 7 of the 93 mothers (8 per cent) and 12 of the 81 fathers (15 per cent) who addressed this issue during the interview indicated that they had ever talked to their son about the physical changes associated with puberty. Narratives highlight the limited communication, and where communication took place, it was restricted to 'safer' topics such as voice change and facial hair growth:

> I have never talked, and he also has not asked about his *valarchi* [growth] and about *uravumurai* [sexual relationship]. (Father, Tamil Nadu, urban, age 41 years, education level up to Class 10.)

> Yes, he asked me why his voice was getting heavy. I told him not to worry as things would get normal pretty soon. (Mother, Bihar, rural, age 55 years, education level up to Class 10.)

While communication on the physical changes associated with puberty was clearly gendered, this was not so evident in parents' narratives about communication on sexual and reproductive matters relating to sex, pregnancy, and/or sexually transmitted infection/HIV. A great majority of parents who were interviewed in-depth reported that matters relating to sex, pregnancy, and/or sexually transmitted infections/HIV were rarely discussed with their children. Indeed, of the 164 mothers and 137 fathers who discussed this topic in the course of the interview, just 12 (7 per cent) and 13 (10 per cent), respectively, reported that they had talked to their children about such matters. Indeed, narratives from mothers and fathers, whether they were poorly or better educated or whether they were from the north or south highlight that communication is limited:

> I have never done such a thing [talk about sex]... Everything need not be talked about. (Mother, Bihar, rural, age 45 years, no education.)

> No, he hasn't asked me [about sexual matters]. We haven't told him. We don't talk about these things to our children. (Father, Andhra Pradesh, urban, age 52 years, no education.)

Among the few who had discussed matters relating to sex, pregnancy, and/or sexually transmitted infections/HIV with their children, the overwhelming majority had spoken in generalities—warnings about 'staying away' from the opposite sex, not engaging in 'bad' behaviour, not watching films with sex scenes, and so on.

> I told my daughter before her marriage [about marital relations]. I told her she should not be afraid and should not shout loudly. (Mother, Andhra Pradesh, rural, age 46 years, education level up to Class 5.)

> I have warned him. I have asked him not to go around with friends, not to go to the cinema, and not to watch sex movies. He has not watched such movies but when he mingles with friends he may feel inclined to do so. So, I have warned him not to do so. (Father, Tamil Nadu, rural, age 48 years, education level up to Class 5.)

Occasionally, parents appeared to have conveyed information that was inaccurate.

> Yes. I had explained to her that she... should drink only one cup of tea as drinking more tea leads to white discharge and frequent periods because it increases the heat in one's body. (Mother, Rajasthan, urban, age 45 years, education level up to Class 5.)

> I have told my son that if there is a problem in passing urine, circumcision must be done. (Father, Tamil Nadu, urban, age 55 years, education level: graduate.)

Obstacles to Communication about Matters of Sexual and Reproductive Health

Parents were probed about the reasons for their limited discussion on the physical changes associated with puberty and/or sexual and reproductive matters such as sex, pregnancy, and infection. A total of 145 mothers and 97 fathers elaborated on the reasons for their limited communication with their children on these matters, and their preferences on whether their children should obtain this information (Table 10.3).

Reasons for not communicating with children on sexual and reproductive health matters fell into four major groups:

1. That such discussion is against cultural norms; discussion on such matters is unacceptable; children, girls in particular, should not know about sexual matters until marriage; or that they should not be informed about these matters till they are much older.
2. That most parents were uncomfortable because of shame or shyness about holding such discussions with their children and, alternatively, for much the same reasons, children were also uncomfortable about doing so with a parent.
3. That young people these days become aware of these issues on their own.
4. Explaining these matters to children would lead them to engage in sexual activity.

TABLE 10.3 Reasons for Absence of Discussion between Parents and Children on Puberty and/or Sexual and Reproductive Health

Reasons revealed	Mother	Father
Total whose narratives contained reasons for absence of discussion	**145**	**97**
Against cultural norms	80	55
Discomfort, shyness		
Parent shy	50	22
Child shy	42	8
Children get to know on their own	95	56
From friends, environment	70	47
From school and media (TV, newspapers, films)	25	9
Informing children leads them astray	9	15

Source: In-depth interviews with parents.

While not an obstacle, several parents cited young people's preference for obtaining this information from extended family members as a reason for not communicating with their children about sexual and reproductive matters.

Cultural Norms and Unacceptability of Discussion on Matters of Sexual and Reproductive Health

A large group of parents—80 mothers and 55 fathers (55 per cent of the 145 mothers and 57 per cent of the 97 fathers)—who had elaborated on their reasons for not communicating with their children about SRH matters, reported that it was not culturally appropriate for them to provide their children with information about such matters. Several of these parents noted that discussion about sexual relations was unacceptable socially and culturally and, hence, not done in their settings. For these parents, sexual matters were clearly a matter of shame and were not something to be discussed within parent–child relationships. For example, narratives from mothers highlight the following:

> No, all these things [discussing about physical relationship with children] don't work in our village. No, all this does not work in our society. (Mother, Jharkhand, rural, age 39 years, no education.)

> It's wrong. Parents should not tell [their children about sexual matters]. (Mother, Andhra Pradesh, rural, age 50 years, education level up to Class 10.)

Narratives from fathers about discussing sex-related matters with their children were less expansive, but suggested a similar perception:

> To talk (*pause*) with your sons and daughters is not possible. Parents will not talk like that because our culture is not that type. (Father, Maharashtra, rural, age 55 years, education level, graduate.)

> In the community, you will never find any mother or father who speaks to their children on this topic. (Father, Rajasthan, urban, age 42 years, education level not available.)

Parents' narratives further suggested that marriage is a marker legitimizing the provision of information on sexual relations to children. For example, 18 mothers (and two fathers) clearly indicated that children should not be given such information until after marriage, and some others noted that once married, their children would come to know about these matters on their own. For example:

> No. One should not tell them about these things [sexual relations]. When they get married, they will themselves come to know about these things. No. One should not tell boys either before they get married. (Mother, Bihar, rural, age 45 years, no education.)

> A girl must not be given this information before marriage; [she will] automatically come to know after marriage. (Mother, Maharashtra, rural, age 40 years, education level up to Class 5.)

Despite the fact that all parents were referring to children who were 15 years or older, several suggested that in their setting, discussing sexual matters was only acceptable at an older age. For example:

> How do we discuss such private issues? He is only a 15–16 year-old boy. As of now, what can I tell him? (Mother, Bihar, rural, age 35 years, no education.)

> She is a small girl and she need not know about these things [sexual relations]. (Mother, Tamil Nadu, urban, age 35 years, education level up to Class 5.)

Discomfort in Discussing Matters of Sexual and Reproductive Health: Lack of Awareness and Embarrassment

Closely related to cultural norms that dissuaded parents from speaking to their children on SRH matters was the discomfort they experienced, either because they lacked awareness themselves or, more frequently, because they were shy or embarrassed to communicate on such matters with their children. A large group of 50 of the 145 mothers (34 per cent) and a smaller group of 22 of the 97 fathers (23 per cent) also reported the same hesitation in discussing SRH matters with their children. For some, discomfort arose from their own lack of awareness about SRH matters, as these narratives suggest:

> This education has to be given. How to go about it? What can I tell him when I myself am not able to understand? (Father, Jharkhand, rural, age 48 years, education level up to Class 3.)

> If he asks me, I don't have much knowledge about that [sexual matters] to explain to him. (Mother, Maharashtra, urban, age 31 years, education level, postgraduate.)

For many parents—rural mothers in particular—there was a sense of embarrassment or awkwardness about discussing sexual and reproductive matters with both sons as well as daughters, which was clearly related to the cultural norms prohibiting discussion between parents and children about the physical changes associated with puberty and/or sex and reproduction. With regard to shyness in discussing these matters with their daughters, mothers expressed the following:

> I would not ask her anything about it [menstruation]. I would feel bad [to ask]... Yes, I would feel very shy. When one's daughter grows up, one is bound to feel shy... (Mother, Bihar, rural, age 45 years, no education.)

> I feel a little awkward about talking about it [sexual matters]. Yes, I was feeling shy to discuss it with Shivani. (Mother, Bihar, urban, age 32 years, education level, postgraduate.)

Mothers were even shyer about discussing sexual matters with their sons:

> No. He is a boy and I am his mother; so I can't talk to him regarding all this. (Mother, Rajasthan, urban, age 40 years, education level up to Class 8.)

> Once he saw a 'Carefree' [sanitary napkin brand] advertisement on TV and asked me what it is. He was studying in the eighth standard [then]. I did not know what to answer; I asked him to go away. (Mother, Tamil Nadu, rural, age 40 years, education level up to Class 12.)

While few fathers who expressed shyness expanded on their perceptions, one father lamented his shyness as:

> [It is] good to tell them [about sexual matters]. But we feel shy. Both the listener and the one who tells feel shy. (Father, Andhra Pradesh, rural, age 60 years, no education.)

Some parents whose narratives elaborated on the nature of discussion—considerably more mothers (42 of 145 or 29 per cent) than fathers (8 of 97 or 8 per cent)—reported that communication was limited because their son or daughter was too shy to engage in a conversation with them about sexual and reproductive matters. For example, mothers reported the following with regard to their daughters:

> I wanted to ask. One day I even sat [with my daughter] to ask about it, but she got up and ran away. I have tried to ask her, but she doesn't tell me. (Mother, Jharkhand, rural, age 36 years, no education.)

But when I try to tell her, she tells me to keep quiet; that she knows everything. Girls feel shy to share with their parents; they can speak freely with their friends but they feel shy to speak to their mother. (Mother, Maharashtra, urban, age 38 years, education level not available.)

Regarding discussions with their son, mothers reported thus:

Whenever he asks questions, we are able to reply to him properly. He doesn't talk much because he is the eldest son and feels very shy towards us. But sometimes he talks to us... She [daughter] too doesn't speak much. She also feels shy. They are all kids. (Mother, Jharkhand, rural, age 35 years, education level up to Class 2.)

He does not talk as he feels shy. Even with his father, he feels shy. No; he should not talk about these things. We all feel shy, be it him or us. (Mother, Rajasthan, rural, age 48 years, education level not available.)

The few fathers who perceived that their children were too shy to communicate on sexual and reproductive matters reported as follows:

Girls feel shy to talk about such things with their father. (Father, Rajasthan, urban, age 37 years, education level up to Class 12.)

These questions should be asked but in a high-society family. In such families, they [parents and children] don't feel shy. In our middle-class families, children will not ask their parents as they feel bad to ask them. Our children will not ask us and we will not tell them. (Father, Maharashtra, rural, age 55 years, education level not available.)

Several parents who reported that they or their children were too shy to discuss these matters appeared to rely on extended kin to assume the role of informing their children about sexual and reproductive matters. In general, these parents suggested that their children were more comfortable communicating on these matters with extended family kin and that they themselves could not approach their children on these matters. Several women (and not a single father) reported that their daughter—and, in a few cases, their son—discussed these issues with a relative rather than their own mother. For example:

He has an elder brother [cousin] with whom he discusses these matters. (Mother, Jharkhand, rural, age 34 years, education level up to Class 6.)

All this can be told by the grandmother. Her grandmother and girl friends should advise her properly... Or, her grandmother should ask her about it; her grandmother can speak about it (*smiles*). How can

I ask my daughter about it? (Mother, Maharashtra, rural, age 42, no education.)

No. Girls feel shy to talk to their mother about such things; they talk to their aunt who is of their age and discuss what is to be done. (Mother, Rajasthan, urban, age 40 years, education level up to Class 8.)

While not an obstacle as such, young people's preference for obtaining this information from extended family members rather than their own parents was clearly a factor underlying parents' limited communication with their daughters and sons on sexual and reproductive matters.

Children Come to Know about Matters of Sexual and Reproductive Health on Their Own

A large group of parents argued that young people came to know of sex and reproduction on their own: through friends, through the mass media, notably TV, and simply because they are more educated than earlier generations, and hence parents need not provide this information. This perception was articulated by 95 of the 145 mothers (66 per cent) and 56 of the 97 fathers (58 per cent) from the six states. About half the number of parents, both among mothers and fathers, who reported that they had not spoken to their children about these sensitive matters, perceived that their sons and/or daughters had been informed about sex and reproduction by their friends, their siblings, siblings-in-law, and so on. This was reported by 70 of the 145 mothers (48 per cent) and 47 of the 97 fathers (48 per cent).

She will talk to her brother's wife or her friends. (Mother, Jharkhand, rural, age 39 years, no education.)

She gets to know about such things from her friends and through the TV. (Mother, Bihar, urban, age 45 years, no education.)

These days, boys and girls come to know everything by themselves, they talk amongst themselves. (Father, Rajasthan, rural, age 43 years, no education.)

About sexual topics, they do not speak to anybody; not even their father. They have got a few friends from whom they come to know. Not from the parents; in rural areas, it [speaking to parents about such matters] doesn't happen. (Father, Maharashtra, rural, age 40 years, no education.)

Further, several fathers and a few mothers spoke about how today's youth understand sexual and reproductive matters from their social environment.

> What does one have to tell children of today's generation? They know everything, I feel. They have developed maturity; so I hope they know everything. (Mother, Jharkhand, urban, age 40 years, education level up to Class 10.)

> Nowadays there is no need to tell the children; they understand everything. When we see animals having sex; then, we understand ourselves. That's why I feel there is no need to tell the children. Boys and girls come to know through their friends, or by watching television or animals and birds. There is no need for parents to tell them. (Father, Maharashtra, urban, age 43 years, education level not available.)

> There is no need to tell our children. Children are observing what is happening. They are learning from others about how to behave. So, there is no need to tell them anything. There is no need to tell children of the present generation. (Father, Andhra Pradesh, urban, age 38 years, education level up to Class 8.)

A relatively smaller number of parents (25 of the 145 mothers and 9 of the 97 fathers, or 17 per cent and 9 per cent, respectively) also suggested that their children may have learned about sexual and reproductive matters from TV, books, and newspapers. For example:

> Children these days get to know so much from TV and school. There is no need to tell them anything. (Father, Bihar, urban, age 44 years, education level up to Class 10.)

> Now, what will I tell her beforehand? Nowadays, educated children get to know all this beforehand. Earlier, because children were uneducated, they had to be told all this; but girls today read all this in books and come to know about it. (Mother, Jharkhand, rural, age 36 years, no education.)

> Nowadays, with increasing age they watch everything on TV. Therefore, it is not necessary to tell them about it. Earlier, as children were married at a very young age, and there was no TV, they were not aware [of sexual matters]. Now, they get married much later. Therefore, it is not so necessary to tell them about it. (Mother, Maharashtra, rural, age 50 years, education level up to Class 11.)

> They know everything as they watch TV and cinema. In the past, parents used to tell [their children] how a wife and husband should be

> [husband–wife relationship]. There is no need to tell present-day children. They know everything. (Mother, Andhra Pradesh, rural, age 45 years, no education.)

Several parents who argued that young people came to know of sexual and reproductive matters on their own acknowledged a generational difference. They alluded to the fact that their children were well-educated and exposed to mass media which provided vast information and by virtue of this better education and mass media exposure, the children were better aware than their parents about sexual and reproductive matters. For example:

> They know everything. We may not know about it [sexual and reproductive matters] but children know about everything. Still, we ask them to behave in a certain manner. (Mother, Tamil Nadu, rural, age 45 years, education level up to Class 6.)

> No, I didn't say anything to him. Nowadays, children are smart because they watch TV, and know all this before marriage. As the new generation is educated, they must explain to us—the world has changed. The children are smart and they don't get scared to do anything wrong. (Mother, Maharashtra, urban, age 55 years, education level not available.)

> She is an intelligent girl and has knowledge about all these things; [in fact] it [knowledge] is a little more than normal or required. What can she ask her mother? She had studied about all these things in 12th class, and so she has increased her knowledge about these things. So what could she ask her mother? She knew it very well. (Father, Bihar, urban, age 45 years, education level, graduate.)

Fears That Children Will Go Astray if Given Information about Matters of Sexual and Reproductive Health

A few parents expressed concern that communicating with children on SRH matters would encourage young people to engage in sex or perceive the communication as parental approval of such activity. While not expressed, it is possible that many of those who reported that communicating with children on SRH matters was culturally unacceptable or was unnecessary were also expressing this concern indirectly. A total of nine of the 145 mothers (6 per cent) and 15 of the 97 fathers (15 per cent) articulated this view. Mothers and fathers responded thus:

> No. No. I have not told them those matters, as I am their mother. I have told them about all other thing... Not necessary. It is like parents teaching that. (Mother, Andhra Pradesh, rural, age 45 years, no education.)

> No. They will become spoilt. They will go in the '*galat*' [wrong] line [path]. (Mother, Bihar, urban, age 45 years, no education.)

> Yes. If the one who doesn't have any knowledge is taught about this he would start doing *chettai* [mischief]. This education would give youngsters the opportunity to *kettu poka* [become bad]. (Father, Tamil Nadu, rural, age 48 years, education level up to Class 10.)

> He will be curious to know what will happen next. The chances of going on the wrong path are greater. Therefore, we don't discuss such topics. (Father, Maharashtra, urban, age 44 years, education level up to Class 7.)

> If at all our daughter asks us such questions [about sexual and reproductive matters], our first duty would be to look at her and read her face, and try to analyse why she is asking such questions. (Father, Maharashtra, rural, age 46 years, education level not available.)

> In a village, parents will never tell their children about such matters... They don't realize that it is good if children know about these things. They fear that their children will engage in such activities if they know. (Father, Andhra Pradesh, rural, age 55 years, education level up to Class 1.)

> No. It is wrong. If we discuss about that, they may think about that. If we tell him not to go in a particular way, he will think about it and go that way. (Father, Andhra Pradesh, urban, age 54 years, education level up to Class 9.)

> We should not teach them. It would be like spoiling our own children. If we teach them about it, they may try to experiment. Even now, school students read all kinds of dirty magazines, and if we teach them, they will get even more spoilt. (Father, Tamil Nadu, urban, age 49 years, education level up to Class 8.)

MOVING FORWARD

Parent–child communication on matters of sexual and reproductive health was clearly limited, apart from the large number of mothers who reported having discussed menstruation with their daughters.

Even discussions between mothers and daughters on menstruation, however, focused more on the mechanics of menstruation and the dos and don'ts traditionally associated with menstruation, rather than on the meaning of menstruation and the menstrual cycle and its links with pregnancy. The kinds of obstacles to discussing sexual and reproductive health matters—largely sex, pregnancy, and infection, but also, in several instances, the physical changes associated with puberty—described by mothers and fathers and by rural and urban parents were, on the whole, similar. Mothers were, however, considerably more likely than fathers to report discomfort and shyness experienced by themselves as well as their children as an obstacle, and somewhat more likely than fathers to suggest that children came to know these matters on their own. Fathers were more likely, in contrast, to report fears that children would go astray if informed by their parents about SRH matters.

Recommendations

A number of recommendations based on the findings of this survey are discussed in this section. For one, while acknowledged by relatively few parents, it is likely that a key obstacle to communication may be parents' own lack of knowledge of SRH matters and their perceived inability thus to respond to their children's questions. Indeed, even among those who did provide information to their children, this information was not always accurate. These findings call for programmes that address parents' lack of awareness on SRH matters, including sex and reproductive processes, pregnancy and infection, reproductive rights, and the physical changes associated with puberty.

Second, it is clear that parents hold many misconceptions, for example, girls should not be informed about menstruation until it happens or young men and women, particularly young women, about sex and reproduction until marriage; and youth will interpret any communication on matters relating to sexual life as a licence to experiment with sex; and young people are well-informed about sexual matters through the media and friends. Programmes for parents need to dispel these misconceptions and highlight the need for and acceptability of providing their children this information themselves.

Given the lack of communication on menstrual matters, it is not surprising that many women described their daughters' first experience of menstruation as traumatic, characterized by tears, fears that their parents would be angry, and concerns that the blood signified ill health. Our third recommendation calls for programmes that inform parents about the need for providing timely information to girls before they start menstruating and not after, and that age-appropriate information is provided that explains the menstrual cycle and its links to pregnancy.

Fourth, efforts must also be made to reduce discomfort, embarrassment, and shyness among both parents and children about talking with each other about the physical changes associated with puberty and/or sex. Lessons may be drawn from programmes for young people—particularly for the school-going children—conducted elsewhere that include activities or homework for young people to do with their parents that enable learning and, at the same time, provide an opening for parents to initiate discussion on SRH matters with their children. Lessons may also be adapted for mothers and fathers from life-skills education models implemented among the young, with some sessions devoted exclusively to parents and others that bring parents together with their sons and/or daughters.

Finally, as described earlier, policies formulated by several ministries—Health and Family Welfare (MoHFW), Youth Affairs (MoYAS), and Women and Child Development (MWCD)—have recognized the need to engage parents meaningfully in enabling young people to make a successful transition to adulthood. The findings presented in this chapter underscore the limited extent to which these commitments have been realized in the lives of young people and parents themselves. These findings call for increased investments by these ministries in pilot-testing models to encourage supportive supervision and trusting relationships between parents and adolescent children and scaling up lessons from these pilots.

Before concluding, we note an important limitation of our data. The way topics were covered differed across states and reflected, in many instances, the respondent's willingness or unwillingness to discuss various topics and the interviewer's ability to draw out pertinent experiences from the respondent. Indeed, narratives show that in several instances, particularly with regard to communication on sensitive SRH matters, responses were monosyllabic or deviated from the question posed. As a result, responses were not equally expansive in all settings. The discussion and the depth of narratives differed, with responses in some settings richer than those in others, and with narratives relating to parent–child communication on the physical changes associated with puberty being more expansive than those relating to sex, pregnancy, and sexually transmitted infections/HIV. We acknowledge that, as a result, narratives from some states are richer than from some others; and that narratives on some topics are richer than on other topics.

In conclusion, we note that there is enough evidence from around the world that supportive communication between parents and children enables young people to make a safe and confident transition to adulthood. This chapter, one of the first from India to probe parental perspectives, suggests that parents are constrained by traditional norms, lack of information, and limited skills from communicating with their children and providing them the supportive environment needed to make this transition. It is important that efforts are initiated that enable parents to overcome these constraints.

REFERENCES

Abraham, L. and K.A. Kumar. 1999. 'Sexual Experiences and Their Correlates among College Students in Mumbai City, India', *International Family Planning Perspectives*, 25(3): 139–46.

Alexander, M., L. Garda, S. Kanade, S.J. Jejeebhoy, and B. Ganatra. 2006. *Formation of Partnerships among Young Women and Men in Pune District, Maharashtra*. New Delhi: Population Council.

Altekar, A.S. 1962. *The Position of Women in Hindu Civilization*. Delhi: Motilal Banarsidass.

Aspy C.B., S.K. Vesely, R.F. Oman, S. Rodine, L. Marshall, and K. McLeroy. 2007. 'Parental Communication and Youth Sexual Behaviour', *Journal of Adolescence*, 30(3): 449–66.

Bettinger, J.A., D.D. Celentano, F.C. Curriero, N.E. Adler, S.G. Millstein, and J.M. Ellen. 2004. 'Does Parental Involvement Predict New Sexually Transmitted Diseases in Female Adolescents?' *Pediatrics and Adolescent Medicine*, 158: 666–70.

Biddlecom, A., K. Awusabo-Asare, and A. Bankole. 2009. 'Role of Parents in Adolescent Sexual Activity and Contraceptive use in Four African Countries', *International Perspectives on Sexual and Reproductive Health*, 35(2): 72–81.

Blum, R.W. and K.N. Mmari. 2005. *Risk and Protective Factors Affecting Adolescent Reproductive Health in Developing Countries*. Geneva: World Health Organization.

Cui, N., M. Li., and E. Gao. 2001. 'View of Chinese Parents on the Provision of Contraception to Unmarried Youth', *Reproductive Health Matters*, 9(17): 137–45.

Garda, L. and M. Alexander. 2009. '*Parent-child Connectedness: A Pressing Need to be Addressed in Rural and Urban India*', Paper presented at the XXVI IUSSP International Population Conference, Marrakech, Morocco.

Hollander, D. 2007. 'Program for Fathers Helps Them Talk to Young Sons about Sex and HIV Risk', *Perspectives on Sexual and Reproductive Health*, 39(4): 248–9.

International Institute for Population Sciences (IIPS) and Population Council. 2010. *Youth in India: Situation and Needs 2006–2007*. Mumbai: IIPS.

Jejeebhoy, S.J. and K.G. Santhya. 2011. *Parent–child Communication on Sexual and Reproductive Health Matters: Perspectives of Mothers and Fathers of Youth in India*. New Delhi: Population Council.

Joint United Nations Programme on HIV/AIDS (UNAIDS). 2008. *Report on the Global AIDS Epidemic*. Geneva: UNAIDS.

Kiragu, K., C. Watson, M. Muhwezi, A. Akia-Fiedler, R. Kibombo, T. Nelson, and M. Juma. 2007. *Straight Talk Campaign in Uganda: Parent Survey*. Washington, DC: Population Council.

Kirby, D. 2007. 'Emerging Answers 2007: Research Findings on Programs to Reduce Teen Pregnancy and Sexually Transmitted Diseases', The National Campaign to Prevent Teen and Unplanned Pregnancy. http://www.thenationalcampaign.org/ea2007/, last accessed on 21 July 2011.

Kumi-Kyereme, A., K. Awusabo-Asare, A. Biddlecom, and A. Tanle. 2007. 'Influence of Social Connectedness, Communication and Monitoring on Adolescent Sexual Activity in Ghana', *African Journal of Reproductive Health*, 11(3): 133–47.

Lambert, H. and K. Wood. 2005. 'A Comparative Analysis of Communication about Sex, Health and Sexual Health in India and South Africa: Implications for HIV Prevention', *Culture, Health and Sexuality*, 7(6): 527–41.

Lederman, R.P., W. Chan, and C. Roberst-Gray. 2004. 'Sexual Risk Attitudes and Intentions of Youth Aged 12–14 Years: Survey Comparisons of Parent-teen Prevention and Control Groups', *Behavioural Medicine*, 29(4): 155–63.

Li, X., B. Stanton, and S. Feigelman. 2000. 'Impact of Perceived Parental Monitoring on Adolescent Risk Behaviour Over 4 Years', *Journal of Adolescent Health*, 27: 49–56.

Luwaga, L.C.N. 2004. *Parent–adolescent Communication on Sexuality in the Context of HIV/AIDS in Uganda: An Exploratory Study*. Bergen: Research Centre for Health Promotion.

Mahajan, P. and N. Sharma. 2005. 'Parents Attitude towards Imparting Sex Education to Their Adolescent Girls', *Anthropologist*, 7(3): 197–9.

Mehra, S., R. Savithri, and L. Coutinho. 2002. 'Sexual Behaviour among Unmarried Adolescents in Delhi, India: Opportunities Despite Parental Controls', Paper presented at the 2002 IUSSP Regional Population Conference, Bangkok, June.

Meschke, L.L., S. Bartholomae, and S.R. Zentall. 2000. 'Adolescent Sexuality and Parent–Adolescent Processes: Promoting Healthy Teen Choices', *Family Relations*, 49: 143–54.

Miller, K.S., B.A. Kotchick, S. Dorsey, R. Forehand, and A.Y. Ham. 1998. 'Family Communication about Sex: What Are Parents Saying and Are Their Adolescents Listening?' *Family Planning Perspectives*, 30(5): 218–22, 235.

Ministry of Health and Family Welfare (MoHFW). 2000. *National Population Policy 2000*. New Delhi: MoHFW, Government of India.

———. 2002. *National Health Policy*. New Delhi: MoHFW, Government of India.

———. 2006. *Implementation Guide on RCH II Adolescent Reproductive Sexual Health Strategy for State and District Programme Managers*. New Delhi: MoHFW, Government of India.

Ministry of Human Resource Development (MHRD). 1998. *National Policy on Education 1986 (as modified in 1992) with National Policy on Education, 1968*. New Delhi: MHRD, Government of India.

Ministry of Statistics and Programme Implementation (MoSPI). 2008. 'New Series (1999–2000) Statement: Gross State Domestic Product at Current Prices'. New Delhi: MoSPI, Government of India. www.mospi.nic.in/6_gsdp_cur_9394ser.htm, last accessed on 27 March 2008.

Ministry of Women and Child Development (MWCD). 2005. *National Plan of Action for Children 2005*. New Delhi: MWCD, Government of India.

Ministry of Youth Affairs and Sports (MoYAS). 2014. *National Youth Policy 2014*. New Delhi: MoYAS, Government of India.

Mohammadi, M.R., S. Alikhani., F.K. Abadi Farahani, and A. Bahonar. 2007. 'Parents Attitudes towards Adolescent Boy's Reproductive Health Needs and Practice in Tehran', *Iran Journal of Psychiatry*, 2: 13–24.

National AIDS Control Organisation (NACO). 2002. *National AIDS Prevention and Control Policy*. New Delhi: NACO.

National Council of Educational Research and Training (NCERT). 2005. *National Curriculum Framework 2005*. New Delhi: NCERT.

Ngom, P., M.A. Magadi, and T. Owuor. 2003. 'Parental Presence and Adolescent Reproductive Health among the Nairobi Urban Poor', *Journal of Adolescent Health*, 33(5): 369–77.

Office of the Registrar General and Census Commissioner, India. 2001. *Age Groups*. New Delhi: Office of Registrar General and Census Commissioner. http://www.censusindia.gov.in/Census_Data_2001/Census_

Data_Online/Social_and_cultural/Age_Groups.aspx, last accessed on 27 November 2008.

Office of the Registrar General and Census Commissioner, India. 2011. *Provisional Population Totals Paper 2 of 2011 (India & States/UTs).* http://www.censusindia.gov.in/2011-prov-results/paper2/census2011_paper2.html, last accessed on 14 December 2011.

Rajya Sabha. 2009. *Hundred and Thirty-fifth Report on Petition Praying for National Debate and Evolving Consensus on the Implementation of the Policy for Introduction of Sex Education in the Schools and Holding Back Its Introduction until Then.* New Delhi: Rajya Sabha Secretariat.

Roche, K.M., S. Ahmed, and R.W. Blum. 2008. 'Enduring Consequences of Parenting for Risk Behaviours from Adolescence into Early Adulthood', *Social Science and Medicine*, 66(9): 2023–34.

Ryan, S., K. Franzetta, J. Manlove, and E. Holcombe. 2007. 'Adolescents' Discussions about Contraception or STDs with Partners before First Sex', *Perspectives on Sexual and Reproductive Health*, 39(3): 149–57.

Shekhar, M., S. Ghosh, and P. Panda. 2007. 'Exploring Safe Sex Awareness and Sexual Experiences of Adolescents in Patna', *Economic and Political Weekly*, 42(48): 48–55.

Shetty, P., S. Kowli, and V. Patil. n.d. 'Attitude of Mothers towards Sex Education of Adolescent Girls', *Regional Health Forum WHO South-East Asia Region* (Volume 3). http://www.searo.who.int/en/Section1243/Section1310/Section1343/Section1344/Section1351/Section1686_7197.htm, last accessed on 29 March 2011.

Soletti, A.B., V. Guilamo-Ramos, D. Burnette, S. Sharma, and A. Bouris. 2009. 'India–US Collaboration to Prevent Adolescent HIV Infection: The Feasibility of a Family-based HIV-prevention Intervention for Rural Indian Youth', *Journal of the International AIDS Society*, 12(1): 35.

Whitaker, D.J., K.S. Miller, D.C. May, and M.L. Levin. 1999. 'Teenage Partners' Communication about Sexual Risk and Condom Use: The Importance of Parent-teenager Discussions', *Family Planning Perspectives*, 31(3): 117–21.

World Health Organization (WHO). 2007. *Helping Parents in Developing Countries Improve Adolescents' Health.* Geneva: WHO.

Zhang, L., X. Li., I. Shah, W. Baldwin, and B. Stanton. 2007. 'Parent–Adolescent Sex Communication in China', *European Journal of Contraception and Reproductive Health Care*, 12(2): 138–47.

11 Universal Day-care Services

Meeting the Intersecting Needs and Rights of Women and Children

Neeta Misra and Ramya Subrahmanian[1]

The first six years of a child's life are critical for her future development. The provision of inputs related to care, education, nutrition, and health, often collectively referred to as Early Childhood Care and Education (ECCE), determines path dependence for children, particularly between the ages of 0–3 years.[2] Social policies that promote ECCE can act as a powerful tool in addressing poverty and social exclusion and in developing human capital by building stable foundations for growth and development of all children.

[1] The authors are grateful to Ragini Saira Malhotra for her contribution to and feedback on earlier drafts of this chapter. The authors are also grateful to Mina Swaminathan, Sudeshna Chatterjee, Ratna Sudarshan, Shraddha Chigateri, Mridula Bajaj, Rajni Palriwala, and several others who have helped shape the perspective reflected in this chapter through several discussions on the issues of balancing women's unpaid care work and child rights, though they bear no responsibility for the arguments put forward in this chapter.

[2] The concept of ECCE refers to a holistic approach to child development that recognizes the interrelatedness of different inputs; it is the equivalent of international terms such as Early Childhood Development (ECD) or Early Childhood Care and Development (ECCD). This chapter will refer to the holistic approach as ECCE (UNICEF 2013).

Effectively targeted ECCE interventions can play a central role within welfare regimes to reduce poverty and inequality by providing the building blocks of physical and emotional well-being to enable poor children to climb out of poverty. Conversely, inadequate or insufficient ECCE interventions lead to negative consequences across the life cycle for the populations involved. Thus, the centrality of ECCE to human development, poverty elimination, social justice, and, ultimately, human rights is the framing argument of this paper. In particular, the chapter argues for an approach that is both gender-sensitive and child-focused in ensuring ECCE services reach all children.

The chapter looks at one aspect of ECCE, that of providing child-care services, and how it can meet the needs of young children in India. Childcare refers to the physical and emotional aspects of care that are essential for a child's development. Care inputs are required the most between 0 and 3 years of age when proper nutrition, emotional security, and dedicated attention from caregivers need to be ensured. Scientific evidence has shown that the foundation of a child's emotional, intellectual, social, and physical development is laid during the first six years of life and particularly within the first two years when significant development of the brain occurs (NSCDC 2007). Where quality attention and inputs from caregivers are not received, children's growth and well-being are compromised, often irreversibly so. Therefore, the time and attention of dedicated caregivers is central to this period of a child's life.

Given that the gender division of labour results in women being largely responsible for children within the home, the time required of women to provide this unpaid work makes 'caregiving' fundamentally a gender issue. Women, and particularly poor women, face the challenge of balancing multiple yet distinct roles of earners, caregivers, and home-makers whose value is rarely recognized by policymakers (Swaminathan 1993). Given the gender dimensions of childcare, designing and implementing appropriate social policies to provide universal quality care to children would provide women with support and choice and reduce long-term gender inequality, whilst preventing the underdevelopment of children. Women's rights and opportunities are also fundamentally strengthened if they are supported in their maternal and caregiving roles.

The key nutrition and poverty indicators for children in the ages 0–6 in India, detailed by Rustagi et al. in Chapter 2 of this volume, highlight the crises of development that children in India face. High levels of poverty and social exclusion limit opportunities and choices of poor households to provide for the basic ECCE needs of their children. The provision of quality childcare services within this context is a primary social exigency in national poverty eradication strategies and for reducing social exclusion. Aside from facilitating the development of young children's core capacities, the provision of childcare allows women to take up economic activity, and contributes to their economic empowerment. The provision of universal childcare thus has individual and society-wide benefits and can be promoted both from the perspective of children's and women's rights and from the perspective of the benefits and returns to society and individuals from investments in such services to human development. These arguments are laid out below.

CHILDCARE FROM THE 'RIGHTS' PERSPECTIVE

Placing the need for childcare services within a rights-based framework derives from the notion that access to quality childcare is a basic citizenship right of both women and children. Quality care is essential for children's development, and it needs to be advocated as a fundamental right on their behalf. Diversifying access to trained caregivers enables the mother to pursue activities that guarantee her greater freedoms within patriarchal settings. Further, the amount and quality of care the girl child will receive is contingent on her status within the family, which needs to be addressed to prevent the perpetuation of inequitable gender practices. The rights-based framework also includes the rights of children to pursue their own development and be freed from the tasks of childcare of siblings that may be imposed on them.

Access to quality childcare services can therefore be considered a basic citizenship right that allows women to exercise their rights to work or for leisure, whilst ensuring that their children are provided with quality care.

The rights-based approach to childcare is therefore based on the interconnected and interdependent nature of women's and children's needs and rights around childcare. Accordingly, if childcare is seen as a fundamental citizenship right for both women and children, then states have an obligation to fulfil the realization of this right through legal reforms and regulatory frameworks and allocate sufficient resources, whilst setting up necessary governance and accountability structures to ensure the efficacy of care policy (Goonesekere and Silva-De Alwis 2005).

The Case for Universal Services for Young Children

Conclusive scientific medical evidence supports early childhood intervention by the targeting of ECCE efforts on children in the critical ages of 0–3 years and then from 3–6 years. Research shows that a child's development in the early stages of the care continuum, that is, from the womb to 3 years, is the most critical period for brain development, because much of the loss of development during this period is irreversible.

Early experiences shape and develop circuits within the brain. Limited or inadequate experiences lead to underuse of the brain circuits that once neglected cannot be re-developed. Some people refer to this as 'use it or lose it' (NSCDC 2007, p. 2). Brain circuits are built in a hierarchical fashion, starting with the simplest to the more complex circuits. Sensory pathways for basic vision and hearing are the first to develop, followed by early language skills and higher cognitive functions. Every new skill is built upon competencies that come before, and development peaks at the age of 3 years (NSCDC 2007, p. 3).

The evidence shows that the brain is much more malleable at the early stages of formation, and, over time, a layering process allows the brain to take on complex functions. Later, this malleability decreases and the brain becomes more rigid and difficult to influence and alter.

Another key finding, particularly for childcare, is the importance and interrelatedness of both cognitive and non-cognitive inputs in early childhood.

> Research shows that cognitive, emotional, and social capacities are inextricably intertwined in the brain, and, in like fashion, learning, behaviour, and both physical and mental health are highly interrelated throughout the life course. (NSCDC 2007, p. 5)

Investing in Children: A Feminist Response

The 'human capital argument', which states that investment in all the components of ECCE develops future generations of dynamic workers and that investing in ECCE is a social investment, has driven the focus towards the provision of ECCE. Thus, the widely made argument that early child development is the foundation of human capital formation and has the highest rate of return to economic development (Young and Richardson 2007, p. 1). Human capital accumulation is also viewed as a dynamic and synergistic process and early investments contribute significantly to raising the productivity of later investments (Carneiro and Heckman 2003, p. 5).

However, who bears the responsibility of providing the care for children that contributes to these human capital returns? This is a central question that is seldom addressed in economic literature. Social norms and values assign the responsibility of childcare to 'families' (Strober 2004). Within families, women generally assume the unpaid role of carers, including the care of children. Feminist economists have gone deeper into the human capital debate by interrogating the role of the state vis-à-vis children, their welfare, families, and women. They argue for treating children as a public good as societies benefit from the contributions of working adults, although not everyone contributes to the care of those future adults during childhood. Thus families and particularly women unduly bear the burden of creating a society-wide shared benefit. Included in this argument is the need to recognize the contribution of non-market labour to the development of human capital in society (Folbre 1994; Strober 2004).

When extending this debate to developing countries, the human capital approach must further accommodate the constraints that poverty places on the livelihoods, health, and education of poor households in shaping parental strategies for children in those households. Poor households that do not have access to food, housing, and health would be unable to provide their children with basic care and education and, in turn, would be unable to break the cycle of intergenerational transmission of values, poverty, and disadvantage (Kabeer 2000, p. 17). Thus, high levels of poverty and exclusion require that the well-being of children be framed as a public good, and the role of the state as a provider of services for childcare assumes central importance.

WOMEN, WORK, AND CARE

Gender and Care

Social values and norms often place childcare within the ambit of the family and, more specifically, as part of the role of women within the household. The introduction of time-use surveys has revealed the extent to which women continue to shoulder responsibilities for unpaid care work. A time-use survey conducted in 1998–9 in India shows that while 74 per cent of men participated in SNA-defined work (that is, work defined as job by the System of National Accounts), only 51 per cent participated in unpaid care work; for women, 43 per cent participated in SNA and 91 per cent in unpaid care work. When assessing the weekly time spent on unpaid work, the differences were significant with women spending 5.5 (rural) and 6.1 (urban) hours of the day on unpaid care work and men spending 1.2 (rural and urban) hours. These numbers varied across social groups based on caste and religion (Palriwala and Neetha 2008, p. 2).

Another dimension to gender and care is the non-recognition of care work in national policy and statistics. Conventional economics and national statistics and policy tend to overlook the unpaid work in the economy or the extended economic work, which contributes as much to human well-being and human capital as 'economic work' does, but, being largely unpaid, it remains unaccounted for. This aspect of women's work has been largely excluded from SNA, and it is only in the recent decade that the United Nations has begun to account for Extended SNA (ESNA), which is yet to be uniformly applied across countries to capture the extended economic work done by both men and women (Hirway 2005, p. 4).

The time use study, referred to earlier, estimates that unpaid care work contributes an estimated 29 per cent of India's total GDP (Palriwala and Neetha 2008, p. 3). The two types of work (SNA and ESNA) are also interrelated in terms of opportunities and upward mobility (Hirway 2005).

Since liberalization and globalization, the debate on gender and care has gained prominence, because of the increasing numbers of women entering the labour force. The 'era of flexibility' became characterized as 'the era of more generalized insecurity and precariousness' in which many more men as well as more women were pushed into precarious forms of labour (Standing 1999, p. 583).

Traditional economic theory that saw the potential of the labour power of women to be a transmission mechanism, transforming labour into paid work and, in turn, paid work into improved levels of livelihood and security, was questioned, since this transformation had to interface with existing gender relations that made it complex and constrained:

> These constraints relate to social norms and values which govern the gender division of labour in production and reproduction in different regions of the world. In general, these tend to assign primary responsibility for the reproduction and care of the family to women and overall decision-making authority to senior males... (Kabeer 2008, p. 3)

Women often entered the labour market forced by economic need rather than choice, and gender-based inequalities resulted in the majority of women in developing countries entering the labour force with low levels of education and skills accessing substandard types of employment that were casual, low paying, and vulnerable. These types of jobs did not provide enough sustenance to sufficiently contribute to sustainable livelihoods, but came with the additional burdens of childcare (Kabeer 2008).

Women and the Workforce in India

The labour market in India is overwhelmingly situated in the informal sector, which accounts for over 90 per cent of the workforce (GoI 2012, p. 1). The majority of the labour force is located in rural areas that account for 73.4 per cent of all employment and 82.1 per cent of women's employment (Chowdhury 2011, p. 23). The primary categories of employment for both men and women are 'self-employment' and 'casual labour'. On the whole, the category of 'regular' workers has shown little movement for either men or women over the past decade, although for urban women, the share of regular employment as a percentage of rural employment has increased by 6 per cent from 2000–10 (Mazumdar and Pillai 2011, p. 119).

Overall, long-term trends of women's employment in India paint a picture that is inconsistent with development theories of increased participation in the labour force and the feminization of the labour force thesis. The female labour force participation rates (LFPRs) over a 25-year period have shown a long-term downward trend for rural women and relative stagnancy for urban women with a brief increase in 2004–5 (Mazumdar and Pillai 2011, p. 119).

Although the country has experienced unprecedented growth in the past two decades, the statistics paint a fairly bleak picture of employment since 2004–5; limited creation of jobs, widespread withdrawal of women from the labour force, and slow growth of employment in the non-agricultural sector. An increase in the labour force of 22.3 million by men was virtually cancelled out by a decrease in the female workforce of 21 million (Mazumdar and Pillai 2011, p. 1). The decrease was likely to have been caused by the financial crises in 2008, which made women more vulnerable to losing their jobs, particularly in the export sector (Chowdhury 2011).

A more detailed look at 2009–10 employment data for women shows that the bulk of women's employment falls within self-employment (53.3 per cent) and casual work (36.6 per cent), with regular workers accounting for only 10.1 per cent of women's employment. The self-employed category consists of three categories; the own account worker, the employer, and a third category—the unpaid helper working in family enterprises. This third category dominates the self-employed category, consistently accounting for over 70 per cent of self-employment amongst rural women. When the unpaid worker category is removed from self-employment and compared with all other categories of employment for women, it emerges as the dominant category of employment for rural women, accounting for over 40 per cent of employment between 1993 and 2008. This has significant implications for accessing childcare services (Mazumdar and Pillai 2011, p. 4).

The sectoral distribution of women's employment shows a stagnant and highly segregated picture, with women concentrated in the primary sector where they are denied basic economic and social protections, including childcare and maternity entitlements. Staying home to care for children has high opportunity costs, and mothers are often compelled to compromise children's care needs in favour of economic survival.

There are also several supply-side issues around childcare and women's work. The private provision of childcare is a burgeoning source of employment for women and particularly poor women who are affected by lower job security and benefits (Rustagi 2010). The dynamics that arise from these conditions need to be understood in terms of the regulation of private care services, setting quality standards, training, and linking better standards with work conditions for caregivers, who are predominantly women shouldering the double burden of care by both being providers of care and continuing to be responsible for the care of their own children (Moghe 2005).

ECCE AND PROVISION OF CHILDCARE

'Care' is a key component for early child development. There are three significant aspects of childcare:[3]

1. *Presence*: Continuous and constant (though not permanent) and available at short notice
    - close and constant interaction, supported by body contact, leads to psychic bonding between mother and child, forming the base for human relationships
    - presence also implies responsiveness to need
    - the need for presence is inversely related to the age of the child
2. *Relationship*: A warm and caring one, expressing affection and concern through body language, gestures, tone, expression, touch, and language.
3. *Caregiving activities*: Caregiving routines and activities, such as feeding, bathing, grooming, toileting, putting to sleep, comforting, amongst others.

The delivery of this care varies depending on the age of the child, and a generally used model to distinguish between different stages of care is the 'continuum of care' (Figure 11.1), which would help social policy to be structured according to the changing needs and requirements of the different stages. A complete package of services should

[3] This definition was presented by Mina Swaminathan in a presentation titled 'Framework for ECCD' at an ISST-UNICEF workshop in New Delhi, December 2012.

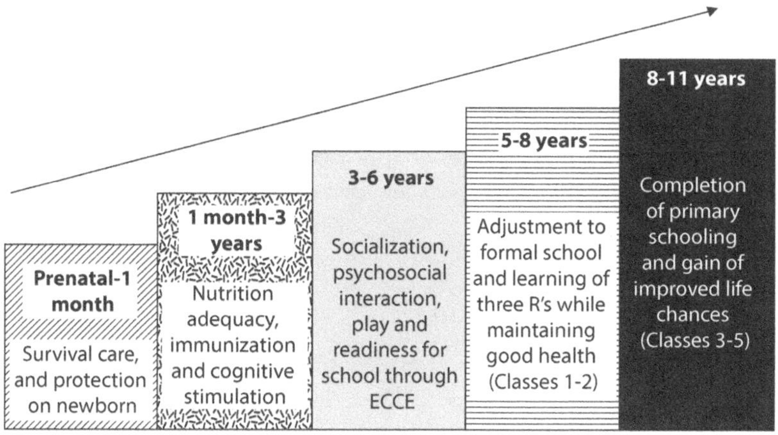

FIGURE 11.1 The Continuum of Care and Early Interventions
Source: World Bank 2004.

have maternity benefits, antenatal care, postnatal care, home-based services for children and infants, and care services with effective transition to crèches, where along with physical care delivery, monitoring of key nutrition, health, and education benchmarks for children occurs. The continuum of care identifies the key differentiated stages of early childhood development and the necessary inputs for each stage. Most models for early childcare extend from the third trimester of pregnancy up to the time the child is of school age, that is, 5–6 years old (Swaminathan 1993, p. 1).

This provision of childcare services across the care continuum requires regulation of the care sector, creation of a set of suitable standards, a curriculum, and benchmarks for minimum inputs for children under 6 years. The creation and regulation of standards for caregivers is an important element of this, requiring minimum wages, fixed work hours, suitable ratio of caregivers to children, and adequate resources, curriculum, and infrastructure for training caregivers. Creating benchmark indicators will also make it easier to assess whether the needs of children under 6 years are being met.

The provision of universal childcare across the continuum of care, this chapter argues, is a core entitlement. The debate in favour of replacing childcare services with cash transfers in this context is misguided, because it needs to recognize that at different stages in this continuum, a cash transfer would not meet the qualitative care needs of young children. A combination of cash transfers (such as those for maternity benefits), infrastructure, and delivery of services tailored to specific age groups is a sounder approach than cash transfers alone to provide a comprehensive package of key inputs for children under 6 years.

COMMUNITY-BASED CRÈCHES

A community-based crèche is an essential service and must be viewed as a right, especially for poor families. Apart from being a place where children are left for care, such crèches potentially play a role in the provision and monitoring of the ECCE needs of young children. Community-based crèches provide a broader service along with the delivery of childcare; they are an institutional mechanism for ensuring quality provision of the ECCE needs of children, and, particularly in poor communities, they have the potential to prevent the underdevelopment of children. A community-based crèche is also a gendered response to childcare as it can support women to use their time for productive work or also for required rest and leisure.

While home-based care for nursing infants in their first six months carries the optimum benefit, an ideal crèche model would have provisions to accommodate all children from new-born infants to 6-year-olds to provide an alternative to home-based care for even the most vulnerable and at-risk babies. The community-based crèche forms the meeting point for determining community need, community participation, and monitoring and accountability of all ECCE services, so that there is a continuum between home-based care and access to services at the crèche centre.

Understanding these multifarious roles a community crèche plays, planners need to design universal crèche care within a broad framework of essential infrastructure, adequate resources, quality standards, and decentralized governance and budgeting to allow crèches to sufficiently meet the needs of children, mothers, and poor households. To prevent social exclusion, a community crèche must ensure that marginalized groups use this service, and social policy must be designed to ensure universal access. An integrated ECCE framework in designing crèches allows it to act as an early intervention towards reducing poverty and social exclusion.

UNIVERSAL DAY CARE: THE ARCHITECTURE OF PROVISION

State and the Provision of Childcare

The state will have a central role to play, if access to childcare services is to be treated as a right. The state is a key institution for the prioritization and delivery of childcare as a key component of social welfare. The state must be the driver of policy, its regulation, creation of universal services, and access to childcare within the rights-based approach.

The 'care diamond'—a stylized conceptualization of provision of care by various institutions—which places care at the intersection of and interplay between the state, markets, not-for-profit sector, and families (Razavi 2007) is a useful analytical tool for understanding how a society prioritizes childcare. Within the interplay of the four institutions, the level of regulation, expenditure, and funding by the government becomes a useful indicator of how care is prioritized within a society and of the balance of responsibility between the various providers. Government provision of funding is also an indication of its commitment to assist women to enter the labour force by reducing their burden of childcare.

In order to frame childcare as an essential right, social policy needs a framework in which the responsibility for and socialization of the child are no longer the responsibility of the family alone but that of the society as well. A reframing of childcare within this context would broadly require:

1. A redefinition of public (state) and private (family) relationships concerning children's affairs;
2. The recognition of the right of the child to be cared and socialized in a wider social context than that of the family;
3. The recognition of the family's right (and specifically women's) to share the care of their children with society;
4. The recognition that childcare is a professional task, which along with education, in a broader sense, promotes the child's full development.

The provision of childcare services in this context calls for the reframing of state responsibility, administrative links, target population and age groups, funding policies, types of provision, professional profile and training, physical environment, pedagogical guidelines, and parental involvement (Haddad 2002, p. 27).

Status of Childcare Services in India

As argued above, high levels of poverty and social exclusion make a strong argument for regarding the welfare of children and specifically childcare in India as a fundamental citizenship right. Resource allocation becomes a key starting point to assess the importance of childcare within social policy.

A recent study looks at budgetary allocation for children under 6 years and at the adequacy of funds and their utilization. The study finds that allocations for the Integrated Child Development Services (ICDS), health, nutrition, child protection, and others have risen from close to 1 per cent of the total outlays in the 1990s to almost 5 per cent of the total outlays in 2006–7. However, the bulk of these expenditures is focused on elementary education (70 per cent), with other child-related expenditures rising only incrementally and being still under 1 per cent (Kaul and Sankar 2009, p. 43). State-level spending far outpaces central allocation, and wide differences across states account for the uneven delivery of ECCE services across the country (Kaul and Sankar 2009). The study finds that a higher investment in education and a relatively lower investment for ICDS and other services mean that the children in the critical early years are not getting as much attention as they are getting in later stages in life. Additionally, these amounts when translated into per child expenditure, though improved over time, are far from the desired levels.

> Overall, while the allocations per child increased in all sectors...the gaps in the provision per child in the early age group and those in the school-going age group are wider; this in spite of the international evidence to focus on early ages, especially before three years of age... (Kaul and Sankar 2009, p. 45)

The extent to which government incorporates childcare in social policy is an acknowledgement of the role of childcare in, and a measure of commitment to, reducing poverty and increasing human development. Although there are a number of policies on childcare in India, their provision has been largely piecemeal, uneven, and inadequate.

State efforts to intervene in childcare, such as the Rajiv Gandhi National Crèche Scheme, 2005, Mahatma Gandhi National Rural Employment Guarantee Act (MGNREGA)—where childcare is part of the work programme—and the National Rural Health Mission (NRHM): Reproductive and Child Health Scheme (RCH), 2005, are limited in their reach. A recent assessment of the Rajiv Gandhi National Crèche Scheme for Children of Working Mothers initiated in 2006, which was meant to cater to the needs of working mothers, showed that it has had inadequate outreach. According to the 2009–10 *Annual Report of the Ministry of Women and Child Development* (MWCD), 0.08 million children had been reached through 31,718 crèches, as against 22,599 crèches in 2012 (Sharma et al. 2012).

New opportunities exist to improve on this record. In the Twelfth Five-Year Plan (2013–17), the government has stated that the existing provision for crèches at the worksite in MGNREGA 'will be implemented on a priority basis'. This could see the scheme institutionalize the delivery of care services as part of the provision of 100 days of work per household (GoI 2013). The private sector has played a large role in the provision of childcare services, but these remain largely unregulated and, more importantly, beyond the financial reach of the majority of poor households. The non-governmental organization (NGO) sector reaches anywhere between 3–20 million children and has played an important role in bringing the issue of childcare to the forefront, involving the government, and designing and implementing interventions in childcare that could act as models for large-scale interventions in the future (Sinha 2009).

The urgent need for ECCE is gaining currency within social policy. The Twelfth Plan recognizes the importance of ECCE and undertakes to deliver universal access to ECCE with inclusion (GoI 2013). The ECCE policy drafted by the Ministry of Women and Child Development (MWCD) is the most ambitious and comprehensive policy on childcare to date; if implemented it will have far-reaching implications for the regulation of the childcare sector in both public and private domains (MWCD 2012).

The focus of this policy is to deliver ECCE primarily through the existing ICDS programme: 'The policy seeks to universalize the provision of ECCE for all children mainly through the ICDS in the public sector and other service provisions across systems' (MWCD 2012, p. 7). It further states that 'the ICDS Anganwadi Centre would be repositioned as a vibrant child friendly ECD [Early Childcare and Development] centre with adequate infrastructure and resources for ensuring a continuum of ECCE in a life-cycle approach and child-related outcomes' (MWCD 2012).

Childcare features as a significant issue in the policy document. The policy envisions 'facilitating comprehensive childcare supports, infrastructure and services aimed at holistic well-being of children and responsive to their developmental needs' (MWCD 2012). The document also proposes to ensure quality standards, strengthen capacity, and monitor, evaluate, and take up advocacy on ECCE. It includes convergence with existing programmes, institutional and implementation arrangements, increased investments, and periodic reviews. It is by far the most ambitious policy on childcare developed by the government.

The policy overwhelmingly favours ICDS as the vehicle to deliver ECCE. Of the nearly 160 million children under 6 years, almost 48 per cent are currently covered by the ICDS (MWCD 2012, p. 5). This is a likely factor in selecting the ICDS to deliver comprehensive ECCE as well as to provide crèches.

Integrated Child Development Scheme

The ICDS, launched in 1975, is one of the older flagships programmes of the Government of India. The programme offers six broad services that range from supplementary nutrition, immunization, health check-ups, referral services, preschool education, and nutrition and health education. In 2011, the ICDS covered 75 million young children below the age of 6 years and close to 16.7 million women and nursing mothers through 6,722 projects and a network of 1.26 million operational anganwadi centres (AWCs) across the country. Over 2.5 million anganwadi workers (AWWs) and anganwadi helpers (AWHs) (community-based local women childcare workers/helpers) constitute the core of these services (Planning Commission 2011).

In November 2001, the Supreme Court of India ordered the government to universalize the ICDS. The entitlements of the children under 6 years were further improved in 2006 in a ruling that ordered the government to ensure 'universalization with quality' by 2008. The order stated that all ICDS services must be extended to every child under the age of 6 years, all adolescent girls, and all pregnant women and nursing mothers (Right to Food 2007).

Over the past decade, as evidence of underdevelopment of children has increased, a large number of studies have focused on the ICDS, because it is the largest scheme targeting children under 6 years of age. A number of studies have shown that the ICDS, in its current form, is severely resource constrained, lacks adequate infrastructure, and does not sufficiently deliver on its mandate. In 2005, the Comptroller and Auditor General (CAG) released a comprehensive report on the ICDS that pointed out serious accountability and financial issues of the scheme

> serious irregularities like failure to avail Central assistance, diversion of funds, mismanagement, disregard of Central guidelines, improper maintenance of various registers at AWCs, etc., thereby defeating the basic objectives of the scheme... Medicine kits and pre-school kits were not supplied to AWCs every year as prescribed by GoI. (CAG 2005, p. 43)

In 2011, the National Advisory Council (NAC) released a substantive report on the ICDS that underlined the following:

> In many states, the ICDS has got reduced to a feeding programme operated through an overburdened and underpaid anganwadi worker (AWW); linkages with the public health system have been weak; the pre-school component is missing; early childhood care has never got the attention it deserves; anganwadi centres (AWCs) have not had the physical space to operate efficiently and effectively; community engagement and participation are virtually non-existent. Falsification of data, poor management information systems (MIS), and delays in release of funds and payments to AWWs are also reported from different states. Little attention has been paid to the needs of working women for whom access to a crèche is an urgent priority. (NAC 2011, p. 2)

Can the ICDS Deliver Universal Quality Childcare?

The NAC recommendations further provide detailed suggestions to reform the ICDS and make it the vehicle for universal provision of ECCE in India. Some of the broad measures are institutional convergence with various government departments and programmes working on nutrition, health, and education, the participation of mothers and communities in strengthening the scheme, a nationwide information campaign to prevent malnutrition, piloting reformed ICDS programmes in 200 high-burden districts, and formation of a national nutrition mission. Added to these are nine areas listed for programmatic reforms, with detailed recommendations for each section. The NAC report, however, cautions that the ICDS reforms require a comprehensive overhaul as opposed to a piecemeal approach to achieve its goals. The NAC report also suggests framing a mission document through a consultative process engaging stakeholders to assess resources, develop a vision, goals, strategies, and detailed time-bound plans to be put into action through pilots in 200 districts prior to rolling out the revamped ICDS (NAC 2011, p. 14).

It remains to be seen if there is enough political will for this vast task that the government is undertaking of reforming the ICDS and including universal crèche care services as part of its restructuring. The greatest argument for using the existing ICDS to deliver comprehensive and quality universal crèche services is that the ICDS already has institutional structures in place across the country with reach to a large number of children (48 per cent) under 6 years of age. To begin a crèche service of the scale and scope necessary to reach the majority of the population would be a far greater challenge than to revamp an existing system of delivery. Putting pressure on the government to undertake a comprehensive reform that includes universal crèche care is the biggest challenge. Within this context a greater challenge and of immense importance is the need to design specific policies for the 0–3 years' age group, that factor in the complex interplay between home-based maternal care and the provision of crèches for at-risk children of the age group of 0–3 years, while meeting the needs of the 0–3 years' age group that tend to get overlooked in favour of more standardized solutions for the older age group who are ready to enter the educational system.

However, as the ICDS is being reformed, government can draw on the well-developed models for crèche delivery in the not-for-profit sector. Mobile Crèches, one of the leading NGOs in the childcare sector, has over many decades developed a model of quality care for the children of migrant workers on construction sites. More recently, *Jan Swasthya Sahyog* (JSS) has implemented crèche-care services in tribal communities, using an integrated ECCE approach. They start with the age group of 0–3 years for nutrition and cognitive stimulation. The government could provide resources to expand the outreach of these and other initiatives. The government could also begin to channel funds through Panchayati Raj Institutions (PRIs) for the creation of community crèches.

★ ★ ★

Given the levels of poverty, exclusion, and malnourishment of children under 6 years of age in India, this chapter has laid out a rationale for the provision of universal childcare for children from at least 6 months of age, that accommodates the intersecting needs of women and children, both in the provision of quality care and in receiving care, and that allows women the freedom to pursue their multiple roles as caregiver, breadwinner, and homemaker. It also accommodates the human capital arguments for ECCE intervention.

The section on women and labour market in India shows that the majority of women in India are employed in low-skilled and predominantly unpaid work in the informal sector. With low levels of education and skills and limited opportunities to advance, these women are primarily employed in unregulated sectors where they have no access to care services and maternity entitlements.

Contrary to the feminization of the labour force thesis, women in India are leaving the labour market and there needs to be more detailed assessment of the causes for this. Access to decent, affordable childcare services is likely to be a major factor. Paradoxically, the evidence shows that many poor women who are entering the labour force are doing so as domestic workers, caring for other people's children even as they compromise the care of their own children. Older siblings, particularly girls, take up the task of caregiving, compromising their own development. This leads to intergenerational poverty and transmission of gender values that impede long-term development and keep people trapped in a cycle of poverty.

Dual crises in women's work and the widespread underdevelopment of young children call for a gendered response that meets the intersecting needs of women and children. The provision of universal childcare in these circumstances needs to be seen as an essential right and entitlement for poor families. The delivery of community-based childcare services through crèches is a key intervention towards attaining long-term national goals of poverty reduction, social inclusion, and gender equity.

REFERENCES

Budlender, D. 2011. 'Measuring the Economic and Social Value of Domestic Work', Domestic Work Policy Brief No. 3, International Labour Organization (ILO). http://www.ilo.org/wcmsp5/groups/public/---ed_protect/---protrav/---travail/documents/publication/wcms_156071.pdf, last accessed on 6 October 2014.

Comptroller and Auditor General of India (CAG). 2007. 'Performance Audit', Chapter 3 in *Audit Report (Civil) for the Year Ended 31 March 2007*, pp. 43–127. New Delhi: Government of India.

Chowdhury, S. 2011. 'Employment in India: What Does the Latest Data Show?' *Economic and Political Weekly*, 46(32): 23–6.

Daly, M. (ed.). 2001. *Care Work: The Quest for Security*. Geneva: ILO.

Folbre, N. 2004. 'Children as a Public Good', *The American Economic Review*, 84(2): 86–90.

Gooneskere, S. and R. De Silva-De Alwis. 2005. 'Women's and Children's Rights in a Human Rights Based Approach to Development', UNICED Policy and Planning Working Paper.

Government of India (GoI). 2012. *Report of the Committee on Unorganised Sector Statistics*, National Statistical Commission. http://mospi.nic.in/Mospi_New/upload/nsc_report_un_sec_14mar12.pdf, last accessed on 6 October 2014.

———. 2013. *Draft 12th Five Year Plan 2012–2017, Social Sectors*, Volume 3. http://planningcommission.nic.in/plans/planrel/12thplan/welcome.html, last accessed on 22 March 2013.

Haddad, L. 2002. 'Integrated Policies for Early Childhood Education and Care: Challenges, Pitfalls and Possibilities', Paper. www.scielo.br/pdf/cp/v36n129/en_a0236129.pdf, last accessed on 5 November 2012.

Heckman, J. and P. Carneiro. 2003. 'Human Capital Policy', National Bureau of Economic Research (NBER) Working Paper 9495. http://www.nber.org/papers/w9495, last accessed on 5 November 2012.

Hirway, I. 2005. 'Integrating Unpaid Work into Development Policy', Paper presented at the Conference on Unpaid Work and the Economy: Gender,

Poverty, and the Millennium Development Goals, Levy Economics Institute, NewYork, October. http://www.levyinstitute.org/undp-levy-conference/program_documents.php, last accessed on 5 November 2012.

Kabeer, N. 2000. 'Intergenerational Contracts Demographic Transitions and the "Quantity-Quality" Trade-off: Children, Parents and Investing in the Future', *Journal of International Development*, 12(4): 463–82.

———. 2008. 'Gender Labour Markets and Poverty: An Overview, Poverty in Focus, Gender Equality', International Poverty Center, No. 13, January.

Kaul, V. and D. Sankar. 2009. *Early Childhood Care and Education in India*, New Delhi: National University of Education Planning and Administration (NEUPA).

Mazumdar, I. and N. Pillai. 2011. 'Gender Dimensions: Employment Trends in India, 1993–94 to 2009–10', Centre for Women's Development Studies, Occasional Paper No. 56.

Ministry of Women and Child Development (MWCD). 2012. *Draft National Early Childhood Care and Education (ECCE) Policy*. New Delhi: MWCD, Government of India.

Misra, Neeta, R.S. Malhotra, and R. Subrahmanian. 2012. 'Women, Children and the case for universal daycare in India', mimeo. New Delhi: UNICEF India.

Moghe, K. 2005. 'Shouldering the Double Burden: Experiences of Organising Domestic Workers in Pune City', Paper presented at the seminar on Globalisation and the Women's Movement, 20–22 January, organized by the Centre for Women's Development Studies, New Delhi.

National Advisory Council (NAC). 2011. *Recommendations for a reformed and strengthened Integrated Child Development Services (ICDS)*. New Delhi: NAC, Government of India.

National Scientific Council on the Developing Child (NSCDC). 2007. 'The Science of Early Childhood Development (ECD), Core Concepts', pp. 1–7. http://www.developingchild.net.

Neetha, N. and R. Palriwala. 2008. 'The Political and Social Economy of Care: Analysis of Time Use Data Report 2', UNRISD.

Planning Commisssion. 2011. Report of the Inter Ministerial Group on ICDS Restructuring, p. 5. http://www.planningcommission.nic.in/reports/genrep/rep_icds2704.pdf, last accessed on 5 November 2012.

Razavi, S. 2007. 'The Political and Social Economy of Care in a Development Context: Conceptual Issues, Research Questions and Policy Options', UNRISD Gender and Development Program Paper No. 3.

Right to Food. 2007. *Anganwadi's for All—A Primer*. http://www.sccommissioners.org/FoodSchemes/Documents/icds_primer.pdf, last accessed on 5 November 2012.

Rustagi, P. 2010. 'Employment Trends for Women in India', ILO Asia-Pacific Working Paper Series.

Sharma, K., V. Raman, and P. Dhawan. 2012. *Need Assessment for Creches and Childcare Services*. Ministry for Child and Women's Development, Government of India.

Sinha, D. and V. Bhatia. 2009. 'Learning from Models of ECCD provision in India', Paper presented to the Kusuma foundation.

Standing, G. 1999. 'Global Feminization through Flexible Labor: A Theme Revisited', *World Development*, 27(3): 583–602.

Strober, M. 2004. 'Children Should Be Considered Public Goods', *Dissent*, Fall, 2004. http://www.dissentmagazine.org/author/myrahstrober, last accessed on 5 November 2012.

Swaminathan, Mina. 1993. 'The Continuum of Maternity and Child Care Support', Centre for Women's Studies, Indian Association of Women's Studies, Sixth National Conference on Women's Studies, *The Dynamics Of the New Economic Policy: Implications for Women*, pp. 186–217.

UNICEF. 2013. 'Early Childhood Care and Education', Concept Paper for UNICEF-India Country Office.

World Bank. 2004. *Reaching Out to the Child: An Integrated Approach to Child Development*. New Delhi: Oxford University Press.

Young, M. and L. Richardson (eds). 2007. *Early Child Development from Measurement to Action: A Priority for Growth and Equity*. Washington, DC: World Bank.

12 Conditional Cash Transfers for the Welfare of the Girl Child

The Indian Experience[1]

T.V. Sekher

Introduction of conditional cash transfer schemes (CCTs) is a marked departure from the traditional approaches in social programming. Through provision of financial incentives to poor families following the fulfilment of certain verifiable conditions, CCTs seek to provide short-term income support and at the same time promote long-term behavioural changes. CCTs therefore have the potential to become an effective means of channelizing the limited resources available to the poor and socially disadvantaged sections; more specifically to girls and women. In the context of persisting gender inequalities in India, the girl child is at a disadvantage and faces discrimination at every stage of her life—from sex-selection procedures at conception and

[1] This study was commissioned by the United Nations Population Fund, India, at the request of the Planning Commission, Government of India. I am thankful to Syeda Hameed, N.K. Sethi, Firoza Mehrotra (Planning Commission), Ena Singh, Dhanashri Brahme, K.M. Sathyanarayana, and Sanjay Kumar (UNFPA), state-level programme officials and NGOs for useful discussions and suggestions. For a detailed discussion on each scheme, refer to the report of the study (Sekher 2010).

female infanticide to little or no access to education, lack of health care and nutrition, child marriage, and teenage pregnancy later in her life. The conditionality-linked cash transfer attempts to correct such discriminations. These programmes represent a shift in the government's approach of focusing on the supply-side to a demand-driven approach. Experiences from various countries illustrate that conditional cash transfer programmes were successful in increasing enrolments in school, improving immunization of children, and raising household consumption levels. This is true for poor and low-income countries as illustrated from the experiences of Brazil, Columbia, Mexico, and Nicaragua (Briere and Rawlings 2006; Fajth and Vinay 2010; IFPRI 2002; Son 2008). Poor mothers received financial incentives conditional to their promoting certain activities on behalf of their children.

In the Indian context, the adverse influence of negative social attitudes towards girls has left many girl children vulnerable and disadvantaged. Their survival, education, health care, development, security, and well-being are a matter of national concern. A significant impact of this discrimination is reflected in the deterioration of the male–female ratio, particularly among children. The 1991 Census of India indicated the worsening trend in the child sex ratio (CSR), and the 2001 Census revealed that the situation was alarming in some states. The dwindling number of girl children on account of increasing incidences of female foeticide is a matter of great concern nowadays (Sekher and Hatti 2010). Even after legislations such as the Pre-conception and Pre-natal Diagnostic Techniques Act of 1994, popularly known as the PC-PNDT Act, and many campaigns to promote the value of the girl child, the scenario has not improved and, in fact, has further deteriorated as evident from the 2011 Census. Programmes and policies clearly state that it is necessary to empower girl children in all aspects of life, so that they become equal partners with boys and enjoy freedom and equal opportunity. Thus, special measures are required to protect the survival and security of the girl child from conception to birth, in infancy, and throughout the period of her childhood. It is a fact that in many families, poverty is the major constraint in raising and educating girl children. Given the limited financial resources available to these families, they would prefer a son to a daughter. With this in mind and against the background of the deteriorating condition of girls in India as reflected in the worsening male–female ratio, the Government of India (GoI) and many state governments have introduced innovative schemes of conditional cash and non-cash transfers. By providing a set of staggered financial incentives to encourage families to retain the girl child and to educate her, the ultimate objective of these schemes is to change the attitude and mindset of parents towards the girl child (GoI 2007). In most traditional Indian families, girls are considered a liability and a burden. By providing cash inflows to the girl's family, these schemes seek to create and reinforce the idea in parents that having a girl is an asset to the family. The CCT is subject to the completion of certain requirements such as birth registration, institutional delivery, childhood immunization, school enrolment, completing school education, and delaying marriage until 18 years of age. This would result in improvements in the value of the girl child, more specifically measured through improved sex ratio at birth (SRB) and CSR; increased enrolment in schools; attendance in primary, middle, and high schools; and marriage at or above the legal age.

This study was undertaken to examine the extent to which financial incentive schemes have contributed towards enhancing the value of daughters within a family. These incentive-based schemes aim at improving the value of the girl child on the premise that financial benefits would trigger behavioural changes among parents and communities. In the long run, such initiatives hope to ensure the survival and well-being of girls. However, with very limited or no documentation/assessment in place, the first task initiated under this study was to gather information about different incentive schemes aimed at the welfare of the girl child. Discussions with a few non-governmental organizations (NGOs) and government officials implementing the schemes provided a general idea about the functioning of each scheme. Interactions with few beneficiary families also helped in gaining useful insights. The findings presented here rely heavily on interactions with officials and analysis of the scheme-related available data at the state level.

Though most of these schemes are steps in the right direction, very little is known about their implementation and effectiveness. Through a desk review and interaction with government officials and NGOs, this study examines operational aspects of 15 selected girl-child promotion schemes across the states and gathers first impressions regarding the performance of these schemes. The schemes selected for secondary review are Dhan Laxmi Scheme of the Government of India, Ladli Scheme of Delhi, Ladli Lakshmi Yojana of Madhya Pradesh, Bhagyalakshmi Scheme of Karnataka, Balri Rakshak Yojana in Punjab,

Ladli Scheme of Haryana, Kanyadan Scheme of Madhya Pradesh, Girl Child Protection Scheme in Andhra Pradesh, Indira Gandhi Balika Suraksha Yojna in Himachal Pradesh, Mukhya Mantri Kanya Vivah Yojana of Bihar, Rajalakshmi scheme in Rajasthan (discontinued), Balika Samridhi Yojana (BSY) in Gujarat and Himachal Pradesh, Kunwarbainu Mameru scheme in Gujarat, Beti Hai Anmol Scheme in Himachal Pradesh (initiated in 2010), and Mukhya Mantri Kanya Suraksha Yojana of Bihar. The number of beneficiaries enrolled during the last three years under each of these schemes is presented in Table 12.1. That the Ladli Lakshmi Yojana (Madhya Pradesh), Bhagyalakshmi Scheme (Karnataka) and Mukhya Mantri Kanya Suraksha Yojana (Bihar) have more than four lakh girls who registered within a span of three years is indicative of the huge popularity of some of these

TABLE 12.1 Girl Child Schemes: Number of Beneficiaries

Name of the Scheme	Number of Beneficiaries		
	2007–8	2008–9	2009–10
Dhan Lakshmi Scheme (Govt. of India)	–	79,555	42,077
Bhagyalakshmi Scheme (Karnataka)	123,789	297,764	144,749
Ladli Lakshmi Scheme (Madhya Pradesh)	214,134	209,848	40,854
Girl Child Protection Scheme (Andhra Pradesh)	96,487	72,046	70,302
Ladli Scheme (Delhi)	–	135,645	140,006
Balika Samridhi Yojana (Gujarat)	26,031	30,263	132,684
Balika Samridhi Yojana (Himachal Pradesh)	7,955	13,031	17,038
Ladli Scheme (Haryana)	49,558	72,624	105,113
Balri Rakshak Yojana (Punjab)	62	53	62
Mukhya Mantri Kanya Suraksha Yojana (Bihar)		475,220*	
Kunwarbainu Mameru Scheme (Gujarat)	8,762	6,775	7,628
Mukhya Mantri Kanyadan Yojana (Madhya Pradesh)	32,621	43,297	19,579
Mukhya Mantri Kanya Vivah Yojana (Bihar)		157,256*	
Indira Gandhi Balika Suraksha Yojana (Himachal Pradesh)	152	318	233

Source: Compiled by the author based on state government documents and discussions with officials.

Note: *Total number of beneficiaries since inception.

schemes. Recently in 2012, the new government in Goa had launched the Ladli Lakshmi Scheme with much fanfare.

INTENT AND OBJECTIVES

The schemes that were reviewed had varying objectives, and they set preconditions upon fulfilment of which benefits were provided. In general, all schemes attempted to enhance the value of the girl child in terms of her being considered as an asset to the family. It intended to empower girls and ensure their survival through cash transfers that are linked to fulfilling certain conditions such as birth registration, immunization, and education of the girl child. However, a review of the objectives of the different schemes reveals that the multiplicity of outcomes expected from the schemes somewhat diffused the focus of achieving the original objective behind the provision of these incentives—to induce a change in the perceived value of daughters by the family. For example, some schemes provide the incentive only if the couple accepts sterilization after two children, others extend the incentive to only two girls in a family, with a larger incentive for the first girl than for the second. Dhan Lakshmi is the only scheme that provides incentives to all girls born in the family. Clearly, the intention behind some of the schemes is also to ensure smaller families and promote family planning alongside ensuring the birth of girls.

ELIGIBILITY

Table 12.2 provides the eligibility criteria to avail benefits at different stages under each scheme. Apart from fulfilling the eligibility criteria, the beneficiary families need to produce a set of documents to register for each scheme (see Table 12.3). This varies from birth certificate to income certificate to proof of undergoing sterilization by any one of the parents. Most of these schemes are specifically aimed at people belonging to the poor families—below poverty line (BPL) households. There are a few schemes that are open to all categories of households irrespective of education, income levels, and caste. An analysis of the CSR data from the 2001 Census has revealed variations, which need further analysis. Thus, though ratios are lower amongst the educated and affluent in urban areas, the rural areas are surprisingly not far behind. Given this, it is critical to revisit the target groups under

TABLE 12.2 Girl Child Schemes: Eligibility Conditions to Avail Benefits

Name of the scheme	Registration of birth	Immunization	Family planning (sterilization)	Anganwadi enrolment	School enrolment	Completion of standard 10	18 years of age and unmarried
Dhan Lakshmi Scheme	✓	✓	–	–	✓	✓ (8th standard)	✓
Bhagyalakshmi Scheme (Karnataka)	✓	✓	✓	✓	✓	✓ (8th standard)	✓
Ladli Lakshmi Scheme (Madhya Pradesh)	✓	–	– (withdrawn)	✓	✓	✓	✓ (after 21 yrs)
Girl Child Protection Scheme (Andhra Pradesh)	✓	✓	✓	–	✓	✓ (12th standard)	✓ (after 20 yrs)
Ladli Scheme (Haryana)	✓	✓	–	✓	✓	✓	✓
Balika Samridhi Yojana	✓	–	–	–	✓	✓	–
Ladli Scheme (Delhi)	✓	–	–	–	✓	✓	✓
Indira Gandhi Balika Suraksha Yojana	–	–	✓	–	–	–	–
Mukhya Mantri Kanyadan Yojana	✓	–	–	–	–	–	✓
Balri Rakshak Yojana (Punjab)	✓	–	✓	–	–	–	–
Beti Hai Anmol Scheme	✓	–	–	–	–	–	✓
Rajalakshmi Scheme (Discontinued)	✓	–	✓	–	–	–	–

Source: Compiled by the author based on documents of various schemes of state governments.

TABLE 12.3 Girl Child Schemes: Documents Required

Name of the scheme	Birth certificate	Domicile certificate	Income certificate	Sterilization certificate	Immunization certificate	Marriage certificate
Dhan Lakshmi Scheme	✓	✓	–	–	✓	–
Bhagyalakshmi Scheme (Karnataka)	✓	✓	✓	✓	✓	–
Ladli Lakshmi Scheme (Madhya Pradesh)	✓	✓	–	✓ (withdrawn)	–	–
Girl Child Protection Scheme (Andhra Pradesh)	✓	✓	✓	✓	✓	–
Ladli Scheme (Haryana)	✓	✓	–	–	✓	–
Balika Samridhi Yojana	✓	–	✓	–	–	–
Indira Gandhi Balika Suraksha Yojana	–	✓	–	✓	–	–
Ladli Scheme (Delhi)	✓	✓	✓	–	–	–
Mukhya Mantri Kanyadan Yojana (Madhya Pradesh)	✓	✓	✓	–	–	✓
Balri Rakshak Yojana (Punjab)	✓	✓	✓	✓	–	–
Beti Hai Anmol Scheme (Himachal Pradesh)	✓	✓	✓	–	–	–
Rajalakshmi Scheme (Discontinued)	✓	–	–	✓	–	–
Mukhya Mantri Kanya Suraksha Yojana	✓	✓	✓	–	–	–
Mukhya Mantri Kanya Vivah Yojana	–	✓	✓	–	–	✓
Kunwarbainu Mameru Scheme	–	–	✓	–	–	✓

Source: Compiled by the author based on documents of various schemes of state governments.

these incentive schemes based on the perception of the value of the incentive by different income groups. Even for lower-middle-class or middle-class households, the more immediate perceived benefit from not having a daughter may appear more tangible than a final benefit that will accrue only after their daughter turns 18. Only through a systematic evaluation can it be established whether the incentives help to address both pre- and post-birth discrimination against girls. In other words, it is not clear yet whether these incentives ensure that girls survive and receive better care and attention or that they also ensure their birth itself. Again, by limiting the benefit to two girls or by providing a larger incentive to the first girl child, the scheme inadvertently ends up valuing girls differentially depending on their position in the birth order. Therefore, the eligibility criteria potentially may lead to mixed perceptions about the intent of the scheme.

VIEWS OF THE IMPLEMENTING OFFICIALS

Involvement of the State Governments

It is interesting to note that most state governments took pride in implementing the scheme and publicizing it as one of their biggest achievements. The chief ministers of many of the states have launched these schemes and have had a close association with them, sometimes even monitoring them. Ladli Lakshmi Yojana of Madhya Pradesh, Ladli Scheme of Delhi, and Bhagyalakshmi Scheme of Karnataka are a few examples. The state governments are ready to invest huge amounts for implementing these schemes. For example, the Madhya Pradesh government spent Rs 250 crore in 2007–8 for the Ladli Lakshmi Yojana. For the Ladli Scheme of Delhi, Rs 87 crore were spent in 2009–10. The Government of Haryana spent Rs 52 crore for the Ladli Scheme in 2009–10 (Table 12.4). Karnataka government has earmarked Rs 358 crore for the Bhagyalakshmi Scheme for the year 2010–11. Chief ministers also made public announcements that money will not be a constraint in expanding these 'popular' schemes. Some of the state governments are also seriously considering increasing the cash incentives to make the schemes more attractive. Hence, proper negotiations with financial agencies for ensuring the promised terminal benefits are important, as demonstrated by previous experience with the well-known Rajalakshmi Scheme in Rajasthan that had to be discontinued

TABLE 12.4 Girl Child Schemes: Annual Budget and Expenditure, 2007–11

Name of the scheme	2007–8		2008–9		2009–10		2010–11
	Budget	Expenditure	Budget	Expenditure	Budget	Expenditure	Budget
Dhan Lakshmi Scheme (Govt. of India)	–	–	10 crore	5.95 crore	10 crore	5 crore	–
Bhagyalakshmi Scheme (Karnataka)	150 crore	132.43 crore	266.65 crore	316.65 crore	229.89 crore	229.64 crore	358 crore
Ladli Lakshmi Scheme (Madhya Pradesh)	276 crore	250 crore	135 crore	100 crore	24 crore	26 crore	302 crore
Ladli Scheme (Delhi)	–	–	81.30 crore	86.44 crore	83.17 crore	86.97 crore	–
Ladli Scheme (Haryana)	21 crore	25.1 crore	29 crore	29.61 crore	34 crore	52 crore	38.65 crore
Balika Samridhi Yojana (Gujarat)	50 lakh	51.4 lakh	1 crore	2.38 crore	10 crore	1.36 crore	–
Balika Samridhi Yojana (Himachal Pradesh)	40 lakh	60.88 lakh	75 lakh	59.01 lakh	80 lakh	80.92 lakh	–
Balri Rakshak Yojana (Punjab)	1 crore	9.48 lakh	50 lakh	24.26 lakh	60 lakh	12.13 lakh	–
Mukhya Mantri Kanya Suraksha Yojana (Bihar)	–	–	28 crore	27.44 crore	67 crore	65.66 crore	42 crore
Mukhya Mantri Kanya Vivah Yojana (Bihar)	10 crore	10 crore	40 crore	39 crore	80 crore	79 crore	60 crore
Mukhya Mantri Kanyadan Yojana (Madhya Pradesh)	19.20 crore	19.57 crore	26.18 crore	25.98 crore	25 crore	14.88 crore	–
Indira Gandhi Balika Suraksha Yojana (Himachal Pradesh)	95 lakh	93 lakh	91.10 lakh	33 lakh	95.50 lakh	33 lakh	–

Source: Compiled by the author based on documents of various state governments.

for financial reasons. Though the scheme was attractive and many clients were hoping to reap the benefits, the Rajalakshmi Scheme was discontinued in 2000 owing to perceived losses (from falling interest rates) by the Unit Trust of India (UTI). The premature closure of the scheme disheartened the beneficiaries, and people lost interest and faith in similar schemes (Sharma et al. 2003). Before terminating the scheme, the state government should have considered alternatives such as investing in mutual funds, increasing the deposit amount, reducing the total maturity amount in their tie-ups with banks or other financial institutions.

The CCT is subject to the completion of certain verifiable conditions such as parents accepting sterilization after a maximum of two children. In most of the schemes, the terminal benefits can be availed only when the girl completes 18 years of age and is still unmarried (Table 12.5). Discussions with the implementing officials provided very useful insights into the functioning of the schemes. Most of the schemes are administered by state governments through the Departments of Women and Child Development. Two schemes that are under review here are sponsored by the Department of Health and Family Welfare of Punjab and of Himachal Pradesh. Dhan Lakshmi is the only scheme which is fully supported by the Government of India and is implemented as a pilot in eleven backward blocks in seven states. The Balika Samridhi Yojana (BSY) was originally initiated by the Government of India in 1997, but since 2006, it has been taken over by the state governments. It was also observed that in some cases, the state governments changed the name of the scheme and implemented it under a new name with additional financial incentives. The BSY was discontinued in Himachal Pradesh in July 2010, and the state government launched a new scheme called Beti Hai Anmol with similar objectives and benefits as that of BSY. In many states such as Odisha, the BSY has been discontinued owing to lack of funds.

Coordination between Departments

It is important to mention here that most of these schemes are implemented through the vast network of *anganwadi*s and the Integrated Child Development Services (ICDS) machinery. Successful implementation of the scheme also requires support and cooperation from other departments, such as education, health, and panchayats.

TABLE 12.5 Girl Child Schemes: Year of Initiation, Implementing Agency, Terminal Benefits, and Financial Institutions

Name of the scheme	Year of initiation	Implementing agency	Terminal benefit		Financial institution
			Age	Amount	
Dhan Lakshmi Scheme (Govt of India)	2008	Dept of Women and Child Development	18 years	Rs 100,000	Nationalized Bank/ Post Office
Bhagyalakshmi Scheme (Karnataka)	2006	Dept of Women and Child Development	18 years	Rs 100,000	LIC
Ladli Lakshmi Yojana (Madhya Pradesh)	2006	Dept of Women and Child Development	21 years	Rs 118,300	Post Office (NSC)
Girl Child Protection Scheme (New) (Andhra Pradesh)	2005	Dept of Women Development and Child Welfare	20 years	Rs 1 lakh for one girl child and (in case of two girl children) Rs 30,000 for each	LIC
Ladli Scheme (Haryana)	2005	Dept of Women and Child Development	18 years	Rs 96,000	LIC
Rajalakshmi Scheme (Discontinued)	1992	Dept of Medical, Health, and Family Welfare	20 years	Rs 21,000	UTI
Balika Samridhi Yojana (transferred to states in 2006)	1997	Dept of Women and Child Development	18 years	Rs 6,700 (with maximum rate of interest)	Nationalized Bank/ Post Office
Ladli Scheme (Delhi)	2008	Dept of Women and Children Development	18 years	Rs 100,000	SBI/SBIL

(Continued)

TABLE 12.5 *(Continued)*

Name of the scheme	Year of initiation	Implementing agency	Terminal benefit		Financial Institution
			Age	Amount	
Balri Rakshak Yojana (Punjab)	2005	Dept. of Health and Family Welfare	18 years	Rs 100,000	Nationalized Bank/Post Office
Mukhya Mantri Kanya Suraksha Yojana	2008	Social Welfare Department/ State Women Development Corporation	18 years	Rs 18,000	UTI Children's Career Plan Growth Option
Mukhya Mantri Kanya Vivah Yojana	2007	Social Welfare Department	18 years	Rs 5,000	Bank
Kunwarbainu Mameru scheme	1995	Social Justice and Empowerment Department	At marriage	Rs 5,000	Bank
Indira Gandhi Balika Suraksha Yojana	2007	Health and Family Welfare Department	At marriage or maturity	Rs 25,000 to one girl child and Rs 20,000 to both in case of two girl children	Bank
Mukhya Mantri Kanyadan Yojana	2006	Dept. of Social Justice	At marriage	Goods worth of Rs 9,000	–

Source: Compiled by the author based on documents of various schemes of state governments.

Note: LIC: Life Insurance Corporation of India; NSC: National Savings Scheme; UTI: Unit Trust of India; SBI: State Bank of India; SBIL: State Bank of India Life Insurance.

The officials responsible for implementing the schemes spoke about their not receiving the necessary support from other government departments, which resulted in delays and difficulties. For example, if the birth certificate is not received on time, it delays the financial incentive that the family will receive following the birth of a girl. Sometimes there are problems with financial agencies like banks and the Life Insurance Corporation (LIC), including delays in opening zero balance accounts. Lack of coordination between departments and financial institutions, such as the LIC and UTI, has led to delays in issuing bonds/certificates to the beneficiaries in some states. Bonds/certificates of a certain value are given by the state government with a lock-in period from the date of issuing the bonds to the date when the girl as a beneficiary has turned 18 or older. This can then be encashed at the maturity value of the bond and given only to her. In some instances, the infrastructure bottlenecks at the level of banks, post offices, and insurance companies also contributed to the unnecessary delay in providing financial assistance.

Implementation, Allocation, and Disbursements

According to the information available, very little money is spent on the administrative cost of implementing the schemes. Most state governments utilized the existing infrastructure and manpower (mainly ICDS or health workers). In most of these schemes, the involvement of local panchayats, NGOs, and women's groups was said to be limited. The scheme has been largely implemented as a programme of the given department. However, in some cases, the local panchayat leaders and NGOs have helped in popularizing the schemes and identifying the beneficiaries. State governments have also helped in the publicity of the schemes by distributing certificates/bonds in mass public gatherings and, at times, in the presence of the chief minister. While fund allocation for schemes has been substantial in the initial years, proper monitoring mechanisms are few or absent, and schemes lack procedures for addressing grievances of beneficiaries in most states. Progress has been reviewed through routine department-level meetings. Some of these schemes underwent modifications with regard to the eligibility criteria, required documentation, and the amount of incentives provided. Officials feel that procedures and eligibility conditions need to be further simplified to make the schemes more citizen friendly and accessible. However, systematic monitoring remains an urgent need to allow proper implementation of schemes, gain a better understanding of bottlenecks, and to obtain a sense of the total impact. So far no review or evaluation has been conducted to examine whether the financial incentives provided through the schemes have had an impact on the parental attitude and behaviour towards girl children.

VIEWS OF THE BENEFICIARIES AND CIVIL SOCIETY

The discussions with beneficiaries revealed that there were considerable delays in registration under some of the schemes as well as in the distribution of certificates. Some beneficiaries stated that they had to pay money to the local functionaries to get registered under the scheme. Also, in a few cases, the officials admitted that those who were not eligible received benefits under the scheme, which points to corrupt practices that prevent the benefits from reaching the intended target group. Though random verification is carried out by district-level officials to examine the authenticity and eligibility of applicants, it is possible for some to misuse the scheme in connivance with local officials. For example, it was found that some of the beneficiaries of Bhagyalakshmi Scheme were not from BPL households and that the parent of the girl child had not undergone sterilization as required (Government of Karnataka 2010).

Nonetheless, one advantage of CCTs is that the money directly reaches the households and beneficiaries, at least minimizing the possible leakages in the process. Some beneficiaries felt that the financial incentives provided through the schemes have helped them to provide an education for their daughters. Some of them even stated that girls are perceived as less of a liability, since the government is meeting the cost of their education and marriage. This could perhaps mean that the families appreciated the role of the state in helping to offset the liabilities involved in educating girls and getting them married rather than regarding the incentives as a way of persuading them to recognize the value of their daughters.

NGOs and women's groups felt that state governments are not able to utilize their services for better implementation of schemes. Few NGOs also believed that some of these schemes need to be better targeted with focused attention on specific groups. For example, under the Ladli Scheme of Haryana, the cash incentives are provided to all irrespective of caste or income criteria. In a way, this helps to reach out to all socio-economic groups as seen in the data that show a decline in the CSR across the state. However, financial incentives are likely to be of greater value to poorer households than affluent ones. Also, given the quantum of benefit, the scheme needs to take this aspect into consideration while determining the eligibility criteria. Some NGOs also felt that providing gifts in kind to the girl at the time of her marriage may send out a wrong message to the community, which may perhaps perceive it as an implicit involvement of the state in covering marriage-related financial transactions.

USEFULNESS OF THE INCENTIVE SCHEMES

On the whole, both the government officials and the beneficiaries acknowledged the positive aspects of the incentive-driven schemes. Clearly, direct financial support for girls, with funds being transferred to the bank account in the name of the girl child, was seen as a useful mechanism. Further, cash transfers were possibly proving to be a motivational factor for at least poor families to invest in the education of their daughters, where the tussle was always about prioritization of limited resources for the son. A majority of the beneficiary families have spoken about the need to simplify the schemes to further enhance its usefulness and thereby expand its reach too. For example, schemes such as Dhan Lakshmi and Bhagyalakshmi can be simplified for operational purposes by cutting down on the number of conditions attached to various levels of immunization and school attendance, because with every conditionality the beneficiaries have to provide proof of fulfilment of the conditions to complete the corresponding documentation and certification formalities (see Table 12.6 for Dhan Lakshmi Scheme). Likewise, domicile certificate is mandatory for many schemes, and poor migrant families are likely to be excluded from the schemes. Inflexibility in the stipulated time for joining the scheme is also a major deterrent for availing benefits among illiterate families. Barring Ladli Scheme of Delhi, most other schemes insists on registration of girl child within a year of birth.

A common complaint from the beneficiaries across the states is the difficulty to obtain various documents required to register, such

TABLE 12.6 Dhan Lakshmi Scheme

A. Selected Districts and Blocks

State	District	Block
1. Andhra Pradesh	Khammam Warangal	Aswaraopeta Narsampet
2. Chhattisgarh	Bastar Bijapur	Jagdalpur Bhopalpattnam
3. Odisha	Malkangiri Koraput	Kalimela Semiliguda
4. Jharkhand	Giridih Kodarma	Tisri Markachor
5. Bihar	Jamoi	Sono
6. Uttar Pradesh	Rae Bareilly	Shivgarh
7. Punjab	Fatehgarh Sahib	Sirhind

B. Financial Benefits

Conditions	Amount (in Rupees)
All girl children born after 19 November 2008 and registered	5,000
Immunization	
In 6 weeks	200
In 14 weeks	200
In 9 months	200
In 16 months	200
In 24 months	200
On completion of full immunization	250
Education	
On enrolment to primary school	1,000
In class 1 + attendance	500
In class 2 + attendance	500
In class 3 + attendance	500
In class 4 + attendance	500
In class 5 + attendance	500
On enrolment to secondary school	1,500
In class 6 + attendance	750
In class 7 + attendance	750
In class 8 + attendance	750
Insurance maturity cover*	100,000

Source: Ministry of Women and Child Development, Government of India, 2008.

Note: *LIC will provide lump sum of Rs 1 lakh per girl child on completing 18 years. Cash incentives in classes 9 to 12 will be borne by the Ministry of Human Resource Development.

as birth certificate, income certificate, immunization certificate, school attendance certificate, and sterilization certificate. Officials and some NGOs also pointed out how money was being paid at times by the beneficiaries to hasten the documentation. There is a need to minimize the number of cash transactions per beneficiary. An option of clubbing together some of the conditions and enhancing the incentive provided at that stage could be considered. The emergence of Panchayati Raj Institutions (PRIs) at the local level provides an opportunity for implementing these schemes through local bodies. They are in a better position to identify the beneficiaries, monitor the progress of implementation, and ensure the transfer of funds to the rightful beneficiaries. Though some of the schemes presently involve PRIs and NGOs to a limited extent, there is a need to formulate clear guidelines for their direct involvement and active participation.

PLUGGING THE IMPLEMENTATION GAPS

The schemes are introduced with a specific set of objectives in order to have a desired impact. In many instances, it is too early to say whether the desired impact is visible or not. This desk review of the select schemes has its own limitations. Based on the available information and feedback from the officials and NGOs, certain drawbacks in the programme implementation of every scheme were identified and corrective measures were suggested (Sekher 2010, 2012). However, a thorough assessment of the effectiveness of the scheme and its impact can only be ascertained through a detailed evaluation and beneficiary assessment. Each of these schemes requires independent review and evaluation by taking into consideration the views of beneficiaries, local NGOs, panchayats, and functionaries. This will help in identifying the problems in programme implementation, such as the need to simplify the eligibility conditions and the required number of documents, ways and means of involving NGOs, women's groups, and panchayats, and optimum utilization of funds.

GIRL CHILD SCHEMES AND FAMILY PLANNING

The acceptance of the terminal method of family planning is one of the eligibility criteria in many schemes. It also raises a larger question—why is family planning linked with girl child promotion schemes? It is possible that many poor families with strong son preference and who have only daughters (often more than two) are unlikely to be enrolled under the scheme. An appraisal of the Girl Child Protection Scheme in Tamil Nadu (Srinivasan and Bedi 2009) observed that two conditions of the scheme—sterilization and 'no sons in the family'—need reconsideration, as it may actually work against daughters and may force families to choose between the schemes (daughters) or sons. If the basic philosophy of these schemes is to promote birth and survival of girl children particularly from poor families, why restrict the benefits to only one or two girls? In other words, in reality, many of these schemes may attract those who do not have a strong son preference. Most of the schemes are mainly focused on poor households, whereas son preference and daughter elimination are widespread across different economic categories. The girl child promotion incentive schemes can have potentially far-reaching implications, and therefore financial constraints should not come in the way of their implementation. It may be appropriate to consider a proposal where both the central and state governments jointly finance these schemes through improved targeting of beneficiaries and attractive incentives. With regard to the impact of these schemes, it is true that the promise of cash transfers has provided a sense of security and confidence among families to invest in girls.

KEY FINDINGS

Study findings point to the need to simplify the eligibility criteria and conditionalities and also the procedures of registration under each of these schemes. Though, year after year, substantial financial resources have been directed towards promoting these schemes, there is a lack of field-level monitoring. In the absence of a proper grievance redressal mechanism the challenges often multiply. In some states, the lack of coordination across different sectors such as health, education, and social welfare is adversely affecting programme implementation. The implementing officers complain that they are not receiving the required support from other agencies, which causes delays and difficulties. In some states, the lack of coordination between implementing departments and financial institutions (LIC, UTI, banks, etc.) also led to delays in issuing bonds/certificates and dispersal of funds. In most of these schemes, the involvement of local panchayats (PRIs), NGOs, and women's groups is rather limited. PRIs may be in a better position to identify the beneficiaries, monitor the progress of implementation, and ensure timely transfer of funds. Some of the state officials highlighted the issue that in many cases, the guidelines for implementation are not clearly understood and the staff is not aware of the different aspects of the schemes. In India, the government has greater familiarity with delivering physical goods and services to enhance well-being and has very little experiential learning on providing and monitoring income transfers closer to the point of impact (Prabhu 2009). In that sense, the introduction of CCTs implies a formidable capacity development challenge.

REFLECTIONS AND RECOMMENDATIONS

These promotional schemes for the girl child could have potentially far-reaching positive implications in enhancing the value of a daughter within a family. Therefore, financial constraints should not come in the way of implementation of such initiatives. The study discovered that the promise of cash transfers provided a sense of security and instilled a sense of confidence in these families to invest in their girls. Wherever benefits were availed, to a large extent families ensured birth registration, immunization, school enrolment, and delayed age of marriage of their daughters. It may be appropriate to consider a proposal wherein both the centre and the state governments jointly finance these schemes through improved targeting and attractive incentives. Schemes aimed at improving the value of the girl child and addressing the decline in sex ratio may not meet these objectives in their entirety if they target BPL families alone. This could be attributed to the adverse sex ratios across different economic classes in the country. A majority of the beneficiary families have spoken about the need to simplify the schemes to further enhance its usefulness and thereby its reach too. For example, schemes such as Dhan Lakshmi and Bhagyalakshmi can be simplified for operational purposes by cutting down on the number of conditionalities attached to various levels of immunization and school attendance. With every conditionality, the beneficiaries have to provide proof of fulfilment of the conditions to complete the documentation formalities. Likewise, domicile certificate is mandatory for many schemes and poor migrant families are likely to be excluded from these schemes. Inflexibility in the given time span for joining the scheme is also a major deterrent for availing benefits among illiterate families. It was felt that enhancing the cash incentives, simplifying the registration procedures, and perhaps minimizing the number of conditionalities would make these schemes more attractive. The multiplicity of outcomes expected to be achieved by a single scheme is likely to somewhat diffuse the focus in achieving the original objective behind the provision of incentives, that is, change in the perceived value of daughters by the family.

Though CCTs offer governments the scope to positively discriminate in favour of girls, it is not clear how far CCTs have led to a change in parental preferences and attitudes towards their daughters. This desk review has helped to highlight the operational challenges in the implementation of such schemes. However, the effectiveness and impact of these initiatives towards ensuring desirability of daughters cannot be absolutely established. An impact evaluation and an analysis of beneficiary perspective would be undertaken in the second phase of the study. An in-depth analysis would also help in addressing certain unanswered questions on the perception of these families towards such schemes. Issues such as perceptions regarding linkages between incentives and family planning, differential incentives for the first and the second daughter, marriage incentive and whether it helps to value delayed marriage or whether it only offsets marriage costs need to be explored. More importantly, such an analysis would help establish whether CCTs in the long run could lead to a significant change in the attitude towards daughters.

REFERENCES

Briere, B.D.L. and L.B. Rawlings. 2006. 'Examining Conditional Cash Transfer Programmes: A Role for Increased Social Inclusion?' Social Protection Discussion Paper, No. 0603, Social Safety Net Primer Series. Washington, DC: World Bank Institute.

Fajth, G., and C. Vinay. 2010. 'Conditional Cash Transfers: A Global Perspective', *MDG Insights*, No. 1, February.

Government of India (GoI). 2007. *Girl Child in the Eleventh Five Year Plan (2007–2012)*. New Delhi: Working Group on Development of Children, Ministry of Women and Child Development.

Government of Karnataka. 2010. *Ninth Round Sample Check on Selected Developmental Programmes—2008–09*. Bangalore: Directorate of Economics and Statistics.

International Food Policy Research Institute. 2002. *Progresa: Breaking the Cycle of Poverty*. Washington, DC: International Food Policy Research Institute.

Prabhu, Seeta. 2009. 'Conditional Cash Transfer Schemes for Alleviating Human Poverty: Relevance for India', Discussion Paper No. 1. New Delhi: United Nations Development Program, India.

Sekher, T.V. 2010. 'Special Financial Incentive Schemes for the Girl Child in India: A Review of Select Schemes'. New Delhi: International Institute for Population Sciences, Mumbai and United Nations Population Fund. http://www.unfpa.org/gender/docs/sexselection/UNFPA_Publication-39772.pdf, last accessed on 14 July 2014.

———. 2012. 'Ladlis and Lakshmis: Financial Incentive Schemes for the Girl Child', *Economic and Political Weekly*, 47(17): 58–65.

Sekher, T.V. and Neelambar Hatti (eds). 2010. *Unwanted Daughters: Gender Discrimination in Modern India*. Jaipur: Rawat Publications.

Sharma, R., R. Goel, and H. Gupta. 2003. 'Rajalakshmi—An Initiative for Improving the Status of Girl Child in Rajasthan', *The Journal of Family Welfare*, 49(1): 66–72.

Son, H.H. 2008. 'Conditional Cash Transfer Programmes: An Effective Tool for Poverty Alleviation?' Manila: Economics and Research Department, ERD Policy Brief Series No. 51, Asian Development Bank.

Srinivasan, S. and A.S. Bedi. 2009. 'Girl Child Protection Scheme in Tamil Nadu: An Appraisal', *Economic and Political Weekly*, 46(48): 10–12.

Part IV

Social Exclusion and Human Development

13 Engaging with Caste

Academic Discourses, Identity Politics, and State Policy[1]

Surinder S. Jodhka

Children are often viewed merely as a demographic or age category. However, childhood has always been socially/historically constructed and constituted. The social and historical context plays a critical role in the way societies look at children and approach their concerns. Given that caste has been, and continues to be, an important institution in the Indian context, it is bound to shape our notions of childhood and the development outcomes. Data from multiple sources confirm that children from formerly 'untouchable' castes, that is, the castes now known as Dalits or Scheduled Castes (SCs), suffer from multiple development deprivations. While broadly it is understood that it is discrimination based on a prevailing set of caste relations that underpins

[1] I would like to express my gratitude to Ramya Subrahmanian for her active involvement in the writing of this chapter. She has been constantly reminding me of the responsibility of the social sciences towards informing state policy and engaging with questions of poverty and deprivation. I also thank her for the useful comments on an earlier draft of this chapter. I have also learnt a great deal from S.K. Thorat and members of faculty at the Indian Institute of Dalit Studies.

these deprivations, the concept of 'caste' itself needs to be revisited to put into perspective the reasons for these caste-linked outcomes and also to identify the kinds of discourses and strategies that can inform public policy efforts to address and change these outcomes.

The dominant view of caste has tended to see it in cultural terms; a uniquely Indian practice that distinguished the traditional social organization of India from the West. In this popular understanding, caste is an ancient institution of the Hindus, based on the ideas of varna, karma, and dharma pronounced in a text called the *Manusmriti*. These ideas translated into a hierarchical society, structured around the notions of purity and pollution. The varna system divided the Hindus into four or five mutually exclusive categories, the Brahmins, the Kshatriyas, the Vaishyas, and the Shudras. Beyond the four varnas were the *achhoots* (the untouchables). These four or five categories occupied different positions in the status hierarchy, with the Brahmins at the top, followed by the other three varnas in the same order as mentioned above, with the achhoots occupying a position at the very bottom.

As an aspect of traditional culture and ideology, it was to change on its own, with the process of modernization and urbanization. This however has not happened. Even more than six decades after Independence, the institution of caste survives in India in many different ways. In some ways, its presence in the popular and political discourses is much more pronounced today than it was during the 1950s or 1960s, when the institutional hold of caste was perhaps much stronger.

While caste continues to be present in the Indian public (and personal) life, the way it is understood has indeed changed. As mentioned above, the classical view of caste, articulated mostly during the colonial period and by early generations of social anthropologists, was viewed purely as a traditional system of hierarchy based on the ideas of purity and pollution. This view has been best articulated by Louis Dumont in his book called *Homo Hierarchicus: The Caste System and Its Implications* (first published in English in 1970). By the late 1960s, sociologists and political scientists also started looking at the way caste interacted with democratic political process in India and how caste communities reinvented themselves in the form of caste associations (Jodhka 2010; Kothari 1970; Rudolph and Rudolph 1967; Shah 2002). The decade of the 1980s witnessed some major shifts in Indian society.

A new kind politics began to take shape around questions of identity and marginality. By the early 1990s, the question of caste was being increasingly articulated mostly by those who had been its 'victims', the 'low' caste.

Even though the Indian Constitution provided reservations for the SCs and also abolished the practice of untouchability, the mainstream process of development planning until the 1980s had mostly been 'caste blind'. Development machinery worked with categories like rich and poor or peasant, farmers and labourers, etc. During the initial decades, caste was rarely treated as a relevant variable in the visualization, designing, or administration of various developmental schemes and programmes.

Caste too has distributive and material dimensions, which produces diverse developmental outcomes for different categories of population located at different locations in the system of caste hierarchy. The institution of caste operates through its intricate relationship with other social institutions such as the patriarchal family system, agrarian economy, and patterns of settlements. Along with its ideological hold over the minds and mentalities of the Indian people, it is through these social institutions that caste reproduces itself in everyday life. However, the everyday aspects of caste, the manner in which it structures and shapes our notions of good and bad, and right and wrong, and its micro-practices have been relatively less-researched and discussed subjects.

However, as mentioned above, over the last two decades or so the nature of academic and popular discourses on caste have been determined from the margins and increasingly through the engagement of those who have been at the receiving end of the 'traditional' systems of hierarchy and exclusions. This perspective from the margins raises the question of revisiting caste, not because it needs 'revival', or 'recognition' as a system (as a marker of 'cultural difference'), but because of its oppressive character, and the fact that it influences development outcomes. In other words, the emphasis of the caste-based movements representing marginal groups, such as the Dalits, is on the need to recognize the continued presence of caste as a reality of Indian society, as a system of power and domination. This articulation of caste has also opened up spaces for engagements with the state for policy intervention on caste lines.

CONCEPTUALIZING CASTE

The history of modern-day theorization of caste begins with Western and colonial engagements with Indian civilization (Cohn 1996; Dirks 2001).[2] Categories such as varna (the four theoretical occupation-based classes of Indian society), jati or *zat* (endogamous group) and the corresponding social divisions and hierarchies of status have indeed been present in different parts (though not everywhere) of the South Asian region for a very long time. They have also been a source of contestations. For example, several social and religious movements during the 'medieval' times questioned the legitimacy of such divisions and offered alternative ways of imagining the human universe based on egalitarian ideals.[3]

The Western idea of 'caste' simplified the diverse and often contested realities of the 'native' social order as a neatly marked out division of groups. Drawn mostly from the ancient 'Hindu' texts, these 'orientalist' writings theorized caste as a hierarchical system through the idea of varna, a substantive category where Brahmins were always placed at the top of the hierarchical order, with Kshatriyas immediately below them, followed by Vaishyas, and last of all, Shudras. The untouchable communities were outside the formal hierarchy, but their status also followed this neat hierarchical ordering derived from the logic of purity and impurity.

Though not all colonial observers agreed on the nature of the Indian caste system, a dominant view on the subject evolved over

[2] However, this is not to suggest that divisions that came to be described as the caste system did not exist earlier or that they were a creation of colonial rule.

[3] A good example of this can be seen in the writings of fifteenth-century poet–saint Ravi Das. Born into an 'untouchable' caste in Banaras, the *Chamars*, he critiqued Brahminical ritualism and articulated a utopia in his famous poem, '*Begumpura Shehr*' ('A City without Sorrow'),

> *where none are third or second—all are one;*
> *Its food and drink are famous, and those who live there*
> *dwell in satisfaction and in wealth.*
> *They do this or that, they walk where they wish,*
> *they stroll through fabled places unchallenged*
> (Hawley and Juergensmeyer 1988, p. 32).

Also see Jodhka 2009 and Omvedt 2008.

the years. The beginning of a systematic theory of caste could be seen in the writings of C. Bougle. In an essay first published in 1908, he contested views that looked at caste merely as a system of occupational specialization. He defined caste as a system consisting of hierarchically arranged hereditary groups, separated from each other in certain respects (caste endogamy, restrictions on eating together, and on physical contact), but interdependent in other respects (traditional division of labour). The word 'caste', he emphasized, involved not only hereditary specialization of occupations but also differential rights. Different occupations were arranged in a hierarchical order that made their occupants socially unequal. Inequality was an essential feature of the caste system. Along with inequality, he also underlined the element of pollution as an important feature of caste. Different groups in a caste society tend to 'repel each other rather than attract, each retires within itself, isolates itself, makes every effort to prevent its members from contracting alliances or even from entering into relation with neighboring groups' (Bougle 1971, p. 65). Thus Bougle identified three core features of the caste system, namely, hereditary occupation, hierarchy, and mutual repulsion.

For the colonial rulers, such theorization of the Indian social order was not merely an academic exercise. This helped them make sense of what seemed like an incomprehensible reality. They also deployed their notion of caste hierarchy in their administrative system for classifying the native communities and determining their qualities and traits. As Sharma points out

> the British took the existence of caste very seriously. Successive censuses of India attempted to classify the entire population by caste, on the assumption that everyone must belong to some caste or other and that castes were real identifiable groups. As a result this objectification of caste actually made it more real and liable to rigidification... (Sharma 2002, p. 8)

This 'book view' of caste also constructed India as the 'other' of the West. Even though they were divided on class lines, modern Western societies were culturally or ideologically governed by the idea of equal citizenship. Caste was a peculiar feature of the subcontinent, where the social order had been static for ages and held no possibility of change emanating from internal contradictions. This view of caste served a useful ideological function. It helped colonial rulers present a positive image of their rule. The normative order of caste was so strong that it made it impossible for 'natives' to change their traditional system on their own, or as Inden would argue, they had no agency of their own (Inden 1990, p. 65). Even radical thinkers like Marx and Engels were influenced by such views about the Indian social order, and they affirmed in their writings the need for a colonial intervention that alone could disturb the equilibrium that had kept the Indian village community static for centuries (Marx 1853).

The influence of colonialism and its forms of knowledge, to use Bernard Cohn's expression (Cohn 1996), was also quite significant for the way professional sociology and social anthropology developed its understanding of caste and the Hindu social order. Even when the postcolonial 'native' sociologists and social anthropologists advocated a shift away from the 'book view' of India, towards a 'field view', the categories through which a majority of them imagined India invariably remained the same. For example, the village typically became a convenient methodological entry point for anthropologists interested in understanding the dynamics of Indian society (Jodhka 1998). Similarly, sociologists and social anthropologists universally assumed that the caste system was fundamental to Indian social structure, which in turn also synonymized Hindu religion with Indian culture.

More recent historical research on the subject has seriously undermined this common-sense view of the caste system. The colonial rulers not only raised consciousness about caste through a process of enumeration and ethnographic surveys, but also produced social and intellectual conditions where 'caste became the single term capable of expressing, organizing, and above all "synthesizing" India's diverse forms of social identity, community and organization' (Dirks 2001, p. 5). A good example of this can be found in Peter Mayer's work on the *jajmani* system (a caste-based system of patron–client relations that defined duties and responsibilities of different caste groups in a village setting/agrarian economy and tied the lower castes with the landowning dominant *jajmans*). As he argues, though the jajmani system is popularly believed to be an ancient and pan-Indian reality, in fact it originated in northern India during the late nineteenth century (Mayer 1993).

THE POPULAR TEXTBOOK VIEW OF CASTE

Notwithstanding these critical writings, the dominant textbook view of caste has continued to be based largely on the classical colonial understanding of 'Hindu India'.[4] Caste, according to this dominant view, was not merely an institution that characterized the structure of social stratification; it represented the core of India. It was both an institution and an ideology. Institutionally, 'caste' provided a framework for arranging and organizing social groups in terms of their statuses and positions in the social and economic system. As an ideology, caste was a system of values and ideas that legitimized and reinforced the existing structures of social inequality. It provided a world view around which a typical Hindu organized his/her life.

Apart from being an institution that distinguished India from other societies, caste was also an epitome of the traditional Indian society, a 'closed system', where generation after generation of individuals did similar kinds of work and lived more or less similar kinds of lives. In contrast, modern industrial societies of the West were projected as 'open systems' of social stratification, societies based on class, where individuals could choose their occupations according to their abilities and tastes. If they worked for it, in such open systems of stratification, they could move up the social hierarchy and change their class position. Such mobility at the individual level was impossible in the caste system.

Putting it in the language of social science textbooks, G.S. Ghurye (1991) identified six different features of the Hindu caste system, namely, segmental division of society; hierarchy; restrictions on feeding and social intercourse; civil and religious disabilities and privileges of different sections; lack of unrestricted choice of occupation; restrictions on marriage.

Though seemingly simple and obvious, this list represented caste as a total and unitary system. Thus, it was possible to define caste and

[4] Students of India have also offered alternative formulations, which did not become popular. Some scholars, for example, stress that the origin of caste system lay in the nature of agrarian production and generation of surplus in early agrarian systems (see Klass 1980; Yurlova 1989). Similarly, some others have pointed to primacy of the political in structuring caste hierarchies in India (see Quigley 1993; Raheja 1988).

to identify its core features, which were presumably present everywhere in the subcontinent. Similarly, caste was also not merely about occupational specialization or division of labour. It encapsulated within it the features of a social structure, normative religious behaviour, and even provided a fairly comprehensive idea about personal lives of individuals living in the Hindu caste society.

Indian sociologists also pointed out the difference between varna and jati. While in the popular understanding there were only four varnas, the actual number of caste groups was quite large. According to one estimate, in each linguistic region 'there were about 200 caste groups which were further sub-divided into about 3000 smaller units each of which was endogamous and constituted the area of effective social life for the individual' (Srinivas 1962, p. 65).

Perhaps the most influential theoretical work on caste has been of Louis Dumont. He approached the Hindu caste system from a structuralist perspective that focused on the underlying structure of ideas of a given system, the 'essential principles', which may not be apparent or visible in its everyday practice. Invoking Max Weber, he described his theory of caste as an ideal-type.

Caste, according to Dumont, was above all an ideology, and the core element in the ideology of caste for Dumont was hierarchy. Hierarchy was not merely another name for inequality or an extreme form of social stratification, but a totally different principle of social organization founded on the idea of opposition of the pure and the impure. Pure was understandably superior to impure (Dumont 1998, p. 43).

Another important aspect of his theory was the specific relationship that existed between status and power in Hindu society. Unlike the West where power and status normally went together, in the caste system there was a divergence between the two. In caste-based society, status as a principle of social organization was superior to power.

Such theorizations of caste were extensively criticized for their ideological bias and weak empirical groundings (see Berreman1971; Beteille 1979; Gupta 1984; Mencher 1974). However, they have continued to be popular and influential. Why does this happen? As argued elsewhere (Jodhka 2004), the idea of caste has been deeply embedded in the modern Indian self-image, which is itself a mirror reflection of the orientalist and colonial images of India. The Indian past is thus constructed as an unchanging tradition and the future is imagined through an evolutionary schema where Western society is presented as a model for imitation in the name of modernization.

In such an evolutionary imagination, caste was part and parcel of the traditional culture of India, which was supposed to eventually disappear with the unfolding of the processes of industrialization, urbanization, and modernization. Not only did such theorizations of caste simplify the complex systems of inequality, they rarely looked at it critically. It was a descriptive account of the classical anthropological eye, a Western view of the 'other cultures'. Even something like the practice of untouchability was not seen critically as an oppressive system with an agency that enforced codes of behaviour and reproduced regimes of subordination and domination.

DEMOCRATIC POLITICS AND CHANGING CASTE RELATIONS

Notwithstanding their faith in the scientific value of the classical anthropological theorizing, the encounter of social scientists, social anthropologists, and political scientists working on India during the post-Independence period produced very different accounts of caste. Even when they worked with evolutionist models of social change, they recognized the tremendous resilience that caste was showing on the ground. Caste as a source of mobilization could enter the 'modern' institutions of democracy, and survive or could even find a new life for itself. The rise of non-Brahmin movements in southern and western Indian provinces provoked Ghurye to argue that their attack on Brahmin dominance did not necessarily mean the end of caste. These mobilizations generated a new kind of collective sentiment, 'the feeling of caste solidarity' which could be 'truly described as caste patriotism' (Ghurye 1932, p. 192).

M.N. Srinivas developed this point further in his writings during the late 1950s. Focusing specifically on the possible consequences of modern technology and representational politics, both of which were introduced by the colonial rulers in India, he argued that far from disappearing with the process of modernization, caste was experiencing a 'horizontal consolidation'. Commenting on the impact of modern technology on caste, he wrote:

> The coming in of printing, of a regular postal service, of vernacular newspapers and books, of the telegraph, railway and bus, enabled the representatives of a caste living in different areas to meet and discuss their common problems and interests. Western education gave new political values such as liberty and equality. The educated leaders started caste journals and held caste conferences. Funds were collected to organize the caste, and to help the poorer members. Caste hostels, hospitals, co-operative societies etc., became a common feature of urban social life. In general it may be confidently said that the last hundred years have seen a great increase in caste solidarity, and the concomitant decrease of a sense of interdependence between different castes living in a region. (Srinivas 1962, p. 74–5)

This horizontal solidarity of caste, which also meant a kind of growing 'competition' among different castes at the politico-economic plane, eventually weakened the vertical solidarity of caste (Bailey 1963; Srinivas 1962, p. 74). The process of horizontal consolidation received further impetus with the introduction of democratic politics after India's Independence. On encountering the question of change in caste order, Louis Dumont too followed Srinivas and speculated on similar lines. Castes, he argued, did not disappear with the process of economic and political change, but its logic was altered. He described this process as change from 'structure' to 'substance'. This substantialization of caste indicated

> the transition from a fluid, structural universe in which the emphasis is on interdependence and in which there is no privileged level, no firm units, to a universe of improbable blocks, self-sufficient, essentially identical and in competition with one another, a universe in which the caste appears as a collective *individual* (in the sense we have given to this word), as a substance. (Dumont 1998, p. 222 emphasis in original)

These attempts at theorizations of the changing realities of caste opened up many new possibilities for looking at the dynamic relationship of caste with the democratic political process. Thus, by the 1960s, sociologists and political scientists began to talk about caste and politics in a different language. Discussions shifted from a predominantly moral or normative concern about the corruption that caste brought into democratic political processes to more empirical processes of interaction between caste and politics. The gradual institutionalization of democratic politics changed caste equations. Power shifted from one set of caste groups, the so-called ritually purer upper castes, to middle-level 'dominant castes'. However, as caste encountered democratic political process, it also began to change, both internally as well as externally, in terms of social relations and political equations of jatis and *upjati*s (sub-castes). The accompanying processes of economic development also introduced a process of differentiation within and across caste communities, which influenced structures of local power. The democratic state institutionalized new institutions of representations. Though they were visualized as secular institutions, caste soon entered in their working.

However, the authority of these institutions had to be reproduced differently. Electoral process could not be completely neutralized by the existing structures of caste power. For example, though traditional sources of power continued to be relevant, introduction of universal adult franchise also made the numerical size of caste communities in a given local setting critical. The dominant caste communities or individual families of traditional patriarchs could control the new institutions, such as the panchayats, only if they were able to gather support of 'others', including those who had until now been completely outside the domain of politics, such as the 'untouchable' communities. Power could now be reproduced only through mobilizations, vertically as well as horizontally. This also gave birth to a new class of political entrepreneurs. Over the years some of them have begun to work successfully without confining their political constituency to a single caste cluster, thus undermining the logic of caste politics (Krishna 2001).

CASTE POLITICS FROM THE MARGINS AND ITS IMPLICATIONS FOR STATE POLICY

As the politics of caste and community identities begins to get differentiated, we witness the growing emergence of newer forms of caste clusters. This time it is the caste communities located on the margins of the social order of caste, the 'backwards' and 'Dalits', who collaborate with and mobilize their caste members for electoral battles.

Articulations of caste politics from the margins also introduced a new language of caste.

This phase took off during the decade of the 1980s, with the introduction of separate quotas for the other backward classes (OBCs) by the then prime minister, V.P. Singh, based on the recommendations of the Mandal Commission in 1990. Though the introduction of the Mandal Commission Report invoked a lot of opposition from the middle- and upper-caste groups, there was virtually no open opposition from any of the major political parties to the introduction of new quotas.

At another level, implementation of the Mandal Commission Report and the casteist mobilizations against it raised questions about caste to which professional sociology had no clear answers. Though caste-based quotas had already been in existence for the SCs, they were seen more as exceptions than the rule. Reservations for the SCs and Scheduled Tribes (STs) were in the nature of targeted programmes. Their extension to the other backward classes meant an acceptance of caste as a legitimate aspect of state policy and a possible indicator of 'development' or the lack of it.

Until the 1980s, the discourse of development had largely remained 'caste blind'. Even within electoral politics, the SC communities were mostly aligned with the mainstream political formation, the Congress party. The question of autonomous Dalit politics and identity was confined only to a few pockets in states such as Maharashtra, Karnataka, or Andhra Pradesh, largely as a concern of urbanized individuals who articulated the question of Dalit identity through literature and other cultural forms (Mendelsohn and Vicziany 2000).

However, over the years, the size of the Dalit middle class has grown, thanks largely to the policy of reservations in government jobs and educational institutions. As they grew in numbers, they also felt more confident to articulate their experiences of discrimination at the workplace and the continued caste-based prejudice against their communities in society at large. They began to form separate associations of SC employees and mobilized themselves in the event of any discriminatory experiences (Mendelsohn and Vicziany 2000). It was about this time that Ambedkar was rediscovered as a universal icon of Dalit identity and as symbolizing their aspirations (Zelliot 2001).

More recently, studies have pointed to a process of loosening of traditional structures of power/domination. On the basis of his work in Rajasthan, Oliver Mendelsohn, for example, argued that though Srinivas was right in talking about 'dominant caste' during the 1950s, such a formulation makes less sense in the present-day rural India. The 'low caste and even untouchable villagers were now less beholden to their economic and ritual superiors than was suggested in older accounts' (Mendelsohn 1993, p. 808). Similarly, 'land and authority had been de-linked in village India and this amounted to an historic, if non-revolutionary transformation' (Mendelsohn 1993, p. 807).

Similarly, writing on the basis of his field experience in Karnataka, Karanth argued that the traditional association of caste with occupation was weakening and that the jajmani ties were fast disintegrating (Karanth 1996). In an extensive survey of 51 villages of Punjab, this author also found a similar kind of change taking place in rural Punjab where the older structure of jajmani relations had nearly completely disintegrated (Jodhka 2002). As in Karnataka, in rural Punjab too, with the exception of a few occupations, there was hardly any association between caste and occupations. Further, Dalits in Punjab had also begun to distance themselves from the village economy and disliked working in farms owned by the local Jat community. They were also trying to construct their own cultural centres like religious shrines and community halls in order to establish their autonomy in the rural power structure. In the emerging scenario, local Dalits have begun to assert demands for equal rights and a share of resources that belonged commonly to the village but had so far been in the exclusive control of the locally dominant caste groups or individual households. This new-found awareness of entitlements and assertions of claims among the Dalit communities were directly responsible for the frequent cases of caste-related conflicts and violence being reported from rural Punjab (Jodhka and Louis 2003). A study from rural Bihar also similarly reported an erosion of traditional jajmani ties. Here too, the hold of the village community over the individual's choice of occupation was virtually absent (Sahay 2004).

It is in this changed context of a combination of factors that the new agency among the Dalits has to be located. The new class of political entrepreneurs that has emerged from amongst the ex-untouchable communities used the idea of 'Dalit identity' and mobilized the

SC communities as a united block on the promise of development with dignity. Some of them, such as Kanshi Ram and Mayavati have been quite successful in doing so (Pai 2002; Shah 2002).

DALIT DEPRIVATIONS AND THEORIZING CASTE FROM THE MARGINS

Notwithstanding the success of Indian democracy and the increasing participation of the historically marginalized groups/communities in the electoral process, along with more than six decades of development and quotas for SCs, caste-based disparities have not disappeared. In other words, caste discrimination continues to be an important indicator of deprivation and marginality, both at the macro-level reflected in national-level data (see Thorat 2009) and at the micro-level (see Jodhka 2002; Shah et al. 2006). Caste also plays an important role in the modern urban economy. For example, ownership of industry in India has historically been concentrated in the hands of a few social/cultural groups and jobs at the top were always kept within the family or community (Munshi 2007; Rutten 2003). Recruitments for other jobs were opened to outsiders only when the required personnel were not available within the community or the wider kin-group. The negatively associated social identity of Dalits is a barrier when they wish to enter the modern/urban labour market (Jodhka and Newman 2007) or business (Jodhka 2009).

The caste system has three core defining features when it is viewed from the context of the margins. The first and above all is that caste is about *dominations*. Max Weber's distinction between coercive power and authority/domination is invoked here to demonstrate that caste has historically been an institutionalized form of domination, supported by a set of values, norms, and institutions, some of which continue to be present even today, while others have weakened or disintegrated (Weber, in Gerth and Mills 1946). However, a radical break with the caste system has not yet taken place. In the absence of comprehensive structural change, caste asserts itself as coercive power, perhaps more often than before, because of the weakening of its ideological hold. Increase in the incidences of caste-based atrocities is evidence of this.

The second related dimension of caste is its role in creating *disparities*. Caste does not simply imply power in a cultural sense of the term.

It is also a structural reality where inequality is institutionalized in terms of unequal distribution of resources. Inequality seen in terms of disparities refers to a very different set of attributes when compared with the Dumontian notion of inequality that refers to a cultural notion of hierarchy, something which exists only as an ideological category, derived from the dialectical opposition between pure and impure as it exists in the Hindu mind. Disparities, on the other hand refer to inequalities in terms of entitlements and ownership of resources, closer to the Marxian notion of 'means of production'. However, the nature of disparities and inequalities in the caste society is different. They are 'graded inequalities', to use Ambedkar's expression (Ambedkar 1936).

The third related dimension of caste is that it is an institutionalized system of discrimination and denials. Discrimination and denial have been socially and culturally institutionalized in India and it has been group specific. It produced a pattern of disadvantages that in turn produced deprivations and poverty among certain groups. Denial was culturally institutionalized in the sense that it had legitimacy and long-term implications for the social and economic status of caste groups/communities. For example, the ex-untouchable communities were not allowed to own and cultivate land and become peasants. Such customary practices could not be explained away by referring simply to the dialectics of pure and impure. It defined and limited rights of different groups of people. More importantly perhaps, the effects of such past tradition is felt even today by a large majority of Dalits. Absence of assets, such as agricultural land, makes them much more vulnerable, economically as well as socially.

★ ★ ★

Caste has for long been a subject of inquiry with sociologists, social anthropologists, and political scientists. However, they have invariably looked at it as a traditional system of social hierarchy and culture that would inevitably weaken and eventually disappear with the process of development or modernization. Caste was thus researched in relation to rural social order, kinship networks, religious life, or traditional occupations, and mostly by social anthropologists and sociologists. The economists who worked on 'hard' questions of development rarely treated caste as a relevant area of inquiry. In the mainstream understanding of textbook economics, development or markets were essentially secular and anonymous processes. Poverty and deprivation were attributes of individuals or households and those possessing such attributes could be classified and clubbed together using purely secular and economic categories. The 'secular economists' argued that using caste and community in policy discourse was akin to giving them legitimacy and strengthening hierarchical social order and traditional cultural practices.

However, over the years scholars have come to recognize the crucial importance of the 'non-economic' factors such as caste, race, ethnicity, or gender in structuring market and determining economic outcomes. Following this realization, mainstream development studies have also undergone a complete paradigm shift over the last two decades or so with 'human' rather than 'economic' development becoming the focus and index of growth and progress.

On the one hand, we saw this paradigm shift taking place from above through UN agencies and academic debates on how best to understand development. On the other hand, India also witnessed a social and political churning thanks to the forces unleashed by democratic political processes. The rise of autonomous Dalit movements during the late 1980s did not simply ask for recognition and state power. They also raised questions about the meanings of caste, and how they continue to experience it even in secular/modern spaces of the contemporary. They also wish to actively engage with the state system on its policies for development and laws against discrimination.

Over the last two decades, the academic understanding of caste has also been undergoing change. There is an increasing recognition of the fact that caste is not simply a question of past tradition and Indian/Hindu culture, or that it would disappear on its own once modern forces of industrial development and democratic politics appear on the scene. The popular understanding of caste is also beginning to recognize that talking about caste is also talking about power and powerlessness. It is also talking about disparities, discrimination, and denial of access to resources and entitlements for some. The rise of autonomous Dalit voice also articulated a new vision of citizenship where recognition of community identities becomes essential for addressing the question of denial.

REFERENCES

Ambedkar, B.R. 1936. *Annihilation of Caste.* Jallandhar: Bheem Patrika.

Bailey F.G. 1963. 'Closed Social Stratification in India', *European Journal of Sociology*, 4(1): 107–24.

Berreman, Gerald D. 1971. 'The Brahamanical View of Caste', *Contributions to Indian Sociology* (n.s.), 5(1): 16–25.

Beteille, A. 1979. 'Homo Hierarchicus, Homo Equalis', *Modern Asian Studies*, 13(4): 529–48.

Bougle, C. 1971 [1908]. *Essays on the Caste System.* Cambridge: Cambridge University Press.

Cohn, B. 1996. *Colonialism and its Forms of Knowledge: The British in India.* Princeton: Princeton University Press.

Dirks, N.B. 2001. *Castes of Mind: Colonialism and the Making of Modern India.* Princeton: Princeton University Press.

Dumont, L. 1998 [1970]. *Homo Hierarchicus: The Caste System and Its Implications.* New Delhi: Oxford University Press.

Gerth, H.H. and C. Wright Mills (eds). 1946. *From Max Weber: Essays in Sociology.* Oxford: Oxford University Press.

Ghurye, G.S. 1932. *Caste and Race in India.* London: Kegan Paul.

———. 1991. 'Features of Caste System', in Dipankar Gupta (ed.), *Social Stratification*, pp. 35–48. New Delhi: Oxford University Press.

Gupta, D. 1992 [1984]. 'Continuous Hierarchies and Discrete Castes', in Dipankar Gupta (ed.), *Social Stratification.* New Delhi: Oxford University Press.

Hawley, J.S. and M. Juergensmeyer. 1988. *Songs of the Saints of India.* New Delhi: Oxford University Press.

Inden, R. 1990. *Imagining India.* Oxford: Blackwell.

Jodhka, S.S. 1998. 'From "Book-View" to "Field-View": Social Anthropological Constructions of the Indian Village', *Oxford Development Studies*, 26(3): 311–31.

———. 2002. 'Caste and Untouchability in Rural Punjab', *Economic and Political Weekly*, 37(19): 1813–23.

———. 2004. 'Sikhism and the Caste Question: Dalits and Their Politics in Contemporary Punjab', *Contributions to Indian Sociology* (n.s.), 23(1 and 2): 165–92.

———. 2009. 'The Ravi Dasis of Punjab: Global Contours of Caste and Religious Strife', *Economic and Political Weekly*, 44(24): 79–85.

Jodhka, S.S. and Prakash Louis. 2003. 'Caste Tensions in Punjab: Talhan and Beyond', *Economic and Political Weekly*, 38(28): 2923–6.

Jodhka, S.S. and Katherine Newman. 2007. 'In the Name of Globalisation: Meritocracy, Productivity and the Hidden Language of Caste', *Economic and Political Weekly*, 42(41): 4125–32.

Juergensmeyer, M. 1982. *Religious Rebels in the Punjab: The Social Vision of Untouchables*. Delhi: Ajanta Publications.

Karanth, G.K. 1996. 'Caste in Contemporary Rural India', in M.N. Srinivas (ed.), *Caste: Its Twentieth Century Avatar*, pp. 86–109. New Delhi: Penguin.

Klass, Morton. 1980. *Caste: The Emergence of the South Asian Social System*. Philadelphia: Institute of Study of Human Issues.

Kothari, Rajni. 1970. *Caste in Indian Politics*. Hyderabad: Orient Longman.

Krishna, Anirudh. 2001. 'What Is Happening to Caste? A View from Some North Indian Villages', Working Paper SAN01-04. Duke: Terry Sanford Institute of Public Policy.

Marx, Karl. 1853. 'The British Rule in India', *New York Daily Tribune*, 25 June. http://www.marxists.org/archive/marx/works/1853/06/25.htm, last accessed on 12 February 2013.

Mayer, Peter. 1993. 'Inventing Village Tradition: The Late 19th Century Origins of the North Indian "Jajmani System"', *Modern Asian Studies*, 27(2): 357–95.

Mehta, Pratap Bhanu. 2003. *The Burden of Democracy*. New Delhi: Penguin.

Mencher, Joan. 1974. 'The Caste System Upside Down, or the Not-So-Mysterious-East', *Current Anthropology*, 15: 469–93.

Mendelsohn, O. 1993. 'The Transformation of Authority in Rural India', *Modern Asian Studies*, 15(4): 805–42.

Mendelsohn, O. and M. Vicziany. 2000. *The Untouchables: Subordination, Poverty and the State in Modern India*. Cambridge: Cambridge University Press.

Munshi, K. 2007. 'The Birth of a Business Community: Tracing Occupational Migration in a Developing Economy'. www.econ.brown.edu/fac/Kaivan_Munshi/diamond10.pdf, last accessed on 10 November 2008.

Omvedt, Gail. 2008. *Seeking Begumpura: The Social Vision of Anti-caste Intellectuals*. New Delhi: Navayana.

Pai, S. 2002. *Dalit Assertion and the Unfinished Democratic Revolution: The Bahujan Samaj Party in Uttar Pradesh*. New Delhi: Sage Publications.

Quigley, D. 1993. *The Interpretations of Caste*. New Delhi: Oxford University Press.

Raheja, G.G. 1988. *The Poison in the Gift: Ritual, Presentation and the Dominant Caste in a North Indian Village*. Chicago: University of Chicago Press.

Rudolph, Lloyd I. and Susanne H. Rudolph. 1999 [1967]. *The Modernity of Tradition: Political Development in India*. Hyderabad: Orient Longman.

Rutten, Mario. 2003. *Rural Capitalists in Asia: A Comparative Analysis on India, Indonesia, and Malaysia*. London: Routledge.

Sahay, Gaurang R. 2004. 'Hierarchy, Difference and the Caste System: A Study of Rural Bihar', *Contributions to Indian Sociology* (n.s.), 38(1 and 2): 113–36.

Shah, G. 1975. *Caste Associations and Political Process in Gujarat: A Study of Gujarat Kshatriya Sabha*. Bombay: Popular Prakashan.

———. 2000. 'Hope and Despair: A Study of Untouchability and Atrocities in Gujarat', *Journal of Indian School of Political Economy*, 12(3 and 4): 459–72.

——— (ed.). 2002. *Caste and Democratic Politics in India*. Delhi: Permanent Black.

Shah, G., Harsh Mander, and Sukhadeo Thorat. 2006. *Untouchability in Rural India*. New Delhi: Sage Publications.

Sharma, Ursula. 2002. *Caste*. New Delhi: Viva Books Private Limited.

Srinivas, M.N. 1962. *Caste in Modern India and Other Essays*. Bombay: Media Promoter and Publishers.

Thorat, Sukhadeo. 2009. *Dalits in India: Search for a Common Destiny*. New Delhi: Sage Publications.

Yurlova, Eugenia S. 1989. *Scheduled Castes in India*. New Delhi: Patriot Publishers.

Zelliot, E. 2001. *From Untouchable to Dalit: Essays on the Ambedkar Movement*, 3rd edition. New Delhi: Manohar Publishers.

14 Assessing the Inclusiveness of Government Flagship Programmes

The Case of National Rural Health Mission

Kaveri Gill

This chapter seeks to develop a conceptual understanding and an analytical framework for assessing social exclusion that is then applied as an illustrative case study to the central government's flagship health programmes, the National Rural Health Mission (NRHM), and, within it, the Reproductive and Child Health (RCH) programme. The next section contextualizes the current emphasis on inclusiveness in the policy sphere, against the broad mandate of 'inclusive growth' first elaborated in the Government of India's Eleventh Five-Year Plan (2008–12), and continued in the current (Twelfth) Five-Year Plan (2013–17).[1] It then explores the concept of social exclusion, and how it is transmitted in actuality, both at the 'macro institutional bias' level and at the 'meso unruly practices' level, which in turn impact flagship programmes in

[1] In this chapter, the Eleventh Five-Year Plan is being used as the frame of reference given its elaboration of the policy aspiration of 'Inclusive Growth'.

various ways. Based on an understanding of the aforesaid, a framework for assessing social exclusion—or its obverse, inclusiveness—in the flagship programmes is developed.

The framework's focus areas are: flagship policy, delivery and implementation, and the beneficiary perspective. Further strands of interest emerge under each heading: on policy, the concerns are on its design, participation and coverage norms, budgetary resources and utilization, and monitoring and evaluation; on implementation, the areas of interest are opportunities for discretionary delivery performance dependent on whether ongoing services through repeat delivery and interaction are required or not, shortfall in quantity and quality of services, provider discrimination, and accountability; and on the beneficiary perspective, the concerns are on access, (un)equal treatment, and decentralized community involvement. The next three sections demonstrate how this framework is used to assess social exclusion in the flagship programmes of health alone—such as RCH (NRHM)—that is, in isolation from the other programmes. The data for this assessment are based on existing secondary literature. The final section presents findings, gaps in the literature, and the way forward.

FLAGSHIP PROGRAMME POLICY

Policy Context of 'Inclusive Growth', Eleventh Five-Year Plan, Planning Commission

Titled 'Inclusive Growth,' the Eleventh Five-Year Plan of the Planning Commission, Government of India (GoI), begins its vision and strategy chapter with the explicit recognition that while the country recorded an average rate of growth of 7.7 per cent during the Tenth Plan period, a major shortcoming is that this growth is not perceived as being 'sufficiently inclusive for many groups, especially Scheduled Castes (SCs), Scheduled Tribes (STs), and minorities. Gender inequality also remains a pervasive problem…' (Planning Commission 2008, p. 1). Citing the National Sample Survey Organisation (NSSO, now renamed as the National Sample Survey Office) and other data evidence in support of this statement, the Planning Commission argued that during the last decade and a half, the rate of decline in poverty has not been commensurate with the growth in Gross Domestic Product (GDP), and that the incidence of poverty amongst certain hitherto excluded groups, especially the Scheduled Tribes, has shown hardly any decrease at all (Planning Commission 2008).

The central vision of the Eleventh Five-Year Plan is to 'trigger a development process which ensures broad-based improvement in the quality of life of the people, especially the poor, Scheduled Castes (SCs) and Scheduled Tribes (STs), Other Backward Classes (OBCs), minorities and women' (Planning Commission 2008, p. 2). Moreover, the target is 'inclusive growth, that is, a growth process which yields broad-based benefits and ensures equality of opportunity for all' (Planning Commission 2008). For the purposes of this analysis, amongst the interrelated components seen to further this vision and listed in the Plan documents, the most relevant are access to services, social justice and empowerment, and governance.

On how access to services is conceived as a means to inclusive growth, the Plan document argues that while in the short run, access to basic facilities, such as health, education, clean drinking water, and sanitation impact welfare, in the long run, they determine economic opportunity, and more importantly, equal opportunity. Since, for the majority of the population, access to services depends on not just their income levels, but also upon their delivery through public-funded systems, the Eleventh Plan envisages a major expansion in the supply of these services. These are to be funded, sustainably, through tax revenues generated from faster growth and funnelled towards increased Plan expenditure.

The vision of the Eleventh Plan explicitly mentions social justice and empowerment of excluded groups as a means to inclusion. The latter is to be achieved through affirmative action for SCs, STs, OBCs, minorities, and women, leading to equality of opportunity and possibilities for economic and social mobility. Empowerment is to be further facilitated through participation in the third established layer of democracy, that is, the Panchayati Raj Institution (PRI) level, wrought through reservation for SCs, STs, and women in these bodies. In particular, 'it is absolutely critical for the inclusiveness of our growth process that these large numbers of elected representatives in our PRIs are fully involved in planning, implementing and supervising the delivery of the essential public services' (Planning Commission 2008, p. 23).

Finally, the vision for the Eleventh Plan acknowledges that government-funded social sector programmes have suffered from poor design, lack of accountability, corruption, and ineffective implementation. Accordingly, it cites the importance of improved governance by involving communities in the design and implementation of programmes, as also better scientific evaluation, which it is hoped will again feed back into their superior design and implementation.

Looking back on the performance of India's economy under the Eleventh Plan on the eve of the Twelfth Plan, the Deputy Chairman of the Planning Commission notes,

> It is more difficult to assess performance on inclusiveness than on growth for three reasons. First, inclusiveness is a multidimensional concept and progress therefore needs to be assessed in many different dimensions. Second, the data relating to various aspects of inclusiveness become available only after a considerable lag, and information for the Eleventh Plan period is often not available. Third, most policies aimed at inclusiveness have an impact only over a relatively long term, and this means that even when policies are moving in the right direction, the results may only be evident much later. (Ahluwalia 2011: 89)

These are the challenges this chapter seeks to address, albeit only in the limited domain of flagship programmes of the government.

Social Exclusion and Flagship Programmes

As suggested above and as envisaged under the Eleventh Plan, improved access to services is one of the lynchpins for achieving inclusive growth. Most flagship programmes address inclusion by building in regional equity components or targeted components, sub-plans, or earmarked funds for traditionally excluded groups such as the SCs or the STs. This is by design. Yet, others try and reach them through innovations in implementation on the ground. Before we assess the extent to which the health flagship programmes of our interest have been able to address exclusion, it is critical that we first understand the concept of social exclusion—what it means and what operational implications it can potentially have.

THE CONCEPT OF SOCIAL EXCLUSION

Social exclusion has been defined as 'the process through which individuals or groups are wholly or partially excluded from full participation in the society within which they live' (de Haan 1999, p. 6). Although often conflated with poverty, social exclusion is different in the sense that it focuses not just on poor outcomes (for example, low incomes, consumption, as seen in monetary definitions of poverty). Rather, it focuses on the institutional processes—in the economic, social, or political sphere—that lead to poor outcomes (de Haan 1998). Its potential value addition to previous approaches, especially to monetary poverty, thus lies in the fact that it highlights the nature of disadvantage and deprivation as being multidimensional, relational, and processual and, in doing so, adds scope for temporal and causal analyses (de Haan 1998).

Drawing out the analytical basis of the social exclusion approach in finer detail, Kabeer posits that different forms of disadvantage stretch along a spectrum, with economic injustice ('what you have') at one end, cultural injustice ('what you are') at the other, and hybrid forms lying somewhere in between (Kabeer 2000). The latter give rise to 'bivalent collectivities', that is, social groups for whom economic disadvantage is bound up with cultural-valuational disadvantage (Kabeer 2000, p. 85). A key example of such bivalent collectivities is gender and, in the context of South Asia in particular, caste or, more precisely, SCs and ethnicity, which alludes in this instance to STs.

Gender, caste, or ethnic disadvantage translates into social exclusion when the 'institutional mechanisms through which resources are allocated and values assigned operate in such a way as to *systematically* deny particular groups of people the resources and recognition which would allow them to participate fully in the life of that society' (Kabeer 2000, p. 86; emphasis added). The key ideas emphasized by this definition are those of the processes of disentitlement, 'given' group characteristics (as opposed to chosen ones), and faulty (or a lack of) access for them, which are reinforced across multiple domains.

Systematic exclusion has been documented in several studies in India. Among the most notable of them is the longitudinal study by Drèze et al. (1998), which documents economic development and societal change over five decades in Palanpur village of Uttar Pradesh. The authors found that an SC identity, as a 'predetermined characteristic' or 'given group', engendered radically different endowments and opportunities in various spheres, resulting in a systemic poverty trap for them. Moreover, entire generations of SC families were unable to move out of poverty suggesting intergenerational transmission of inequalities (Drèze et al. 1998).

APPLYING A SOCIAL EXCLUSION LENS TO FLAGSHIP PROGRAMMES

In terms of actual practices through which social exclusion is transmitted, two are especially relevant to the subject of this chapter. First, at the macro-policy level, is the mobilization of institutional bias, that is, a predominant set of values, beliefs, rituals, and institutional procedures or rules of the game that operate systematically and consistently to the benefit of certain persons and groups at the expense of others (Kabeer 2000, p. 91). These are insidious in that they can operate to exclude those who threaten the status quo without conscious decisions or awareness by status quo representatives. Second, at the meso-level, are unruly practices, that is, gaps between rules and their implementation, which occur in all institutional domains (Kabeer 2000, p. 92). The latter are especially relevant to the flagship programmes, where unofficial norms are likely to shape actual (non) provision and mediate people's (in)ability to gain access to goods to which they are technically entitled.

In sum, and as is appropriate for the remit of the present chapter, which is to apply the concept of social exclusion to flagship programmes of health, the following points emerge. First, we are to focus on the 'bivalent collectivities' of gender and excluded categories (for example, SCs and STs) that are explicitly named as priority beneficiaries in each of the central government's flagship programmes. Second, we are to recognize and explore the extent to which—for these 'given groups'—social exclusion is possibly reinforced across multiple sectors, which leads to poverty traps and intergenerational transfer of inequality. Third, our analysis should look for evidence, if any, of a 'macro institutional bias' operating against these groups, and which is sought to be compensated for by explicitly naming them as priority categories in terms of the macro-vision, design, and budget allocation of flagship programmes. Finally, we need to focus also on 'meso unruly practices', if we find any in the implementation of flagship programmes, which result in outcomes other than those intended (here, outcomes may even allude to access to inputs promised by the programme, not necessarily the final development outcomes).

Keeping these factors in mind, exclusion in flagship programmes can be studied in terms of (i) policy; (ii) delivery system and implementation; and (iii) what target group representatives themselves have to say about exclusion in these programmes, that is, a beneficiary perspective. Appendix A14.1 summarizes this analytical framework in tabular form, including the sub-strands falling under each of the above categories that need scrutiny.

Four issues arise at the policymaking stage itself: (i) design and strategies; (ii) guidelines for participation and coverage norms; (iii) budgetary resources and utilization; and (iv) monitoring, evaluation, and assessment documents. A look at the programme-specific policy documents can throw considerable light on whether they are indeed inclusive by design—for example, do they target SC and ST populations in their objectives? Do the programme guidelines include coverage norms for excluded groups? Are adequate resources allocated for covering them? Is there a provision for gathering disaggregated data on services and inputs reaching these groups?

When it comes to actual delivery or implementation, this chapter will assess findings on the following social exclusion strands identified: (i) opportunities for variable performance dependent on whether the flagship programme provides for one-off or on-going delivery; (ii) shortfall in quantity and quality of services and physical infrastructure and other resources available to provide these services; (iii) provider discrimination; and (iv) checks and balances for accountability in terms of supervision and punishment for malfeasance in delivery.

In terms of assessing the beneficiary perspective, issues of exclusion can be broken up in the following manner: (i) access, especially to components of the flagships programmes that are meant for certain 'given' groups, such as Janani Suraksha Yojana (JSY) for women under the NRHM; (ii) (un)equal treatment and opportunity; and (iii) knowledge, participation, agency, voice and empowerment in specific PRIs, for example, Rogi Kalyan Samitis (RKSs), and Village Health and Sanitation Committees (VHSCs).

The rest of this chapter uses existing secondary material on flagship programmes to review exclusion through these three aspects, that is, policy, implementation, and beneficiary perspective. The secondary material encompasses government documents, external evaluations of the chosen flagships (by practitioners, academics, and Comptroller

Auditor General [CAG] accountability authorities), civil society and activist-group documentation, and United Nations (UN) and international body studies. The aim is not to undertake an impact evaluation of outcomes and how they differ for different groups. Rather it is to assess how flagship programmes of the RCH (NRHM) are faring on the goals they have defined for themselves, namely, reaching out to excluded groups through inputs and service delivery.

EXCLUSION IN POLICY

Policy: Reproductive and Child Health, National Rural Health Mission[2]

Reproductive and Child Health (RCH II) is a comprehensive sector-wide programme that comes under the umbrella of the GoI's flagship programme, the National Rural Health Mission (NRHM). Launched in 2005, similar to the RCH I that was launched in 1998, the RCH II had the primary objective of bringing about improvements in the three critical health indicators, that is, total fertility rate (TFR), infant mortality rate (IMR), and maternal mortality rate (MMR) by reducing social and geographical disparities in access to and utilization of quality reproductive and child health services.

Marked points of departure from RCH I are: a greater and more explicit pro-poor focus; a concern with outcomes, as opposed to inputs; using an evidence-base to prioritize interventions and shift resources to where health outcomes are the worst and need is the greatest; encouraging innovative approaches, including public–private partnerships (PPPs), to improve reproductive and child health among SCs and STs; and monitoring of the programme by multiple internal and external organizations to track equitable access by and outreach to excluded groups.

[2] RCH and NRHM fall under the Ministry of Health and Family Welfare (MoHFW), GoI. This section is based on MoHFW 2005, as well as RCH II and NRHM programme documentation obtained from the official website of the MoHFW, http://mohfw.nic.in/NRHM/RCH/index.htm, last accessed on 21 June 2010.

The United Progressive Alliance (UPA) government launched NRHM in 2005, undertaking an 'architectural correction'—decentralization and communitization, in institutional terms—of the public health system to provide access to affordable and accountable primary health care services to poor households in remote parts of rural India.

Some new strategies under NRHM include the creation and upgrade of health centres; using untied flexi-pool grant and maintenance funding; JSY, which provides cash incentives to BPL women for institutional delivery; introduction of Accredited Social Health Activists (ASHAs)—a female interface between the health system and the community; Village Health and Nutrition Days (VHNDs) to educate and mobilize the community; Hospital Development Societies (HDSs) or RKSs, and Village Health and Sanitation Committees VHSCs, all of which encourage the involvement of the community at decentralized levels; and District Health Plans (DHPs), which converge health, nutrition, water, sanitation and hygiene activities.

DOES RCH (NRHM) POLICY TAKE ACCOUNT OF SOCIAL EXCLUSION?

Taking the issues of design and coverage norms together, we find that while the NRHM policy framework is targeted at the BPL rural households in general, with universal access for women and children as a particular goal, there is no explicit mention of groups, such as SCs and STs. On the contrary, RCH II formulates a comprehensive and well-articulated plan to tackle social inclusion (MoHFW 2004).

In a document titled, 'Project Implementation Plan for Vulnerable Groups under RCH II' (MoHFW 2004), 'vulnerable communities' are identified as those groups that are 'underserved due to problems of geographical access (even in better-off states), and those who suffer social and economic disadvantages, such as SCs/STs and the urban poor' (MoHFW 2004, p. 3). Interestingly, the RCH II is the only policy document that not only acknowledges differential outcomes for certain groups, but also identifies various causal pathways that result in exclusion. Accordingly, it states, 'marginalisation results in poorer indicators for these groups, including maternal and child health indicators. This can be as much a result of service provider behaviour, as of health seeking behaviour and capabilities' (MoHFW 2004, p. 3). Other identified causal factors include: poor connectivity to health centres because of distance, topography, and a lack of public transport; social and cultural barriers, especially for women; lack of flexibility and reduced responsiveness to local diversity and needs; scarcity of funds for non-salary expenditure, including innovative activities; lack of an appropriate human resource (HR) policy to encourage and motivate service providers to work in understaffed remote and tribal areas; and weak monitoring and supervision systems (MoHFW 2004, p. 4).

It is argued that RCH II 'seeks to address the above issues systematically' (MoHFW 2004, p. 4) and that the Vulnerable Communities Health Plan

> adds value by acting as a 'conscience' within the Department of Family Welfare to ensure that RCH II is progressively more focused on reaching those least served, and by earmarking a separate pool of resources that will enable innovative solutions to be implemented—in monitoring systems; behavioural change communication; service delivery; PPPs; demand-side financing, such as insurance and voucher programmes; training and supervision of professional, auxiliary and administrative staff; research on tribal systems of medicine, planning capacities, disseminating good practice etc.

In terms of actual strategy, the document puts the onus on states to identify the vulnerable groups and include in their Project Implementation Plans (PIPs) a strategy to prioritize them, that is, what will be done to improve their health status and how it will be done. Moreover, state PIPs are mandated to reflect this strategy in an appropriate monitoring and evaluation (M&E) mechanism; capacity development; behaviour change communication; flexible state and district plans; converging health activities with those of ICDS (Integrated Child Development Services), as well as water and sanitation; and weighting of resource allocations towards vulnerable groups. Lastly, RCH II has a performance fund that gives additional funds to states and districts that provide evidence of 'significant improved performance', where the majority of indicators for success are based on quality and convergence of services for the vulnerable (MoHFW 2004, p. 5).

For STs, in particular, state and district plans are to include a special health plan in accordance with the PIP for Tribal Health (Annexure I of MoHFW 2004). The Tribal Health Annexure reads like any other PIP, except for the following:

1. Under strategies—to promote and encourage a tribal system of medicine.
2. Under human resources—to give additional incentives to health service providers who are working in tribal areas and to provide Auxiliary Nurse Midwife (ANM) training to tribal girls by relaxing educational standards.
3. Under coverage—to implement the programme in a phased manner, eventually covering all 600 Tribal Blocks, with initial priority to blocks having Primitive Tribal Groups (PTGs).

Turning to NRHM, budget allocations under the flagship privilege heavily populated poorer 'focus' states by allocating centre plan funds to individual states according to a weighting system dependent on the population and category of state (whether a focus or a north-eastern state). Under RCH II, a sum of Rs 115 crore has been earmarked for the Tribal Health Program (over and above the budget for taking up activities covered under other programmes of RCH II in tribal areas). Additional funds are also available out of the 10 per cent of the budget earmarked especially for north-eastern states for taking up said activities in areas covered by this programme. On the basis of an average cost of Rs 40 lakh per block per year, and coverage of all 600 tribal blocks over a period of five years, the total proposed allocation is estimated at Rs 688 crore (MoHFW 2004, p. 18).

As for actual allocation, release and expenditure, an evaluation report suggests that despite the privileges accorded to poorer focus states while making budgetary provisions, allocations in fact have not been in line with the proposed weighting system (CAG 2010). Instead, a vicious cycle appears to be in place where a lack of capacity inhibits acceptable levels of expenditure in focus states, which in turn fail to attract release of funds as they are entitled to under the weighting system. On the other hand, non-focus states, such as Andhra Pradesh, Gujarat, Kerala, and Tamil Nadu, obtained larger grant releases than warranted on the basis of better prior utilization records. Furthermore, in 2007–8 only four states (Andhra Pradesh, Bihar, Gujarat, and West Bengal) made their financial contribution of 15 per cent as per the

MoU between the centre and states (CAG 2010). Low expenditure levels, in general, and in focus states, in particular, is a finding which is borne out by numerous other assessments of NRHM—both internal (MoHFW 2009a) and external (Gill 2009). But, for the purpose here, neither the mid-term review of the RCH II (MoHFW 2009a) nor the joint review mission of NRHM/RCH II (MoHFW 2009b) makes any mention of actual budgetary allocation, release, or utilization for the vulnerable communities, in general, or the Tribal Health Plan, in particular.

Finally, on monitoring and evaluation, it remains the case that such tracking, if it is occurring routinely, remains unavailable in the public domain. For example, neither the MoHFW website nor the NRHM/RCH II pages lead to any documents. Although there are links to state PIPs and to the M&E Framework for RCH II—monthly, quarterly, and annual reporting formats—they lead to blank pages. Consequently, despite many promises of enumerating excluded communities in State and District Health Plans and of undertaking subsequent regular sensitive M&E in the programme documentation of RCH II, including the call for such exercises to gather disaggregated data on the utilization of services and outcomes by SCs, STs, and other excluded communities (MoHFW 2004, pp. 6, 7), it thus far remains an unfulfilled claim.

EXCLUSION IN IMPLEMENTATION AND DELIVERY

Much has been written on implementation and delivery performance—or the lacunae and inadequacy thereof—of the flagship programmes of the government. These will not be discussed, since to do so would actually overwhelm and detract from the focus of this section, which is to unearth and shed light on the 'meso unruly practices' affecting implementation of flagship programmes and resulting in unintended outcomes for excluded groups. No doubt, general implementation and governance failures—especially as vast and intractable as they appear to be in the context of many flagship programmes—do, in turn, negatively impact outcomes for groups such as SCs and STs, and indeed it would be hard to separate out the causation, but they will not be explored in any detail here.

RCH (NRHM) Implementation and Delivery Performance through a Social Exclusion Lens

As a key social sector, implementation and delivery performance under the flagship programmes for health—NRHM, and by extension, RCH II—have been the subject of a number of external academic assessments. However, few have adopted an explicit social exclusion lens in their analysis. For instance, while there is considerable evidence on the performance of ASHAs across the country, there is little or no research on their social identity background, and whether that has facilitated or detracted from serving sections otherwise excluded, such as SCs and STs.

The scarcity of human resources—both medical and paramedical, and in the context of RCH services, female doctors and adequately trained obstetricians and gynaecologists, in particular—in rural primary public health care is found to be a complicated and key driver of less than ideal implementation of NRHM (Gill 2009). We know that health care in general involves the most repeat delivery and intensive interaction between provider and beneficiary compared with other programmes. Thus, it is unique in being especially prone to asymmetry in information and hence to principal agent problems, such as moral hazard.

A recent innovative project in Chhattisgarh looks at the human resources issue in detail. It flips the usual absent and absconding question to ask instead why some qualified health workers continue to remain and work in otherwise underserved rural and remote areas of Chhattisgarh, with its significant tribal population of poor economic status (IIPHD, PHFI, NHSRC, and SHRC Chhattisgarh, 2010). The answer for a subset of the total respondents (N=37), of whom (n=5/37) share ethnic (tribal) affiliations, and of whom (n=14/37) were brought up in the same district or region of their present habitation and duty, was articulated as being these very factors, that is, shared identity and belonging, which fuels greater duty and obligation, and which helps to inhibit moral hazard in frontline provider behaviour.

Borooah (2010) explores the social gradient to certain health outcomes in India, of which the two that have a direct health care focus is mentioned here, that is, after controlling for several non-group factors that affect health outcomes, what is the likelihood that treatment for the ailing elderly and pre and postnatal care for women are significantly influenced by their social group identity? Using the Morbidity and Health Care Survey for January–June 2004, conducted across the country by the NSSO, Borooah found that living in a forward state (compared with living in a backward state), affluence, household-living conditions, and education significantly improved the probability of receiving treatment and care. Even controlling for all these factors, however, the social group to which people belonged had a significant impact, with Adivasis, ST Christians, Dalits, Muslim OBCs, and non-Muslim OBCs faring worse than their Hindu counterparts in the likelihood of their elderly taking treatment, and ST Christian, OBC Muslim, and non-OBC Muslim women faring worse than their Hindu counterparts in receiving prenatal care. Study limitations notwithstanding, he shows group identity is the main cause of health inequity (that is, the part of inequality generated by factors beyond a person's control).

Excluded communities probably suffer to a greater degree from both quantity and quality shortage under NRHM and RCH II than the rural poor in general (and Borooah's study does not directly speak of public service delivery under these programmes, though tangentially it does, alluding even to better outcomes in forward states). The poor as a whole suffer enough of a degree of lack on both accounts to make a separation of general implementation and governance failure from particular social exclusion rather difficult, though it is important to be able to do so. Baraik and Kulkarni's (2006) study uses secondary NFHS data to record poorer access to public maternal and child health care services of SCs and STs as compared with 'Others', with STs faring the worst. However, it pre-dates the rolling out of NRHM and overlaps with the first year of RCH II. The precise nature and scale of the lack of excluded communities vis-à-vis service delivery under the flagship programmes, therefore, is still a subject for further enquiry.

As for provider discrimination, Acharya (2010) records the prevalence of discriminatory behaviour by dominant castes and resultant beneficiary experiences of unequal and unsatisfactory delivery of health care to SC children in 12 villages of Gujarat and Rajasthan.

Such a study, which attempts to measure discrimination and construct an index for an essentially behavioural and subjective phenomenon, remains to be replicated on a much wider scale and also to be applied to communities other than SCs.

Finally, as regards accountability, community monitoring as a means of engendering accountability is negligible or less than effective at the moment (CAG 2009–10). It is argued that 'monitoring mechanisms in the NRHM should include systems and processes...so as to involve community-based representatives, including women and those from marginalised groups. This is extremely critical because these systems and processes will have to move beyond existing power dynamics in the community to ensure that...[all] their health needs are met' (OCPMTAEFYP 2010a, p. 13).

The MoHFW named the following priority actions for the annual plans of 2010–11:

1. Clear action plan for backward districts as part of the PIP—the state must identify the backward areas for greater attention (difficult, left-wing affected, minority, tribal, SC/ST, gender, etc.). Special incentives to medicos and para-medicos, for performing duties in difficult areas, which was part of 100 days agenda of the Ministry, may be made part of the state PIPs for the year 2010–11 (MoHFW 2010, p. 29).
2. Constitution of district planning teams and ranking of backward districts for planning—235 high-focus districts identified on the basis of ranking of 13 indicators from DHLS III,[3] districts with 35 per cent or more SC/ST population, and 33 left-wing extremists-affected districts. District planning teams have been constituted for visiting the high-focus districts to observe and ensure adequate attention to these districts in the planning process. The entire process has been coordinated by NHSRC (National Health Systems Resource Centre). (MoHFW 2010, p. 30)

Since this is a plan yet to be carried out, its success may be judged only in future.

[3] District Level Household and Facility Survey, DLHS III 2007–8.

EXCLUSION FROM THE PERSPECTIVE OF BENEFICIARIES

The phenomenon of social exclusion has a large experiential dimension, where the positionality and identity of the individuals in the 'given' groups is key to their reflexive perception of differential and unequal treatment meted out to them. Where certain individuals fall in multiple 'given groups' experiencing discrimination, for example, being SC and a woman, one would expect that this cumulative identity would influence the degree of disadvantage they face and make it more extreme. This certainly appeared to be the case on listening first-hand to the testimonies of Muslim women's groups, such as Awaaz-e-Niswan. The women were living in deprived and congested slum neighbourhoods in Mumbai, such as Cheetah Camp and Dharavi, and they recounted their experiences of service delivery in education and health.[4]

Muslim women recalled how they routinely faced highly derogatory stereotypes with respect to perceptions about their community when they went to public health facilities. Some common examples were when doctors and frontline health providers told pregnant women that they opted to have 'too many children and ultra-large families' or that certain commonplace stomach and other ailments were due to their 'unclean habits and meat-eating ways'. Similarly, in the sphere of education, they would be confronted with questions from government school teachers about whether they 'did not prefer to send their children to *madrassas*'. In cases of domestic violence, they were so afraid of their men being booked and taken away under the draconian Maharashtra Control of Organised Crime Act (MCOCA), 1999, that they would hesitate to report such cases to the police (demonstrably privileging their minority identity over their gender rights concerns, so wary were they of a disproportionately harsh response to the menfolk of their community by the state law and order machinery).[5]

[4] Workshop on 'The Sachar Report: A Women's Perspective', organized by UNICEF Mumbai and the Minorities Development Department, Government of Maharashtra, October 2009.

[5] Workshop on 'The Sachar Report: A Women's Perspective', organized by UNICEF Mumbai and the Minorities Development Department, Government of Maharashtra, October 2009.

From such accounts, it would appear that the beneficiary perspective is especially important in trying to assess how social exclusion affects service delivery under the flagship programmes, and in accordance with the structure of this chapter, would be the final aspect in seeking to do so. Participant perspectives on their experiences of exclusion could serve to triangulate the evidence-based data gathered from previous exercises, too. Two such excellent studies look at: the experience of Dalit children in schools (Nambissan 2010) and in the government's flagship programmes of mid-day meal schemes; and at the public distribution system (Thorat and Lee 2010).

Turning to our flagship programmes of interest, anecdotal evidence of lesser treatment meted out by public health providers to groups such as women, SCs, and STs does exist (Gill 2009; PHFI, NHSRC, and SHRC Chhattisgarh 2010). A detailed analysis of the beneficiary perspective on the discrimination faced, however, is at present restricted to a study looking at the experience of SC children in a few villages of Gujarat and Rajasthan (Acharya 2010). It is particularly important to unearth social exclusion in the delivery of health services, because the latter is not a routine commodity, but one that ethics dictate is a universal right from a social justice perspective. Moreover, its delivery often involves actual physical contact, which in the face of caste discrimination might mean that SC beneficiaries face acute disparity in service delivery from dominant-caste providers in this sphere.

It is easy to see why scholars have shied away from seeking to capture in detail the elements of social exclusion, as experienced by members of 'given groups', in the delivery of public services. Other than anthropologists or sociologists, social scientists have in general been wary of systematically studying an ideologically charged phenomenon such as discrimination. There is enough evidence, however, in the specific Indian contexts of caste and minority identity, of how prevalent identity-based discrimination is and how deeply damaging experiences of exclusion can be even in the public policy sphere. There is little excuse, therefore, to refrain from undertaking such studies, though they should be done using sound qualitative methods as very meaningful supplementary data to rigorous quantitative studies.

★ ★ ★

There is widespread agreement amongst academics, practitioners, and policymakers in India today that available data categorically show that development outcomes across sectors are consistently differential and disproportionately worse for certain groups, that is, SCs, STs, women, and minority communities when compared with the mainstream. This may be ascribed in part to the phenomenon of social exclusion, which may operate in any or many spheres (World Bank 2011). Systematic and sustained inter-group inequalities based on identity are problematic not just because they have interrelation effects and intergenerational consequences (Thorat and Newman 2010), but because if it is established that it is indeed discrimination (rather than neutral factors, such as a skill gap) causing disparities between groups, then there are very strong policy implications, such as reservation for the socially excluded (Deshpande 2011).

Given the government's recent emphasis on inclusive growth and on service delivery through flagship programmes as a key channel to bring about more broad-based development, it is surprising that in fact there is little substantive research and there are few in-depth studies on the phenomenon of social exclusion in the flagship programmes. Civil society and activist-group literature, to the extent that it is available in this broad area, is focused more on the general shortcomings of centrally sponsored government programmes—their faulty design, inadequate funding, limited scope, targeted approach as opposed to universalization, lackadaisical implementation, failures in capacity, governance, and accountability—than on social exclusion, perhaps because they see a focus on the latter as detracting from their larger and more pressing cause.

But what does available secondary literature—howsoever limited in its remit on the exclusionary aspects of flagship programmes—tell us? In terms of the 'macro institutional bias' against 'given' groups, we can conclude that there appear to be two routes prevalent in flagship programme policy. The first is that of explicitly recognizing groups, such as the SCs and STs, and naming them as priority beneficiaries for the programmes (RCH II). The second is of targeting rural BPL households, and, since certain marginalized groups, such as SCs or STs, are over-represented amongst this target group, assuming that social exclusion concerns are thus tangentially addressed (NRHM). The macro bias also emerges at the level of utilization. Very few budget analyses are able to disentangle the reasons for underutilization of budgetary allocations for centrally sponsored flagship programmes, especially in poorer focus states. That is, they are unable to separate the capacity constraints and governance failures leading to such an outcome from specific social exclusion factors. There is no disaggregated tracking of budgetary allocation, release, and expenditure for groups such as SCs and STs. Further, there is a tendency to judge performance based on counting of physical inputs (number of beds, mobile units, doctors), even though theory tells us these might only have a tangential bearing on outcomes. Here too, there is no disaggregated data on service delivery to specific social groups (with the exception perhaps of some DLHS III data on health) and how this relates to their outcomes.

In terms of the 'meso unruly practices', one can conclude that general governance and other failures in implementation and delivery, both in quantity and quality, are significant across flagship programmes. It is therefore imperative, but very difficult, to distinguish the effects of these from specific social exclusion factors that negatively influence implementation and service delivery. That is to say, lack of proper implementation and delivery of flagship programmes is a generalized malaise in poorer focus states and is not restricted to the experience of SCs, STs, and women. So how do we segregate and assess the contribution of general factors versus causation due to social exclusion factors? Secondly, it is hard to unearth and pick out exclusionary behaviour from ordinary survey data, a simple reading of which might even lead to misleading and perverse conclusions. Conversely, robust studies and indicators designed to capture subjective phenomenon, such as discriminatory behaviour, are difficult to find.

Clearly, evidence on exclusion per se is lacking. In undertaking future research on social exclusion in the flagship programmes, two challenges must be overcome.

First, groups suffering from social exclusion are many in the Indian context—SCs, STs, women, minority groups, and less often considered but equally valid groups, such as differently-abled people, the aged population, and migrant workers. Government policy in general and flagship programmes in particular focus on some of these groups, for example, SCs and STs, far more than others. When gender is taken into account, it complicates the picture, because in many instances, there might be cumulative identity problems, that is, being a poor Dalit woman might intensify one's negative experience of service delivery in the public health system. Good research must be able to separate the effects of each. Also, the historical trajectory of social exclusion faced by SCs is very different in nature and causation to that faced by STs, and again variable for subgroups within these broad categories. Research on exclusion must therefore be sensitive to and reflect the nuanced contexts of disaggregated groups.

Secondly, in undertaking future research on social exclusion in flagship programmes, there is a need for interdisciplinary collaboration. Recently, the publication of two books marked the beginning of the field-building task of developing an interface between economics and the broader social sciences in order to better understand and capture the phenomenon of discrimination, as well as foreground research on it and get greater attention from policymakers (Deshpande 2011; Thorat and Newman 2010). It is a great start, but much remains to be done, for there is little in either volume on the government's flagship schemes and discrimination therein—whether it exists, its nature and extent, and the institutional processes which explain, at least in part, how and why development outcomes for certain groups continue to be consistently dire.

APPENDIX A14

Table A14.1 Assessing Social Exclusion in a Generic Flagship Scheme

RCH (NRHM)	Focus on, in recognition of	Strands	Constraints, caution, and challenges
Flagship programme (FP) policy	• Women, SCs, STs • 'Macro institutional bias' against 'given' groups implicitly recognized by government in naming above priority categories in FP	• Design and strategies • Guidelines for participation, coverage norms • Budgetary resources and utilization • Monitoring and evaluation/assessment	• Constraint: Availability of authenticated official secondary data on budgetary allocation and utilization, M&E for social exclusion strands in particular
Implementation/delivery system	• Women, SCs, STs • 'Meso unruly practices' in implementation of FP so that outcome other than intended	• Repeat (RCH [NRHM]) delivery • Quantity vs quality shortfall • Provider discrimination, types of exclusion (active/passive, etc.) practiced • Checks and balances for accountability, in terms of supervision and punishment for malfeasance in delivery	• Caution: How to separate general implementation and governance failures from specific exclusion ones, that is, lack of proper delivery not restricted to SCs, STs, women, etc., rather is a generalized malaise in poorer focus states • Challenge: To capture provider discrimination and accountability, which are intangible, in quantitative, objective indicators design for field instruments, both qualitative-quantitative, that is, including interviews and questionnaires

Beneficiary perspective	• Women, SCs, STs • Participant perspective on experiences of exclusion, triangulate previous evidence-based data	• Access (especially on strands of FP weighted towards certain 'given groups', for example, JSY for women) • (Un)equal treatment and opportunity • Knowledge, participation, agency, voice and empowerment in specific PRIs	• Caution: Not much out there • Challenge: To capture perceptions and subjective phenomena, such as agency and voice, in quantitative, objective indicators design for field instruments, both qualitative-quantitative, including exit interviews/questionnaires

REFERENCES

Acharya, S.S. 2010. 'Caste and Patterns of Discrimination in Rural Public Health Care Services', in S. Thorat and K.S. Newman (eds), *Blocked by Caste: Economic Discrimination in Modern India*, pp. 208–29. New Delhi: Oxford University Press.

Ahluwalia, M. 2011. 'Prospects and Policy Challenges in the Twelfth Plan', *Economic and Political Weekly*, 46(21): 88–105.

Baraik, V.K. and P.M. Kulkarni. 2006. 'Health Status and Access to Health Care Services—Disparities among Social Groups in India', Working Paper Series, 1(4), pp. 1 37. New Delhi: Indian Institute of Dalit Studies.

Borooah, V.K 2010. 'Inequality in Health Outcomes in India: The Role of Caste and Religion', in S. Thorat and K.S. Newman (eds), *Blocked by Caste: Economic Discrimination in Modern India*, pp. 179–207. New Delhi: Oxford University Press.

Comptroller and Auditor General of India (CAG). 2009–10. Performance Audit of the National Rural Health Mission (Ministry of Health and Family Welfare), 'Report of the Comptroller and Auditor General of India Union Government (Civil) No. 8 of 2009–2010', pp. 1–115.

Deshpande, A. 2011. *The Grammer of Caste: Economic Discrimination in Contemporary India*. New Delhi: Oxford University Press.

Drèze, J., P. Lanjouw, and N. Sharma. 1998. 'Economic Development in Palanpur, 1957–1993' in P. Lanjouw and N. Stern (eds), *Economic Development in Palanpur over Five Decades*, pp. 114–234. Oxford: Clarendon Press.

Gill, K.A. 2009. 'Primary Evaluation of Service Delivery under the National Rural Health Mission: Findings from a Study in Andhra Pradesh, Uttar Pradesh, Bihar and Rajasthan', Planning Commission of India Working Paper 1/2009—PEO, pp. 1–92. http://planningcommission.nic.in/reports/wrkpapers/wrkp_1_09.pdf, last accessed on 21 June 2010.

de Haan, A. 1998. '"Social Exclusion": An Alternative Concept for the Study of Deprivation?' *IDS Bulletin*, 29(1): 10–19.

———. 1999. 'Social Exclusion: Towards an Holistic Understanding of Deprivation', Background Paper prepared for the World Development Report 2001 Forum on 'Inclusion, Justice and Poverty Reduction', pp. 1–19.

Indian Institute of Public Health, Delhi (IIPHD); Public Health Foundation of India (PHFI); National Health Systems Resource Centre (NHSRC) and State Health Resource Centre (SHRC), Chhattisgarh. 2010. 'Report: Why Some Doctors Serve in Rural Areas? A Qualitative Assessment from Chhattisgarh State'. New Delhi: PHFI.

Kabeer, N. 2000. 'Social Exclusion, Poverty and Discrimination: Towards an Analytical Framework', *IDS Bulletin*, 31(4): 83–97.

Ministry of Health and Family Welfare (MoHFW). 2004. 'Project Implementation Plan for Vulnerable Groups Under RCH II'. New Delhi: MoHFW, Department of Family Welfare, Government of India.

———. 2009a. 'Reproductive and Child Health Program II Mid Term Review Draft Aide Memoire' (Version, 6 May 2009). New Delhi: MoHFW, Government of India.

———. 2009b. 'National Rural Health Mission Reproductive & Child Health Program Phase II 6th Joint Review Mission Aide Memoire', 25 May to 7 July 2009. New Delhi: MoHFW, Government of India.

———. 2010. 'National Rural Health Mission: Meeting People's Health Needs in Partnership with States—The Journey So Far 2005–2010'. New Delhi: MoHFW, Government of India.

Nambissan. 2010. 'Exclusion and Discrimination in Schools: Experiences of Dalit Children', in S. Thorat and K.S. Newman (eds), *Blocked by Caste: Economic Discrimination in Modern India*, pp. 253–86. New Delhi: Oxford University Press.

Organising Committee of the People's Mid-Term Appraisal of the Eleventh Five Year Plan (OCPMTAEFYP) (Centre for Budget and Governance Accountability; National Social Watch Coalition; and Wada Na Todo Abhiyan). 2010a. 'How Inclusive Is the Eleventh Five Year Plan? People's Mid-Term Appraisal—A Review of Selected Sectors'. New Delhi: OCPMTAEFYP.

Planning Commission. 2008. *Eleventh Five Year Plan 2007–2012: Volume I Inclusive Growth*. New Delhi: Oxford University Press.

———. 2010. 'Mid-Term Appraisal Eleventh Five Year Plan 2007–2012'. New Delhi: Planning Commission (spiral-bound copy).

Public Health Foundation of India (PHFI); National Health Systems Resource Centre (NHSRC) and State Health Resource Centre (SHRC), Chhattisgarh. 2010. 'Report: Which Doctor for Primary Health Care? An Assessment of Primary Health Care Providers in Chhattisgarh, India'. New Delhi: PHFI.

Thorat, S. and J. Lee. 2010. 'Food Security Schemes and Caste Discrimination', in S. Thorat and K.S. Newman (eds), *Blocked by Caste: Economic Discrimination in Modern India*, pp. 287–307. New Delhi: Oxford University Press.

Thorat, S. and K.S. Newman (eds). 2010. *Blocked by Caste: Economic Discrimination in Modern India*. New Delhi: Oxford University Press.

World Bank. 2011. *Poverty and Social Exclusion in India*. Washington, DC: World Bank.

15 Caste and Social Exclusion

Concept, Indicators, and Measurement

Sukhadeo Thorat and
Nidhi Sadana Sabharwal

We have now begun to recognize the linkages between social exclusion and high levels of deprivation and poverty of social groups that have suffered such exclusion and differential treatment in different spheres. It has also been recognized that unfair exclusion or inclusion results in low access to income-earning assets, employment, social needs like education, health services, food, and housing; unequal access to civil, religious, cultural, and political rights; and unequal participation in governance, which ultimately cause high poverty and low human development among the excluded groups.

Notwithstanding this recognition, there are an extremely limited number of empirical studies that actually capture this linkage between social exclusion and poverty and deprivation. The study of 'exclusion induced human poverty' of excluded groups is something which has been neglected in mainstream Indian economic discourse. The lack of empirical studies on the nature of social exclusion and its consequences on excluded groups has constrained not only the efforts of new researchers to enter this field, but also the efforts of the government and other bodies to develop evidence-based inclusive policies. For a researcher, the main difficulty is lack of a relevant theoretical concept of caste-based, ethnicity-based, or religion-based social exclusion, indicators (or identifiers) of social exclusion, methods for measurement of social exclusion, and methods to capture the consequences of social exclusion on the poverty, livelihood, and human development of excluded groups. The lack of studies has limited government capacity to develop appropriate policies against discrimination in private employment, business, social need sectors such as education, health, housing, and other spheres.

In this chapter our purpose is to address some of these neglected issues. The main focus of the chapter, therefore, is to have a discussion on:

1. The concept of social exclusion—drawing mainly from the present theoretical social science literature;
2. The concept of caste-based and ethnicity-based social exclusion—using relevant literature on the caste system;
3. The indicators or identifiers of social exclusion and discrimination in multiple spheres;
4. The method for measurement of social exclusion and discrimination.

CONCEPT OF SOCIAL EXCLUSION

In social science literature, there is a general agreement on the core features of social exclusion (Buvinic 2005). Social exclusion is defined as a social process that involves denial of equal rights and opportunities, which others enjoy, resulting in the inability of individuals from excluded groups to participate in the basic political, economic, and social functioning of the society that, in turn, results in high human poverty and deprivation among them. The concept of social exclusion is essentially a group concept. Amartya Sen (2000) has brought in more clarity to the general concept of social exclusion; he has drawn distinctions between 'unfair exclusion' and 'unfair inclusion'. Sen's concept of unfair exclusion implies that not all exclusions are unfair. Not all exclusions are social exclusion. Theoretically, it is reasonable to assume that only those exclusions that exclude people of certain social groups from having access and entitlements or rights, where such exclusion violates the recognized and accepted principles, rules, and norms and practices of fairness may be considered as 'unfair exclusion'. Similarly, not all inclusions are unfair: only those inclusions that provide access and entitlement to persons from certain social groups but on different terms and conditions—different from that of the accepted principles, rules, and norms and practices of fair inclusion (as well as different from those used for other persons)—maybe considered as unfair inclusion. Sen's concept of unfair inclusion is similar to the concept of discrimination that is used in social science literature, particularly in the discipline of economics, as a form of market discrimination.

Two other dimensions involving the notion of exclusion need to be recognized—it involves 'societal institutions' of exclusion (which operate through inter-social relations), and it involves their 'outcome' in terms of deprivation. In order to understand the dimensions of exclusion, it is necessary to understand the societal interrelations and institutions that are instrumental in bringing exclusion of certain groups into multiple spheres—civic, cultural, political, and economic. Thus, insights into the societal processes (rules and customs governing social relations) are as important as the outcome in terms of deprivation for groups that face exclusion.

This concept of social exclusion clearly makes a distinction between group exclusion and exclusion of an individual. In 'group exclusion', all persons belonging to a particular social/cultural group are excluded, based on their group identity and not their individual attributes. Exclusion of an 'individual' is fundamentally different from exclusion of a 'social group'. Individuals (both from excluded and from non-excluded groups) often get excluded from access to economic and social opportunities for various reasons specific to them (and not because of their group, social, or cultural identity). Individuals, for instance, may be excluded from employment owing to lack of requisite education and skills; individuals may face exclusion in access to education because of lack of requisite minimum qualification or merit or high education costs; individuals may get excluded from access to input and consumer markets because of lack of income and purchasing power. It is important to note that, conceptually speaking, exclusion of an individual has necessarily no connection with the social and cultural identity of a person. On the other hand, in the exclusion of a social group, variables associated with social and cultural identities, such as caste, ethnicity, religion, gender, colour, and race, become important and result in exclusion of all persons belonging to specific social groups. Thus, the group characteristics of exclusion are based on social and cultural identities and not on individual attributes.

CASTE-BASED SOCIAL EXCLUSION

In India, exclusion revolves round the social interrelations and institutions that exclude, discriminate, isolate, and deprive some groups on the basis of their group identity like their caste, ethnic, and religious identity. Historically, the caste system has regulated the social, economic, and political life of not only Hindu society, but also non-Hindu societies through a spill-over effect of the caste system.

Theoretical formulations by social scientists have recognized that in its essential form, caste as a system of social and economic governance or organization is determined by certain customary rules and norms that are unique and distinct (Akerlof 1976; Ambedkar 1936, 1987; Lal 1988; Scoville 1991, 1996). The organizational scheme of the caste system is based on the division of people into social groups (or castes) in which the civil, cultural, and economic rights of each individual caste are predetermined or ascribed by birth and made hereditary. The assignment of civil, cultural, and economic rights among castes is, however, unequal and hierarchical. The most important feature of the caste system, however, is that it provides for a regulatory mechanism to enforce social and economic organization through the instruments of social ostracism (or social and economic penalties). The caste system is reinforced further with justification and support from philosophical elements in the Hindu religion (Ambedkar 1936, 1987; Lal 1988).

The caste system's fundamental characteristics of fixed civil, cultural, and economic rights for each caste with restrictions on change implies 'forced exclusion' of some castes from the equal rights that other castes enjoy. Exclusion and discrimination in civil, cultural, and particularly in economic spheres (such as occupation and labour employment) are therefore internal to the system and a necessary outcome of its governing principles. In the market economy framework, restrictions would operate through denial of access to various markets such as land, labour, credit, and services necessary for any economic activity. Labour, being an integral part of the production process of any economic activity, would obviously become a part of market discrimination. Exclusion of some castes would also cover other spheres such as education, health, housing, and similar social needs. This implies that the caste system involves negation of not only equality and freedom, but also basic human rights, particularly of the low caste/'untouchables' (Scheduled Castes [SCs] or Dalits) and thereby impeding personal development.

Untouchability-based Social Exclusion

In the traditional scheme of the caste system, the untouchables who are at the bottom of the caste hierarchy suffered the most from unequal assignment and entitlement of rights. They were denied right to property along with occupation (except so-called polluting occupations and manual labour), education, civil, and cultural rights. It is necessary to recognize other channels through which 'untouchables' faced denial of rights and entitlements. The graded inequality in rights implies that every caste, except the caste located at the top of caste hierarchy which is the Brahmin caste, suffered from exclusion in terms of denial of some rights, although the type of rights denied varies depending on the social location of the caste in the caste hierarchy (Ambedkar 1987). Thus, like other lower castes, the 'untouchables' also suffered from denial of certain rights. However, the 'untouchables' also suffered from the notion of 'untouchability', which is unique to them (from which other castes do not suffer). On account of this unique stigma of untouchability, the 'untouchables' are considered to be impure and polluting, and they have suffered from physical and social segregation and isolation. Physical and social isolation is unique to the caste system. The isolation and segregation lead to suppression of freedom and restriction on physical and social mobility, resulting in denial of equal access in various spheres of society, culture, and economy. In this sense, the untouchable suffered from double denial, namely, denial of equal rights, which are clearly specified in the customary laws of the caste system, and denial of rights owing to their untouchable status involving 'forced non-association' and lack of participation in various spheres of society, culture, and economy. The lack of participation in the communal life of society resulting from the notion of untouchability is widespread in Indian society in so far as it involves restrictions on physical and social mobility, which take various forms and dimensions.

Forms of Caste-based and Untouchability-based Social Exclusion

The practice of caste-based and untouchability-based exclusion and discrimination thus necessarily involves failure of entitlements, to not only economic rights, but also civil, cultural, religious, and political rights. It involves what has been described as 'living mode exclusion' (UNDP 2004). Caste-based and untouchability-based exclusion thus reflect the inability of individuals and groups like former 'untouchables' and similar groups to interact freely and productively with others and to take full part in the economic, social, and political life of a community (Bhalla and Lapeyre 1997). Incomplete citizenship or denial of civil rights (freedom of expression, rule of law, right to justice), political rights (right and means to participate in the exercise of political power), and socio-economic rights (economic security and equality of opportunities) are key drivers of impoverished lives (Zoninsein 2001).

In the light of the above, caste-based and untouchability-based exclusion and discrimination can be categorized in the economic, civil, cultural, religious, and political spheres as follows:

1. Exclusion and the denial of equal opportunity in the economic sphere would necessarily operate through market and non-market transactions and exchange.
   (i) Exclusion may be practised in the labour market through denial of jobs; in the capital market through denial of access to capital; in the agricultural land market through denial of sale and purchase or leasing of land; in the input market through the denial of sale and purchase of factor inputs; and in the consumer market through the denial of sale and purchase of commodities and consumer goods;
   (ii) Discrimination can occur through what Amartya Sen would describe as 'unfavourable inclusion'—for example, through differential treatment in terms and conditions of contract or that reflected in discrimination in the prices charged to and received by groups that are discriminated against. This can be inclusive of the price of factor inputs, and with regard to consumer goods, price of factors of production such as wages

for labour, price of land or rent on land, interest on capital, rent on residential houses, and charges or fees on services such as water and electricity. Such groups can get lower prices for the goods that they sell, and could pay higher prices for the goods that they buy as compared with the market price or the price paid by other groups.

(iii) Exclusion and discrimination can occur in terms of access to social needs supplied by the government or public institutions or by private institutions in education, housing, and health, including common property resources (CPR) like water bodies, grazing land, and other land of common use.

(iv) A group (particularly the 'untouchables') may face exclusion and discrimination from participation in certain categories of jobs (the sweeper being excluded from jobs inside the house), because of the notion of purity and pollution of occupations and engagement in so-called unclean occupations.

2. In the civil, cultural, and religious spheres, the 'untouchables' may face discrimination and exclusion in the use of public services like roads, water bodies, temples, and institutions delivering services such as education and health.

   Because of the physical (or residential) segregation and social exclusion due to the notion of untouchability, 'untouchables' can suffer from a general societal exclusion. Since there is a societal mechanism to regulate and enforce the customary norms and rules of the caste system, the 'untouchables' usually face opposition in the form of social and economic boycott and violence, which acts as a deterrent to their right to development.

3. In the political sphere, the 'untouchables' can face discrimination in access to political rights and participation in the institutions of governance and decision-making processes.

This overview of the development of the concept of 'exclusion' in general and that of caste-based or untouchability-based exclusion in particular highlights various dimensions of the concept in terms of its nature, forms, and consequences. Caste-based and untouchability-based exclusions are essentially 'structural in nature' and are, therefore, comprehensive and multiple in coverage, involving denial of equal opportunities, particularly to excluded groups like the former 'untouchables'.

IDENTIFYING BEHAVIOUR (OR IDENTIFIERS) RELATED TO SOCIAL EXCLUSION

The conceptual analysis of social exclusion given in the previous sections provides an insight into the nature of social exclusion in the institution of caste and in the practice of untouchability. In this section, identifying social behaviour of people with regard to social exclusion is addressed. For this, it is necessary to draw a distinction between unfair exclusion and inclusion (UEI) and other forms of exclusion. The definition of social exclusion encompasses both unfair exclusion and unfair inclusion:

1. Unfair exclusion is the complete denial of access to various rights and entitlements in unfair ways to members of certain social groups.
2. Unfair inclusion is access (or inclusion) to rights and entitlements but with unequal terms and conditions or differential treatment in accessing the rights and entitlements.

Identification and specification of general indicators of UEI that enable quantitative and qualitative estimation are necessary. This would help to also establish what forms of action constitute UEI.

The preceding discussion has shown how caste-based and untouchability-based exclusion and discrimination have permeated the economic, civil, social, religious, and political spheres. Economic exclusion, both market and non-market, is discussed in the following sections.

Economic Exclusion (or Discrimination)—Market and Non-market

Economic discrimination operates mainly through various markets. People belonging to low castes may experience discrimination in market and non-market transactions. In this context, market exclusion would include (i) labour markets; (ii) land markets, both for agricultural and for non-agricultural use; (iii) credit markets; (iv) input markets (needed in any production and business activity); (v) markets in services necessary for businesses; (vi) products and consumer markets in goods and services; and (vii) housing markets.

Non-market transactions may include several public goods offered by government and public institutions. These may include (i) social needs like education, housing, health services, public roads, electricity, drinking water, and fair price shops in consumer goods, and other services; (ii) common property resources in the villages like irrigation, grazing lands, forests, etc., and (iii) various schemes and programmes operated by government or other agencies on behalf of government.

Given the preponderance of social exclusion and discrimination in multiple spheres in which it may be practised, it is rather difficult if not impossible to typify various forms of economic discrimination and specify criteria to identify and measure discrimination effectuated through market and non market exchanges and transactions. However, the following two indicators capture the behaviour described as UEI:

1. *Unfair Exclusion from Access to Markets*: Unfair exclusion may be practised through complete exclusion of members of certain groups from having access to various market and non-market exchanges, such as hiring of labour, sale and purchase of factor inputs, supply of credit, sale and purchase of product and consumer goods, and supply and demand of social services, which are unrelated to normal terms and conditions of exchange.
2. *Unfair Inclusion*: Unfair inclusion (or access to various market and non-market transactions) may be practised through selective access to market and non-market transactions, but with differential treatment reflected in different prices charged for factor inputs, and goods and services to certain groups. Unfair inclusion may also operate through unequal terms and conditions (for SC persons) in transactions carried through various market and non-market exchanges.

In light of the above criteria, *labour market discrimination*, as a concept, can be conceived as:

1. complete denial to certain social groups of opportunities of being hired or employed by higher castes that is unrelated to productivity;
2. selective hiring but with lower wages for SC workers (lower than market wages or the wages given to workers from higher castes) that is unrelated to productivity;

3. employment or hiring (often forced) bound by caste obligations and duties reflected in, firstly, overwork, loss of freedom leading to bondage and attachment and, secondly, in differential treatment at the workplace; and
4. denial of jobs or work in certain categories of jobs and services to those SCs who are in so-called hereditary 'unclean or polluting occupations' (such as sanitation jobs, leather-processing jobs). This is in addition to the general exclusion or discrimination that persons from this caste would face for being low castes.

There are two measurable criteria that could be used to define and measure exclusion with regard to *other market* (other than the labour market) and *non-market* transactions. These are:

1. denial (or complete exclusion) to members belonging to SCs with regard to the sale and purchase of factors of production necessary in any production and business, such as agricultural lands, land for business or production activities, credit and other inputs, and services necessary for production and business; and denial with regard to the sale and purchase of consumer and other goods produced or offered by SC producers or business persons; and
2. inclusion (or access) with differential treatment in market and non-market transactions, which may entail:
   a. differential treatment reflected in different prices charged or received by a particular group where these prices are different from market prices (or prices charged or received by higher caste persons), including prices of factor inputs required in production and businesses such as price of land or rent on land, interest on capital, rent on residential houses, and charges or fees on services that are privately owned, such as irrigation, etc.; and
   b. differences in terms and conditions of contracts in market and non-market transactions, which may be unfavourable to persons from particular social groups.

Thus, theoretically speaking, although the markets are supposed to be neutral in their functioning (in the sense that all those who have purchasing power could enjoy equal access to markets for sale and purchase of factors of production, including services required in occupations and sale and purchase of consumer goods) access may be denied to certain castes on account of their social background.

MARKET-WISE IDENTIFIERS OF SOCIAL EXCLUSION

As mentioned above, it is difficult to typify various forms of economic discrimination. However, within the broad framework of market and non-market exchanges, one can categorize market and non-market discriminations associated with caste and untouchability.

The nature of discrimination involved in market and non-market transactions is discussed below.

Labour Market

Discrimination in the labour market would mean denial of employment to certain groups, employment at lower wages that are unrelated to productivity, denial of employment in certain types of jobs and work, differential treatment in the workplace and in other terms and conditions of work.

Land Markets

With regard to land markets, members of low caste communities and 'untouchables' may experience discrimination in the form of denial in (i) sale and purchase of land for agricultural and non-agricultural usage (for production/business location and residential housing); and (ii) prices paid and received by the SCs in the event of sale and purchase of land.

Discrimination may also persist in leasing of land by members of SC or Dalit communities for agricultural use and for renting of houses for residential purposes. Discrimination in lease markets may be practised in the form of denial of leases for agricultural lands and houses for residential purposes, charging of higher prices or rents on leased land for agriculture use, or on the rents of houses for residential purposes compared with other social groups for similar services.

Credit Markets

Discrimination in credit markets may take the form of denial of credit to SCs, such as charging higher interest rates for SCs in the event of their having taken loans, and also discrimination in other terms and conditions of loans.

Factor Input Markets

Discrimination may prevail in sale and purchase of input factors required in production and services. These include various material inputs and services required in the production processes and businesses. Discrimination may be either denial of sale of such inputs to the SC producer or business persons or not purchasing inputs from SC sellers and producers, and in the event of purchase by the SCs, they would be required to pay a higher price than those paid by others for identical inputs and services. Similarly, in the event of sale, the SCs may be required to sell at prices lower than the market price.

Consumer Goods Markets

Lastly, the SCs may face discrimination during the sale and purchase of consumer goods. As in input markets, discrimination in the consumer goods market may take the form of restrictions in purchase from and sale to SC producers or business persons. Charging higher prices for goods that SCs purchase and low prices for goods they sell is again a form of discrimination.

Non-market Transactions and Discrimination—Goods and Services Supplied Directly by Government or by Government-approved Suppliers

Non-market transactions include goods and services supplied by the government or state-supported public organizations and agents at fixed prices. However, individuals from excluded groups may face discrimination in access to these services. These publicly supplied services include education, health facilities, drinking water, public roads, electricity, public housing, etc. These may also include village-level common property resources like canals, tank water, grazing lands, forests, etc.

Social exclusion through non-market channels takes place when there is complete denial of access to the services offered by government and government-supported public institutions or if there is access, but with differential treatment reflected in price paid or services received and in other terms and conditions.

CASTE AND PRIMARY HEALTH CENTRES

The IIDS (Indian Institute of Dalit Studies) had sponsored a study on discrimination faced by the Dalits in accessing health services from Primary Health Centres. The study developed the concept of discrimination in health service sectors, identified indicators of discrimination, and formulated the method of its measurement (see Acharya 2010).

Discrimination in access to health care may occur at the health care centre because of neglect by the providers—doctors and the supporting staff; and at home during a visit by the health worker. Discrimination is likely to be practised during diagnosis and counselling, dispensing of medicines, or laboratory tests, and even while waiting in the health centre and when paying the user fee. Discrimination during diagnosis may take the form of time spent in asking about the problem, or may be manifest in avoiding touch of the user during diagnosis. Discrimination during dispensing the medicine may be practised in the way the medicine is given to the user—kept on the palm, or on the windowsill/floor, or when someone else is asked to give the medicine to the 'untouchable' customer to avoid physical touch. Duration of waiting, separate space for waiting, waiting till dominant castes have been attended to, and the care and attitude of the paramedics towards the SCs while they wait are reflective of discrimination and exclusion. Discrimination during payment of user fee, if any, will reflect in actual amount being paid, time spent waiting to pay, space for waiting, and a separate queue for payment.

Discrimination at home during the visit by the health worker may occur while entering the house, touching the user, sitting, drinking/eating in the user's house, and giving medicine and information regarding health camps/programmes to them. It may also take the form of selective dissemination of information regarding health camps and programmes, such as exclusion of SCs in accessing certain type of services where touch is involved (such as vaccination). Thus, discrimination can be practised by different providers in various spheres, and it may take different forms.

FOOD SECURITY SCHEMES IN SCHOOL

The IIDS also conducted a study to understand the nature of discrimination faced by children of the SCs in the Mid-Day Meal Scheme

(MDMS) and discrimination faced by SCs at fair price shops. The study by Thorat and Lee (2005) studied how, where, and to what degree caste discrimination and untouchability operate in the government-run MDMS in 531 villages across five states, namely, Rajasthan, Andhra Pradesh, Tamil Nadu, Uttar Pradesh, and Bihar.

In order to assay caste discrimination and exclusion in the MDMS, the survey considered the following three factors: Dalit children's access to meals, Dalits' participatory empowerment/ownership of MDMS, and the treatment of Dalits in MDMSs. In gauging Dalit children's access to MDMS, three measurable indicators were applied to the scheme's actual material presence in the village: the existence of a functioning MDMS, its physical setting, and its location in terms of caste geography. First, is there a functioning and implemented MDMS in the village? Second, is the MDMS held in a physical setting accessible to Dalit children, for instance, in the school building as opposed to a Dalit-exclusive temple? Third, is the physical setting of MDMS situated in the village's dominant caste locality, in the Dalit colony, or in some third area?

Two measurable indicators were used to evaluate Dalits' participatory empowerment/ownership of MDMSs. First, in all the MDMSs, what percentage of the cooks belonged to the Dalit community? Second, in all the MDMSs, what percentage of the organizers belonged to the Dalit community (in a decision-making role: those ultimately responsible for ensuring the smooth functioning of the MDMS—usually teachers, but sometimes sarpanches or public distribution system [PDS] dealers)?

Finally, in order to measure treatment of Dalits in the MDMSs, the following indicators were considered. First, do dominant castes oppose the hiring of Dalit cooks? Second, do Dalit and dominant caste children sit and eat together in MDMS, or is some form of segregation practised?

The Indian government's public distribution system (PDS) is reputed to be the largest system of controlled food distribution in the world. In it, the government stocks of essential food commodities, notably, rice, wheat, sugar, and oil are distributed to needy areas, where people of below poverty line (BPL) status can purchase the goods at subsidized, below-market prices fixed by the government. At the local level, stocks are provided through government-recognized 'fair price shops' or PDS shops run by the local government-recognized PDS dealers.

As with the MDMS, access, participatory empowerment/ownership, and treatment are the factors according to which the IIDS survey evaluated caste discrimination and exclusion in the PDS. Two measurable indicators were employed to gauge Dalits' access to PDS: existence and number of functioning PDS shops in the village, and location in terms of caste geography. Are there PDS shops operating in the village, and are these shops located in dominant-caste localities, Dalit quarters, or elsewhere?

Dalits' participatory empowerment and ownership of the PDS was measured by percentage; out of all PDS shops in respondent villages, what percentage of PDS shops were owned by Dalits?

Finally, treatment of Dalits at PDS shops was measured by quantifying respondents' responses to questions about various reported forms of caste discrimination in the context of PDS distribution, namely, discrimination in price and quantity, caste favouritism by PDS dealers, and the practice of 'untouchability' by PDS dealers.

DISCRIMINATION AND SCHOOLS

The IIDS had sponsored another study to capture discrimination experienced by Dalit children in schools, which was undertaken by Geeta Nambissan (2009). The objective of the study was to identify spheres of exclusion, discrimination in education, and practices and processes in which exclusion manifests in schools and the subsequent impact of these on Dalit children's full access and participation in the school. An attempt was made to explore whether Dalit respondents experienced/perceived unequal or differential treatment vis-à-vis their non-Dalit peers in school. The study was conducted taking a sample size of 234 Dalit households (129 urban and 105 rural households from the village and *Tila* or settlement, respectively) in Rajasthan.

Spheres of Exclusion

The study identified how access by Dalit children is exclusionary and discriminatory in nature in certain spheres. It established identifiers of discriminatory behaviour and the spheres and indicators of discrimination. These were delineated as access to water, participation in the classroom and teacher–student relationship, responsibilities and tasks given in the classroom, participation in school functions and games, responsibilities of performing rituals linked to the Hindu religion in the daily routine of the school, sharing/serving food in school, MDMS, peer relations, and peer and academic support.

CONSEQUENCES OF SOCIAL EXCLUSION AND DISCRIMINATION

Another issue that needs consideration is estimating the consequences of various types of exclusions and differential treatment on access to education, health services, and food security schemes. The consequences of economic discrimination on unemployment, income and earnings, land and business ownership need to be also captured.

The labour and other market discrimination entails denial of equal economic rights and opportunities to SC groups, and it reduces access to income-earning capital assets like agricultural lands and non-land assets, employment, social needs such as education and health, housing, and other needs, which lead to lower income and high poverty among the discriminated groups.

The adverse consequences of labour market discrimination are fairly obvious. The denial and exclusion in employment in general and in certain categories of work result in higher unemployment and underemployment among the discriminated groups. Lower wages reduce income; and compulsory involvement in work because of traditional caste obligations makes discriminated groups liable to exploitation and this often leads to unpaid labour.

The consequences of occupational discrimination through denial of access to land, credit, factor inputs, product and consumer goods, restrictions on sale of products, consumer goods and services, and differential treatment in terms of prices paid in purchase of capital goods, inputs, and services are equally adverse. Further, various types of restrictions on the purchase of income-earning capital assets and non-land assets reduce the ownership of these assets and increase the incidence of asset-less persons among the discriminated groups. Also, restrictions on the purchase of inputs and services affect the scale, viability, and profit of firms and businesses.

The most adversely affected businesses owned by discriminated groups are likely to be the ones dealing in consumer goods, in which the restrictions on purchases by higher castes from lower castes may be more pronounced and pervasive because of the notions of purity and pollution. As a corollary, few persons from discriminated groups are likely to engage in businesses dealing with the sale of consumable items. Therefore such restrictions will affect the magnitude of sale of consumer goods and incomes of businesses owned by SCs/'untouchables'.

Discrimination in terms of selective restrictions in purchase of consumer goods by SC consumers from higher-caste businesses will affect their consumption level. Also, higher prices will lead to lower consumption.

The discrimination in non-market transaction channels takes effect when there is complete denial of access to services offered by government and government-supported public institutions or access with differential terms and conditions.

Discriminatory access to social needs, such as education, health services, food security schemes, housing, and common property resources, will lead to consequences such as lower education levels and lower access to food and public housing. These consequences need to be measured in quantitative terms in order to capture the magnitude of 'exclusion induced deprivation' of SCs. The likely consequences of discrimination in school education and in access to public and private health services and its impact on poverty are given in detail below.

Discrimination in schools in a village setting may take the form of denial of access to education and skill development and/or discriminatory treatment in school. This may reduce the quality of human resource and reduce the employability for quality jobs and force Dalits to fall back on low-earning manual wage labour in farming and non-farming activities. Specifically, denial of access to education leads to high illiteracy, low functional literacy, high dropout rates, limited skill development, and low human capital. The impact of limited skill development and low human capital because of discrimination in education may cause high representation in menial jobs, low wages, low income, and ultimately high poverty.

Lower access to public health services and private health services affects the health status, increases the number of non-working days because of illness, lowers the days of employment, and ultimately affects income levels negatively. Denial of access to public health services or improper services leads to the dependence on private health service providers and expensive medical treatment. This results in borrowing money for treatment, high debt, and it ultimately affects the income levels.

The likely consequences of discrimination on poverty, as seen in terms of provision of safe drinking water, civic amenities, and common property resources, may get reflected in denial of access to safe drinking water and other civic amenities, which, consequently, is likely to result in poor health, increasing the number of non-working days because of illness, lowering the days of employment, and, ultimately, impacting income levels negatively.

* * *

Given the adverse consequences of economic and social discrimination on human poverty, reducing discrimination is necessary to enhance access to economic and educational rights and help reduce poverty and inter-group inequalities.

The excluded groups therefore require dual policy measures: general economic empowerment (pro-poor policies) that is supplemented by policies to safeguard against discrimination in market and non-market transactions to ensure non-discriminatory access. The complementary nature of these two policies will ultimately help the historically discriminated groups not only to improve their capabilities, but also to receive their fair share in economic and social progress of the country.

REFERENCES

Acharya, S. 2010. 'Public Health Care Services and Caste Discrimination: A Case of Dalit Children', in Sukhadeo Thorat and Katherine Newman (eds), *Blocked by Caste: Economic Discrimination and Social Exclusion in Modern India*, pp. 208–29. New Delhi: Oxford University Press.

Akerlof, George. 1976. 'The Economics of Caste, the Rat Race and Other Woeful Tales', *Quarterly Journal of Economics*, 90(4): 599–617.

Ambedkar, B.R. 1987. 'The Hindu Social Order—Its Essential Features', in Vasant Moon (ed.), *Dr. Babasaheb Ambedkar Writing and Speeches*, Volume 3, pp. 95–129. Mumbai: Department of Education, Government of Maharashtra.

Becker, Gary S. 1957. *The Economics of Discrimination*. Chicago: University of Chicago Press.

Birdsall, Nancy and Richard Sabot. 1991. *Unfair Advantage: Labour Market Discrimination in Developing Countries*. Washington, DC: World Bank Sectoral and Regional Studies.

Buvinic, Mayra. 2005. 'Social Inclusion in Latin America', in Mayra Buvinici and Jacqueline Mazza (eds), *Social Exclusion and Economic Development*, pp. 3–32. Mayra Baltimore: The Johns Hopkins University Press.

Nambissan, Geetha. 2009. 'Exclusion and Discrimination in Schools—Experiences of Dalit Children', 1(1), IIDS–UNICEF Working Paper Series, New Delhi.

Romer, David. 1984. 'The Theory of Social Customs: A Modification and Some Extension', *Quarterly Journal of Economics*, 99(4): 717–27.

Scoville, James G.L. 1991. 'Towards a Model of Caste Economy', in James G. Scoville (ed.), *Status Influences in Third World Labour Markets: Caste, Gender and Custom*, pp. 386–93. New York: Walter de Gruyter.

———. 1996. 'Labour Market Underpinnings of a Caste Economy Failing the Caste Theorem', *The American Journal of Economics and Sociology*, 55(4): 385–94.

Sen, Amartya. 2000. 'Social Exclusion: Concept, Application, and Scrutiny', Working Paper, Social Development Paper No. 1, June. Bangkok: Asian Development Bank.

Subrahmanian, Ramya. 2003. 'Exploring Processess of Marginalisation and Inclusion in Education', in 'Education Inclusion and Exclusion: India and South Africa Perspectives', *IDS Bulletin*, 34(1): 1–8.

Thorat, S.K. and Joel Lee. 2005. 'Caste Discrimination and Food Security Programme', *Economic and Political Weekly*, 40(39): 4198–201.

Thorat, S.K. and Katherine Newman. 2010. *Blocked By Caste: Economic Discrimination in Modern India*. New Delhi: Oxford University Press.

Thorat, S.K. and Nidhi Sadana Sabharwal. 2009. 'Caste and Social Ownership of Private Capital', *Economic and Political Weekly*, 41(23): 14.

———. 2009. 'Discrimination and Children's Nutritional Status in India', *IDS Bulletin*, 40(4): 25–9.

Thorat, S.K., Motilal Mahamallik, and Nidhi Sadana Sabharwal. 2010. 'Caste System and Patterns of Discrimination', in Sukhadeo Thorat and Katherine Newman (eds), *Blocked by Caste: Economic Discrimination in Modern India*, pp. 148–76. New Delhi: Oxford University Press.

UNDP. 2004. *Human Development Report 2004: Cultural Liberty in Today's Diverse World*. New Delhi: Oxford University Press.

16 The Political Economy of Development and Adivasi Children and Society

Virginius Xaxa

Tribals or Adivasis are one of the most exploited and deprived sections of the population in Indian society. In all indicators of development, they remain the most excluded, despite the fact that various kinds of policies and programmes have been pursued for their upliftment in post-Independence India. Needless to say, exclusion from the fruits of development has adversely affected the quality of life of the tribal people. Tribal children are no exception. This chapter makes an attempt to identify and understand the multidimensional problems of the tribal children in the wider context of the political economy of development.

The tribal populations in India are also known as Adivasis, meaning the original or indigenous peoples. Even tribal people refer to themselves as such and have been making claims for official recognition of their status in the international fora. The Indian State finds these claims problematic and refuses to extend Adivasi status (that is, recognition of their rights as indigenous people) to tribal people, though their economic, political, social, and cultural situations are similar to those of other people described and identified as indigenous elsewhere in the world. It sees no problem, though, in describing and addressing them as tribes. In more recent years, however, there seems to be some shift in India's position on the question of 'indigenous peoples' in the international fora. This is to be inferred from the fact that India has been a signatory to the UN declaration of the Rights of the Indigenous Peoples in September 2007. India, thus implicitly recognizes the status of tribes as indigenous people, though there may not be an explicit endorsement of this identity. An important point to note is that, since tribes in India are listed in the Schedules of the Indian Constitution for the purposes of receiving administrative and political benefits, they are delineated as the 'Scheduled Tribes' (STs). Though each of the terms—tribes, STs, and Adivasis—has distinct connotations, there is an overlapping of their characteristics. That explains why the three terms have been interchangeably used in popular discussion and social science literature in India.

At the eve of Independence, though much of the tribal community had come under colonial rule over different phases, they lived in relative isolation from the rest of the Indian society. If at all this isolation was broken, it was because of the extension of roads, railways, and, more importantly, because of land, labour, and credit markets, which were predominantly exploitative. As for infrastructure such as education and health, agricultural development and irrigation facilities, tribal communities, however, remained completely neglected.

The condition in which tribes found themselves at Independence was primarily attributed to their social and geographical isolation. In fact, the use of the category 'tribe' has greatly shaped the discourse on tribes in India. From this angle, the critical issue is their isolation, both geographical and social. The onus of locating the problems of the tribals is squarely put on their isolation and economic, social, and cultural features of their societies. While this has been the dominant view, exploitation of tribes by non-tribals especially in the form of alienation of land has not altogether been overlooked. It is within this backdrop that the state's agenda towards tribes in post-Independence India needs to be understood.

The different measures taken for the upliftment of the tribal people are usually divided into three categories. These are (i) protective measures; (ii) mobilization measures; and (iii) developmental measures. The protective measures include constitutional and legislative rights that safeguard the interest of the tribals. Keeping this in mind, almost all the states where there are tribal populations have enacted laws for the protection of tribes against alienation of their land by non-tribes. In the post-Independence period, legislations have been enacted also for the restoration of tribal land. Protection is provided in terms of special administration of tribal areas. In administrative parlance, such areas have been referred to as the Fifth or Sixth Schedule Areas—Articles 244 and 244(a). The Fifth Schedule has a provision giving special regulatory power to the Governor of a state with Schedule Areas, provision for a Report by the Governor to the President regarding administration of Schedule Areas, and, most importantly, provision for constituting tribal advisory councils. The Sixth Schedule has provisions for autonomous district councils (ADCs) and hence provides scope for self-governance. The Sixth Schedule, in general, is for the northeastern region and the Fifth Schedule is for other regions of India where tribes, either in a district or parts of a district, form a majority.

Mobilization refers to the reservation extended to the tribals in the domains of politics, government employment, and educational institutions. In each of these spheres, a certain percentage of seats are earmarked for the STs.

Developmental measures comprise programmes and activities that are initiated for promoting the welfare and development of the tribal people. As a first step to developmental initiatives, special multipurpose development projects as supplements to the community development projects were introduced in the tribal areas. This strategy was continued with some modifications until the Fifth Plan period (1974–9). The Fifth Plan is taken as a landmark for tribal development. It not only made a shift in policy perspective from welfare to development, but also adopted a new approach of Tribal Sub-plans (TSPs) and Integrated Tribal Development Projects (ITDPs). The TSPs had a separate budget head in Plan documents for the purpose of earmarking funds, which were to be in proportion to the ST population. The immediate objective of this strategy was to eliminate forms of exploitation that existed in the tribal areas and accelerate the process of development. The TSP, thus, primarily focused on the socio-economic development of Schedule Areas and on improving the quality of life of the tribal communities. Its main components were the ITDPs; modified area development approach (MADA); and cluster and primitive tribal group projects.

Under the broad strategy of TSPs, a number of schemes have been introduced periodically with the purpose of improving the condition of the tribal people. Broadly, the schemes fall under two categories—economic and social. Social development has been pursued along two lines—education and health, which include the issues of women and children. For promotion of education, in addition to the introduction of schools of various levels, various schemes have been worked out to give a boost to education among tribal children. Some of the key schemes have been residential schools, vocational education, scholarships, book grants, free uniforms, mid-day meals, among others. In the sphere of health, emphasis has been laid on extending and improving health infrastructure such as primary health centres (PHCs), and community health centres (CHCs), as well as prevention and control of communicable and non-communicable diseases. Many of the schemes under health and education exclusively deal with issues concerning women and children. In economic development, the issues taken up include mainly activities such as employment and income generation, credit and market support mechanisms, and skill and vocational training. Within such activities, different schemes have been formulated from time to time.

The development schemes under the TSP have been in operation for about 36 years. Still, the results are very disheartening. In 2004–5, the share of the tribal population living below the poverty line was 46.5 per cent as compared with 27.6 per cent for the country as a whole (Mathur 2008). Thus, although there has been a decline, the level of poverty in the tribal population is still much higher than the national average and the gap between the two continues to be one of the major issues of concern in poverty discourses in India.

The same is true with regard to other indicators of social development such as education and health. In 2001, the literacy rate for the general population had jumped to 68.81 per cent as compared with 47.1 per cent for the tribal population. The gap between the two has been somewhat bridged, but the difference of 21.71 per cent is still very large (GoI 2007). The picture is no different with respect to health of the tribal population. The percentage of institutional deliveries was a mere 17.1 per cent among tribes as compared with 33.6 per cent for the general population. As for antenatal care (ANC) check-ups, the figure was 56.5 per cent for the tribal population, the same being 65.4 per cent for the general population.

IMPLICATION FOR CHILDREN

Such a state of development in tribal society is a combination of various factors that have a bearing on the well-being of tribal/Adivasi children. One of the features that marks tribal children is widespread malnutrition. Poverty, low literacy, unsafe drinking water, environmental conditions, lack of sanitation, unavailability of basic health services, as well as traditional beliefs and customs, all add to malnutrition of tribal children. The outcome is that they become easily exposed to attacks of infection and infectious diseases resulting in high mortality among them. Infant mortality, for example, was 84.2 in comparison with 67.6 per 1,000 live births for the total population in 2002. Child mortality was 46.3 in comparison with 29.3 per 1,000 for the total population. Under-5 mortality rate (U5MR) among tribals was as high as 126.6 per 1,000 live births as compared with 94.9 per 1,000 live births for the total population. The percentage of undernourished children (weight for age) was 64.9 per cent among tribes and 51.8 per cent for the total population. Childhood vaccination (full immunization) was a mere 26.4 per cent among tribes in comparison with 42 per cent for the total population (GoI 2007). Tribal people on the whole also show low health status. Health indices like birth-weight, life-expectancy at birth, infant mortality rate (IMR), and prevalence of various diseases have pointed to lower health status. The tribal population is also affected by chronic energy-deficiency in school-going children, adolescent boys, and girls and women of reproductive age. They also suffer from various types of anaemia—mild, moderate, and severe. As high as 70–80 per cent of the population seem to be affected by it (GoI 2007).

Even in the sphere of education, the status of tribal children is far from satisfactory. Even after so many years, enrolment in schools is still a problem. However, since the last decade or so, enrolment of tribal children has shown a rate of increase that has been higher than the enrolment of other categories such as the Scheduled Caste (SC) and the general population in primary, upper primary, and even in other categories of education such as secondary, senior secondary and higher education (GoI 2007). Enrolment figures are taken to bolster reports of the progress made in expanding school education in India. But enrolment is a very unreliable basis for assessing the degree of access to education (Dubey 2010). What is important for assessing the progress in expanding education is figures showing attendance and dropout rates rather than enrolment. Though the enrolment of tribal children in school is not that low, dropout rates are extremely high. It is the dropouts that constitute the most serious problem as far as tribal children's education is concerned. Dropouts at primary, upper primary, and secondary school levels were as high as 52.3, 69.5, and 81.2 per cent, respectively, as compared with 39, 54.6, and 66 per cent, respectively, for the total population in 2001–2. In 2002–3 dropouts had declined by mere 1 per cent at all three levels (GoI 2007).

The question is how this poor and deplorable status of social development of tribal population in India is to be explained. Can these be placed in perspective so that we have a better understanding and analysis? The chapter aims at providing this perspective.

The tribal situation that prevailed at the dawn of independence was attributed to their geographical and social isolation from the rest of the Indian society. Hence, the whole thrust of policy towards tribes in post-Independence India was centred on their integration—economic, political, social, and cultural—with the larger Indian society. This idea continues till the present day, and much of the problems tribals face are still attributed to this phenomenon. Intricately tied to this is also the idea that if tribes suffer from low income and poor educational and health status as well as various kinds of diseases, these are due to their tradition, culture, and style of life. A way out of this problem is discussed in terms of modernization of traditional societies, that is, in the adoption of new ideas, knowledge, and values. This is the modernization perspective that has been in currency the world over. Though this argument is applicable for the whole of the Indian society, it has been sharply problematized in the context of the tribal society. While there is a relationship between the lack of development and traditional social structure and culture, this aspect needs to be further probed and carefully examined. After all, lack of development may not be so much due to their social structure and culture as to the structure of the wider development process. This chapter attempts to place the Adivasi situation in general and Adivasi children in particular in the larger perspective of the political economy of India's development.

HISTORICIZING CHANGE AND DEVELOPMENT

The British rule drove tribes out of their isolation and incorporated them into the larger political and economic framework. It was not the first time the tribes had such encounters. Many tribes in different parts lived under alien political suzerainty at some point in time or other. The suzerainty ranged from symbolic gestures of loyalty to the payment of tribute/tax to the political authority. The extension of British rule was, however, different. It introduced new laws and regulations—civil and criminal—in tribal areas. It set up an administrative structure that was alien to them. As in many other parts of India, the British imposed upon the tribes the notion of private property and landlordism in place of lineage or community-based ownership of land. This led to large-scale eviction of tribes from their land and installation of non-tribes in their place. In places where tribes still had control over land, massive transfers of land took place from tribes to non-tribes through fraud, deceit, mortgage, etc. Over and above this, the colonial state took upon itself the right over forests, thereby denying tribes the right to collect fuel and other daily necessities of life for which they were so heavily dependent on forests (Bosu Mullick 1990; Singh 2002).

Now, much of the discussion on development of tribes, including issues of children, tends to be ahistorical and in the process tends to ignore placing it in the context of the wider political economy. How the larger economic, political, social, and cultural processes have impacted tribes is an aspect that has received little attention. To understand this impact, it is important to situate their development status prior to their being incorporated into the wider economic and political structure. This is important as the wider social structure has invariably been tied to loss of their life support system, namely, land, forest, water, and other resources. This has had adverse effects on tribes and a bearing on their condition of living and health. Hence, it is important to capture the material and social well-being of the tribals (nature of poverty; health status—fertility, infant mortality, child mortality, morbidity, gender difference, diseases suffered), however limited the information may be, prior to their integration into wider economic and political structures.

Unfortunately, there is a paucity of literature for reference on the material and social well-being of the tribals under colonial rule and administration. The colonial literature on tribes generally deals with the land and revenue settlement, or labour and credit situations, or the customs and traditions of the tribal people. Even anthropological studies have been little concerned with the material and social well-being of tribals. Rather, they focused more on the study of tribal social structure. In the process, they provided a systematic account of tribal social institutions, such as family, and kinship, and institutions in other spheres such as the economic, religious, and political spheres. They also provided accounts of tribal culture—material and non-material. In dealing with material culture, they gave an account of their houses, tools, implements, dresses, ornaments, etc. This gave some idea about the condition of their life and being (Fürer-Haimendorf 1933; Hutton 1921; Roy 2004). Even when anthropological literature provided a description of the conditions of tribes, it has been done more in terms of landlessness, indebtedness, bondage, wages, etc., and not so much in terms of hunger, poverty and access to food, quality of diet and nutritious value of food consumed, and health status such as longevity, rates of mortality, morbidity, and birth. The literature is also conspicuous by an absence of accounts on illness and diseases. Further, all previous studies have been qualitative, making it difficult to gauge the extent and magnitude of such problems in the society (Elwin 1986). As noted earlier, tribal society was marked by low development, with tribals existing at bare subsistence levels. The houses they lived in and clothes they wore were elementary and simple; but, it is important to probe if the deprivations they suffered then were of the same order and type as the deprivations they have begun to suffer after they have been incorporated into the wider world.

EXPLORING SOCIAL DEVELOPMENT STATUS PRIOR TO STATE INTERVENTION

The standard of life of tribes in their traditional social system may have been low and poor, but the poverty was not so extreme as to cause starvation deaths. If at all there were starvation and hunger deaths, it was more on account of natural calamities, and the community as a whole suffered. In fact, tribes as a whole suffered substantial decline in their absolute numbers during 1891–1901, 1911–21, 1921–31 owing to famine or epidemics in mainland India (Maharatna 2005).

Otherwise, survival was not threatened in tribal society, and there has been a general increase in the population. In fact, the proportion of tribal population had increased from 2.26 to 3.26 per cent during 1881–1941, whereas the Hindu proportion had steadily declined from 75.1 per cent to 69.5 per cent during this period. This difference, according to Davis, was due to the high fertility levels of the tribal population as compared with the Hindu population. However, it was probably due to relatively low mortality and high fertility levels of the tribal population compared with those of the mainstream population (Maharatna 2005).

Fertility and mortality rates are used as important indicators for ascertaining the health status of the population. This in turn is related to its nutritional status. Mortality rates have already been referred to earlier, and these point to a lower mortality rate among tribes than among the general population. More direct evidence of lower mortality rates, however, comes from the tribal regions of Nagaland, which has been one of the least integrated tribal regions in India. It is worth noting that Nagaland for several years has had the lowest death rate in the country, even though modern health coverage and status of potable water supply was extremely unsatisfactory (Roy Burman 1990, p. 213). With regard to mainland India, this is what Maharatna (2005, p. 134) has to say:

> As tribes are generally less modernized and have less exposure to modern health provisions, they can be hypothesized to experience a higher mortality as compared to the mainstream. However, because of greater intimacy with the natural environment in a primitive habitat with less crowding and pollution, as well as because of healthy life style pattern and practices, such as child care and use of indigenous herbal/natural medicines, tribes could be expected to experience a (relative) mortality advantage.

In fact, whatever, information we have on the nutritional status of tribes in their traditional setting has been positive. The given information points to remote areas as offering a healthy way of life in many important respects, such as having a clean environment and access to a nutritious diet (for tribals). This has been possible, because of easy access to forest and forest resources, but which has slowly been denied to tribals since the time of colonial rule. Caloric intake of many traditionally food-gathering tribes is entirely from the natural produce of forests. Even settled agriculturist tribes derive a substantial amount of nutrition from jungle products. Tribes, in fact, subsisted for generations with a reasonable standard of health, because forests provided food, such as fruits, leafy vegetables, honey, game, and fish. Medicinal plants, which they have been using for treatment of diseases and maintaining health, are today a source of modern medicine. Tribal children are not only familiar with any number of biological species around them, but they also have an understanding of the ecological relationships between various components in the forest. In areas where forests exist, the able bodied, as also the old, infirm, and the children bring something, however modest it may be, to the household, giving them a sense of satisfaction (Roy Burman 1990).

CONSEQUENCES OF STATE POLICIES AND DEVELOPMENT PROJECTS

Tribes, as observed earlier, were societies unto themselves with a distinct territory, language, culture, and political and economic demarcation of their own. By virtue of existing as a self-contained unit, they held control over land and forests in their territory. The coming of British rule drastically altered all such relationships. Traditionally, these resources were either individually or collectively owned. Even if they had no such rights, they at least had usufructuary rights over these. But, owing to the policies and measures pursued during colonial rule and its continuation in post-Independence India, there has been a steady erosion of control over and restrictions on use of these resources by tribes. Despite much protective and even restorative legislation to stop land alienation in the post-Independence period, there has been little success to this effect. Of course, the major source of land alienation in the post-Independence period is not so much the encroachment of the non-tribals into the tribal land as the process of development that the Indian State has followed during the period. The large-scale industrialization and exploitation of mineral resources and the construction of irrigation dams and power projects that the tribal areas have witnessed during this period have been the most disruptive factors that have uprooted more people out of their lands than the transfer of land from tribals to non-tribals on an individual basis. Assessment of displacement studied over a decade ago point to the fact that more than 8.5 million tribal people have been displaced, which constitutes over 40 per cent of all persons displaced in the country. In the face of this scale of displacement, it is estimated that the extent of land acquired during the colonial period was a small fraction of what has been acquired in post-Independence India (GoI 2007). During the first-three Five-Year Plans, more than 50,000 ST and 10,000 SC families in the Jharkhand area of Bihar[1] were uprooted from their ancestral homes to make land available for the construction of public sector industrial projects alone. The total number of displaced families would be much higher if one were to consider the private sector projects and coal mines, which were during that phase with the private sector. The process of land acquisition for industrial purposes has remained high even after the first three Plans (Sengupta 1979).

Tribes underwent change not only in their relationship to land but also in their relationship to the forest. Tribes were greatly dependent on the forest for their day-to-day needs such as their food, shelter, instruments, medicine, and even clothing in some instances. But, as long as tribes were in control of forests, in the sense of unrestricted use of forest and its produce, they had no difficulty meeting these needs. The entry of the British, however, drastically altered this relationship. To the British, the forest was an important source of revenue and commercial exploitation. Hence, the forest policy enunciated by the British introduced state control over forest resource and imposed curtailment of rights and privileges over forest resources. The policy pursued by the British was continued in the post-Independence era of economic development with even stricter regulation and enforcement. All these were justified on the grounds that these were necessary in the wider and national public interest. However, this had/has serious consequences on access to basic necessities of life such as food and shelter for the tribals.

Both displacement and denial of access to forests, especially the former have impacted children in a significant way. Displacement has invariably led to dislocation of sources of livelihood resulting in food insecurity in families. Even when there has been rehabilitation and resettlement, this problem is still present. Needless to say, this

[1] Jharkhand was carved out as a new state on 15 November 2000. Till then it was a part of Bihar.

has adversely affected children's nutritional status and their health. Displacement has also uprooted them from their traditional habitat and environment and pushed them into an environment that they were not only unfamiliar with, but was often even hostile resulting in social and psychological adjustment problems. It disrupted the schooling of school-going children and, more often than not, was a factor of their discontinuation of schooling. Even in restriction of access to the forests, tribal children are affected, though not as severely as when there is displacement, since tribal life, even if based on settled agriculture, is intricately linked with the forest.

Jharkhand and Odisha illustrate the various aspects and consequences of development, such as the setting up of industries, construction of dams, and mineral exploitation and mining better than any other states in India. And yet, the two states have the highest percentages of tribal people living below the poverty line. In 1993–4, in the state of Odisha, 71.26 per cent of tribals lived below the poverty line. In Jharkhand, which was then part of Bihar, the share of tribal people living below the poverty line was 69.75 per cent. These figures were higher than the all-India tribal average of about 50.58 per cent. In contrast, Andhra Pradesh with 25.66 per cent, Kerala and Karnataka with 37.34 per cent, and Gujarat with 31.20 per cent fared better than the eastern states (GoI 2001). The northeast region, especially tribal population majority states, has fared even better. The percentage of people below the poverty level was 37.92 per cent in Meghalaya and Nagaland, 25.66 per cent in Mizoram, and 39.55 per cent in Arunachal Pradesh (Nagdeve 2008).

With respect to literacy, the percentage was a mere 27.5 per cent in 1991 and 40.7 per cent in 2001 in Jharkhand. The corresponding figure for Odisha was 22.3 per cent in 1991 and 37.4 per cent in 2001. Maharashtra and Gujarat had better tribal literacy rates than the eastern states, and the north-eastern states like Nagaland, Manipur, and Mizoram were even ahead of the national average at 64.8 per cent (GoI 2007). The picture was no different in the sphere of health. Odisha had an infant mortality rate and under-5 mortality rate of 79 and 136, respectively, per 1,000 live births as compared with the all-India tribal average of 62 and 96, respectively, per 1,000 live births for the year 2005–6 (UNICEF Inclusive Programming Roadmap Workshop of 2010). The figure had been far better for the north-eastern states.

In fact, in all tribal states, the percentage of stunted, wasted, and underweight tribal children has been lower than the all-India tribal average of 54, 28, and 55 per cent, respectively (Pala and Khongjoh 2009). What this shows is that states with large development projects and mineral exploitation have done poorly in human development indicators. In contrast, where such development has been relatively absent, such as in Maharashtra, Gujarat, Rajasthan, Madhya Pradesh in mainland India or the states of north-eastern India, the share of tribal people living below the poverty line is significantly small and levels of literacy and health indicators have been better (GoI 2001).

LARGE DEVELOPMENT PROJECTS AND PREVALENCE OF DISEASES

Development in tribal regions has primarily taken the form of dam projects, irrigation, industries, power projects, and more importantly mineral exploitation. Such developments have led to extensive environmental degradation in tribal areas. Rivers and streams which were the lifeline of the tribes have dried up. The remaining water bodies have been highly polluted, because of effluence from industries and mines. The air also has been drastically affected, because of these development projects. Dust and smoke emanating from industries, thermal projects, and mineral extraction have given rise to diseases that were hitherto unknown in the region. Infectious diseases like malaria, dysentery, diarrhoea, tuberculosis, leprosy, and nutrition-deficiency diseases such as anaemia, goitre, and diseases of the eye have been on rise. In fact, malaria and dysentery, followed by polio, leprosy, diarrhoea, filariasis are prevalent among children up to four years of age leading to high infant mortality rates, various disabilities, low efficiency, etc. Respiratory diseases have also been reported as being prevalent in tribal areas. Such diseases get aggravated among female children and aged women because they cook food using firewood in the traditional *chulhas* (stoves). What is important to note here is that many of the diseases that the tribal population is currently encountering stems from the change in environment arising from development projects in the tribal region. In fact, efforts at improving the health status of the tribal population is often countered or neutralized by environmental problems caused by such development projects.

CHILDREN AND ARMED CONFLICT

The problem of poverty, unemployment, deprivation, and exploitation experienced by tribes as a part of the larger agenda of industrialization, mineral exploitation, and infrastructure development all through the post-Independence period has given rise to general restlessness in the tribal society in recent years. This has led to resistance and struggle of various forms—resistance against development and mineral projects and rights to access of forests being the more dominant ones. Such a situation in tribal areas has created suitable conditions for the Maoists to entrench their base in these regions. In this fight of the Maoists against the State, which has taken the form of armed conflict, ordinary people including children have invariably been drawn as either participants or victims. The Maoists recruit children, who have to undergo rigorous training in combat warfare in severe circumstances quite early in life. They then engage in war with the state armed forces. At times even the state armed forces recruit children as militia to fight insurgent groups. This is most evident in the war against the Naxalites in Chhattisgarh where children have not only been recruited for combat, they have been used both by the insurgents and by the state armed forces in various ways in their war against each other. Often this results in harassment and violence (physical and mental) from both sides of the warring parties. Children, however, suffer most as victims. They have found themselves not only orphaned because of the deaths of their parents, but also physically assaulted, raped, tortured, and even permanently impaired by the security forces or the insurgents. Often they have found their habitats destroyed and are confined to camps without adequate food, water, sanitary facilities, and schools (ACHR 2006, 2013).

LITERACY AND EDUCATION

The status of literacy and educational attainment of tribals has already been referred to in the earlier sections. Low enrolment and high dropout rates, especially the latter, continue to be the main problem of school education among tribal children. The important question is why the attendance is low and the dropout rates high among them. Such problems in the general population have been attributed to poor curriculum and syllabus, deficient pedagogy, or negligent teachers. Parents, too, are held accountable for their children dropping out (Dubey 2010). Now, if this is the case with the larger population in whose language and ethos school education is imparted and whose history and culture the school curriculum and syllabus represents, with even teachers belonging to same cultural group as the students, then one can imagine the state of tribal children for whom the education that is imparted at all levels is alien to their life, history, and experience.

It is a fact that the educational systems into which tribes have been incorporated have been developed to correspond with the interest, language, culture, and history of the dominant linguistic communities. The result was that modern education in tribal society became an alien phenomenon. The language in which reading and writing skills were taught was not only alien, but what came to be taught was alien too. Even those engaged in imparting such instruction were strangers to the tribal society. This partly explains why tribal children found education far from attractive. Low enrolment but, more importantly, such high dropout rates in tribal society had to do with these factors to a great extent. The number of tribal children who have crossed such barriers to education has been small, but subsequently they have moved to occupations other than agriculture and have been the pillar of the new middle class in tribal society.

EXPLAINING SOCIAL EXCLUSION AND DEPRIVATION

The issue of deprivation and social exclusion is thus intricately linked with the larger question of the political economy and development in the form of large-scale development projects, such as dams, irrigation, power plants, roads, railways, industry, mineral exploitation, and state control over forest resources; and, with regard to children, in the structure of the educational system. The development projects and state control of forest have invariably taken the form of appropriation of tribal land, forests, and other resources that had begun under colonial rule and continued through the post-Independence era, though under the garb of national and regional development. The benefits of this development, which Jawaharlal Nehru, the country's first prime minister, described as the temples of modern India, did not accrue to the tribal people. Rather, tribal people were deprived of their livelihoods and left without any alternative avenues of employment and food security despite special Constitutional provisions for their protection and special affirmative action programmes for their economic and social development. The latter, have been portrayed as the signpost of tribal development. A close examination shows, however, that affirmative action for tribes tends to be no longer an affirmative action, as it does not lift them from the given social base in which they were traditionally located. Rather, affirmative action has been pushed through after their existing social base has been eroded causing their deterioration and exposing them to greater vulnerability. In the light of development such as this, any benefit that may accrue from various state-initiated tribal development projects, either in the economic sphere or social sphere, gets neutralized. As a consequence, they remain where they are or move to a situation worse than they were in. This paradox of development needs to be resolved.

REFERENCES

Asian Centre for Human Rights (ACHR). 2006. *The Adivasis of Chhattisgarh: Victims of the Naxalite Movement and Salwa Judum Campaign*. New Delhi: ACHR.

———. 2013. *Nobody's Children: Juveniles of Conflict Affected Districts of India*. New Delhi: ACHR.

Bosu Mullick, S. 1990. 'Jharkhand Movement: A Historical Analysis', in M. Miri (ed.), *Continuity and Change in Tribal Society*, pp. 437–62. Shimla: Indian Institute of Advanced Study.

Dubey, Muchkund. 2010. 'The Right of Children to Free and Compulsory Education Act: 2009: The Story of a Missed Opportunity', *Social Change*, 40(1): 1–13.

Elwin, Verrier. 1986. *The Baiga* (1939, reprint, London: John Murray). Delhi: Gyan Books.

Fürer-Haimendorf, Christoph von. 1933. *Naked Nagas*. Calcutta: Thacker, Spink & Co.

Government of India (GoI). 2001. *Report of the Steering Committee on Empowering the Scheduled Tribes for the Tenth Five Year Plan (2002–07)*. New Delhi: Planning Commision, GoI.

———. 2007. *Report of the Working Group on Empowerment of Scheduled Tribes for the Eleventh Five Year Plan (2007–12)*. New Delhi: GoI.

Hutton, J.H. 1921. *The Sema Nagas*. London: Macmillan.

Maharatna, Arup. 2005. *Demographic Perspectives on India's Tribes*. USA: Oxford University Press.

Mathur, Ashok. 2008. 'An Overview of the Jharkhand Economy and Perspectives for Human Development', National Seminar on Growth and Human Development in Jharkhand, 4–5 July.

Nagdeve, Dewaram A. 2008. 'Population, Poverty and Environment in India', IIPS Research Brief, No. 6.

Pala, Veronica and I.P. Khingjoh. 2009. 'Calorie Deficiency among Scheduled Tribes in the North-Eastern Region of India', International Seminar on Adivasis/ST Communities in India: Development and Change, 27–29 August, New Delhi.

Roy, S.C. 2004. *The Mundas and Their Country*, 10th edition (1912, reprint, Calcutta: Kuntaline Press). Ranchi: Crown Publications.

Roy Burman, B.K. 1990. 'Tribal Population: Interface of Historical Ecology and Political Economy', in M. Miri (ed.), *Continuity and Change in Tribal Society*, pp. 175–216. Shimla: Indian Institute of Advanced Study.

Sengupta, N. 1979. 'Class Structure in Jharkhand', *National Labour Institute Bulletin*, 5(7–8): 217–31.

Singh, K.S. 2002. *Birsa Munda and His Movement 1872–1901. A Study of a Millenarian Movement in Chotanagpur*. Kolkata: Seagull Books.

17 Literacies and Power

Looking for Adivasi Voice in Education[1]

Shivali Tukdeo

For Adivasi children, opening their textbooks often means encountering isolation, images of themselves that are frozen in time, and histories that are invisible or at best appear as tokens. Powerful and evocative imagery accompanies the introduction of 'tribes' in the textbooks. With feathers in their hair, and faces painted, the Adivasi communities are presented as 'being part of the jungle'—primitive in every sense of the term. For all children, such encounters are problematic on many levels. To start with, such images reconfirm the age-old taken-for-granted misunderstanding about Adivasi communities. Second, the imagery is introduced amidst an absence of recognition for Adivasi cultural heterogeneity. Given that the enterprise of formal education is deeply involved in the production of appropriate behaviours,

[1] Most of the arguments in this chapter are part of a larger report (2012) entitled, 'The Education Question from the Perspectives of Adivasis: Conditions, Policies and Structures'. The report was developed by the National Institute of Advanced Studies and UNICEF, following fieldwork and consultations that took place over 18 months. I thank all the team members on the report: P. Veerbhadranaika, Revathi Sampath Kumaran, A.R. Vasavi, and Rina D'Souza; special thanks to A.R. Vasavi for introducing me to the nuances of education among the Adivasis.

norms and moral citizenry, the 'representation' of Adivasis in our textbooks and in schooling practices needs to be understood within the larger social and political contexts. What we see as part of school knowledge is hardly innocent of the broader histories of isolation, erasure, and invisibilization.[2]

Epistemic and actual violence, forced displacement, and land alienation have been part of the stories of marginalized communities in India. A comparison of every possible indicator of development and educational attainment finds the Adivasi communities always at the very bottom of the index. This chapter focuses on the narrative of 'failure' that has been integral to the ways in which the Adivasi communities' relationship with education has been understood. Numerous accounts of educational access, retention, and achievement elaborate on statistics showing low educational attainment of the Adivasis. These empirical descriptive works are of importance for obvious reasons. But, for the purposes of this chapter, my objective is to move away from the focus on 'educational outcomes' and, instead, pay attention to the history and sociology of policy in India that has contributed to the current conditions of education among the Adivasis. This enquiry, thus, begins by asking a set of opening questions: Given that the present era is obsessed with literacy and our institutions are heavily invested in enumerating literacy levels in order to connect them to educational achievements or deficit, how do we make sense of communities that do not possess the right kind of literacy? To what extent do factors such as lack of food security, health care and livelihood security contribute to decline in school attendance? How can Adivasi knowledge systems find space and recognition within the mainstream curricula?

For as long as the modern, institutionalized forms of education have existed and proliferated, a series of interventions have consistently pointed out that neither learning nor school education are external to

[2] A rather common experience during our fieldwork was of Adivasi youth recalling their experiences of shock and disbelief on seeing the stereotypical images in textbooks. A young activist remarked, 'We don't look like *that* [the stereotypical image] and don't ride elephants'. Yet, the image of an Adivasi person as necessarily anti-modern and different from the rest of India continues to hold.

the power relations that are at work.[3] Schools are sites that transmit, disseminate, and shape knowledge and social practices. Taken in this context, then, 'reading' and 'writing' are more than a set of skills with instrumental value attached to them. Acquisition of literacy opens up an ability to act, interpret, opine, and engage. It opens the world before the learners as it also covers up and conceals. Extending the idea of 'literacy' in order to connect it to reflection, interpretation, and action, this analysis focuses on education policy in India and the place of Adivasis therein.

The relationship between Adivasis and the Indian State has been fraught with many tensions and contradictions. While recent attempts at introducing decentralized governance and greater autonomy—with the introduction of Panchayats (Extension to the Scheduled Areas) Act (PESA), Forest Rights Act, along with the formation of Ministry of Tribal Affairs (MoTA) and National Council for Tribal Welfare—are useful steps towards realizing actual meaningful autonomy for Adivasi communities, such attempts are accompanied by conflicting and contradictory structures, schemes and programmes. For instance, the initiation of Integrated Action Plan (IAP) in Naxal-affected tribal regions undermines autonomy and decision-making power at local levels. Similarly, the entry of transnational corporations in tribal regions along with the development models including mega dams and industries have also been given clearance without consent from local authorities. As documented by several scholars, activists, and civil society groups, these interventions have resulted in large-scale migration, displacement, and violence in Adivasi areas. In particular, following are some of the trends that have occurred in the Adivasi regions as a result of long-standing interventions on the state's part:

1. Different economic/industrial models have been superimposed on erstwhile indigenous ways of livelihoods. In the reorganization of

[3] The work of Brazilian educator and thinker, Paulo Freire, has been an important testament to thinking of the ways in which modern, institutionalized forms of education are connected to marginalization. His most famous work, *Pedagogy of the Oppressed* (1970) uses knowledge to understand the relationship between the colonizer and the colonized. Inspired by Freire's work, the intellectual tradition in critical pedagogy has pointed out how social and political components affect and shape education.

the tribal region, opinions and interests of Adivasis have not been given their rightful place.

2. Community-based indigenous social organizations and practices have been lost (such as collective food security) and the State has stepped in with its provisions that are of an uneven quality and are unreliable.
3. There has been a historic rise in migration and displacement in Adivasi regions owing to a range of factors. Most notably the nexus between the State and transnational corporations has contributed to this. As surplus migrant labour, the Adivasis are being absorbed in the urban, informal economy.
4. There are serious issues of quality, transparency, and monitoring in providing basic services, including health, food, education, water, and sanitation. As far as education is concerned, schools in the interior parts have severe teacher absenteeism.

These trends manifest a trajectory of policy development over the course of last century resulting in the ambivalence of integration/isolation of Adivasi communities.

HISTORY OF POLICY PRODUCTION

A quick glance at the history of education tells us the ways in which restrictive caste codes operated in India for centuries and how they gave selective access to learning, knowledge production, and practice. In the nineteenth century, with institutionalization of teaching and learning in India under the British, schools became places to educate young learners in a variety of subjects and skills. For the historically outcaste communities however, the caste character of the formal schooling system became a crucial determinant that affected their access, understanding, and participation in education. By design and through overt and covert practices, education became part of the systematic exclusion of non-elite students. For instance, the present formal education system is such that Adivasis can hardly identify, enjoy, thrive, and participate in educational institutions. Neither the make-up of the education system nor the lack of participation by Adivasis is by accident. This brings us to the condition of 'invisibilization' that also marks the educational experience of the disadvantaged. Even as they participate in formal education as students, teachers, parents, staff, and school administrators, Adivasi people can never hope to find Adivasi knowledge, ethos, traditions, histories, and languages as part of their educational experience.

India's public policy on indigenous populations shares close links with that of the colonial policy that sought to plug the tribal economies into Western models of capital accumulation. The colonial regime exercised massive land grab in the tribal belt, simultaneously attempting to 'settle' the tribes and classify them. The Criminal Tribes Act of 1871 became part of the successive legislation that described some tribal communities as 'habitually criminal', thereby enforcing restrictions on their movement and keeping them under surveillance. The criminalization of tribes occurred in the aftermath of several tribal revolts against the British on issues of land, forests and autonomy. The Bhil revolt (1818), the Kol rebellion (1833), the Santhal rebellion (1855), the rebellion of 1857 and the Birsa Munda rebellion (1895) were among the many forms of organized resistance against the British, the moneylenders, and outsiders. In the early twentieth century, a number of tribal communities joined forces with the non-cooperation movement and attempted to forge a political space within the Congress party around Adivasi issues. The colonial policy on education was driven by forces of enlightenment and the necessity of workforce creation. The first policy document dealing with education, the Charter Act (1813), hoped to revive 'the encouragement of the learned natives of India...for the introduction and promotion of knowledge of the sciences among the inhabitants of the British territories in India' (Kumar 2006, p. 24; Naik 1997). Taking the argument of 'cognitive superiority of English education' further, the first education commission chaired by F.W. Hunter (1882) called for a 'downward filtration of western scientific knowledge' with tribals at the very end of the hierarchy. A blend of English and vernacular schools were established by the end of nineteenth century, and these institutions catered to different types of needs. The idea of forming a national system of education also began to take root about this time, largely as a response to the political climate that tied reforms to nationalism. Consequently, the first Congress of National Education at Wardha in 1937 approved the proposals on 'free and compulsory education', 'mother-tongue as the medium of instruction', skill-based education, and self-sufficient schools. Building on the concept that mass education is a political project, the Central Advisory

Board of Education (CABE) was formed and the committee drafted a report on Post-War Educational Development in India, also called the Sargent Report, in 1944. The committee put forward the idea of equality of educational opportunity, calling explicitly for a common system. But as these documents reveal, the expected and desired students/beneficiaries of English education were upper castes and classes who were historically part of the process of teaching and learning. While missionary schools had been set up in several predominantly tribal regions since the nineteenth century, the policy and public texts on education rarely paid attention to the particularities of tribal education.

POST-INDEPENDENCE ERA

The imprints of colonial governance accompanied by logics of unbridled capitalism can be seen easily in the official discourse, particularly as it relates to questions of Adivasi autonomy, self-governance, legitimacy, and claims of authentic history. The official stance of the independent Indian State on issues such as land tenure, natural resources, and cultural identity of Adivasis is fraught with tensions and contradictions. An analysis of education policy in the last five decades can be done by deploying the following conceptual categories: (i) Nationalism, (ii) Culturalism, and (iii) Development Discourse.

Nationalism and Educational Policy

Adivasis have found themselves to be the object of state-crafted knowledge regarding administration, policy, legal provision, and general discourse on welfare. In response to the large tribal population and their demands, the postcolonial state positioned itself within the two opposite ends of policy—integration and isolation. The ambivalence becomes especially clear in the context of the 'five principles of governance of Adivasi region' proposed in 1955. The 'Panchsheel' principles, often hailed as a welcome step towards the policy of respect and autonomy of tribal regions, were a product of the changed geopolitics, including decolonization and recognitions of autonomy in/of newly emerging frontiers. The five principles include:

1. No direct imposition of rules on tribal areas
2. No encroachment of tribal lands and forests

3. Encouragement of tribal administrative structures
4. Refrain from over-administration of tribal areas
5. Long-term development strategies over short term

In reality, however, the Indian state is engaged in a host of actions contrary to the five principles mentioned. As highlighted earlier, a series of policies, political trends, and economic priorities have been put in place, but they have not led to the realization of the stated policies of tribal autonomy, self-determination, and rights to sustainable living. The impact of these have been that educational policies have also reflected the larger subversions of Adivasi interests, and have not recognized the autonomy and specific requirements of Adivasis, and have instead made them an appendage of a larger dominant system.

Culturalism

A rather loaded word, the construct of 'culture' is used liberally and loosely to define and identify the Adivasis. The folklore, art, and the cultural practices of 'tribals' are, often, the only ways in which their lives are understood by dominant groups. Their culture is seen as either exotic and unique or as backward and outside modernity. Such representations overlook the diversities and the specificities of cultural complexes of different tribal societies. In addition, the history of change within these societies and the relationships of tribal societies to dominant societies have been neglected. In such contexts, the deployments of culture as a tool of resistance and assertions for new identities have been also overlooked. While most policies in India recognize the rights of Adivasis to a culturally embedded education (including language), in reality much of it has not been realized. The fact that the content, orientation, curricula, syllabi, and texts are all primarily from the dominant society testifies to this.

Development Discourse in Education

In the last two decades, there have been some shifts in the objectives and goals associated with the promotion of mass elementary education. For one, it is firmly embedded within the growing currency of the discourse on development and economic growth that rests on a set of identifiable and measurable traits. Simply put, greater access to and higher levels of education are understood to be connected to informed personal and public choices, democratic participation, and economic betterment. Articulated initially by numerous international and transnational groups, the development discourse in education has now become commonplace. The Millennium Development Goals (MDGs), minimum levels of learning (MLL), education for development (E4D), and education for all (EFA) are some of the major turns in this shift. While the discourse is logical and well intentioned, it has slowly shifted the perception of education towards being primarily a measurable enterprise. The instrumentality attached to learning, as per this model, renders education into a goal-specific process.

Additionally, being a prized 'development' cause, the field of education has become susceptible to large numbers of private, commercial, and philanthropic interests. In the context of promoting education among Adivasis, the logic of 'development' shares its purpose with long-standing views that necessitated mainstreaming Adivasis 'for their own good'. Thus, education is considered to be the staircase that will lead Adivasis towards development and out of poverty. In this case, the conceptions of 'development' and 'education' are rather constraining and generate two contradictions. On the one hand, the focus on the developmental model seeks to integrate Adivasis into the dominant society/nation through forms of submissive assimilation. On the other hand, since the dominant education system does not challenge structural inequalities, the subordinate position of these marginalized groups is reproduced.

PROVISIONS AND POLICY PROCESS

Clauses (1) and (2) of Article 342 of the Constitution lay out the context in which 'tribal' groups can be notified as scheduled tribes (STs). Accordingly, the Parliament can determine the list of scheduled tribes from time to time. Similarly, the provisions for administration of scheduled areas and STs have been incorporated in the Fifth and Sixth Schedule of the Constitution.[4] Taking stock of the education

[4] See Article 342(1): The President may with respect to any State or Union territory, and where it is a State, after consultation with the Governor thereof, by public notification, specify the tribes or tribal communities or parts of or

of Scheduled Castes (SCs) and STs, the position paper developed by the National Council of Education Research and Training (NCERT)[5] states that the main challenge before the newly independent Indian state was to address the historical wrongs through policy measures in education. 'In its effort to offset educational and socio-historical disadvantage, the Indian state conceived a range of enabling provisions that would facilitate access to and ensure retention of SC and ST children in school'. Provision of basic access remained the priority during initial Five-Year Plans, with considerable expansion of enabling interventions after the Fourth Plan.[6]

The following Constitutional provisions are useful in thinking about the guarantee of education for Adivasis. In more general terms, the fundamental right to education has been incorporated under Article 21A of the Constitution, and education in the mother tongue for minority groups is ensured under Article 350A. Articles 15(4), 29(1), 29(2), 30(1), 30(1A), 30(2), and 46 of the Indian Constitution contain the State's commitment to education of SC and ST children. For instance, Article 15 highlights the State's commitment for the advancement of '...socially and educationally backward classes of citizens or for the Scheduled Castes and the Scheduled Tribes'. Cultural and educational rights of the minorities have been protected under Articles 29(1), 29(2), 30(1), 30(1A), and 30(2), including the right to set up educational institutions. Finally, Article 45 focuses on the

---

groups within tribes or tribal communities which shall for the purposes of this Constitution be deemed to be Scheduled Tribes in relation to that State or Union territory, as the case may be.

Article 342(2) 'Parliament may by law include in or exclude from the list of Scheduled Tribes specified in a notification issued under clause (1) any tribe or tribal community or part of or group within any tribe or tribal community, but save as aforesaid a notification issued under the said clause shall not be varied by any subsequent notification'.

[5] For a list of position papers prepared by NCERT, see http://www.ncert.nic.in/rightside/links/focus_group.html, last accessed on 27 October 2014.

[6] See National Focus Group on Problems of Scheduled Caste and Scheduled Tribe Children at http://www.ncert.nic.in/new_ncert/ncert/rightside/links/pdf/focus_group/position_paper_on_sc_st.pdf, last accessed on 27 October 2014.

promotion of 'educational and economic interests of Scheduled Castes, Scheduled Tribes and other weaker sections'.[7]

One of the serious challenges of education policymaking in India is the concurrent listing (as both a central and a state subject) of education, which does generate a variety of schemes and programmes, but does not necessarily lend itself to integrated reviews, accountability, development of programmes or cater to the needs of the marginalized in respective states or regions. This ultimately affects the educational experience and opportunities, especially of marginalized populations. Issues of school-distance, language, and nutrition continue to be important determinants of access to education in tribal areas. But these issues rarely receive adequate attention. Reflecting the diversity of structures in different states, a growing trend in recent years can be seen in the uneven growth of private voluntary organizations in the education sector.[8]

In 64 years since Independence, low levels of enrolment at the primary levels and lower learning achievements were two of the biggest challenges for the Indian education system. Non-universalization of primary education and uneven selective expansion of education institutions continue to have a severe impact on disadvantaged communities. While the National Policy on Education (NPE), 1968 recommended 6 per cent of the GDP expenditure on education, in reality the state spent just about 2.5 per cent on an average over the years. In the 1960s, the Kothari Commission (1966) and the National Policy on Education, 1968, made a convincing case for universalization of elementary education and formation of a common school system.[9] The three-language formula advocated by the Kothari Commission has been responsible for the current multilingual educational model in states, as the three-language position was upheld by subsequent

[7] See The Constitution of India (as of December 2011), Government of India, Ministry of Law and Justice at http://lawmin.nic.in/olwing/coi/coi-english/coi-indexenglish.htm, last accessed on 27 October 2014.

[8] Despite the spread and presence of various national and international aid and philanthropic groups in tribal and Adivasi education, there have been no systematic reviews or assessments of these programmes.

[9] See 'Education Commissions and Committees: A Retrospect' at http://www.education.nic.in/cd50years/g/W/16/0W160301.htm, last accessed on 27 October 2014.

education commissions.[10] In doing so, however, questions of Adivasi languages have been put on hold or have never been factored in adequately. In a move towards increasing decentralization, on the one hand, and reduced State-provision, on the other, the National Policy on Education, 1968 had a set of provisions impacting tribal education:

1. Elementary schools in Adivasi areas a priority
2. Curricula and instruction in Adivasi languages
3. Increase in ashram schools
4. Tribal youth to be encouraged to take up teaching in schools
5. Introduction of non-formal system of schooling in Adivasi areas
6. Schemes at the centre and state levels for ST students

The NPE 1968 brought up the idea of 'non-formal' stream of education as a viable policy option. Following the NPE provisions, local districts became important units in educational management. During this time, India's economic policy began to witness a shift from a state-interventionist model restricting foreign direct investment and foreign trade to that of liberalization of nationally controlled services.

In addition to education access, which has dominated policy attention for a long time, matters of pedagogy, curriculum, language of instruction, and teacher education also deserve focus and attention. In this respect, the position paper on 'Tribal Education' prepared by members of the National Curriculum Framework, 2005 highlighted a workable direction that would involve:

1. Emphasis on multilingual education not only as instructional strategy, but also as a 'holistic approach.'
2. Textbook production, publication at large in tribal languages.
3. Curriculum needs to shift from the promoter of high culture to that of depiction of tribal life.
4. Inclusion of tribal/Dalit folklore, lesser-known languages.

With the passage of the Right to Education (RTE) Act, 2009, Article 21A has now been translated into legal obligation on the part of the State. In what follows, we present three significant policy

[10] See the summary of Kothari Commission report at http://www.education.nic.in/cd50years/g/W/16/0W160401.htm, last accessed on 27 October 2014.

initiatives of recent times that will have an impact on education among Adivasis.

Policy Moment: Right to Education

Passed in 2009, the Right of Children to Free and Compulsory Education Act, or simply Right to Education (RTE) Act provides for free and compulsory education for children between the ages 6 and 14. The Act includes a range of measures that are important in thinking of education of the disadvantaged communities:

1. Local authority is responsible for providing education.
2. Steps to be taken to enrol dropout students in age-appropriate classes.
3. Infrastructural support including buildings, learning materials.
4. Necessary teaching support, including well-trained teachers.
5. Establishment of norms for teacher training and certification.
6. Greater role of School Management Committees in:
   - (i) Monitoring the workings of the school;
   - (ii) Recommending school development plan; and
   - (iii) Monitoring grants.
7. Comprehensive Quality Enhancement plans for ST areas.

While the RTE fulfils the Constitutional mandate and provides grounds for recognizing education as 'non-purchasable' and a 'right for all', some provisions in the Act raise concerns. Fixed norms about school infrastructure, greater standardization of teaching, recruitment, teacher education and credentials are cases in point. Given that an alternative sustainable vision of Adivasi and tribal pedagogy opposes standardization and regimentation of learning, some of the provisions of RTE need to be thought over. In a short report, 'A Space for Alternate Schools', the alternative educators in the country lay out the perils of standardization, and its anticipated impact on the very philosophy of non-mainstream alternative education.[11]

[11] The note titled 'A Space for Alternate Schools': Note on behalf of alternative schools with regard to certain provisions of the Right of Children to Free and Compulsory Education Act, 2009, was put together by several organizations and individuals working in the domains of alternative education. The document can be found at http://www.swaraj.org/shikshantar/RTE_alt.pdf, last accessed on 27 October 2014.

Greater standardization, the report cautions, does not translate into greater levels of actual learning. Further, the most significant contribution by alternative schools has been their curricula that have been local, diverse, and experiential. As for the education of Adivasis, the 'one size fits all' approach to teacher education, pedagogy, curriculum, and classroom instruction has demonstrably failed and it need not be reinforced through RTE.

Some of the points outlined above are corroborated in a recent research report carried out by Dhaatri Resource Centre for Women and Children (DRCWC) (2012), based on their work in tribal districts of Odisha and Andhra Pradesh. Based on their findings, regarding the enforcement of provisions of RTE in select districts of the two states, the report states that a large number of Adivasi children who should be enrolled in elementary schools continue to be outside, not enrolled, or are dropouts. The following findings of the report particularly stand out:

1. Quality of educational institutions for ST children is low. In particular, the quality of residential schools/*Ashramshalas* 'is shockingly below the minimum standard of human dignity for any child' (DRCWC 2012, p. 13).
2. In what seems to be a serious violation of the right to education, the primary schools in Adivasi districts have almost become dysfunctional.
3. The levels of retention, qualification, and quality of the teachers in the region are abysmally low.
4. Arbitrariness and ad hoc decisions continue to play a role in teacher recruitment.
5. Mid-Day Meal programmes have been crucial in increasing enrolment in rural and tribal areas. However, the facilities and management of the programme leave much to be desired.

New Policy Directions: Decentralization and Local Governance

Large-scale reforms, loosely based on the ideas of decentralization, participatory governance, and public–private partnerships have dominated the Indian political universe since the late 1980s. The passage of the 73rd Constitutional Amendment in 1992 is historic in the experimentation of political decentralization in the country. The subsequent reorientation of public policy introduced three significant units of administration—village, block, and districts through which decentralization could operate. Devolution of powers, democratization of the delivery system, and greater role(s) of the gram sabhas are some of the ways in which the transfer of power has taken shape. In line with the 73rd Amendment, the subsequent enactment of Provisions of PESA 1996 sought to provide legislative powers in gram sabhas, particularly in matters of planning and management of natural resources and adjudication of disputes in accordance with prevalent traditions. With the model of self-governance at its core, PESA presented political opportunities for Adivasi communities that were a clear break away from erstwhile policies that (in principle) supported the Adivasi right to self-rule, but never enabled it to become a reality. PESA viewed Adivasi communities as legitimate units of governance, who have voice in exercising their command over natural resources and who can make use of the minor forest produce. Similarly, the panchayats at various levels and the gram sabhas have been given powers to monitor the performance of state institutions including schools, health centres, drinking water facilities, etc.

Community-driven management and decentralized power structures have been common threads between PESA, Joint Forest Management (JFM) programmes, and Forest Rights Act (FRA), 2006. Through the JFM, the forest department and village community enter into an agreement to jointly protect and manage the forest. Despite its departure from complete State control of the forests, JFM practices are yet to be fully participatory and democratic. In their review of the JFM, the Campaign for Survival and Dignity (CSD) states that 'despite many claims about its "success" and "people friendly nature", in practice, JFM has proven to be a dangerous scheme that has been used mainly to deprive people of their rights'.[12] The much talked about FRA recognizes three types of rights: (i) land rights, (ii) use rights, and (iii) rights to protect and conserve. By way of land rights, the Act recognizes an individual's rights to live in and cultivate forest land that was occupied prior to December 2005. Those without

[12] See http://www.forestrightsact.com/index.php?option=com_content&view=article&id=73&Itemid=400055, last accessed on 27 October 2014.

a land record at hand, but who have cultivated land can claim up to 4 hectares (Section 3, clause 1), and this also includes the land that is part of the dispute between forest department and cultivators. Since its inception in 2006, numerous studies on FRA (legal analysis, case studies, and fact-finding reports) have drawn attention to the ways in which the 'horizontal decision-making' gets routinely sidestepped in practice, with forest officers taking the lead in decision-making. The decentralized governing structures, be it PESA, JFM, or FRA, present huge gaps between the objectives and reality. The subversion of stated provisions is not simply the matter of 'what plays out on-the-ground politics', it can also be seen as a part of the design.[13]

To return to the question of Adivasi voice in education, the invisibility exists in textbook contents, administration of education, and in general policy formulation. While a host of schemes and programmes are introduced for the ST communities, there are no enabling structures for true participation. The newly introduced participatory models of development and governance hardly have a space for considering the structural issues that go into producing non-participation and silence on the part of Adivasis. The participatory development models have been accompanied by a much stronger and contradictory push towards private interests and capital that are given an easy entry in the Adivasi regions. In this chapter, I have paid attention to the historical contexts as well as social and political conditions that have influenced educational policy for Adivasis. Within the contemporary education regime, with its numerous hierarchies, a truly democratic Adivasi voice needs to be fostered and supported. First steps in this endeavour can be to develop creative programmes that are built around knowledge, identity, and languages of Adivasis.

REFERENCES

Dandekar, Ajay and Chitrangada Choudhuri. 2010. 'PESA, Left-Wing Extremism and Governance: Concerns and Challenges in India's Tribal Districts'. New Delhi: Ministry of Panchayat Raj.

[13] For an excellent analysis of the politics of local governance in PESA areas, see Dandekar and Choudhuri 2010. Also, for the critique of FRA, see Gopalakrishnan 2006.

Dhaatri Resource Centre for Women and Children (DRCWC). 2012. 'A Report on the Status of Primary Education of Adivasi Children in Andhra Pradesh and Orissa in the Context of the Right to Education Act 2009', Unpublished report.

Freire, Paulo. 1970. *Pedagogy of the Oppressed*. London: Penguin. Reprint in 1996.

Gopalakrishnan, Shankar. 2006. 'Conservation, Power and Democracy', *Seminar* (613). http://www.india-seminar.com/2010/613/613_shankar_gopalakrishnan.htm, last accessed on 25 October 2014.

Government of India, Ministry of Law and Justice, The Constitution of India (as of December 2011). http://lawmin.nic.in/olwing/coi/coi-english/coi-indexenglish.htm, last accessed on 25 October 2014.

Kumar, Ravi. 2006. *The Crisis of Elementary Education in India*. New Delhi: Sage Publications.

Naik, J.P. 1997. *The Education Commission and After*. New Delhi: APH Publishing.

18 Addressing Deprivations of Scheduled Tribe Children

A Perspective from Odisha

Soumya Kapoor Mehta

The state of Odisha has a peculiarly high share of socially excluded groups, such as the Scheduled Castes (SCs) and the Scheduled Tribes (STs), in its population. According to the 2011 census, STs and SCs constituted 22.8 per cent and 17.1 per cent of the state population, respectively, bringing the total share of these groups to roughly 40 per cent. Further, about 45 per cent of Odisha is classified as scheduled area under the Fifth Schedule of the Constitution, which identifies special privileges for these areas where the majority of the population belongs to scheduled tribes.

Given the high share of tribals in the state's population, tribal development has always been an area of focus in Odisha's policy agenda. But of late, tribal concerns have come to occupy a prime place in policy thinking in the state. This is driven by the fact that Odisha's current source of growth, its mineral resources, lies predominantly in areas where the tribals reside. Setting up mineral-based industries in these pockets has therefore resulted in large-scale displacement of tribals from their traditional lands and accompanying problems of resettlement and rehabilitation. This has fuelled resentment against the government, with several analysts considering such alienation to be the predominant cause of tribal angst and the reason for tribals' joining anti-state groups such as the Maoists. Not surprisingly, calls for identifying the processes that result in tribal deprivation have gained salience in recent years.

The objective of this analysis is to identify the underlying 'processes and pathways' that result in poor outcomes for ST households in Odisha, particularly children residing in them. Its central argument is that policies and programmes aimed at addressing deprivations faced by tribal children (for example, malnutrition) need to be designed keeping in mind the challenging socio-economic context that tribal families find themselves in.

The discussion in the next section of this chapter establishes the extent of the divide between STs and other groups in Odisha along a range of outcomes, particularly those relevant for children. The subsequent two sections present a brief examination of some of the gaps and challenges in addressing exclusion of tribals and their children in Odisha, both on the demand and on the supply side. These are discussed against a broad context of the history, politics, and social institutions of Odisha, which have traditionally constrained access of tribal households to assets, markets, livelihoods, and social service delivery mechanisms and denied them voice and participation. The last section concludes with an elaboration of some principles for promoting the interests of tribals in the state.

The analysis contained in this chapter is based on data from several sources including the Census of India (2011); three rounds of the National Sample Survey (NSS 1983, 1994–5, and 2004–5); three rounds of the Indian National Family Health Survey (NFHS 1992–3, 1998–9, and 2005–6); the Reproductive Child Health (RCH) Survey II (2005); data from the District Information System for Education (DISE) and the e-shishu programme in Odisha; and other independent studies. In addition, it draws on multiple stakeholder interviews conducted by the author during a field visit to Bhubaneswar, Odisha, in October 2009. These interviews held with representatives from the government, civil society, academia, and donor agencies such as Department for International Development (DFID) and UNICEF formed the basis for identifying key demand and supply barriers in existing programmes (as the stakeholders perceived them); wider economic, social, and political economy issues; and areas of opportunities wherein the government could accelerate the agenda of social inclusion in the state. Though stakeholder observations and ideas form the crux of the chapter, they are not attributed to specific persons to protect the identity of the interviewees.

EXTENT OF TRIBAL DEPRIVATION IN ODISHA

One of the first steps to addressing deprivation and exclusion is actually establishing its background. Odisha is among the poorest states in India, with nearly 47 per cent of its rural population below the poverty line (NSS 2004–5). It is also a state with substantial inequalities, which can be seen across its regions, between social groups, and between men and women of the state. At the time of writing this chapter, there were severe disparities, particularly across regions, with coastal and northern Odisha showing much better indicators for health, education, and income than southern Odisha. According to Sharma et al. (2009), the poverty headcount in rural parts of southern Odisha in 2004–5 was a staggering 73 per cent (see Table 18.1). In comparison, rural poverty in coastal Odisha was significantly lower at 27 per cent. The poverty ratio among ST was high across all regions with nearly 83 per cent of them poor in the southern region, which is a pocket of tribal concentration in the state.

It is no wonder then that the ST, despite being one-fifth of Odisha's population, contribute to about 40 per cent of the state's poor (as measured by the state's official poverty line). In fact, Odisha had the dubious distinction of recording the highest poverty rate for STs across India in

TABLE 18.1 Rural Poverty for Various Social Groups, Region-wise

Region	ST	SC	OBC	Others	All
Southern	82.8	67.2	64.7	44.1	72.7
Northern	72.8	64.4	48.6	33.9	59.1
Coastal	67.7	32.8	24.4	19.0	27.4
Rural Odisha	75.8	49.9	37.1	23.5	46.9
Rural India	44.7	37.1	25.8	17.5	28.1

Source: Sharma et al. 2009.

Notes: All numbers are a percentage of population.

SC: Scheduled Caste; ST: Scheduled Tribe; OBC: Other Backward Class.

2004–5, when nearly 75 per cent of tribal population in Odisha was recognized as being below the official poverty line, higher than the poverty ratio for tribals living in any other state.

That children living in poor households are more vulnerable than those living in non-poor households is well established. Nearly 50 per cent (or one of two) children in Odisha live in households that survive on Rs 15 per person, per day, which is close to the lowest international (or extreme poverty) norm of 1.25 purchasing power parity dollar. The fact that tribals comprise a disproportionate share of these poor households makes the condition of tribal children even more precarious.

In contrast to the not-so-encouraging numbers on poverty, Odisha registered significant improvements in several child-related outcomes between 1992–3 and 2005–6: infant mortality rates (IMR) declined from 112 to 65 per 1,000 live births; vaccination coverage improved for all children below 2 years of age from 36 to 52 per cent; and there was reasonable decline in the percentage of children under the age of 3 years who were stunted, wasted, or underweight. Yet, there existed substantial gaps in outcomes between tribal children and children from other groups. While vaccination coverage improved, only 30 per cent of tribal children in Odisha were vaccinated by 2005–6 compared with 59 per cent of non-tribal children. IMR also remained high in districts with tribal concentrations (Figure 18.1). Further, an analysis of age-specific mortality rates for children by social group reveals that

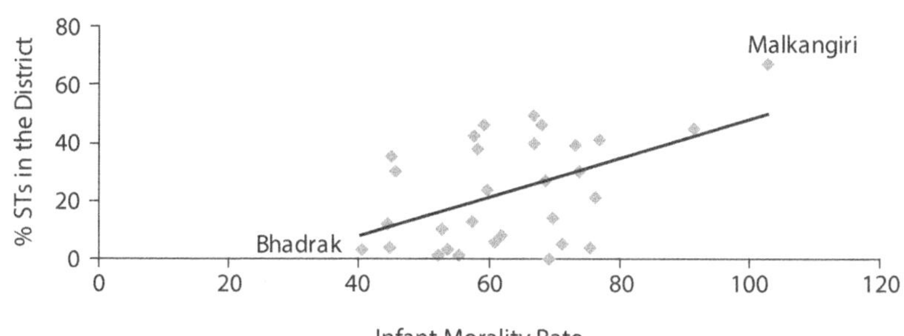

FIGURE 18.1 Odisha: District level Relationship between Infant Mortality and Concentration of Scheduled Tribes

Source: World Bank Staff Calculations from RCH II Survey.

in 2005–6, under-5 mortality rates (U5MR) for tribal children were nearly two times higher than the U5MR for children from other communities (Figure 18.2).

An immediate correlate of high mortality among children is malnutrition or poor maternal health. Malnutrition is endemic among tribals in Odisha, with 57 per cent of ST children showing signs of long-term malnutrition (stunting), 28 per cent showing severe stunting, and 54 per cent being underweight (see Table 18.2).[1] According to the 2007 World Development Indicators, these levels of malnutrition were much higher than in Burundi, Niger, or Afghanistan (World Bank 2007). The Global Hunger Index report on Indian states called the situation in Odisha alarming, ranking the state below Rwanda and Malawi (IFPRI 2009).

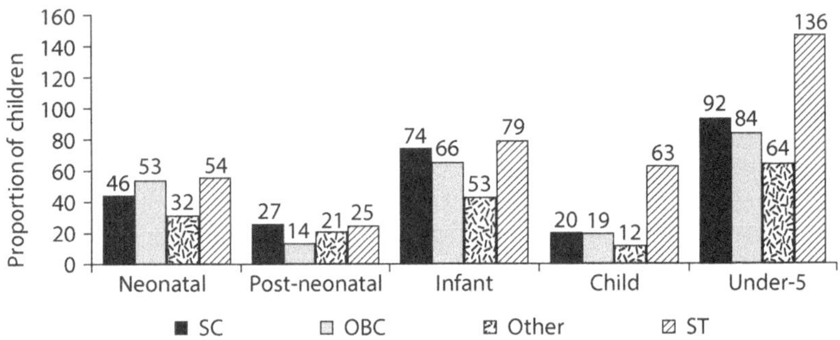

FIGURE 18.2 Infant and Child Mortality Rates for Various Social Groups in Odisha
Source: NFHS-3.

[1] Malnutrition is usually measured along three dimensions: stunting (deficit in height-for-age ratio), wasting (deficit in weight-for-height ratio), and underweight (deficit in weight-for-age ratio). Stunting reflects long-term effects of malnutrition; while wasting measures the current nutritional status of the subject, that is, his/her food intake immediately prior to the survey. The 'underweight' indicator is a combination of the former two and captures both long-term and short-term effects of deficient food intake. A child is considered to be malnourished with respect to each of these measures, if his/her indicator falls below −2 standard deviations from the median (defined for 2006 WHO international reference population). Falling below −3 standard deviations signals severe malnutrition.

TABLE 18.2 Malnutrition among Various Social Groups in Odisha

	ST	SC	OBC	Other
Height-for-age, % below –3 SD	28.4	23.1	16.1	12.3
Height-for-age, % below –2 SD	57.2	49.7	40.8	33.6
Weight-for-age, % below –3 SD	22.9	14.8	9.8	6.5
Weight-for-age, % below –2 SD	54.4	44.4	38.1	26.4
Weight-for-height, % below –3 SD	8.2	2.3	5.9	3.4
Weight-for-height, % below –2 SD	27.6	19.7	17.8	12.2

Source: NFHS-3, 2005–6.

Notes: All numbers are in per cent.

SC: Scheduled Caste; ST: Scheduled Tribe; OBC: Other Backward Class.

As for maternal health, despite improvements over the last decade or so, indicators for tribal women continued to be poor (Table 18.3). In comparison with SCs and Other Backward Classes (OBCs), a relatively smaller proportion of ST women in Odisha reported three or more antenatal visits (46 per cent compared with 59 per cent for SC women and 66 per cent for OBC women). Tribal women also remained less likely to receive a postnatal check-up, give birth at a health facility, and use contraceptives.

Women with more education tend to have better access to maternal health. Female literacy levels, however, remain abysmal among tribals in Odisha. According to the 2011 census, 41.2 per cent of tribal

TABLE 18.3 Maternal Health Indicators for Various Social Groups in Odisha

	ST	SC	OBC	Other
Three or more antenatal visits	46.0	58.6	66.3	74.4
First antenatal visit during first trimester	39.9	47.5	46.6	58.8
Given or bought IFA	76.6	85.8	85.6	84.9
Women with postnatal check-up	25.5	37.3	42.7	56.5
Currently use contraception	35.2	51.1	52.6	59.4
Location of last birth (health facility)	11.7	30.2	40.6	60.4
Birth assisted by health personnel	17.3	39.1	53.6	66.9

Source: NFHS-3, 2005–6.

Notes: All numbers are a percentage of population.

SC: Scheduled Caste; ST: Scheduled Tribe; OBC: Other Backward Class.

women in the state were literate. Tribal residential schools for girls have significantly aided improvement in enrolment levels, as shown by numbers from the DISE. However, dropout rates for tribal girls and the number of children out of school remain high in tribal districts. In 2008, for instance, more than 20 per cent of children were out of school in the tribal-dominated Malkangiri. Numbers indicating the 'out of school' children were higher for girls (Pratham 2008).

This is not to suggest that tribal pockets in Odisha (or elsewhere) are 'holy grails' for those working on human development and are synonymous with all that is bad. Tribal societies are known traditionally for their better gender indicators, particularly late age of marriage and better sex ratios. But sociologists suggest that socio-cultural practices of tribals are changing over time with their entering the mainstream. For instance, they have increasingly started giving dowry and marrying their daughters early. Yet, civic engagement remains strong in tribal societies, expectedly, given their history of communal cultivation.

BARRIERS TO ADDRESSING EXCLUSION OF SCHEDULED TRIBES IN ODISHA: SOME BROADER CHALLENGES[2]

The Indian state has put in place several policies that attempt to redress the disadvantages faced by tribal groups. Besides acknowledging special privileges for areas in which STs are a majority (through the Fifth Schedule of the Constitution), the Indian government extends reservation benefits to scheduled tribes, reserving 7.5 per cent of seats in all government jobs and public educational institutions. In addition, there are earmarked development funds both from the central government and from the state that flow to tribal areas through a special budgetary instrument called the Tribal Sub-plan (TSP). More recently, the Indian government through the Panchayats (Extension to the Scheduled Areas) Act, 1996 (PESA), has acknowledged the 'rights' of STs to Scheduled Areas by taking them towards self-rule. The Act recognizes and stresses on traditional community rights over natural resources. The recent Forest Rights Act or the Tribal Rights Act is a step further,

[2] This section draws from Das et al. 2012.

because it adopts a rights-based perspective and acknowledges the pre-eminent rights of STs to natural resources.

However, implementation of these policies and programmes has been difficult in tribal pockets. Service providers cite barriers both on the demand and the supply side. But these barriers to service delivery need to be located first in the challenging context that the tribals live in.

Poor Access to Assets, Markets, and Livelihoods

Tribal economies are mostly subsistence economies whose survival is closely linked to land and natural resources including forest products. Over one-third of Odisha is covered by forests,[3] and one-half to over one-fifth of annual income of tribal households comes from Non-timber Forest Products (NTFPs).

Even though Odisha has devolved the procurement and marketing of 69 NTFPs to gram sabhas,[4] the government retains control over high revenue-earning products (for example, kendu leaves) which are prone to commercial exploitation. Tribals who do sell on their own, sell in a buyers' market, with no control over prices (Saxena 1999). On the other hand, deforestation continues unabated. It is estimated that Odisha has lost more than a quarter of its forests in the last 25 years resulting in considerable decline in the proportion of tribal income contributed to by NTFPs.[5]

Besides their tenuous hold over NTFPs, another major reason for tribal pauperization is the classification of huge tracts of tribal forest land as state property. Legislation to prevent sale of ST land to non-tribals too has been largely ineffective as witnessed in the large number of cases involving land grabbing by people not belonging to the STs through marriage or through fraud.[6] Worse, the process of

[3] Orissa Eleventh Five-Year Plan 2007–12.

[4] Village assembly to which every resident of the village is a member.

[5] A study for the International Fund for Agricultural Development (IFAD) in Kandhamal and Gajapati districts showed that collection of NTFPs, which previously accounted for a substantial part of household income, now provides only 10 per cent of income. For more details, see RCDC 2000.

[6] Non-STs getting ST certificates and usurping ST lands and other advantages is now a serious political issue in Odisha.

tribal alienation, that is, STs gradually losing their access to traditional commons has accelerated in recent years. The state also has a controversial track record of resettlement and rehabilitation.[7] Most activists and academics working on tribal issues think that it is alienation from these communal resources that has become the fulcrum of tribal angst and revolt.

There are several policies in place to secure the rights of tribals to their land, natural resources, and livelihoods; but, as mentioned above, there is many a slip betwixt the cup and the lip. For instance, several steps have been taken to operationalize PESA—state amendments and rules have been passed and monitoring is underway. However, field studies in Odisha reveal that many people on the ground are not even aware of the legislation (Upadhyay 2007).

Poor Access to Social Service Delivery Mechanisms

The most significant challenge in delivering social services in tribal areas is that of poor physical access. The Special Action Plan for the KBK region[8] (2009–17) indicates that the average road length in KBK districts is only 1.28 km per sq. km of area, which is much below the state average of 2.49 km. Within the KBK region, tribal-dominated districts like Malkangiri and Subarnapur are worse off. Moreover, road quality is poor with many roads being 'nothing but earthen tracks with frequent missing links' (Government of Odisha 2009, p. 124).

Expectedly, transportation costs are high and tribal people think twice before taking people for medical help to public health facilities which are located at a distance. A longitudinal study in Bolangir district found, for instance, that villagers took a young child to the hospital only when the child's condition became critical, because they were deterred by poor road conditions and the expense of hiring a vehicle.

[7] See, for instance, Mishra 2007, pp. 822–5. Also see Actionaid 2007.

[8] The undivided Koraput, Bolangir and Kalahandi districts are popularly known as the KBK districts. In 1992–3, these were divided further into eight districts: Koraput, Malkangiri, Nabarangapur, Rayagada, Bolangir, Subarnapur, Kalahandi, and Nuapada. The region is characterized by a high proportion of ST population—according to the 2011 census, about 38.47 per cent of the population of these districts belongs to ST communities.

They also identified 'giving birth' as a risk, because mothers could not reach health centres on account of inadequate road access, particularly during the rainy season (van Dillen 2006).

While road access is an issue, Odisha has done well in expanding the reach of programmes like Integrated Child Development Services (ICDS) to remote areas. More than 80 per cent of households in the state seem to have an ICDS centre within the village (World Bank 2006). A larger issue that most stakeholders note is one of absenteeism of service providers. A World Bank review of the ICDS/Supplementary Nutrition programme in Odisha found a 30 per cent absenteeism rate among ICDS workers (World Bank 2006).

Functionaries are simply not inclined to be posted in tribal habitations for want of suitable accommodation, access to urban centres, and social support. To address this gap, the Government of Odisha is in the process of creating additional residential infrastructure for service providers working in tribal areas. In very remote areas where this cannot be done, mobile health clinics are becoming a popular option. While mobile units reached about 300,000 people in 1995, by 2009 this number was estimated to have increased to 1.9 million beneficiaries in KBK region alone.[9]

Besides absenteeism, reports from the ground suggest significant mistrust between tribal communities and service providers who are largely non-tribal. A recent primary survey to assess the availability and accessibility of and discrimination in the National Rural Health Mission (NRHM) services found that of the total Accredited Social Health Activists (ASHAs) in the sampled villages, 59 per cent were not from the SCs or STs. Only 26 per cent were from the SCs, and a mere 8 per cent were tribals. Moreover, both ICDS and ASHA workers were reported to have treated children from SC and ST households 'casually', visiting a significantly lower proportion of children in these households than children from households not belonging to the SCs or STs (Development Initiative 2009).

Most stakeholders interviewed by the author agreed that a long-term solution to the problem lies in developing a corps of tribal para-professionals who have filial ties or affinity with the community,

[9] Data given to the author in an interview with the Special Secretary to the Government of Odisha, Planning and Coordination Department.

which would enable building of trust. However, while administrators realize the value of recruiting local residents as field-level personnel, it is a time- and cost-intensive process that requires a completely different paradigm of planning. It is often impossible to find even secondary-level educated ST women who can fill the positions of a nurse or a female health worker (FHW). Yet another issue is getting trained tribal service providers to return once they have become part of the mainstream. As one respondent summarized:

> In the mainstream, they are made to learn one way or another that tribal issues are not important enough. They end up imbibing the dominant paradigm.

Poor Access to Political Voice and Participation

At the time when this chapter was being written, Odisha was witnessing an increasing spate of insurgent incidents, most of them originating from tribal districts. While economic divide is cited as one of the main reasons for such violence, many in the state now acknowledge that such disparities are rooted in a history of 'marginalization', not just economic but also political. Over time, this has led to an increased feeling of alienation and of viewing the politician or administrator as the 'outsider' or the 'adversary' as was prevalent in the colonial past. Tribals look at non-tribals with suspicion and vice versa, particularly the police who suspect tribals to be hand-in-glove with the insurgents.[10] As anger and resentment grow, politicians and administrators, particularly those on the ground, gradually lose the respect of the tribals. Displacement due to industrialization and destruction of forests only adds to such angst.

A majority of the stakeholders interviewed for this chapter agreed that at the core of it all are two larger issues. First, policies directed at tribal self-rule imply a shift in the power axis away from non-tribal

[10] In an interview to NDTV, Prakash Mishra, DG Operations in Odisha Police remarked, 'The Naxalite movement has grown from within the population. There is no clear demarcation between the enemy and non-enemy. The major problem that we face is the local militia, which is growing in the tribal area. There is always a danger of collateral damage in such kind of operations but we are trying to keep it to the minimum' (NDTV 2009).

elite who have represented the tribals thus far. One interviewee said to me:

> It all boils down to whether we want a change in condition of the tribals, or a change in position. And I'm afraid, we never want the latter. It is difficult to break through vested interests.

Second, most policy measures are based on a model of decentralized delivery, which ideally works when Panchayati Raj Institutions (PRI) on the ground have the capacity to deliver services, and citizens are aware of all schemes through adequate availability of information. While decentralized institutions like Palli Sabhas are in place in most tribal areas in Odisha, they are yet to evolve functionally, thus impeding delivery of most programmes. A survey[11] conducted in some of the poorest districts of Odisha before the panchayat elections of 2007 found that only 6 per cent of the gram panchayat representatives were aware of the 73rd and 74th Amendments to the Constitution that empower PRIs. Less than one per cent of the representatives were aware of the provisions included in the extension of PESA. As an interviewee summed up succinctly:

> Though flush with funds, capacity of gram panchayats is limited. It is a classic case of good resources, but no people, no ideas, no utilization, no awareness, no accountability.

Access and Its Relation to Child Mortality among Tribals: A Case Study

Although the challenges mentioned in access seem many, they can all be 'instrumentally a cause of diverse capability failures' (Sen 2000). This section shows how one indicator—U5MR among tribal children—is affected by the socio-economic context of tribal households.

While malnutrition or undernourishment of tribal children; poor maternal health indicators; and inadequate coverage of immunization are some of the more proximate causes of child mortality, those working in the health sector in Odisha attribute these trends to the much wider problem of tribal displacement. Besides, loss of land, displacement

[11] The survey was conducted by the Centre for Youth and Social Development in March 2007 in the districts of Koraput, Keonjhar, Kalahandi, Sundargarh, Rayagada, and Cuttack in 34 gram panchayats.

and forced migration displaces or alienates tribals from public schemes, including vaccination drives. For a tribal family which is displaced, they argue, getting their child immunized is no longer a priority.

Displacement also affects traditional food habits, with most tribals and their children shifting from an earlier balanced diet of fruits, meat and protein-and-iron rich food such as ragi and maize to food supplied by the Public Distribution System (PDS) for cash. Further, the introduction of cash crops instead of local crops, such as ragi and millet, threatens food security, with tribals shifting from a practice of multicropping (which helps regenerate soil nutrients) to a practice of pesticide-based farming.

Finally, destruction of forests over time has resulted in reduced access of tribals to traditional medicines and practices. Tribal activists note the reduction in efficacy of tribal medicines perhaps on account of contamination of the environment because of the rapid growth of mining and other industries.

In addition to displacement, tribal children suffer from poor access to service outposts. Although the incidence of disease among tribal children varies only slightly from those of their non-tribal counterparts (in fact at times it is even lower),[12] they are less likely to receive

TABLE 18.4 Access to Qualified Medical Assistance by Various Social Groups

	ST	SC	OBC	Other
Diarrhoea over last two weeks	12.2	14.9	9.6	11.1
Taken to health facility for diarrhoea	55.2	59.2	66.2	56.8
Received no treatment for diarrhoea	28.1	26.0	25.7	28.0

Source: NFHS-3, 2005–6.

Notes: Among children under age 5, percentage who had diarrhoea in the two weeks preceding the survey and percentage who received advice or treatment from a health provider and who were given no treatment; health facilities exclude pharmacies, shops, any traditional treatments.

SC: Scheduled Caste; ST: Scheduled Tribe; OBC: Other Backward Class.

[12] Until the late twentieth century, tribal mortality (especially infant and child mortality) was observed to be traditionally lower than mortality rates of non-tribals. This was mostly attributed to the ecologically sustainable livelihood patterns of the ST. Since then, child mortality rates for tribals have worsened. Some call it the unfortunate outcome of mainstreaming (Maharatna 2005).

treatment in a health facility than the latter (see Table 18.4). Poor physical access together with high transportation costs implies that tribal families are more resistant to taking their children to health centres for treatment of an illness like diarrhoea. The opportunity cost of the visit is also implicitly weighed against loss in wages for that day. Smaller infections consequently develop into serious ailments resulting in the death of the child.

GAPS IN DEMAND AND SUPPLY OF SCHEMES FOR TRIBALS

Set against these contextual barriers, planners, programmers, and functionaries in Odisha find it difficult to deliver the multiple schemes on offer for tribals, particularly tribal children. When they were asked to sum up their main challenge, the common response was that gaps existed both on the demand and the supply side.

Gaps in Demand

Interviews with those working in the education and health sector indicate that tribal people take up publicly provided services only because they are free or come at a nominal cost. Income poverty; high opportunity and hidden costs for accessing services; and lack of knowledge or information about them are huge dampeners on demand. Lack of demand is also driven by gaps in supply. While open to modern treatment and willing to cover distances to reach primary health centres, tribals often find the centres deserted with no medical workers, no drugs, no equipment, or no water. Unfulfilled promises lead to mistrust of outsiders. Left with no option, tribal families revert to traditional healers.

However, most service providers believe that more can be done to address gaps on the demand side. First, steps can be taken to stimulate demand by offering incentives. For instance, community funds can be mobilized to cater to costs of travel, medicines, books, uniforms, and other direct and hidden costs that keep demand low. Second, demand can be stimulated through awareness building and behavioural change about hygiene (washing hands with soap), water, sanitation, indoor air pollution (use of clean fuels, improved ventilation), malaria (use of bed nets), nutrition and feeding practices, early diagnosis of medical problems, and service provision (what, where, and how). The key however is to have inclusive communication, that is, the messages should be designed in a language (not just Oriya, but local tribal dialects) that can be understood by all stakeholders. Using the spoken word is often better than distributing pamphlets on information, given the poor literacy levels in tribal areas. Some donor agencies are now attempting to address this lacuna by using tools such as community radios and theatre to disseminate information about health issues. The government, on the other hand, is working on organizing right to information clinics about government schemes and entitlements in tribal areas, such as perhaps merging it with weekly markets so more people can attend.

Inclusion—or the demand for it—can also be addressed at the school level where discrimination begins. According to research undertaken by the Odisha Primary Education Program Authority (OPEPA), about 748,000 ST children in Classes 1, 2, and 3 encounter a classroom language other than their mother tongue (OPEPA n.d.). In an effort to make education more inclusive, the Government of Odisha initiated in 2006 a Multilingual Education Intervention (MLE) in the tribal-dominated districts in the state. The intervention focused on developing curricula and teaching in the tribals' own mother tongue. Until 2008, MLE had been introduced in 200 schools, covering 10 tribal language groups across eight districts in Odisha. The scheme has resulted in several positive outcomes. An evaluation in two tribal villages in Keonjhar district shows the positive impact the intervention has had on enrolment rates. Curriculum in their own language has also created a new enthusiasm among tribal people to send their children to school (Cuadra et al. 2008). However, challenges remain. Administrators rue the shortage of qualified tribal teachers. The few that are recruited resort to multiclass teaching, which results in a high student–teacher ratio, which, in turn, affects performance (World Bank 2007). Limited MLE funds, poor school infrastructure, and limited community participation further constrain impact. There is also a misconception among tribal parents that use of a non-dominant language would constrain their children's educational progress and career path. A telling remark by an Alang father sums up their apprehension, 'How will my son leave the village and get a good job if he cannot speak Oriya?' (Cuadra et al. 2008, p. 38).

Gaps in Supply

Efforts to raise demand for and awareness about services may come to naught if they run into gaps in supply. In fact, some programmers working on the ground said it was unethical to raise demand when supply was not assured. This section focuses on a few deeper, underlying issues that constrain effective supply of programmes and schemes for tribals.

CONSTRAINTS IN IMPLEMENTATION OR CONSTRAINTS IN DESIGN?

There is a general consensus among all stakeholders that exclusion starts at the level of policy design itself. Policy prescriptions are rarely disaggregated or targeted and when targeted they are not sufficiently monitored. Moreover, most central government programmes leave little room for local-level interventions or decision-making.

However, it is not that there is a dearth of innovations. In one ICDS centre in Rayagada, Gajapati district, for instance, ICDS functionaries had successfully overcome the constraint of unavailability of pulses caused by the central government's failure to increase the procurement price, by shifting to a community-run nutrition programme using minor millets and pulses that were grown and harvested locally. The programme was therefore not dependent on a centralized supply of grains. It had not only ensured community participation, but had also helped to counter malnourishment among children under 6 years in all the 35 Saora tribe villages under the centre.

PLANNERS' SUPPLY OR SUPPLY DRIVEN BY DEMAND?

The gap in communication between tribal people and non-tribal functionaries implies that the latter fail to relate with tribal people. They deliver programmes in a mechanical, routine way without addressing the specific requirements of the tribals. Thus, for example, water supply schemes that provide tube wells are implemented without consulting people on where they might need the tube wells to be located, which shows that this is carried out merely to meet certain targets. The root cause of such apathy, many think, is the absence of local community-level planning, despite Scheduled Tribes' living in small communities.

Micro-level planning has been successfully tried in some tribal pockets in Odisha and is now being scaled up by the government for delivery of livelihood programmes in the KBK region. One example of successful micro-planning is the UNDP-supported Rural Decentralization and Participatory Planning for Poverty Reduction project in Phiringia block of the Kandhamal district that undertook micro-level planning (MLP) in 236 villages of all the 20 gram panchayats under the block. Studies of the programme establish unambiguously the fact that MLP has 'transformed people into agents of change, contrary to the outcome of the role they play in standardized, blueprint based development planning' (NIPDIT 2008). Villagers involved in the exercise shared that the process of mapping resources and planning for their village in a united manner had given them a common platform to think and plan for the development of the village as a whole. People repeatedly asked about the execution of the plan thus ensuring that it was at all stages a live document.

INFRASTRUCTURE, INCENTIVES, OR SENSITIZATION?

The Government of Odisha in its Special Action Plan for the KBK region (2009–17) is focusing on expanding outreach of services via infrastructure creation in tribal areas, including establishment of hospitals and medical colleges; and improvement in connectivity to remote clusters through construction of arterial roads. However, sceptics think that creation of new infrastructure alone will not help.

To be effective, infrastructure creation needs to be combined with a focus on quality in delivery. Tribal education, for instance, is significantly hampered by lack of funds for curriculum development and human resource development (HRD). Most funds allocated for educational schemes are spent on physical goods—be it construction of a school or hostel or purchase of cycles and uniforms for distribution among children—leaving little or no funds for HRD activities. 'Opening schools alone is not education,' said one respondent.

Similarly, several of the stakeholders interviewed felt that a focus on multiplying personnel (including tribal service providers) in tribal areas or HR reforms using a combination of incentives, punishment, and supervision would not help to address the problem of absenteeism.

Punishment or reward, they asserted, do not work unless service providers, particularly frontline workers and mid-level management functionaries (PRI officials, teachers, and nurses) are trained and made sensitive to the needs of tribal households and tribal children. HR reforms aimed at sensitizing service providers are critical in bringing an inclusionary orientation in their day-to-day work, including equal treatment, by way of behaviour, towards clients. More than empathy, sensitization trainings need to focus on making service providers familiar with the special needs of tribal populations so that they can communicate effectively to tribal communities who are recognized as beneficiaries rather than as social inferiors.

NO DATA, NO MONITORING, NO ACCOUNTABILITY

One of the biggest hurdles in delivering schemes to the tribal populace is the difficulty in getting disaggregated data to monitor inclusion. While data on education outcomes and indicators, disaggregated into SC, ST, and other groups are readily available, no such disaggregation exists for health indicators[13] and water and sanitation—a sector that has fewer foot soldiers to gather data than either health or education. It is also difficult to gather disaggregated data on quality or on allocation of budgets and their utilization for excluded groups. Administrators say that data segregated on the basis of social groups is not captured at facility levels owing to concerns of sensitivity of the population in recording such data. However, the ability to gather similar data in education, but not in other sectors indicates that sensitivity alone may not be the problem.

First, most disaggregated data are available from periodic sample surveys such as the NFHS which are conducted once in five to six years. There is no state-wide regular Management Information System (MIS) that collects data distinguished by SC, ST, and other groups or generates knowledge about day-to-day field operations. This makes

[13] The HMIS for instance has no SC/ST table. However there has been an initiative, recently, to start annual surveys in the health sector. It is possible that they address the gap of disaggregated data in health.

continuous monitoring difficult. Second, while some field assessment studies capture impact by social groups, they are too few and far between and, further, cover only a small sample, with findings limited to only one tribe or a few villages. Finally, data is reliable only as long as it is monitored regularly. The 2007 CAG review of Integrated Tribal Development Agencies (ITDAs) showed that most of them had not prepared annual accounts since their inception and district monitoring committees, though functional in name, had not met even once in seven years (CAG 2007).

Monitoring, however, is a function of accountability from below. Unless it is accompanied by systems of increased voice and accountability—more so accountability ensured through continuous community-based monitoring—no amount of data can help. This brings us back to the issue of capacity-building and engagement with local communities.

IMPLICATIONS FOR POLICY

As the discussion above suggests, there are no easy answers. Most stakeholders acknowledge that both mainstreaming and targeting is essential. The policy for expanding infrastructure or education, for instance, has so far been divided between reaching tribal villages, on the one hand, and keeping intervention at a minimum, on the other, in order to preserve the unique identity of tribals. There is a perception that a generalized uniform routine response does not work in tribal areas given their unique situation. What is needed is focused attention—targeted specialized programmes designed to achieve specific goals—until tribals cross a threshold of progress before they are mainstreamed.

But there are others who argue that inclusion can only happen once equity is achieved in mainstream policies and practices (Kabeer 2006). 'One standard for us and another for another area doesn't work. That by definition is exclusion,' said one government representative interviewed by this author. There is no right or wrong way of achieving inclusion in programmes.

Given the complexity of issues involved and the context of Odisha, this chapter highlights a few principles that can help facilitate inclusive programming for tribals in Odisha.

Principles for Inclusive Programming

MOVE FROM A SHORT-TERM SECTORAL APPROACH TO A LONG-TERM COMPREHENSIVE APPROACH

Although ahead of many other states in the number of schemes it has in place for tribal groups, at the time of writing this chapter, Odisha did not have a cohesive policy for tribal development; for instance, there was no state policy for tribal education nor one for improving tribal health outcomes. Why vision is needed is because achievement of outcomes such as reduced tribal child mortality requires different sectors and programmes (both state and central) to come together. Further, they need to come together from the planning stages itself. Otherwise, roles and responsibilities of each towards the common goal are lost. Stakeholders across the board believe that development of such a cross-sectoral vision or plan is the primary condition for moving forward on an agenda of social inclusion.

There have been initiatives in the government to develop five-year perspective tribal plans which can feed into a state tribal policy. The 2009–17 action plan for the KBK region is one example of a comprehensive approach. However many view it as only adding to the complexity of existing programmes. Further, it still divides tribal development across departments or sectors. Critics argue that what is needed is not an exclusive strategy for ST groups, but how they fit into the overall project implementation plan (PIP) for the mainstream project. One respondent summed up what he thought was the main barrier:

> Development is still about committees and domains—the academic domain; the political domain; the bureaucratic domain; the community domain; and the civil society domain. Seldom do they come together.

There are innovations to learn from, such as the multisector collaboration called ANKUR, a joint initiative of the Odisha Government and UNICEF. Initiated in Koraput, the programme was unique in its not initiating any new activities. Instead, the focus was on establishing linkages between existing programmes (for example, those related to nutrition, education, infant survival, and drinking water and sanitation) to maximize their impact on children. Project activities also included support for micro-planning, capacity-building, training of frontline workers, and coordination.

ENGAGE WITH NON-GOVERNMENTAL ORGANIZATIONS

In most interviews with this author, respondents highlighted that civil society could play a significant role on two fronts—first in sensitizing frontline providers and second in spreading awareness about existing schemes, mobilizing communities, and giving them voice to demand services. There was a general perception that people in tribal villages were at present hesitant to speak out for fear of a backlash against them. Several people thought that while building community organizations and groups was a time-intensive process, it was critical in ensuring accountability from below, and to achieve this, civil society was in a better position to help them. Similarly, having worked intensively in the remotest pockets with tribal groups, non-governmental organizations (NGOs) were also better placed to sensitize functionaries in the field about the special needs of tribals. However, to fulfil these roles objectively, it was stressed that NGOs work independently of the government or programmes run by donors, lest their obligations towards their 'client' have a deleterious impact on their work.

ENGAGE WITH COMMUNITIES

Several examples from across the state suggest that tribal societies if involved can become agents of change. ANKUR, for instance, trained 'child reporters' from within villages in Koraput to report on problems of service delivery in their communities. Children wrote down their observations in a diary, which was collated in the form of a newsletter and distributed to policymakers, functionaries, and the media every month. The reports created a stir with chiefs of departments and bureaucrats asking children to report on progress, if any, in the subsequent bulletins. Some called them the eyes and ears of the village and others referred to them as monitors.

Similarly, in a project facilitated by Actionaid in Kalahandi and Rayagada, local tribal youth were trained to form Swasthya Vahini groups (or health groups) that took up cleanliness drives in their villages, repaired defunct tube wells, disinfected water bodies, and undertook public information campaigns about health and general hygiene.

These and other experiences demonstrate that community participation can be a powerful tool to engage with tribal societies. It creates more foot soldiers; helps establish community information systems; helps monitor programmes through building voice, awareness, and bottom-up accountability; and, most importantly, creates a sense of enthusiasm and ownership of existing programmes. However, mobilization is a time-intensive process. Also, while community forums can be an effective platform for engagement, they need sensitive facilitation. Finally, those at the grass roots need to win the support of the local people by treating them on an equal footing, recognizing their rights as individuals, and ensuring that services are provided on the basis of equal treatment, respect, and dignity irrespective of economic, social, or political status.

IMPROVE MONITORING AND EVALUATION

Almost all evaluations of government schemes in the state stress the need for strengthening internal control and monitoring and evaluation (M&E) mechanisms. At the top, this is reflected in unspent funds for SC/ST programmes and at the bottom in misappropriation. Most stakeholders suggest starting with M&E for underperforming schemes and underserved tribal areas to improve targeting and performance. To help achieve the objective of inclusion though, it is critical that any monitoring system follows two basic principles. One, it should be regular in collecting data disaggregated on the basis of social groups and then, more importantly, following up on progress. Targets and indicators of success should be clearly defined for different points in the programme. Two, it should be accompanied by efforts to increase voice of and accountability for excluded groups and engaging communities as discussed above. Finally, monitoring can lead to actionable change only if there is strong management commitment and follow up at the top. Social audits are an example of good community-based monitoring. However, what happens after a social audit, that is, how programme managers address community concerns, is equally important to maintain people's faith in the monitoring mechanism.

★ ★ ★

In several interviews with me, it was found that the respondents wondered why after so many examples of innovations to reach tribals and tribal children in Odisha, none had achieved scale. Some argued that scaling up required tenacious champions who have the commitment to start, nurture, and spread something that works, with support from the top. However, most importantly, they said, it needed a mindset, an alternate path of treating tribals as part of 'us', not as some people living on the fringes. Interventions for tribal populations unfortunately are still regarded as charity—handouts that need to be doled out to uplift very poor people, with no participation and no monitoring and evaluation.

Developing an alternate path needs a paradigm shift, both in implementation and in thinking. It needs different stakeholders to come together, beyond their ideologies, to work in a cohesive manner, with long-term vision and, most critically, with community participation.

REFERENCES

Actionaid. 2007. *Vedanta Cares? Busting the Myths about Vedanta's Operation in Lanjigarh, India*, Actionaid. http://www.actionaid.org.uk/doc_lib/vedanta_report.pdf, last accessed on 13 September 2012.

Comptroller and Auditor General of India (CAG). 2007. 'Performance Audits', *Orissa CAG Report*, Chapter 3. New Delhi: Government of India.

Cuadra, C., D. Das, N. Goldstein, S.H. Kim, and N. Priyadarshini. 2008. 'Social Inclusion of Children in School, with a Focus on Girls in Tribal Communities, through the Multilingual Education (MLE) Initiative in Orissa', KCCI Paper, 2008/01. Bhubaneswar: UNICEF.

Das, M., G. Hall, S. Kapoor, and D. Nikitin. 2012. 'India: The Scheduled Tribes', in G. Hall and H. Patrinos (eds), *Indigenous Peoples, Poverty and Development*. Washington, DC: Cambridge University Press.

Development Initiative. 2009. *Social Exclusion and Access to Basic Services: A Report*. Bhubaneswar: Development Initiative.

van Dillen, S. 2006. 'Child Health and Mortality in Western Orissa: A Report Based on a Longitudinal Household Survey in Bolangir District', University of Bonn, Mimeo.

Government of Odisha. 2009. *Special Action Plan for the KBK Region: 2009–17*. Bhubaneswar: Government of Odisha.

International Food Policy Research Institute (IFPRI). 2009. *India State Hunger Index: Comparisons of Hunger across States*. Washington, DC: IFPRI.

Kabeer, N. 2006. 'Social Exclusion and the MDGs: The Challenge of the Durable Inequalities in the Asian Context', Institute of Development Studies, Paper presented at the Asia 2015 Conference, London.

Maharatna, A. 2005. *Demographic Perspectives on India's Tribes*. New Delhi: Oxford University Press.

Mishra, I. 2007. 'Heat and Dust of Highway at Kalinganagar', *Economic and Political Weekly*, 10 March, 42(10): 822–5.

National Institute for People's Development, Investigation and Training (NIPDIT). 2008. *Empowering the 3rd Tier: A Compilation of Case Studies and Analysis*. Orissa: NIPDIT.

NDTV. 2009. 'Orissa: Why People Prefer Naxals over the Police', 31 October. http://www.ndtv.com/article/india/orissa-why-people-prefer-naxals-over-the-police-10842, last accessed on 21 October 2014.

OPEPA. n.d. 'Sustainable Community Based Multilingual Education Program Strategy', Unpublished report, Orissa.

Pratham. 2008. *Annual Status of Education Report (Rural) 2008*. Mumbai: Pratham Resource Center.

Regional Centre for Development Cooperation (RCDC). 2000. 'Social and Institutional Analysis and Livelihood Systems Study of Tribal Communities in Selected Villages in Kandhamal and Gajapati Districts', March. Bhubaneswar: RCDC.

Saxena, N.C. 1999. 'Forests in Tribal Lives', Draft. New Delhi: Planning Commission.

Sen, A. 2000. 'Social Exclusion: Concepts, Application and Scrutiny', Social Development Papers, No. 1, Office of Environment and Social Development, Asian Development Bank.

Sharma, M., B.L. Sarangi, J. Kanungo, S. Sahoo, L. Tripathy, A. Patnaik, J. Tewari, and A.D. Rath. 2009. 'Accelerating Malnutrition Reduction in Orissa', *IDS Bulletin*, 40(4): 78, 85.

Upadhyay, S. 2007. 'Assessment of Odisha PESA—Legal Perspective', Draft. New Delhi: World Bank.

World Bank. 2006. *Implementation Completion and Results Report: Orissa Health Systems Development Project*. New Delhi: World Bank.

———. 2007, *World Development Indicators, 2007*. Washington, DC: World Bank.

Index

About the Editors and Contributors

EDITORS

A.K. Shiva Kumar has over 35 years of experience in policy analysis, public management, and evaluation. He has served as Senior Adviser to UNICEF's India country office for over two decades and has been a regular contributor to United Nations Development Programme's (UNDP's) Human Development Reports. As a development economist, his research interests have focussed on poverty, human development, and the impact of development policies on women and children.

Preet Rustagi is Professor, Institute for Human Development (IHD), New Delhi. She has a doctorate in economics from Jawaharlal Nehru University, New Delhi, and has been working on labour, human development, gender, and child-related issues for over 18 years. Her other research interests include urban poverty, violence against women, child labour, poverty and deprivations, education, and food security. She holds the Chair on Human Development Issues and is the Associate Editor of *Indian Journal of Labour Economics* (*IJLE*).

Ramya Subrahmanian is Executive Director, 'Know Violence in Childhood: A Global Learning Initiative', New Delhi. She was the Social Policy Specialist at UNICEF's India country office while working on this volume, and has over 20 years of experience working on issues of social protection, social inclusion, gender equality, and women's and children's rights. Previously, she was a Research Fellow at the Institute of Development Studies, University of Sussex. She has authored several books and papers on issues relating to gender and education, child labour, and social policy.

CONTRIBUTORS

Venkatesh Athreya, a chemical engineer-turned-development economist, is Adviser (Food Security), M.S. Swaminathan Research Foundation, as well as Adjunct Professor, Asian College of Journalism. He retired in 2008 as Professor of Economics at Bharathidasan University, Tamil Nadu. He has written extensively on agrarian change, literacy, gender, infanticide, food security, human development, and political economy.

Asha Bajpai is Dean and Professor of Law, School of Law, Rights, and Constitutional Governance, Tata Institute of Social Sciences, Mumbai. Her teaching and research interests include legislative reforms and rights relating to women, children, youth, and disabled and disadvantaged sections of society. She was a Fulbright Visiting Lecturer at the Washington College of Law, American University. She is currently serving as amicus curiae appointed by the High Court in Public Interest Litigation in the death, abuse, and exploitation of intellectually challenged children in orphanages.

Subrat Das is Executive Director, Centre for Budget and Governance Accountability (CBGA). He studied economics at the Centre for Economic Studies and Planning, Jawaharlal Nehru University, New Delhi. He has worked on India's public spending on social sectors, responsiveness of budgets to disadvantaged sections of population, bottlenecks in planning and budgetary processes, and some of the structural issues in fiscal federalism in the country.

S. Mahendra Dev is Director and Vice Chancellor, Indira Gandhi Institute of Development Research (IGIDR), Mumbai. He received his PhD from the Delhi School of Economics, New Delhi and was at the Yale University, Connecticut for his post-doctoral research. His main areas of interest are development economics, agricultural economics, and rural development. He has been a member of various committees and has held several positions, including Chairman, Commission for Agricultural Costs and Prices, Ministry of Agriculture, in the rank of Secretary, Government of India.

Kaveri Gill is Chief Economist, Oxford Policy Management, New Delhi. She holds a PhD from the University of Cambridge. Her areas of expertise are poverty and deprivation, the informal sector, and the political economy of development and urbanization in emerging economies. Recently, she has worked on flagship government welfare schemes in India, especially those relating to public health.

Shireen J. Jejeebhoy is Senior Associate, Population Council and is also a social scientist with more than 30 years of research experience in the areas of gender and women's agency, adolescent health and development, sexual and reproductive health matters, and gender-based violence both in India and in general. She has written extensively on women's education and empowerment, violence, maternal health, abortion, and youth sexual and reproductive health and rights. Currently, she spearheads the Council's programmes on young people's health and development, addressing violence against women and girls, and increasing access to safe abortion services in India.

Praveen Jha is Professor at the Centre for Economic Studies and Planning (CESP) and Adjunct Professor at the Centre for Informal Sector and Labour Studies (CISLS), School of Social Sciences, Jawaharlal Nehru University, New Delhi. Currently he is also a visiting professor at Rhodes University, Grahamstown, South Africa, and African Institute of Agrarian Studies, Harare, Zimbabwe. His area of research and teaching is Political Economy of Development with focus on Labour Economics, Agricultural Economics, Economics of Education, Public Finance, and History of Economic Thought.

Surinder S. Jodhka is Professor of Sociology at the Jawaharlal Nehru University, New Delhi. He has published widely on the subjects of rural and agrarian change; caste in contemporary India; and social/cultural identities. His publications include *Caste in Contemporary India* (2015); *Interrogating India's Modernity* (ed. 2013); *Caste: Oxford India Short Introductions* (2012); *Village Society* (ed. 2012); *Community and Identities: Contemporary Discourses on Culture and Politics in India* (ed. 2001). He is among the first recipients of the ICSSR-Amartya Sen Award for Distinguished Social Scientists, for the year 2012.

Mary E. John is Senior Fellow at the Centre for Women's Development Studies (CWDS), New Delhi. She was director of CWDS from 2006–12 and the Associate Professor and Deputy Director of the Women's

Studies Programme at Jawaharlal Nehru University, New Delhi, before that. Her recent publications include *Women's Studies in India: A Reader* (2008), and *Planning Families, Planning Gender* (co-authored 2008). She is currently working on a book on the adverse child sex ratio and also working on a book on feminism and the subject of 'women'.

Soumya Kapoor Mehta is an independent development consultant working on poverty reduction, social inclusion, social protection, and social accountability. She has had over 10 years of experience working with organizations such as the World Bank, UNICEF, Food and Agriculture Organization of the United Nations (FAO), Centre for Policy Research, and the Government of India. She is the author of the World Bank's cross-country global study on poverty reduction, *Moving out of Poverty: Success from the Bottom Up* and the forthcoming book *Basic Income: A Transformative Policy for India.*

Sonvi A. Khanna is Advisory Research Associate, Dasra, Mumbai. Her research spans a range of development issues that affect adolescent girls in India. She also provides capacity-building support to non-profits and social businesses on developing logic models as well as pitching their work to funders. Prior to Dasra, she worked with the International Center for Research on Women (ICRW) New Delhi, and contributed to research, particularly in the area of gender-based discrimination against girls and other normative issues that restrict India's progress on development indicators.

Amitabh Kundu is Visiting Professor at the Institute of Human Development, New Delhi, and Senior Fellow at Delhi Policy Group, New Delhi. He served as Professor of Economics and also as Dean of School of Social Sciences at Jawaharlal Nehru University, New Delhi. He has been a Visiting Professor at University of Amsterdam; Maison des sciences de l'homme and Sciences Po, Paris; University of Wuerzburg; University of Kaiserslautern; and South Asian Institute, Heidelberg, Germany.

Balwant Singh Mehta is Associate Fellow at the Institute for Human Development, New Delhi. He specializes in handling unit-level data of the National Sample Survey (NSS). He has worked extensively in the areas of information and communication technology for development, labour, employment, and child well-being.

Sunil Kumar Mishra is currently working as an Associate Fellow at the Institute for Human Development, New Delhi. He has a doctorate in economics and has worked in the areas of rural livelihoods, child labour and trafficking, and food security.

Neeta Misra has worked as a consultant in New Delhi for Oxfam, UNICEF, and the World Bank. Prior to this she completed post-doctoral research in economics at the University of Cape Town where she focused on issues around rural unemployment and small-holder agriculture in a former homeland of South Africa. She holds a PhD in development planning from the Massachusetts Institute of Technology and a Masters in development planning from Cornell University, Ithaca, New York.

P.C. Mohanan, Indian Statistical Service, heads the Computer Centre, Ministry of Statistics and Programme Implementation, Government of India. He has published papers on employment/unemployment, housing, migration, and unorganized enterprises. He headed the secretariat of the first National Statistical Commission. He served on the Expert Committee on Agricultural Statistics as also the Technical Group on Housing Shortage during the Twelfth Five-Year Plan.

Priya Nanda is Director, Social and Economic Development group, International Center for Research on Women (ICRW), Asia Regional Office, New Delhi. She holds a doctorate in health economics from Johns Hopkins University, Baltimore, Maryland and a master's degree in international affairs from Columbia University, New York. Her area of expertise includes measurement and evaluation of women's economic empowerment and access to health services, including reproductive health and HIV.

Nidhi Sadana Sabharwal is Associate Professor at the Centre for Policy Research in Higher Education, National University of Educational Planning and Administration (NUEPA), New Delhi. She has previously served as the Director at the Indian Institute of Dalit Studies (IIDS), New Delhi. She has a PhD in geography from Jawaharlal Nehru University, New Delhi. She has studied inter-group inequalities across human development indicators, focusing on the role of caste- and gender-based discrimination in market and non-market institutions; diversity and discrimination within higher educational institutions,

Mid-Day Meal and Anganwadi programmes; and social protection policies. She has extensive experience in data collection, analysis, and policy advocacy.

Ashwani Saith is professor emeritus at the International Institute of Social Studies of Erasmus University, Rotterdam. He studied Economics at St. Stephen's College, University of Delhi, and Trinity College, Cambridge, where he took his PhD. He has held research and teaching positions at the Delhi School of Economics; Faculty of Economics, University of Cambridge; Queen Elizabeth House, University of Oxford; and the London School of Economics.

K.G. Santhya is Associate II, Population Council and is an economist and demographer with 14 years of experience in designing and conducting rigorous qualitative and quantitative studies on rights of youth, gender equity and women's empowerment, reproductive health, and gender-based violence. She is currently a member of the Scientific Panel on Reproductive Health, the International Union for the Scientific Study of Population, Paris, and an elected member of the Asian Population Association Council.

T.V. Sekher is Professor at the International Institute for Population Sciences (IIPS), Mumbai. Trained in demography and sociology, his areas of research interests are social demography, gender issues, public health, and population ageing. Sekher was a Visiting Fellow at the Wellcome Trust Centre of University College London; Maison des sciences de l'homme, Paris; and Lund University, Sweden. He also served as a Consultant to United Nations Population Fund (UNFPA) and Population Foundation of India to review the girl child promotion schemes in India and South Asia. He is the Managing Editor of the professional journal *Demography India*.

Madhura Swaminathan is Professor at the Economic Analysis Unit of the Indian Statistical Institute, Bangalore. She has authored several books including on the public distribution of food and agrarian relations.

Sukhadeo Thorat is Chairman, Indian Council of Social Science Research; Professor of Economics, Jawaharlal Nehru University, Delhi; and former Chairman, University Grants Commission. He is also a visiting faculty member at the International Food Policy Research Institute (IFPRI). He is the founding Director of the Indian Institute of Dalit Studies (IIDS), New Delhi. He has been awarded the Padma Shri, Mother Teresa International Award for the Weaker Section and Minorities, and Dr Ambedkar Chetna Award. His research areas include agricultural development, rural poverty, institution and economic growth, problems of marginalized groups, economics of caste system, caste discrimination, and poverty.

Shivali Tukdeo is Assistant Professor, School of Social Sciences, National Institute of Advanced Studies, New Delhi. Her scholarly engagements are rooted in diverse disciplinary interactions including education policy, critical social theory, and sociology of education among others. Over the last few years, she has focused her research on the new policy regimes in education in India and their connections with international and supranational policy orientations. Her current work includes education among the disadvantaged communities, ethnography of education, and gender studies.

Rekha Wazir is co-founder and Senior Associate at International Child Development Initiatives (ICDI), the Netherlands, and Deputy Convener of the Postgraduate Diploma on Children, Youth, and Development offered jointly by the International Institute of Social Studies and ICDI. She holds an MA in Sociology from Delhi School of Economics and a PhD from University of Cambridge. She has been active in the field of children and development and has a broad range of research interests that span education, gender, child labour, child abuse, childcare, and child poverty.

Virginius Xaxa is Professor and Deputy Director at Tata Institute of Social Sciences, Guwahati Campus. He has a master's degree in sociology from University of Pune and a PhD from Indian Institute of Technology, Kanpur. He has authored *Economic Dualism and Structure of Class: A Study in Plantation and Peasant settings in North Bengal* (1997) and *State, Society and Tribes: Issues in Post-Colonial India* (2008); co-authored *Plantation Labour in India* (1996); and co-edited *Social Exclusion and Adverse Inclusion: Adivasis in India* (2012).